TALKING ABOUT NOTHING

Talking about Nothing

Numbers, Hallucinations, and Fictions

Jody Azzouni

OXFORD
UNIVERSITY PRESS

UNIVERSITY PRESS

Oxford University Press is a department of the University of Oxford.
It furthers the University's objective of excellence in research, scholarship,
and education by publishing worldwide.

Oxford   New York
Auckland   Cape Town   Dar es Salaam   Hong Kong   Karachi
Kuala Lumpur   Madrid   Melbourne   Mexico City   Nairobi
New Delhi   Shanghai   Taipei   Toronto

With offices in
Argentina   Austria   Brazil   Chile   Czech Republic   France   Greece
Guatemala   Hungary   Italy   Japan   Poland   Portugal   Singapore
South Korea   Switzerland   Thailand   Turkey   Ukraine   Vietnam

Oxford is a registered trade mark of Oxford University Press
in the UK and certain other countries.

Published in the United States of America by
Oxford University Press
198 Madison Avenue, New York, NY 10016

© Oxford University Press 2010

First issued as an Oxford University Press paperback, 2012.

Library of Congress Cataloging-in-Publication Data
Azzouni, Jody.
Talking about nothing : numbers, hallucinations, and fictions / Jody Azzouni.
    p. cm.
ISBN 978-0-19-973894-6 (hardcover); 978-0-19-993768-4 (paperback)
1. Ontology. I. Title.
BD331.A99 2010
111—dc22   2009039246

Printed in the United States of America
on acid-free paper

Acknowledgments

My thanks to Jeff McConnell for convincing me to stop everything I was doing and write this book instead.

I'm grateful to Otávio Bueno and to Tim Crane for a number of constructive suggestions—some heeded and some not. (I expect, in the coming years, to regret not heeding more of their suggestions.) I'm also grateful to Erin Eaker, Thomas Hofweber, and Robert Thomas for constructive suggestions on the article (2009) that eventually matured into chapter 1 of this book.

My thanks to the participants in my class, Talking about Nothing, given in spring 2009.

The idea of figures 1 and 2 are mine. My thanks to Scott Brundage for bringing them so delightfully into existence.

I'm grateful to Peter Ohlin of Oxford University Press for his invaluable and unflagging assistance, both with this book and with the previous books I've published with Oxford University Press.

Finally, a thanks to the folk at Connecticut Muffin, who supplied me with copious amounts of tea while I wrote a large portion of this book.

Contents

TALKING ABOUT NOTHING

General Introduction

The default view is that hallucinations are experiences of nothing at all. "There's nothing there," we'll tell the victim—provided we think the victim is sober enough to respond to the facts. The default view about the denizens of fictional worlds, similarly, is that the characters and events depicted aren't real; they correspond to nothing at all. I'm speaking, of course, of the usual case: real people can and do appear in fiction. So too, hallucinations can occur against a background (or foreground) of things veridically seen.

To say that fictional characters don't exist isn't to say that the words, books, and other art forms (and their parts) that we read, listen to, or watch aren't real. It's to say generalizations of things like this: "Hillary Clinton" is a phrase that refers to someone; "Sherlock Holmes," despite grammatical similarity, refers to nothing at all.

One reason it's fair to call this the default view is that our epistemic practices are so clearly in accord with it. To learn about the solar system, we bring our senses and instruments to bear on the *objects* in the solar system. To learn about Mickey Mouse, we read books and watch cartoons. Of course, some of us can (and do) learn about the solar system in the same way we learn about Mickey Mouse; but a regress of learning about the solar system from others arises, one that ends in the interactions of astronomers (and other scientists) with the solar system itself. In the case of Mickey Mouse, the same regress ends only in the free creations of humans, and not in the interactions of scientists with talking mice. Those humans that participated in the creation of depictions of Mickey Mouse aren't referred to by "Mickey Mouse," nor are those numerous depictions themselves so referred to. The process of learning about Mickey Mouse never involves

Mickey Mouse; we always only study depictions and presentations of him. We can study the history and evolution of his depictions, but *he* never comes into it.

Even so, philosophers might balk at calling these claims "the default position." Consider fiction. Many philosophers are willing to commit themselves in print to the assertion that such things *do* exist. Fictional objects—so some philosophers think—are abstracta, or they are concreta existing in other possible worlds, or . . . Notice how rarified (and rare), how sophisticated—how philosophical—such views are. An ordinary mother, when explaining to her child that the depictions in Disney cartoons are of nothing real, points out that such things are "made up"; she doesn't tell her child that they exist in some other world. That would be misleading. Nor does she call them "abstracta." Such things *don't exist*, the parent (engaged in what's reasonably described as debriefing her child) will explain.

For a position to be the default position, it isn't necessary for views opposing it to bear the burden of proof. (Were that the case, I wouldn't have had to write this book.) There are complications involved in our transactions with the nonexistent that require explanation and philosophical study. Aspects of those complications, especially with respect to how we talk about the nonexistent, very naturally point philosophers away from what I've called the default position and to one or another view that takes hallucinations and fictional objects to exist.

Quine (1953) long ago noted our tendency to confuse unsuccessful reference to the nonexistent with successful reference to something else entirely: images or ideas of such. The tendency to be so confused is widespread; under the right circumstances, public images (such as films or drawings) can be confused with the fictional objects depicted—just as the sculptures of fictional or mythical beings can be confused with what they depict.

But to call this a "confusion," as I just have, and to stop thinking any further about it once the error has been pointed out, is superficial. Confusions are sometimes symptoms of something much deeper, and that's the case here. An indication of this (psychological) depth is our oddly automatic ways of reacting to depictions. Consider two cartoons (figures 1 and 2). If someone is asked, with respect to figure 2, which one is running, he will answer, "that one," or "he is," while pointing to the figure on the right. If he is then asked "who is that?" he will answer "George Bush" (if he knows), and "I don't know," if he doesn't. With respect to figure 1, however, the reaction to the second question will be puzzlement because (of course) "stick figures" are understood not to depict anyone. But if neither stick figure in figure 1 depicts anyone, then *no one is running*. After all, the drawings aren't running. All that can be running—if anything is—is what's depicted.[1] If nothing is depicted, then nothing is running.

We naturally—automatically—shift our property attributions to the depiction when we are aware that no object is depicted by that depiction. But—significantly—we don't recognize this as a shift to a description of a depiction because we don't accordingly adjust our descriptions to accurately fit depictions. We don't say

---

1. Imagine this different case: an e-book that enables figures on the "pages" to move—in which a stick figure itself moves across the page. Now we can say correctly that the stick figure is moving.

Figures 1 (above) and 2 (below).

of the stick figure that it's motionless (rather than running). Rather, we say the "stick figure" is running, and we may also simultaneously (and contradictorily) indicate *its* location on the page. ("Which figure is running?" Pointing: "That one.") In contrast, we won't describe George Bush as on the page, but only describe his caricature as located there.

One thing going on is that we have a powerful intuition that when we talk we always talk *about* things. Our talk is always directed toward one or another topic. This is not the mere grammatical impression that every sentence has a "subject." The intuition runs deeper than that—it's the impression not only that our talk is about things, but that how it is with those things determines the truth or falsity of that talk. If this description of our intuitive impression (of how it is with what we say) is right, then a kind of desperation naturally sets in when we engage in conversation about the nonexistent, for there is nothing for that talk to be directed toward. Further, there is nothing true or false to be said about nothing. If we have nothing as a subject of what we say, then we have nothing meaningful that we can say about *it*.

Quine (1953, 1–2) calls a related issue "Plato's beard" and describes it as having proven historically quite tough to shave. I call his issue "related" because it focuses only on negative existentials: claims that such and such do *not* exist. Quine's worry is this: what is it we are talking about and describing as nonexistent? The quandary I've described is broader than Quine's because we not only deny of the nonexistent that it exists; we simultaneously and naturally make what we take to be other true claims about nonexistent *things*.

The tendency to confuse depictions with what they depict may be described (as I have) as the desperate search to locate a subject matter when we become official about the nonexistence of the topic(s) of our sentences. If we officially take Mickey Mouse not to exist, then our conversation about Mickey Mouse is threatened with a loss of topic. We hang onto there being a topic by switching (or attempting to switch) to Mickey Mouse depictions as the topic (instead of Mickey Mouse). Confusion sets in because we want to hang onto various *truths* as well—ones above and beyond the mere claim that Mickey Mouse doesn't exist. So we describe Mickey Mouse as a mouse, or (relatedly) we describe a stick figure as running, even though a closer inspection shows that these remarks are not true of their subject matter—if (that is) depictions are supposed to be the topic and not what they depict.

Quine makes relatively quick work of the nonexistent. There is nothing to refer to, so any attempt to refer to the nonexistent is naturally confused. There is only one true thing one wants to say "about" Pegasus, say, and that is that he doesn't exist. But this isn't by way indicating *of something* that it doesn't exist— that path leads to Meinongian madness. Rather, one speaks of the failure of certain predicates to be instantiated. We shouldn't say of Pegasus that *it* doesn't exist; we should say instead that there is nothing unique that pegasizes. (Or, it is not the case that there is something unique that pegasizes.) What about the other things we want to say about Pegasus? Quine lets it all go. More precisely, he lets the (first-order classical) logic of this solution about negative existentials dictate the truth values of anything further we might want to say about the matter. Is Pegasus a flying horse? No, because this is false: there is something x that uniquely pegasizes, and x is a flying horse. Is Pegasus a running dog? No, because this is false: there is something x that uniquely pegasizes, and x is a running dog. What about: it is not the case that Pegasus is a flying horse. This is true, because it's the negation of a false sentence. One may balk at some of these translations of English into Logish; but reasons for dissatisfaction involve more than the fact that Quine treats a proper name as a predicate.

What might these reasons for dissatisfaction be? Here's one reason that goes—strictly speaking—beyond issues with vacuous names. Quine's solution plays fast and loose with what we might call "singular reference." We thought we were talking about something specific, Pegasus, but Quine reconfigures our talk as a general existence claim about anything that (uniquely) pegasizes. There seem to be good reasons to deny this as an appropriate reading of the semantics of proper names. Proper names don't (seem to) have quantifiers lurking within them. Indeed, and more generally, there is a class of terms: proper names, demonstratives, certain uses of definite descriptions, that seem to avoid implicit quantification and, apart from this, that seem to lack enough descriptive content to fix what such terms refer to. When I say "Albert Einstein was a physicist," or "That vase is ugly," I seem to indicate specific things (Albert Einstein, a particular vase) not by (implicitly or explicitly) utilizing a description of the form "there is something with such and such" that uniquely holds of what I refer to, but by other means entirely. For example, the object is something I can see, or the person I'm talking about is someone I've witnessed others talking about, and so is someone I've heard something about.

The second reason for dissatisfaction is Quine's "don't care" attitude toward the truth values of discourse about what doesn't exist. Perhaps it's sensible to resist claims about Mickey Mouse being a talking mouse or Pegasus being a flying horse, but it isn't sensible to resist claims about Walt Disney having invented Mickey Mouse, or Pegasus being presented in myth as a flying horse. If we go Quine's way with these statements, we find that it's as true that Disney invented Mickey Mouse as it is that Genghis Khan invented Mickey Mouse. And that won't do. Another option—in the spirit of Quine's approach—is to paraphrase these statements as not about Mickey Mouse or other fictional characters but instead as about Mickey Mouse depictions, and the like. It's been noticed, however, that suitable paraphrases—ones that preserve the appropriate truth values—aren't easily constructed. The true statements we make about fictional characters—knowing full well they don't exist—aren't true statements about the depictions of such characters. I may admire Sherlock Holmes, for example, without admiring any of the Sherlock Holmes depictions (in film or on paper) that I've experienced.

I started this general introduction with the claim that the default view is that fictional items, hallucinations, and the like, don't exist. But I've now indicated some of the ways that make the topic of the nonexistent much more complicated than the default view seems to have the resources to handle. Some aspects of our practices (the epistemic aspects) certainly point us in the direction of taking these things not to exist. But the ways we talk about the nonexistent, and (I will argue) the ways that we need and have to talk about the nonexistent, point us in the opposite direction. Such tangles invite philosophical scrutiny. Indeed, the nonexistent has been a serious topic of inquiry for quite a long time.

The majority tradition, as I call it, is one or another philosophical position in the spirit of Quine. These things don't exist, and we must adjust our ways of talking accordingly. A minority tradition has been the Meinongian one. It's hard to characterize *the* Meinongian position precisely because there are many versions.[2] Roughly, it's to accept that hallucinations, fictional objects, and the like, don't "exist," but then to deny that that's the end of the matter, ontologically speaking. On some Meinongian views, even though such objects don't exist—and, indeed, don't exist *in any sense at all* (as it's often put by proponents of the view)—they nevertheless have properties, and we can nevertheless refer to them. On other Meinongian views, although such objects don't exist, they do have some other sort of ontological value, subsistence, or whatever. As I read this family of views, the idea is this: we ordinarily deny the existence of Santa Claus, Mickey Mouse, and so on, but we can talk about them anyway, as this very introduction amply illustrates. If this talk is genuinely true and false (if we can say things that are true or things that are false about Santa Claus, Mickey Mouse, and so on, and importantly, things that are true of Santa Claus but false of Mickey Mouse, and vice versa) then there are (or there *could be*, or there *might be*) nonexistent things that we talk *about*. Furthermore, the facts about these nonexistent beings are the basis for the truth or falsity of our statements about them.

As I've just intimated, both the minority tradition and the majority tradition share an important and long-standing assumption. This is that there can be no true or false sentences (true or false thoughts) without a subject matter for these things to be true or false *of*. The Meinongian adds the caveat that the topic of conversation needn't exist, but nevertheless how things are with nonexistent things determines the truths and falsities that are *about* those things. If Mickey Mouse doesn't exist, then it's the fact that *Mickey Mouse* (that thing) doesn't exist that determines the truth of the statement "Mickey Mouse doesn't exist." It's worth adding that the Meinongian can thus preserve the apparent singularity of reference even in the case of vacuous names and hallucinations. I say, "Sherlock Holmes doesn't exist," and my remark is about Sherlock Holmes, even though he doesn't exist. I say, of an hallucination I'm experiencing, that "it's an elf I'm seeing over there," and despite my hallucination, my remark is *about* the elf over there that I'm hallucinating. No spurious generality—as in the Quinean view—seeps into what is said in these cases.

---

2. Meinong's own views are fairly subtle and complex. A good discussion can be found in Roderick Chisholm, "Beyond being and nonbeing" (1972), in *Metaphysics: The big questions*, ed. Peter van Inwagen and Dean W. Zimmerman (Oxford: Blackwell Publishing, 2008), 40–50. I always use "Meinongian," not as an indicator that a contemporary position is like Meinong's original one but (similar to how "Platonic" isn't used in metaphysics to assimilate a contemporary position to one of Plato's) as an adjective describing a broad family of contemporary views that—in one way or another, and contrary to my approach—take the metaphysical/semantic position that the truth values of statements about nonexistent objects are in virtue of the properties had by those objects.

Nevertheless, this long-standing shared assumption is what I deny in this book. There can be truths and falsities that are "about" nothing at all. More precisely, there are statements with truth values that are *not* determined by how it is with what the terms within them refer to. (Furthermore, this is because some of the terms within these statements don't refer to anything.) There have been philosophers who—broadly speaking—have denied of *all* of our statements (and of *all* of our thoughts) that they "represent" anything. Instead, what's "true" and what's "false" in what we say and think is determined by other factors entirely—for example, agreement among certain groups (or the eventual agreement among certain experts). Some of these philosophers have additionally suggested that they are proposing a "different" notion of truth—not a "correspondence" notion but a "coherence" notion, or a "pragmatist" notion, or whatnot.

This is decidedly not what I have in mind. Truth, as I argue here and as I have argued elsewhere, is not a family-concept. It is one thing, a logical device for enabling the expression of statements that can't be said directly without it. The ways that our thoughts and statements are made true are numerous. One way, broadly speaking, is by a kind of correspondence. I'm currently typing this sentence on my computer. The previous sentence was made true by how it was with me, my manuscript, and my computer at the moment I typed that sentence. It rightly described the relations between me, my manuscript, and my computer at that time. Such is not the case with $2 + 2 = 4$. Or so I have argued. There are no numbers, and so this statement is made true in some other way entirely—not by any sort of correspondence to the things that it refers to being a certain way.

I've elsewhere argued that the statements of pure mathematics are not about anything, in contrast to statements about me, my computer, or for that matter, in contrast to statements about neutrinos, microbes, and so on. Furthermore, and restricting attention to mathematical statements construed in first-order languages, my nominalism introduces no complications as far as the semantics of mathematical doctrine is concerned. For example, an entirely standard Tarskian semantics, coupled with objectual quantifiers, may be used because, contrary to the suggestions of some philosophers, it imposes no ontological presuppositions whatsoever.

Except for a summary—appended to the end of this introduction—about how my metaphysical views hang together with my views about truth and semantics, this is pretty much all I'll have to say in this book about the background metaphysics that I've argued for over the years. This is because, for the most part, the general focus of this book is quite differently directed. I'm here primarily concerned with what's called (and what I've called earlier in this general introduction) singular reference. There is an important and influential literature in philosophy of language regarding "direct reference," "*de re*" idioms, and so on, with which this book engages. This literature takes it as an evident truism that with respect to certain idioms in natural languages—proper names, demonstrative expressions, and so on—reference to specific objects is achieved without implicit or explicit utilization of quantifiers. As result, some able proponents of these views take the involvement of the objects—the ones referred to—to be constitutive of the success of statements or thoughts using such idioms and even (according to some) constitutive of the statements and thoughts themselves. "Direct reference semantics"—this is one way to put the claim—has built into it, by virtue of that semantics alone, ontological commitments. If what is being spoken of or thought about does not exist, then the singular statement or singular thought is defective. This is taken to mean not only that such statements or thoughts fail to have truth values but, far more dramatically, that nothing meaningful *at all* has been uttered or thought by such. The burden of this book is to show that such a construal of singular reference (that ontological commitments are so constitutively built into it) is utterly misguided.

This raises a point about terminology. In an earlier version of chapter 1 (Azzouni 2009a) I borrowed Tyler Burge's use of *de re* and (perhaps mischievously) extended it to vacuous terms—such as Mickey Mouse—by coining the phrase "empty *de re*." Tim Crane (personal communication) convinced me that this was a mistake: it's too easy for readers to read into my position Burgean views that I don't have (and that I don't want readers to think I have). Of course, in such a heavily plowed area of philosophy of language, it's pretty much impossible to invent a terminology free of unwanted associations. Nevertheless, Tim has suggested that I'll do better at avoiding misinterpretations by speaking of "empty singular reference" and "empty singular thought," instead, and I've gratefully adopted his suggestion.

In that same article I used a second terminological move similar to one found in Putnam (1981).[3] I restricted the use of "refer" and "about" to cases where what a term "is about" or "refers to" exists, and used "refer*" and "about*" instead for terms like "Mickey Mouse" and "Santa Claus." Of course, as we ordinarily use "about," "Mickey Mouse" is about Mickey Mouse even given the knowledge that there is no such object.[4] Tim's complaint is that my terminological choice makes my view look unintuitive when it's not. I've gone along with this suggestion of his as well and adopted conventions for "about" and "refer" that mark ontologically committing and ontologically noncommitting uses of such with superscripts in a way that better fits with the ordinary way we speak.[5]

Let me reinforce the theme that the default view about fictions and the contents of hallucinations is that such don't exist in any sense at all, have no properties, and therefore can't be the grounds for the truth values of sentences or thoughts. Because of this, I see the philosophical job before me to largely be constructive: to present the view, show its internal coherence, its compatibility with our ordinary ways of talking and thinking about the nonexistent, and also to show that it doesn't raise any new insolubilia of its own. In particular, I want to show that philosophical considerations—like the ones indicated earlier in this introduction that seem to create problems for the view—do nothing of the kind. Of course, polemics against alternative views are a requirement—nearly enough—of any

---

3. Hilary Putnam (*Reason, truth and history* [Cambridge: Cambridge University Press, 1981], 1, note 1) writes: "There is a sense of 'refer' in which I can 'refer' to what does not exist; this is not the sense in which 'refer' is used here."

4. As in, "What's everyone talking about?" "Mickey Mouse."

5. I have residual misgivings about this decision because one should avoid changing terminology from publication to publication. Philosophy, I've noticed, is hard enough as it is.

presentation of a philosophical position, and so I do engage in a bit of that. But that proponent, say, of a particular form of Meinongianism who feels that the discussion in this book has not definitively refuted his position should remember the official aim of this book.

Before I turn to an overview of the contents of this book, I want to make a brief autobiographical observation. This book, one might say (provocatively), is about the various kinds of nothing that we talk about: mathematical objects, fictions, and hallucinations. I've had substantial experiences with all three. My interests in mathematics and fiction continue to be ongoing and professional; my experiments with voluntarily induced hallucinations, however, like those of some others of my generation, were a passing occurrence during high school. Although my hallucinatory experiences were induced by the use of only three recreational drugs (as they're sometimes called), I nevertheless have good memories of how far hallucinatory experiences can go. This is importantly related to a line of argument pursued in this book. Let me explain.

As is probably the case with nearly everything that adolescents do, my usage of recreational drugs occurred in public contexts: I used them while others were using them as well—at parties, concerts, and at other social gatherings. One crucial fact about the hallucinations induced by the substances we were using is that to a surprising extent we knew what to expect (and what others were going through), at least at certain stages. This induced a lot of fun and games—where someone would gesture in certain ways or make certain movements, or direct a person to look at certain things, because *it was obvious what he or she would see*.[6] In some cases, these might be described as illusions that were induced by the particular objects seen. In other cases the benign description "illusion" won't do: what the person would see, although primed by what was within his or her visual range, nevertheless wasn't *there* in any sense at all. It's important to realize how much of a shared experience hallucinating can be. I mention this especially because the philosophical literature almost uniformly defines (nearly enough) hallucinations as private experiences.

Let me now turn to a more general methodological point. It seems fair to say that one important impact of our ongoing scientific study of ourselves and our world is the recognition that nothing "supernatural" is to be found there. One thing this means is that various sorts of magical beings (and magical powers) don't exist. Regardless of what rather a lot of Americans (in particular) still think, this indicates a substantial change in what's appropriately described as our current collective worldview. It differs greatly from the various myth-infested perspectives we (broadly speaking) continuously had from the dawn of history (and, no doubt, before) up until only a couple of centuries ago. That is, up until a few centuries ago, it was seen as a genuine (epistemic) possibility that there might be beings with significant intentional powers: abilities to intervene in the physical world in ways similar to how we perceive ourselves as able to spontaneously move our own limbs. Among these powers were thought to be the ability to induce

6. In my circles, we called these "mind games."

illusions or hallucinations in their victims. The striking and ubiquitous presence of beings with such powers in folk tales, poetry, fiction, and philosophy—up until and continuing in our own day—is not merely the invocation of various dramatic devices but a deep-set tendency to think that this is one way things could be (or could have been).

One thing we have learned, very recently, is that hallucinations and illusions generally are much harder to induce in human subjects than one might otherwise have thought. More accurately put, such experiences are more constrained in their possible content, and in the circumstances under which they might arise, than previously expected. Vision science has revealed that optical illusions arise only under very specific circumstances, ones based on the nature and structure of the visual system. One cannot induce illusions, containing any sort of content at all, nor can one induce them in any way at all. Similarly, eliciting hallucinations requires sometimes drastic intrusions in the normal workings of the human brain, and if not, at least what's required are special (and artificial) preparations.[7] In any case, the folk vision of a collective lability in what we can be induced to hallucinate has turned out to be rather wrong.[8]

Two observations need to be made about the foregoing points. The first is that a rather uncritical estimation of the range of possibility of hallucination and error has deep roots in our epistemic tradition. Part of why it's "reasonable" to think we can get it wrong enough that one or another form of global scepticism about the external world is philosophically viable is because it's presumed that—in some sense of "possible"—we could hallucinate *anything*. For the record, I regard this claim as open to serious (philosophical) challenge, and I've indicated where I think the pressure should be applied by the use of quote marks and italics in the previous sentence. That, however, is not the topic of this book. The second point is this. In ways that are hard to pin down precisely, folk-theoretic views deeply infiltrate how our language allows us to talk about the world. In particular, many of the illusion and hallucinogen thought experiments that philosophers have traditionally used for epistemic purposes (e.g., to motivate scepticisms) are appropriate evidence for semantic

7. For example, out-of-body experiences can be induced by magnetically affecting certain parts of the brain. Here, again, the range of the hallucinations experienced (their content) is pretty restricted and has to do with specific neurological aspects of the brain. Similar remarks, I stress, apply to the possible effects of various hallucinogens.

8. Part of what enabled many professional anthropologists (and his larger popular audience) to believe Carlos Castaneda's (*The teachings of Don Juan: A Yaqui way of knowledge* [New York: Washington Square Press, 1968]) descriptions of his purported hallucinations is precisely this folk belief that under certain circumstances one can hallucinate anything at all. This is importantly relevant to why his work was seen to merit dissertation status. (For the record, I regard most of his work as fiction or, less nicely put, fraud.) In any case, what I'm stressing is that what hallucinations we are *capable* of experiencing is open to empirical study. We may (someday) be able to say, about a description of such and such a purported hallucination: given the nature of the brain, it simply isn't possible to hallucinate that. Actually, we can already do this with respect to hallucinations due to certain pathologies and induced by causal interactions with specific aspects of the brain. More general (successfully confirmed) theories of how (certain kinds of) hallucinations arise will concomitantly place further constraints on what sorts of hallucinations are possible. See, for example, Stephen Grossberg, "How hallucinations may arise from brain mechanisms of learning, attention, and volition," *Journal of the International Neuropsychological Society* 6 (2000), 583–92.

claims about language, in sharp contrast to their being unconscionable tools (or so I claim) for epistemology. This must be kept in mind when evaluating the value—for philosophy of language—of the thought experiments presented in this book. For example, it's a folk belief about hallucinations that such can be indistinguishable from ordinary (veridical) experience. This may turn out to be empirically false. If so, this is (arguably) pertinent for epistemology; it isn't pertinent to the use I put thought experiments about hallucinations to in this book. Despite this, I don't ignore the fascinating empirical literature on hallucination.

I'll finish off this introduction with a very brief overview of the chapters to follow. Part I is composed of three chapters, taking up in succession the topics of numerical thought and statement, thought and statement directed toward hallucinations, and finally, those statements and thoughts when directed toward fictional objects. In all three cases, singular reference takes place without the presence of any sort of object; in all three cases, true and false statements (and true and false thoughts) successfully occur without such being made true or false by the referents of terms (that appear in those statements or thoughts) being one way or another. In all three cases, the psychological underpinning for singular reference is object-directed thinking. The chapters aren't meant to be self-contained but to somewhat follow one another in content. Issues and distinctions elucidated in earlier chapters are relied on in later ones. One crucial theme runs through all three chapters—the external discourse demand. The indispensability of mathematics to empirical science has been known and worried over by philosophers for quite some time. And so a number of philosophers have noticed the difficulty of treating mathematical discourse as not truth-apt while still enabling it to play the role it must play in the empirical sciences. It has not been noticed by any philosopher—nearly enough—that something similar is true of discourse about fictions and hallucinated objects. Such discourse must also be truth-apt because of its evidential role for certain specializations (e.g., the neurosciences, psychology, and the various sociological sciences).

Chapter 4 of part II steps back from the three case studies to canvass broader philosophical fallout. Its topic is the evidential and deductive holism of our collective science, seen both through the lens of the external discourse demand and more generally. Because specialized scientific studies employ specialized vocabularies containing (many, sometimes mostly) empty terms, there is a genuine issue of how evidence from one specialized study can be brought to bear on other ones. The primary scientific tools for doing so are what I call gross correlational regularities. These are regularities, roughly, with antecedents couched in the vocabulary of one science and with consequents in another. Examples of such regularities are genotype/phenotype correlations. I show that philosophical approaches to analyzing the relationship between sciences (e.g., molecular biology and classical Mendelian genetics) either by definitional reductions or by supervenience fail—in large measure because of the specialized nonexistent items referred to by the different theories that are to be "reduced" to one another. Where there is no ontology, but there is nevertheless truth and falsity that bears evidentially on other aspects of our scientific doctrine, these forms of reductionism can have no foothold.

Once it's recognized that the primary connective tissue between scientific theories couched in different vocabularies is made up of gross correlational regularities, the way is cleared to seeing the crucial role of blind truth-ascription and deduction in enabling the application of results from one scientific theory to another either as evidence or as part of a background theory. It's shown that blind truth-ascription places strong constraints on the truth idiom: pluralist approaches to truth (which have been fairly popular of late) can't meet these constraints. Similar arguments show that the logical principles governing deduction have to be monistic as well.

Chapter 5 turns to a special science: semantics. It indicates how the foregoing general points about science apply specifically to semantics. In particular, truth-conditional theories of meaning are the focus, and I show that such theories don't have the ontological commitments that almost every philosopher of language has interpreted them as having. The chapter illustrates how empty singular statements may be treated in fairly standard ways by truth-conditional theories of meaning, without requiring such statements to be semantically "incomplete" or "vacuous." This is something of a surprise if only because it's so widely taken for granted that the objects referred to are essential to the semantics of singular expressions. I begin chapter 5 with a discussion of the semantics of ordinary (first-order) quantifiers before turning to proper names and other idioms. Despite semantics and ontology having been intimate for so long, it turns out that divorce (in this case at least) is relatively painless for one of the parties. Those whose work is primarily in semantics won't (really) notice that anything is missing. Those with metaphysical ambitions, however (ontologists, for example), have quite a lot of really hard work ahead of them.

Appendix: A Sketch of Ontology, Truth, Semantics, and Their Interrelationships

Ontology

I claim that we (collectively) subscribe to a particular criterion for what exists. This is that anything exists if and only if it's mind- and language-independent. Dream figures, fictional characters that authors have made up, and hallucinated objects are all, in the sense meant, mind- and language-dependent. Dinosaurs, protons, microbes, other people, chairs, buildings, stars, and so on are (purported) examples of mind- and language-independent objects. There is another way of using "mind-dependent" or "language-dependent," according to which a building or a chair is "mind-dependent" (because these objects wouldn't exist if people hadn't decided to make them). This isn't how these words are being used here. In my sense of "mind-independent" and "language-independent," no one can dictate such an object into existence by (merely) thinking it or symbolizing it as so. For that matter, no one can dictate the properties of such an object by (merely) thinking them as having such or by symbolizing them as having such.[9]

The uses of the word "exist" in this discussion are restricted to ontologically relevant ones. Words such as "there is," "exist," and so on—which can be used in some contexts in ontologically serious ways and in other contexts not so utilized—are linguistically complicated because their literal meaning doesn't require that they be understood one way or the other.[10]

I have long used the phrase "ontologically independent" to describe things that are mind- and language-independent. This is perhaps another bad terminological choice on my part because many philosophers use "ontological independence" and "ontological dependence" in a quite different way (e.g., a trope, some philosophers say, is "ontologically dependent" on the object of which it is a trope).

Leaving terminological issues aside, it may seem that the ontological independence criterion faces difficulties if it's to be understood as a *necessary and sufficient* condition for existence. Consider holes. Holes, let's say, don't exist. Despite that, they hardly seem to be things that are mind- and language-dependent.[11] We must discover the dimensions and contours of any hole in exactly the same way we must discover the dimensions and contours of anything real (a chair, say). Some holes are millions of years old, and their dimensions and contours are surely as independent of our language and our minds as the dimensions and contours of anything that exists. Perhaps there is some controversy about whether holes exist or not, but surely we don't want the adoption of this criterion to dictate that holes exist.

A second objection to the criterion is that problems arise because of variations in how something "depending" on a mind or a language can be understood. Must one think of the item in some detail or name it for it to be so dependent, or need one only quantify over it? On the former, more stringent view, unnamed sets are mind-independent (contrary to the result a nominalist such as myself would want). On the latter, less stringent view, one can think of numerous fictional characters by thinking, say, of "all the detectives that haven't been written about yet." To invent a fictional character, presumably, is to think of him or her—but on this less stringent characterization of mind and language dependence, this is far too easy to do. In addition, the criterion seems to allow all the undesirable mind-dependent objects that Meinong's original position was thought to be plagued with: square circles and the like.[12]

There is a very quick response to both sets of objections. This is that both of them trade on a Meinongian presupposition that the criterion is to be applied to nonexistent things to determine that they don't exist. But that's wrong. If something

---

9. My thanks to Michael Glanzberg for pressing me on this issue.

10. See Jody Azzouni, "Ontology and the word 'exist': Uneasy relations," *Philosophia Mathematica*, forthcoming (a).

11. I owe this choice of example (and the objection) to Ted Sider (personal communication, March 20, 2009).

12. I owe this series of objections to Daniel Nolan (personal communication, March 20, 2009).

doesn't exist, then there is no such thing. There being no such thing means that it has no properties. There is nothing, therefore, to apply the criterion to; there is nothing to discover about what doesn't exist. If holes exist, therefore, they don't violate the criterion. If holes don't exist, they don't violate the criterion either. In neither case is there a violation of the criterion.

This solution only seems to give rise to a further problem.[13] This is that if the criterion is only to be "one-legged," as it were, to only apply to what exists, then there is a worry about what real work the phrases "mind- and language-dependent" (and for that matter "mind- and language-independent") can be doing. For there are many criteria that are coextensive with what exists. In particular, $x = x$ applies to all and only what exists (because it isn't true that items that don't exist are the same as, or for that matter, not the same as, themselves).

Although the ontological independence criterion is a metaphysical one, its value isn't metaphysical. Rather, the criterion is epistemically illuminating. I'll explain the point this way: why is it informative to observe that our community has ontological independence in the foregoing sense as its criterion, and why is it not informative to observe that our community has $x = x$ as its criterion? Because the former criterion and not the latter one explains our epistemic practices when we go about trying to find out what exists (and what doesn't). In our explorations of what there is (and what it's like), we use our senses, which we recognize to operate only in fairly restricted ways, and we use instruments that epistemically generalize on our senses. I call this *thick epistemic access*.[14]

It's an empirical claim that the only way we have to discover anything about objects that are ontologically independent of us is through our senses or instrumentation. It's also an empirical claim that the ways we have of discovering ontologically independent objects and their properties is (roughly) by epistemic access to them or by epistemic access to items that they have affected. As I've stated, these are empirical results about what appropriate forms of epistemic access there are to what's ontologically independent.

Given these empirical results, however, we can see how the mind- and language-independence criterion for what exists can be used to classify an "object" as not existing: it isn't by a direct application of the criterion to the purported object—this is impossible. Rather, we discover that the legitimate methods we use to attribute properties to a purported object don't involve the appropriate forms of epistemic access to that object. For example (in the case of fictions) we or others simply stipulate what properties fictional objects have, or (in the case of holes) the purported properties of the object are derived from the actual properties of other things that are actually the items that we sense (or instrumentally study), or (in the case of hallucinations) the items in question are revealed to be figments of our

13. I owe this objection to Carrie Jenkins and Benjamin Schnieder (personal communications, March 20, 2009).

14. Further discussion of thick epistemic access is found in Jody Azzouni, *Deflating existential consequence: A case for nominalism* (Oxford: Oxford University Press, 2004a) and in Jody Azzouni, "Theory, observation and scientific realism," *British Journal of Philosophical Science* 55 (2004b), 371–92. I've omitted some complexities from this summary.

minds—the properties of which are projected to appearances in the world by our recollections of real objects or by other aspects of our minds.

In all these cases, we thus deduce the mind-dependence or language-dependence of the items in question from the corollary that they don't exist. This latter fact, in turn, is deduced from epistemic facts about how the truths about these objects are established—that the epistemic methods used don't fit the (empirically established) requirements of epistemic access to mind- and language-independent objects.[15]

Language and Truth

In the last section, I talked about there being truths about objects that don't exist. Indeed, we utilize truths about nonexistent objects all the time. We quantify, for example, over mathematical objects; these are items that are denied existence by the foregoing criterion for what exists. Given that talk about mathematical objects is indispensable—it can't be eliminated—my view is that (this is a package deal) Quine's criterion and correspondence views of truth are to be rejected.

These days, however, many philosophers are instead inclined to adopt one or another species of fictionalism,[16] the view that an otherwise indispensable body of discourse needn't be true. Indeed, many are inclined to think that the fictionalist position is forced once (i) one accepts that an indispensable discourse must have nonreferring terms in it, and (ii) one rejects Meinongian approaches. This is because those philosophers think that sentences with vacuous terms in them must be assigned truth values in accord with a vacuous reading of those terms. If there are no mathematical objects, then the statement "There are numbers," for example, is false.

If one rejects Quine's criterion, this is not so. Uses of "there are" needn't presuppose existence. Indeed, the use of names in true and false sentences needn't presuppose that such refer to what exists. But there is more that needs to be said about this. First of all, how are truth and falsity supposed to operate in such circumstances? More specifically, what is the semantics for sentences with vacuous terms supposed to look like, and how does that semantics yield the resulting truth values of sentences? My answer is that this series of questions betrays a confusion—or, more charitably, a programmatic tendency to read metaphysical assumptions inappropriately into semantics. Coupled with this programmatic tendency is a second one: to expect that the truth conditions of sentences suffice to determine the truth values of those sentences.

My first counterclaim is this: regardless of whether or not the terms in a set of sentences correspond to anything that exists, exactly the same semantics can be given to that set of sentences.[17] In general, the semantics of a set of sentences is given by a

15. My thanks to Carrie Jenkins, Daniel Nolan, Benjamin Schnieder, and Ted Sider, for the discussions that eventually gave rise to these eight paragraphs. They are not responsible for the particular form that these remembered objections have emerged on paper.

16. See Mark Eli Kalderon, "Introduction," in *Fictionalism in metaphysics*, ed. Mark Eli Kalderon (Oxford: Oxford University Press, 2005), 1–10.

17. Making this case is the topic of chapter 5.

second set of sentences, and the vacuous terms occurring in the first set of sentences can be appropriately matched with vacuous terms occurring in the second set.

This gives rise to a second, more urgent question. What, then, is the connection between the semantics attributed to sentences and their actual truth values? Consider the sentence, "Zeus was worshiped by the ancient Greeks." Presumably this sentence is true, and presumably the semantics of the sentence provides it with truth conditions. How are its truth conditions—supplied by the semantics of this sentence—connected to its truth?

"Truth conditions" is unfortunate terminology that was originally used to describe a certain (Tarskian) style of semantic theory because of the false impression that such semantic theories must yield the truth values of the sentences the semantic theories are of. On the ontologically neutral view of semantics, as noted, a "truth-conditional" semantics (e.g., a Tarskian theory using objectual quantifiers) can be given to a set of sentences exactly as it's done in the various semantic traditions. Furthermore, these truth-conditions are compatible with the truth values these sentences actually have. For example, on a Tarskian approach, the truth of "Zeus was worshiped by the ancient Greeks" is correlated with the truth of a (meta)language sentence, perhaps of the form, "ZEUS WAS WORSHIPED BY THE ANCIENT GREEKS," where "Zeus" and "ZEUS" are both vacuous terms, and where the two sentences are to have the same truth value (true, in this case).

The question persists: how do the actual truth values of sentences with vacuous terms arise? To enable an illuminating description of how the truth values of sentences with vacuous terms relate to the truth conditions of those sentences supplied by a semantic theory, one should separate talk of *truth conditions* from talk of *truth-value inducers*. The truth conditions of a sentence are the clauses governing that sentence given by a semantic theory. The truth-value inducers are the objects in the world of which the truth values of the sentence are in virtue. In the specific case where *all* the terms in a sentence refer to objects that exist, the truth-value inducers of a sentence can be identified with the objects to which terms in that sentence refer (or with those objects and how they are, etc.).[18]

When a sentence has vacuous terms in it, this isn't the case. Consider mathematical statements. On the nominalist view, the truth-value inducers for "2 + 2 = 4" aren't the numbers and their relationships because there are no such numbers. Rather, the truth-value inducers are a blend of (relevant) objects that exist—us, our language, and our epistemic practices included—and that jointly yield the indispensability of the truth of "2 + 2 = 4," to our assertoric practices in ordinary life and our sciences. Included among the truth-value inducers are physical objects, but nothing corresponding to the terms "2" or "4" are among these truth-value inducers.

---

18. In other words, what the constants in the sentence refer to and what the quantifiers in the sentence range over. In this case, and only in this case, the "truth-value inducers" can be called without it being misleading (and this is currently popular language) "truth makers."

One last point should be stressed to round out this brief summary. The conception of truth being used here isn't meant to replace "correspondence truth" by, say, "permanently indispensable truth." One might think this is the case because one might think that what's on offer is a "pluralist notion" of truth that allows a role for correspondence when terms are nonvacuous, but that utilizes indispensability considerations when terms are vacuous. Instead, my view is a deflationist one where the only characterization of the meaning of "true" is (as a logical device) in terms of a (generalization of) Tarski biconditionals, statements of the form, "'Snow is white' is true if and only if snow is white."[19]

The resulting package of doctrines is surprisingly neat, I think, despite how many traditional philosophical positions have to be jettisoned to construct it. Some omelets, after all, do turn out to be attractive after all the eggs have been broken.

---

19. See Jody Azzouni, "Deflationist truth," in *Handbook on truth*, ed. Michael Glanzberg (Oxford: Blackwell Publishing, forthcoming [b]).

PART I

NUMBERS, HALLUCINATIONS, AND FICTIONS

Kant, in his notion of sensible intuition as a singular capacity, and Russell, in his notion of acquaintance, try to do justice to a common intuition. They believe that we have an epistemically distinctive and important capacity, or set of capacities, to connect our thought to particulars in a singular way. Both philosophers see this sort of capacity as fundamental in understanding human knowledge. Both are opposed to the view that this capacity can be reduced to predicative, attributive capacities. Both seem to be on to something deep about our representational and epistemic relations to objective subject matters. The main reason to reflect on *de re* phenomena is to try to obtain further insight into this "something."

—Tyler Burge (2007b, 67)

Numbers

1.0 An Introduction for Browsers, Grazers, and People Who Like to Know What's Coming before It Arrives

I first describe the *de re*/*de dicto* distinction, as Burge does, in terms of a thought or statement being object dependent, having content that's not fully conceptualized but having to be completed by a corresponding object. As Burge notes, a characterization of the *de re* requiring a demonstrative or indexical element in the *de re* thought or statement doesn't easily apply to mathematical thoughts or statements. For Burge, the *de re*, in the mathematical case, is revealed instead by the "not completely conceptual relation" that's purportedly had "to a *re*"—that is, that mathematical thought and speech seem to intrinsically involve objects that are only incompletely characterized by our conceptions of them. This incomplete conceptualization of numbers, Burge argues, emerges in both the practice of pure computation and in the practice of counting objects (the application of numeral thought to the world).

At this point (by the end of section 1.2), Burge's strategy (one that's very nearly mandatory for anyone who wants to argue for the singular status of numeral thought and speech) has been laid out. In section 1.3, I show that objects are absent from both mathematical practices. This demonstration is facilitated by an application of the epistemic role puzzle (Azzouni 1994, §7). In 1.4, the nature of our involuntary object-directed thought—with respect to numeration—is taken up. It's shown that the psychological impossibility of engaging in numeration without thinking (correspondingly) of objects—numbers—that one is manipulating is entirely compatible with the understanding (or belief) that there are no such things. This motivates the categories of empty singular thought and speech (notions introduced in section 1.5): object-directed thought and speech using referential terminology (e.g., names and demonstratives) coupled with there being no such objects that correspond to those thoughts and statements.

In section 1.6, I turn to polemics, in this case the suggestion that empty singular thought is better described as pretence thought or mock thought. This is a strategy popular enough across so many different philosophical venues—among philosophers with rather different background motivations—that it requires revisiting several times during the course of this book. In this section, it's pointed out that such a perspective on numeration fits very badly with the psychological states we are in when we engage in numeration. It's also indicated how truth-conditional semantic theories for numeration languages can follow standard lines: provide truth conditions for sentences containing vacuous terms (in this case, numerals) that are indistinguishable from those truth conditions provided for sentences containing nonvacuous terms (names). This topic is taken up more fully in chapter 5.

In section 1.7, I turn to Meinongian strategies. Like pretence approaches, these strategies are also very popular, and ones that emerge in many different philosophical venues. This is, therefore, only the first of several discussions of them. Here I restrict myself to attempting to characterize the family of Meinongian approaches in a suitably general way and to distinguishing them from the approach that's taken in this book.

A crucial distinction that arises in this discussion is that between reference^r and aboutness^r, on the one hand, and reference^e and aboutness^e on the other. Reference^r and aboutness^r are restricted to cases where there are genuine relations between terms (names, quantifiers, demonstratives, etc.) and objects—be those objects real or Meinongian. Such relations are taken by realists and Meinongians to be the grounds of or to be that in virtue of which (different philosophers express this differently) statements and thoughts have the truth values they have. That is, it's *those* objects and their properties that the truth and falsity of statements *about them* are due to.

Reference^r and aboutness^r are to be contrasted with reference^e and aboutness^e. The latter are not relations at all. Instead, they are characterizations of certain terms (names, quantifiers, etc.) when such play a certain role in discourse: have grammatical and semantic roles in sentences indistinguishable from otherwise referential^r terms. So when a term is said to refer^e, no relationship to anything is indicated. Nevertheless, we can correctly say: "Pegasus" refers to Pegasus; but this is because of the application of the name-schemata "——" refers to ——, one that applies to every name by virtue of sheer grammatical role. That this name-schemata can be appropriately applied to a name doesn't require a metaphysical state of affairs in which that name is related to an object—in any sense of "object" that attributes a metaphysical status to such (apart from its existing, being, etc., in no sense at all).

The ways we ordinarily speak of reference and aboutness, as the foregoing illustrates, doesn't distinguish between the ʳ- and the ᵉ-notions. We indifferently describe "Mickey Mouse" as referring to Mickey Mouse, just as we describe "Barack Obama" as referring to Barack Obama. Semantic theory, as described in chapter 5, should follow ordinary language in not making distinctions on the basis of ontology.

Another important notion I introduce in this chapter is that of a truth-value inducer. This is to be contrasted with a "truth maker." The truth-value inducers are those factors in the world (objects and relations among such) that—dovetailing with our expressive and inferential needs—force truth values on the sentences we use. In cases where a sentence contains terms that referʳ, the relata of such terms and relations among such can be described as truth-value inducers that are truth makers. But where the terms in a sentence referᵉ, the truth-value inducers are other things (and relations among such) that the terms in such a sentence are neither aboutᵉ nor aboutʳ. "Mickey Mouse was invented by Walt Disney," for example, has among its truth-value inducers, certain objects (Walt Disney, drawings, etc.) that induce its truth value. Mickey Mouse isn't among these.

1.1 Burge's *De Re/De Dicto* Distinction

The *de re*/*de dicto* distinction is perhaps best known in one or another semantic guise. Burge (2007b, 68)[1] offers one semantic account of it on which

> an [attitude] ascription ascribes a *de re* attitude if it ascribes the attitude by ascribing a relation between what is expressed by an open sentence, understood as having a free variable marking a demonstrative-like application, and a *re*[2] to which the free variable is referentially related. The semantical account maintains that an ascription ascribes a *de dicto* attitude if it ascribes the attitude by ascribing what is expressed by a closed sentence—roughly one that involves no applied demonstrative or indexical elements.

A corresponding epistemic account is the following (68–69):

> An attitude is *de dicto* if it is completely conceptualized. An attitude is *de re* if it has a content that is not completely conceptualized (and, it should be added, a not completely

1. These forthcoming *de re*/*de dicto* characterizations originally occur in Tyler Burge, "Belief de re" [1977], in *Foundations of mind* [Oxford: Oxford University Press, 2007], 44–64, and are amplified and evaluated in his postscript (Postscript to "belief de re," in *Foundations of mind* [Oxford: Oxford University Press, 2007b], 65–81). Subsequent references to Burge's work in this chapter, except when otherwise indicated, are to the latter.

2. It has been stressed to me by several people (Tim Crane, Jeff McConnell, and Robert Thomas, among others) that Latin grammar is incompatible with Burge's practice of singularizing the word: *res*. People who know and care about Latin describe Burge's practice as a mistake. (Perhaps, however, Burge has simply "Americanized" the grammar.) In any case, I leave Burge's quotations as is, and either respect the Latin grammar in my own discussion or, more often, substitute the words "object" and "objects"—as appropriate—for his *re* and *res*. In doing so, I'm not presuming that Burge's *res* are objects and not properties. The latter option is evaluated at the end of section 1.3.

conceptualized element in the content succeeds in referring to a *re*). That is, the content contains a demonstrative or indexical element successfully applied to a *re*. The application of the demonstrative or indexical element is the element in the content that prevents the content from being completely conceptualized. This element is formalized by a free variable contextually applied. When successful, such applications are to *res*.

Burge (70) notes that perceptual beliefs constitute a "paradigm case" of *de re* attitudes. *S* sees an urn, and thinks (or says), "that's an urn." The urn (in this case) is the *res* in question; the content of *S*'s thought—however appropriately described—contains a demonstrative or indexical element, and correspondingly, *S*'s utterance contains a demonstrative-like application.

These two complementary accounts don't apply to mathematical thinking: "it is not plausible that demonstratives or indexicals occur in the contents of thoughts in pure mathematics."[3] It's not plausible that the "representational content $\underline{3 + 5 = 8}$" contain demonstratives or indexicals.[4] A second (69) "epistemic account" taken by Burge to remedy this drawback is this: "an attitude is *de re* if it involves an appropriate 'not completely conceptual' relation to a *re*." This is offered as a broader epistemic account that includes the narrower—just described— epistemic account, but in addition is able to handle cases such as pure mathematical thought. Burge writes (70): "The second epistemic account I gave, vague as it was, is more useful than the first as a guide in this enterprise [of characterizing epistemic kinds that are more general, that include the mathematical cases, and that can plausibly be associated with the terms '*de re*' and '*de dicto*']. So I shall take it that at least some simple arithmetical beliefs are singular *de re* attitudes. The *res* are natural numbers. An example might be a belief that $3 + 5 = 8$."

1.2 Burge on "Not Completely Conceptual" Relations to Numbers

How, exactly, is the "not completely conceptual" relation to numbers (as *res*) characterized and established? After all, the presence of a demonstrative or contextual element in a thought looks like a relatively *transparent* indicator of how specific objects intrude into thought and expression.[5] When such elements are absent from thought and expression, more work is needed to reveal the machinations of specific objects, if any. Expressions or thoughts involving names, for

---

3. Burge, 69. The adjective "pure," presumably, is meant to exclude cases where *S* gestures at a blackboard, and thinks: "That number is prime."

4. I follow Burge's implicit convention of indicating "representational content" with underlining. Representational content (Tyler Burge, "Introduction," in *Foundations of mind* [Oxford: Oxford University Press, 2007a], 2) "is a structured abstraction that can be evaluated for truth or falsity, or for perceptual correctness or incorrectness. A propositional attitude, like a belief that not all that glisters is gold, has a propositional representational content. The representational content is that not all that glisters is gold."

5. This claim will be successfully challenged after more attention is paid to the truth values of (and corresponding intuitions about) statements and thoughts directed toward hallucinations and illusions in chapter 2.

example, often lack demonstrative elements (their representational contents can seem completely conceptualized), yet there are widely accepted thought experiments (e.g., in Kripke 1972) that establish their singular character.[6] As Burge (1979, 234) notes, "it seems intuitively implausible that a person who uses proper names . . . always has or grasps abstract thought components ['concepts'] that are sufficiently complete to determine uniquely and in a context-free way the things he refers to." The "not completely conceptual" relations—to the objects referred to by proper names—are taken to be (at least partially) constituted by perceptual, contextual, and other (broader) "causal" relations, for example, sociological/ historical ones.

Even granting, however, the somewhat controversial linguistic claim that numerals are names,[7] one should be cautious about extending claims about names in general to this special case. Not only does the neuropsychology (and neurophysiology!) with respect to numerals differ from that of other names in the vernacular, but intuitions about numerals that bear on the question of whether numerals are genuinely singular ("involving not completely conceptual" relations to objects) differ, too. The case of numerals, therefore, needs independent examination.

There are two abilities connected—in humans—with numeration. The first is (pure) computation: calculations of sums, differences, and so on. Given base 10 notation, for example, there are computational tricks that we learn to exploit, all based on there being ten canonical names for the first ten numbers (including zero, which—in addition—operates as a place-holder), and base 10 concatenation names for the larger numbers.[8] A second ability is the application of numerals to quantities of objects—ones perceptually grasped, for example (three people walking together in a field). One can recognize the quantitative size of small numbers of objects at a glance; larger groups may either be counted explicitly, estimated, or divided into smaller groups that may in turn be recognized at a glance.[9]

Burge's strategy for attributing to us singular attitudes toward the small numbers[10] acknowledges these capacities, and is consequently based on two strategic legs. First, he acknowledges our ability to perceptually recognize applica-

6. I'm attempting to navigate terminological hurdles here with respect to Burge's usage of "*de re*" and my own use of "singular." "*De re*" is contrasted with "*de dicto*"; "singular," correspondingly, is contrasted with "fully predicative," "fully attributive," or perhaps with "fully conceptual." For the purposes of this chapter, the distinction—that both contrasting sets of terms mark out—comes down to whether, in the use of a term, its contribution to the truth value of the sentence it appears in involves what it refers to or instead is entirely in virtue of descriptive content associated with it.

7. As Tyler Burge ("Postscript to 'Frege and the hierarchy,'" In *Truth, thought, reason* [Oxford: Oxford University Press 2005], 173, note 13) is willing to.

8. Any base notation, of course, offers analogous advantages.

9. Significantly, these abilities seem to turn on different subpersonal capacities, and ones that—in cleverly designed experimental situations—interfere with one another. See Stanislaus Dehaene, *The number sense: How the mind creates mathematics* (Oxford: Oxford University Press, 1997).

10. Burge explores—in a somewhat noncommittal way—the attribution of singular attitudes toward larger numbers as well. Since, on his view, such attitudes must rely on singular attitudes toward smaller numbers, I focus my concern on the latter. In any case, the issues I raise will be seen to clearly apply to any full story that anyone tries to give about singular numerical attitudes.

tions of numbers.[11] He writes (71): "Obviously, complex numeral names are formed from simpler ones. I think that the simpler ones are associated with a capacity for immediate, non-inferential, non-computational counting. We have a capacity to count small groups . . . at a glance. We are able to apply the number in counting immediately—non-inferentially through perception."[12]

Second, in his acknowledgment of our computational abilities, Burge (73) notes that "the simple individual concepts, expressed by the numerals, are not products but bases of conceptual computations." This is not a claim about all numerals; rather (72), "canonical concepts for larger numbers are the results of computations on the psychologically simple and immediately applicable (applicable, say, in perception-based counting) canonical representations of smaller numbers."[13]

Crucial to Burge's strategy is that these two abilities (with respect to small numbers) are joined seamlessly in our possession of individual concepts of the (smaller) numbers that aren't descriptive (74–75): "Numerals do not describe numbers. Certainly, the non-complex numerals ($\underline{1}$, $\underline{2}$ . . . $\underline{9}$) do not. Both of these types of *de re* representation are associated with special immediate, non-descriptive powers—understanding and immediate perceptual applicability. These powers are not completely conceptual, in that they involve a relation to the *re* that goes beyond its *merely* being conceived."

He writes further (71): "The equivalences between counting with numerals, on the one hand, and quantificational expressions that capture the counting of objects falling under predicates, on the other, is so close that the relation seems to me to be constitutive."[14]

Once the individual numerical concepts are in place as the sources of our twin abilities with numeration, the objects corresponding to them are not far behind. Because (71) "the capacity to represent the simplest natural numbers . . . is associated with a perceptual capacity for immediate perceptual application in counting[,] there is a relation to these smaller numbers in addition to being able to

11. Adult humans share these abilities with very young children—babies in particular—and with many animals. See Dehaene (1997) for descriptions of empirical results; a more recent discussion occurs in Susan Carey, "Where our number concepts come from," *Journal of Philosophy* 106:4 (2009), 220–54.

12. Burge's discussion intertwines singular attitudes towards numbers and singular attitudes toward thought. The latter raise distinct issues that I'm setting aside, so I'm excising discussion of the latter singular attitudes from the quotations.

13. And (72): "Embedded in the content of a complex numeral individual concept ($\underline{547}$) are simple individual concepts ($\underline{5}$, $\underline{4}$, $\underline{7}$) that involve *de re* application."

14. I won't dwell on objections to this joining of different abilities in the possession of one set of individual numerical concepts—there are more significant problems looming ahead—but it's worth noting that this is offered as a claim about conceptual abilities that are to be so joined. Thus, for Burge to indicate (in note 7, 71) the "familiar fact" that there are three F's is equivalent to the first-order claim that there are F's, x, y, and z, which aren't identical to one another, and so on, hardly suffices as argument. In point of fact, *psychologically speaking*, the abilities in question have been empirically shown to come apart (as noted in note 9) both in the sense that some humans and animals can have one kind of ability without the other, and in the more significant sense that the subpersonal machinery for these differing abilities can operate independently and at cross-purposes. This may not matter if the purpose is only to describe concepts that we are stipulated to possess—that is, if the concepts in question are ones that we are deemed to possess by virtue of our success at various numeration tasks. Such a stipulation won't do if the task is one of explaining how the possession of such concepts involves numerical objects—in that case, the psychological details of exactly how those concept operate is what matters, and not the official stipulations. This point will be made clearer in section 1.3.

conceive them—being able to apply individual concepts of them noninferentially and noncomputationally in counting perceived groups."

He later puts the same point (slightly) differently (75): "We apply the individual concept for the *re* immediately in perception, as well as merely conceive of the *re*. [This type of *de re*] representation on this conception [is] marked by a direct, epistemically basic relation to the *re* that goes beyond merely conceiving of it."

1.3 Does Our Grasp of Numerals (and Numeration Concepts) Really Require a Relationship to Objects?

There is a peculiar—though quite widely shared—tendency to ontological bluffing that occurs in these kinds of ingenious descriptions of our numeration powers. It's one that I hope the deviousness of which is already clear: one can concede to Burge all the elements of his description of how our abilities with small numbers arise from our possession of individual numerical concepts, while simultaneously (and consistently) denying that the *res* postulated by Burge as corresponding to these concepts play any role whatsoever in the description he has given.

One way to see the force of this objection is to notice that the success of the perceptual practices he describes is one that involves not the "application of the number" to small groups of objects but the implementation of the *numeral concept* to small groups of objects. Similarly, the simple computations that Burge alludes to are ones fully explained by a facility with one's concepts and/or notation, when faced with certain numeration task, and regardless of the existence (or not) of the *res* purportedly corresponding to the concepts/notation in question.[15]

A way to see the force of the objection is to imagine that the numbers have changed referential order with respect to the numerals: $\underline{1}$ now refers to 2, $\underline{2}$ to 1, $\underline{3}$ to 4, $\underline{4}$ to 3, etc. Nothing about the mathematical abilities that Burge has described is affected by such a shift; nor would anything in the practice be affected should such numbers happen altogether not to exist. Notice what this objection doesn't presuppose. It doesn't presuppose that numbers are abstracta; and so the objection *isn't* that computational facility or the perceptual recognition of the numerical sizes of small groups of objects seems utterly disconnected from such items (because of

---

15. That these computations are really matters more of notation than of notation-free conceptualizations is clear from the fact that the numerals ($\underline{1}$, $\underline{2}$, . . . $\underline{9}$) being nondescriptive is transparently a matter of base 10 notation. Far more of the numerals are "nondescriptive" in higher base notations, and far fewer are so in base 2 notation. It's hard, I should note, to sustain the claim that computationally complex numerals—relative to a base notation—are nondescriptive given the point, noted by Burge (and cited in note 13), that "embedded in the content of a complex numeral individual concept ($\underline{547}$) are simple individual concepts ($\underline{5}$, $\underline{4}$, $\underline{7}$)." Nevertheless, because the objection being raised in this section doesn't require or presuppose that our mastery of the abilities Burge describes actually turns on notational abilities (as opposed to conceptual ones), I'll accept for purposes of argument that primitive numerical thought-concepts—quite apart from mastery of notation—might be the significant loci of these abilities.

their causal inertness, nonspatiality, nontemporality, etc.).[16] Rather, the point is this: except by the expedient of identifying the numbers with the concepts and/or notation underlying our mastery of computation and perceptual numerical recognition, such numbers visibly play no role in the successful execution of these abilities, regardless of what properties they turn out to have.

Relatedly, it's important that a corresponding role problem for the objects of thoughts (or expressions) doesn't arise with respect to objects in other domains. Should S see an urn, and think, "that's an urn," crucial to his thought being about *that urn* are (nonconceptualized and nonrepresentational) facts about perception that are (at least partly) involved in the relationship between S and the urn. One therefore cannot simply replace the urn with a vase in a thought experiment (corresponding to the referential-order thought experiment above about 1, 2, 3 . . . and 1, 2, 3 . . .), and have everything go swimmingly. The relationship between S and that urn is based partly on the perceptual interactions between S and that urn. It's those perceptual interactions that indicate (in part) "the epistemic role" of the urn itself (since they rely on *its* causal powers—e.g., its opacity, its shape). For when we engage in a detailed study of the perceptual abilities of S, what emerges is a description of—to put it roughly—the sorts of things S is capable of distinguishing by perception (and why). At this point, the actual (and perhaps dispositional) properties possessed by the *urn* become relevant, and *are built into* our explanation of why S sees the urn as he does. It's precisely the absence of any such (epistemic) role, however construed, for numbers in numerical thoughts about them, that the objection—raised to Burge's characterization of numerical objects in numerical cognition—turns on.[17]

For those who like to keep their nomenclature straight, this is—therefore—*not* the challenge that has come to be associated with Benacerraf's name.[18] Rather, it's "the epistemic role puzzle."[19] Benacerraf's challenge turns on a specification of certain properties for the *res* (atemporality, acausality, etc.) and the subsequent

16. Pace Alan Baker ("Mathematical skepticism," in *Scientific papers of Latvia*, vol. 739, ed. Jurģis Šķilters [Riga, Latvia: Latvijas Universitāte, 2008], 15) who assimilates my argument to a quite different one that focuses on the existence or nonexistence of abstracta making no difference to the concrete physical world.

17. Such epistemic roles are present for the theoretical objects that science posits as well, but in such cases (usually) the object's susceptibility to instrumental access (and not perception) reveals such. See Jody Azzouni, "Stipulation, logic, and ontological independence," *Philosophia Mathematica* 3:8 (2000b), 225–43 for further discussion of this.

18. See Paul Benacerraf, "Mathematical truth," *Journal of Philosophy* 70 (1973), 661–80.

19. See Jody Azzouni, *Metaphysical myths, mathematical practice: The ontology and epistemology of the exact science* (Cambridge: Cambridge University Press, 1994), §7, where the epistemic role puzzle first appears and is brought against a wide array of views that attempt to find an epistemic role for mathematical objects in the practice of mathematics. The point (again) isn't that mathematical objects aren't the sorts of things that can have an epistemic role (because they're outside space and time, say); the point is that when we closely look at mathematical practice, we find no epistemic role for mathematical objects howsoever philosophers construe them. See Azzouni (2000b); see as well Yvonne Raley, "Jobless objects: Mathematical posits in crisis," in *Philosophy of mathematics: Set theory, measuring theories, and nominalism*, ed. Gerhard Preyer and Georg Peters (Frankfurt: Ontos-Verlag, 2008), 112–31 (where the epistemic role puzzle is brought to bear against Mark McEvoy, "Is reliabilism compatible with mathematical knowledge?" *Philosophical Forum* 35:4 [2004], 423–37). Another way to see the distinctive insight the epistemic role puzzle offers is to note that the reason that the mathematical tradition had (and has) no problem construing mathematical objects as "outside" time and space is because such objects had (and have) no epistemic role in the practice itself.

raising of the question of how things with those properties can be known (given certain broad but reasonable claims about what knowing about something requires). Part of the (philosophical) popularity of Benacerraf's challenge, no doubt, stems from its formulation rather directly inviting philosophical attempts to circumvent it—either by changing the description of numbers (so that they are more amenable to conditions on knowledge) or by reconceptualizing conditions on knowledge to make the latter more amenable to our knowing about otherwise remote objects. Neither approach responds to the epistemic role puzzle because the latter arises from the recognition that sensitivity to mathematical objects is utterly absent from mathematical practice and mathematical applications. Consciousness of the epistemic role puzzle, therefore, leads to a much more hostile (philosophical) environment for a simultaneous commitment to the existence of mathematical objects.

It may be felt that the epistemic role puzzle, despite my claiming otherwise, trades inappropriately on an implicit characterization of Burge's numerical *res* as objects.[20] That it's constitutively part of our conceptualization of numerical *res* that they are applicable to collections of objects shows—this opponent presses against me—that they aren't objects but instead properties possessed by collections of objects. The thought experiment behind the epistemic role puzzle—one that involves the switching of the references of numerical terms—seems intuitively implausible if what's required is that properties (rather than objects) are to be switched. The objection, therefore, is that someone who counts collections of things does so by (immediately) grasping *numerical properties*, and thus, such numerical properties must certainly be described as having an epistemic role according to this account of numerical abilities.

This epistemic story about one's grasp of numerical properties has the most plausibility in cases of subilizing, where humans and animals recognize small collections of objects.[21] The number of items that can be subilized is apparently three in the case of animals and human children, and four in the case of (most) human adults. It's interesting that numerical properties don't play a role in the neuropsychological theories currently available to explain this ability. One family of views is that subilizing is underwritten by a "parallel individuation system," which—according to Carey (2009, 235)—isn't "a dedicated number representation system" but instead has the purpose "to create working memory models of small sets of individuals, in order to represent spatial, causal, and other relations among them."[22] On this view, although such a system certainly has numerical "content" because it can distinguish objects from one another via indices, it's *not*

20. I owe the following objection to a discussion with Stephen L. White. I have put his objection in my own way, and (as always) there is a danger that this isn't how he would have wanted to put the objection himself.

21. See George Mandler and Billie Jo Shebo, "Subitizing: An analysis of its component processes," *Journal of Experimental Psychology: General* 111:1 (1982), 1–20; Brian Butterfield, *The mathematical brain* (London: Macmillan, 1999); Carey (2009), among others.

22. Also see Stephen Laurence and Eric Margolis, "Number and natural language," in *The innate mind: Structure and contents*, ed. Peter Carruthers, Stephen Laurence, and Stephen Stich (Oxford: Oxford University Press, 2005), 226–29.

directly sensitive to numerical properties of small sets but instead recognizes them on a one-to-one comparison basis.[23]

A second (innate) numerical system is an analog system of magnitude representations. One controversial view is that this latter system enables subilizing capacities, and not the parallel individuation system.[24] In any case, this innate system is certainly used to approximate collections of objects by babies, human adults, and animals, and it's a neurophysiologically based set of abilities that are currently being intensively studied along several evidential dimensions: neuroimaging techniques, studies of the development of basic numerical abilities, the study of various kinds of deficits that arise due to injury or other causes, as well as animal studies.[25] The analog number system is taken to be genuinely sensitive to numerical properties of collections because of empirical evidence that it's amodal, and abstracts away from other variables (e.g., area and distribution of objects, their shapes, etc.).

However, neurophysiological models of how this second innate system operates do not postulate an immediate sensitivity to numerical properties either. Rather, accumulator models postulate that "number is extracted by pooling activation of neural maps of the locations of salient objects, computed preattentively in the parietal lobe."[26] Other models of the phenomenon no more postulate immediate sensitivity to numerical properties. Rather, they postulate various sorts of enumeration.

Enumeration, in any case, is the psychological explanation for successful exact counting beyond the numbers that can be reached by subilization. Such a cognitive process cannot be described as an unmediated relationship to numerical properties—at least, not ones corresponding to the numerical results of the counting process. Enumeration is a cognitive process—par excellence—that doesn't involve Burgean *res*.

It should be clear that even if the various models I've sketched turn out not to be quite right in their depiction of what's going on the brain when someone navigates numerical tasks, the grasping of numerical properties will nevertheless *not*

---

23. This is how it can tell that one small collection is larger than or smaller than another.

24. Lisa Feigenson, Stanislas Dehaene, and Elizabeth Spelke, "Core systems of number," *Trends in Cognitive Sciences* 8:7 (2004), 310, write: "Subilizing has been proposed to depend on the system for representing and tracking small numbers of individuals . . . but this claim remains controversial." See Carey (2009), 232–35 for empirical evidence in favor of the parallel individuation system and against the analog magnitude system, underwriting subilizing abilities.

25. See, for example, Stanislas Dehaene, "Single-neuron arithmetic," *Science* 297 (2002), 1652–53; Stanislas Dehaene, Manuela Piazza, Philippe Pinel, and Laurent Cohen, "Three parietal circuits for number processing," *Cognitive Neuropsychology* 20:3–6 (2003), 487–506; Stanislas Dehaene, Nicolas Molko, Laurent Cohen, and Anna J. Wilson, "Arithmetic and the brain," *Current Opinion in Neurobiology* 14 (2004), 218–24; L. Cohen, S. Dehaene, F. Chochon, S. Lehéricy, and L. Naccache, "Language and calculation within the parietal lobe: A combined cognitive, anatomical and fMRI study," *Neuropsychologia* 38 (2000), 1426–40; Cathy Lemer, Stanislas Dehaene, Elizabeth Spelke, and Laurent Cohen, "Approximate quantities and exact number words: Dissociable systems," *Neuropsychologia* 41 (2003), 1942–58; Stanislas Dehaene and Laurent Cohen, "Cerebral pathways for calculation: Double dissociation between rote verbal and quantitative knowledge of arithmetic," *Cortex* 33(1997), 219–50; and—of course—numerous other articles.

26. Dehaene (2002), 1653.

be part of the empirically corrected story. One might argue, however, that exactly the same is true of anyone's perception of a vase: surely, when all the neurophysiological details are in, what won't be playing a role is the *vase* but, rather, various componental aspects of vases and its effects including photons, surface gradients of pressure, and so on.

The analogy is faulty. One can be described as recognizing that there are three objects there. One can even be described as recognizing this immediately. One does so on the basis of the objects themselves; no immediate grasping of numerical properties is needed to explain this. Instead, what's needed to explain this immediate grasping of a fact are subpersonal explanations of the sorts that researchers—some of whom I've already cited—are developing. In none of this does the immediate grasping of numerical properties come into it.

It also helps to remember where the burden of proof is here. Burge is out to show that our numerical capacities turn on the grasping of numerical *res*. But if it can be shown that such grasping isn't a necessary part of the explanation of our abilities, then his attempted showing fails. One dramatic point that can be made is this: in general, the grasping of properties is never mandatory in psychological explanations. We don't recognize the property *red*; we recognize red objects. We *do* have (conscious and nonconscious) mechanisms by which we recognize and project similarities among such objects. But the descriptions of these mechanisms need nowhere postulate the grasping of properties.

1.4 Involuntary Object-Directed Thinking in the Context of Numerical Computation

Let's now turn to a possible defense of Burge's establishment of a "not completely conceptual" relation to numbers.[27] Perhaps numbers-as-objects come into mathematical practice in the way that an ordinary person, engaged either in computation or in counting, might be thought to (rather automatically) think of them as coming into the practice. *S* thinks: Here are some mathematical thoughts I'm having and that I regard as true (or *S* thinks: Here are some mathematical expressions I'm uttering, and that I regard as true). We do indeed (and rather involuntarily) distinguish *the thought of* one or another number from the numbers *themselves* (we do indeed—and rather involuntarily—distinguish a numeral from the number to which that numeral refers).

Even if we can find nothing more in numerical computation and application for the numbers-as-objects to do than this, still, this is our practice; it looks

---

27. I draw the contours of this forthcoming defense in part from Burge's discussion ("Frege on knowing the third realm" [1992], in *Truth, thought, reason* [Oxford: Oxford University Press 2005], 316) of Frege's rationalism—from the line of thought leading up to the remark (on behalf of Frege) that "questions of 'access' to the third realm are on reflection seen to be misconceived." I do *not* claim that some such defense as the one I give in this section is one that Burge would commit himself to. I'm merely exploring a possible means of defense—one that strikes me as philosophically fruitful. Nevertheless, I would be disappointed were the considerations I raise ones that Burge found entirely alien to his own thinking.

involuntary. That is, one *cannot* think of the process by which one calculates something "with numbers" as just nothing more than a process that (actually) involves only notation on a page that refers to nothing.[28] One cannot think of the numerical thoughts one is having as pure internal thoughts that refer to nothing at all. One, that is, can no more *think* (of one's numerical ruminations) that there is nothing there but pure thought and notation (that there is nothing that such is the thought of, or that it refers to) than one can when perceiving a table. One cannot *experience* the table one sees as just an illusion or an hallucination; similarly, one cannot experience one's thoughts of numbers as (actually) thoughts of nothing at all. One *must* experience them as thoughts of something external— objects. In this sense, it might be said, the object is a constitutive element of numerical thought: one cannot think numerical thoughts at all without thinking of them as about objects.

One can perhaps put the point even more strongly. Such numerical thoughts (that $1 + 1 = 2$) would not be the very thoughts we normally think if we could strip them of the content of being about objects; the numerical thoughts we have are individuated (in part) by their being about objects. To think numerical thoughts *as* sheer notation or concepts without a correspondence to objects would be (actually) to think entirely other thoughts—thoughts that, in fact, *we* are incapable of thinking.

There is a much more ambitious claim that some philosophers might try for. This is that actually thinking numerical thoughts as, say, sheer notation (as object-less thoughts) isn't merely something we can't do; it's something that's rationally incoherent. Constitutive of numerical reasoning as reasoning (and of mathematical reasoning more generally as reasoning) is that the (numerical and mathematical) thoughts have a subject matter. Burge (1992, 316) seems to attribute some such position to Frege. He writes: "being a judging subject is to have or have had some degree of reason. Having or having had some degree of reason requires acknowledging, at least implicitly in one's thinking, the simplest, most basic logical truths and inferences; and doing so commits one to an atemporal subject matter."

There is too much in contemporary mathematics and logic, however, too much about alternative logics, the successful application of semantic notions (such as truth) to languages couched in such logics, and too much by way of systematic studies of sheer notations—as pure sheer notations—to allow such views. It's no longer respectable to claim that if someone somehow were able to think in denotationless terms (of numerals, say, as vacuous notation) when he engaged in computation, or when he recognized quantitative sizes of small groups of perceptible objects, that such thinking (as rational thinking) would fail or fall short in

---

28. This isn't quite fair to the phenomenology of mathematical practice. It's quite common, actually, when engaging in a complex numerical or algebraic computation, to think of the stuff on the page mechanically (and as somewhat uninterpreted), as syntactic signs that one applying rules to, rules that one has (previously) justified or only memorized. Such a mindset is hardly foreign to higher mathematics, by the way: one often engages in notational rule of thumb or calculations that are applied to something that one hasn't any intuitions about. For the purposes of argument here, I treat these cases as exceptions.

some way. Frege's "hitherto unknown form of madness" has turned out rather to be alternative form(s) of reason, and contemporary philosophers have no choice but to acknowledge this rather dramatic development. Still left, of course, are the discoverable but brute psychological facts about our (species-specific?) cognitive constraints: thinking of objects the way we do when we engage in (simple) numerical thinking is indispensable in the sense that this is how we *have* to do it. We have no other cognitive option, given the kind of creatures we are and the kinds of brains evolution has stuck us with.

The point generalizes. We automatically (involuntarily, I'd say) think in terms of objects referred to by our thoughts, when we think at all. Novelists—and perhaps especially poets—think a lot about words; no successful novelist (or poet) succeeds by doing just that. Indispensable here, as well, is object-directed thinking: thoughts about people, the inanimate objects surrounding them, and so on.[29] Thus, specifically in the numerical case, it seems that what we might describe as "pure formalist reasoning" (uninterpreted numerical thought) isn't ruled out because it can be shown to be a species of unreason. It's ruled out (and only ruled out) because (as a matter of contingent evolutionary fact) *we can't do it.*

Until the last couple of paragraphs, I've been treating what we might describe as "notational commitments" to objects and psychological commitments to objects (our experience of our thought being about objects) in—as it were—the same breath. Perhaps considerations about these two kinds of ontological commitments should be distinguished. After all, regardless of what's true about ontological commitments that arise because of notation, it can be argued (one might think) that if we must think in terms of numerical *objects* that are the relata of our numerical concepts or terms to do computation or count objects, isn't that enough for us to take our relevant numerical concepts as indicating those numerical objects? This issue needs exploration independently of the issues of ontological commitments as (purportedly) due to notation. One should not simply borrow a page from how one resolves the sibling ontological issue in the case of notation (e.g., by noticing that quantification needn't be ontologically committing).[30]

29. The "people," the "inanimate objects," and the "etc.," are often (perhaps usually) thought of as fictional, or imaginary creations (as entirely "made up"). But this is to think of them as "fictional *objects*" or "imaginary *objects*"—objects that are (mentally) so labeled. The old Kantian point—Humean, actually—about the imaginary 100 thalers (Immanuel Kant, *Critique of pure reason* (1781), ed. Paul Guyer, trans. Allen W. Wood [Cambridge: Cambridge University Press, 1998], 567) comes to this: to think about 100 imaginary thalers is no different in mental experience than to think about 100 real ones. "Imaginary," "fictional," and so on aren't indicators of ways that we experience the imagined objects—that's not the role of these words. Here's another (useful) way to put the point: the ontological status (the existence or not) of "something" isn't something we *experience* with respect to that candidate item.

30. See Jody Azzouni, "Applied mathematics, existential commitment and the Quine-Putnam indispensability thesis," *Philosophia Mathematica* 3:5 (1997), 193–209, section V; Jody Azzouni, "On 'on what there is,'" *Pacific Philosophical Quarterly* 79:1 (1998), 1–18; Jody Azzouni, *Deflating existential consequence: A case for nominalism* (Oxford: Oxford University Press, 2004a), chapters 3 and 4, for the case that objectual quantification is ontologically neutral. I indicate more about this in chapter 5.

1.5 Recognizing that One's Singular Thought and Speech Can Be Empty

The considerations of sections 1.3 and 1.4 appear to have left us in a quandary. On one hand, it seems to have been cleanly established that the numerical objects themselves play no role in our abilities to compute or to immediately recognize the numerical sizes of small groups of objects. On the other, it seems that our numerical thought requires such objects. Where do we go from here?

Any perceived conflict evaporates on inspection. The important point to make first is that a rather sharp distinction should be drawn between our numerical thought (and correspondingly, our numeration practices) requiring the thought of objects, and our numerical thought (and corresponding practices) requiring the objects themselves.[31] (The discussion in section 1.4 ignored that distinction.) The impossibility of our being able to—as it were—"think away" our thoughts of numbers when we calculate is different from the question of whether there are such things. If our cognitive faculties require our thinking of objects to success-fully do numeration (and other more sophisticated mathematics), this is entirely compatible with our being able to recognize that such a requirement bears not at all on the question of whether these objects exist.[32] The necessity of thinking of objects, as described in section 1.4, to possess mastery of numerical concepts, therefore, is entirely compatible with objects themselves not being required by such mastery and consequently by the possibility of having such numerical mastery while recognizing that the objects in question don't exist.

The psychological state I've described—recognizing that one's thought of objects is involuntarily required in one or another mathematical activity—is real. Consistent with this in the mathematical case, therefore, is the philosophical posi-tion of nominalism: no such objects exist. Nevertheless, philosophers are often tempted to one or another position where the involuntary thinking of objects in numerical thinking (and in experience generally, e.g., perceptual experience) coupled with the nonexistence of those corresponding objects either is (i) taken to be—not genuine thought but—one or another species of "mock" or "pretend" thinking; propositions or complete thoughts don't actually occur in this kind of thinking (because the objects required to complete the thoughts in question are absent); or is (ii) taken to be one or another kind of thinking of objects where those objects—although officially "nonexistent"—must nevertheless be understood in

---

31. Burge, 75, in effect acknowledges this distinction when he repudiates interpretations of his 1977 publica-tion "according to which there is a 'hole' in the representational aspects of the proposition, where the hole corre-sponds to the object (which completes the proposition)." Those who take "Russellean propositions" to be thoughts will, however, have trouble with the distinction.

32. We have the following psychological ability: our recognition that we involuntarily think of (or see) *something* under certain circumstances is compatible with our recognizing—indeed (if it comes to that) with our knowing—that the "something" in question doesn't exist. To know that one is in the grip of an hallucination, and that what one is seeing doesn't exist, isn't an incoherent state of mind (however undesirable it might otherwise be). Knowing that one is in the grip of an hallucination needn't in any way affect the sensory and object-directed experience of that hallucination. It's this psychological datum that (certain) sceptical arguments start from.

an ontologically more robust sense (e.g., a Meinongian sense) than I have argued is necessary.

In the remainder of this chapter, therefore, I discuss the considerations driving philosophers to one or another of these positions, and I explain why we can (and should) resist them. Before turning to this, I develop another point further. Some may claim that if one recognizes that certain objects are irrelevant to one's thinking, it should therefore be possible for one's thinking to be recastable in a form where thoughts of those objects don't arise. This is a psychological or mentalistic version of the Quine-Putnam indispensability thesis. If quantification over certain items indispensably occur in one's (indispensable) theory, then one is "ontologically committed" to such objects. Correspondingly, if one's thinking tasks seem to require the thought of certain objects that don't exist, those thinking tasks should be recastable so that thinking of those objects is eliminated.

There is little independent reason to believe this doctrine, or (for that matter) any doctrine in its neighborhood. For one thing, we don't have that much control over the contents of our psychological states, or—anyway—much control over the contents of such states when they are deployed to enable our success in one or another task. That object-directed thinking—thinking about abstracta—is required to do successful mathematics is hardly surprising.[33] Similarly, that thinking about officially imaginary persons is required to successfully write fiction is also not surprising. In neither case, however (to reinforce the moral of this section), should the mere fact that object-directed thinking is required to execute these tasks be taken to show that there are objects that such thoughts are about. That a distinction between thoughts (of such and such a type) being required to execute a task, and what those thoughts are of instead being so required for the task, is already enough to indicate this.[34] Furthermore, that ordinary people can themselves understand such a distinction (say, in the case of hallucinations) shows that nothing in the neighborhood of an indispensability thesis (for the contents of thoughts and experience) is required.

One may concede the necessity of numerical thought being object-directed but deny that such is appropriately characterized as "singular." After all, mathematical thought (of all kinds) has been successfully axiomatized. Thus, such thought may instead be described as *deferential* to an external body of knowledge, and so only indirectly object-directed. Consider one's thoughts of neutrinos. A crucial aspect of such thoughts is that one recognizes oneself to be partially grasping concepts (e.g., of the quantum mechanical properties of neutrinos). As with singular thought, one's (individual) thought of neutrinos is incomplete and cannot determine what one is thinking of. What determines the references of one's thought, however, aren't the objects (neutrinos) toward which one's thought is

---

33. This is not to say, of course, that it's obviously true. It's an empirical thesis about the nature of the kind of numerical thinking required to execute the twin tasks Burge has described.

34. This isn't a moral just about thought, although the application of the moral to numeration practices may be restricted to thought. The point holds more generally of experience—that is, hallucinogenic experience. My next sentence acknowledges this fact.

directed, but the more conceptually adequate thinking of experts. Call such thought "conceptually deferential."[35]

Despite the presence of successful axiomatizations of, say, number theory, this line should be resisted with respect to numerical thought. Although the involvement of conceptual deference strikes me as operative in one's grasp of certain mathematical concepts—sets, for example—numerical thought is somewhat epistemically independent of subsequent axiomatizations of it. One way to recognize this fact is historically and psychologically: animals successfully engage in numeration practices without such deference. So have humans for most of recorded history. Another point is that the subsequent axiomatizations of numerical thought defer (to some extent) to these numeration practices, rather than the other way around. Thus the strong impression that numerical generalizations can be overthrown by thinking hard about numerical objects and their computationally determined relationships. One's thinking about (small) numbers possesses an immediacy that gives such thought (to some extent) epistemic independence from background expertise.[36] One's impression of the numerals "1" through "9" is that they are names insofar as they lack descriptive content, and so (i) they aren't disguised descriptions, and (ii) they don't involve concepts that invite conceptual deference. Axiomatization is instead seen—even by professional mathematicians—as creative mathematics.

None of this, perhaps, conclusively refutes the suggestion that numerical thought is miscast if it's described as singular.[37] It does suggest, however, that a natural line of thought (call it "the deferred conceptual construal of mathematical thought") with respect to sophisticated and difficult mathematical (and physical) concepts is quite unnatural with respect to numerical (and, I might add, simple geometrical) thought.

---

35. So the suggestion is that one's numerical thought is more appropriately characterized as conceptual rather than as genuinely singular; but the relevant concepts are only inadequately grasped by the individual thinker. My thanks to Erin Eaker for urging me to take seriously in this context the possibility of what I've labeled "conceptual deference."

36. This contributes in no small measure to the impression of apriority of knowledge of items like "$1 + 1 = 2$." Also see Charles Parsons, "Mathematical intuition," *Proceedings of the Aristotelian Society*, NS 80 (1979–80), 151.

37. One important issue Erin Eaker (personal correspondence, April 2008) has raised with me is why "the *de re* status of [numerical] thought is determined by the phenomenology involved when an individual incompletely grasps a thought rather than by the objective nature of the thought content (which may well be *de dicto*)." I cannot give a complete answer to this question here; in one sense, using the psychology of the individual to type thought is (empirically) stipulative. I aim to taxonomize important (epistemic) distinctions that are lost if one individuates "thought" with respect to public knowledge. I am therefore not naively adopting a "Cartesian perspective" toward thought (as, say, Gareth Evans, *The varieties of reference* [Oxford: Oxford University Press, 1982], 45, might put it). I intend to write about this more fully at another time. I should add that we take it as possible to discover that an entire culture is wrong with respect to a mathematical practice. This lends weight against the idea that numerical thought—and mathematical thought in general—should be characterized as conceptually deferential. In any case, as far as my overall ontological aims are concerned, it doesn't matter whether numerical thought is conceptual. In neither case do objects play a role: in the case where numerical thought is regarded as thoroughly conceptualized (treated as not singular), the role of quantification should be construed neutrally.

1.6 Construing Object-Less Thought as "Mock" Thought

Let's turn to the idea that if numerical objects don't exist, then numerical thought is in some way impoverished or defective or mock.[38] A reasonable way to press the idea is to claim that a singular thought essentially involves an object. Absent the object, the corresponding thought must (as it were) contain a blank. Recall the initial (semantic and epistemic) characterizations of *de re* attitudes (by Burge), quoted in section 1.1, where the analogy to an open sentence with a free variable is stressed. If that free variable isn't given an object as an interpretation of it, then the thought is incomplete. It's a thought like "x is prime," an open sentence without an interpretation, and so something that necessarily lacks a truth value.[39]

I won't deny the naturalness (at least for philosophers) of so characterizing singular thought. But doing so doesn't square well with how we ordinarily think and how we ordinarily think about how we think. First, as already noted in section 1.5, it's possible to simultaneously entertain numerical thoughts (ones essentially of objects) while also taking those objects not to exist. In doing so, one's numerical thought doesn't shift in its (apparent) singular character.[40] More strongly (and accurately), numerical thoughts aren't perceived as changing in any way at all in light of (changing) background metaphysical beliefs about numerical objects. Therefore, such thoughts are just as singular, psychologically speaking, after one becomes an official nominalist as they were when one was, say, a metaphysical realist with regard to numerical objects.

Second, such (purely) numerical thoughts—in light of one's changing metaphysical background beliefs—don't shift in their truth-value status. That is, they are still recognized to be just as correctly and incorrectly applicable as they were before; so, too, all the computational truths and falsehoods remain intact. Corresponding to this psychological fact about our perception of the truth values of such object-less statements and thoughts is a semantic fact about the truth conditions for numerical statements. Treating numerals as names, say, enables simple truth conditions like the following. For any predicate G, and for any numeral n, and corresponding predicate $\hat{G}$ and numeral $\tilde{n}$ (in the metalanguage): "Gn" is true iff $\hat{G}\tilde{n}$.[41] Such truth conditions are available regardless of whether numerals refer to anything at all; indeed, the crucial point is that the semantics for numerical

---

38. Such positions are held by Evans (1982) and John McDowell, "Singular thought and inner space," in *Subject, thought, and context*, ed. Philip Pettit and John McDowell (Oxford: Oxford University Press, 1986), 137–68, with respect to thoughts directed toward hallucinations. See chapter 2 for discussion.

39. The view, even for those who find it plausible for thought with demonstrative elements, may nevertheless look implausible in the case of numerical thought which, as Burge notes, looks "fully conceptualized." I'm addressing, for the sake of argumentative completeness, the hypothesis that numerical thought, and thought with explicitly demonstrative elements are both "mock" when the objects in question are absent. (This is acceptable if only because, in the case of hallucination, one's thought still seems fully interpreted even when one knows one is hallucinating.) Notice that my forthcoming objections apply to both kinds of cases.

40. Burge, 68, acknowledges this, writing: "insofar as one is interested in a taxonomy of mental 'natural' kinds . . . non-referring attitudes group with the *de re* attitudes."

41. I'm being sloppy with respect to use/mention. The (simple) point being made doesn't require niceties.

language—and more broadly, mathematical language—is identical regardless of whether or not such terms refer.[42]

Third, all the crucial elements (apart, of course, from the existence of objects) that make numerical thoughts classifiable as singular remain in place. Why? Because such numerical attitudes, although they don't involve referential relations to objects, are nevertheless of singular form and (most important) involve relationships to other things external to the attitude holder by virtue of which the numerical thoughts of the attitude holder are decisively given truth values apart from the conceptualizations of the objects had by the attitude holder.

The point—once seen—is elementary. Numerical attitudes, and mathematical attitudes more generally, are evaluated not in terms of the attitude holder's individual capacities but external to him. This is why computational mistakes are seen as possible. One's computational results can be supplemented and corrected by others, and by the use of (calculating) devices. Notice that these external corrections of one's numeration practices don't (or rarely) involve what's understood to be conceptual misunderstandings (e.g., that one only partially grasps the concept of addition). Rather, mechanical mistakes (of one sort or another) in one's numeration practice are exposed.[43] Strikingly, such small but systematic deviations in computation (e.g., adding 7 to 8 and getting 16) are invariably seen as mistakes about the objects, and not about the notation (e.g., in self-ascriptions: I always add those two *numbers* wrongly).[44]

Another important illustration of the singular nature of numerical thought is this: I think of the only even prime and I think of 2. I may not think these thoughts are about the same object; nevertheless, that I'm wrong about this can be proven to me. More dramatically, certain singular thoughts I have (of certain real numbers, say) being about the same numbers—or not—may turn on whether certain cardinal axioms are accepted. And that may turn on a particular contingent development in mathematical practice.[45]

To sum up, numerical thinking should be described—as I do—as *empty* singular thought. It should be classified with singular thought (where an actual object is involved) precisely because it shares with such thought the property of being "constitutively what [it is] partly by virtue of relations between the individual in those states and a wider reality" (Burge 2007a, 3). However, such relations in the case of empty singular thought, although to objects (of one sort or another), aren't relations of *reference*. The objects that numerical thoughts are related to are those (whatever they turn out to be) involved in an external mathematical practice. Ultimately, the relationship is to the elements of a mathematical practice (including people) that involves families of formal systems. Gödel results guarantee that such systems are augmentable without end. The augmentations, in

---

42. I discuss this further in chapter 5.

43. See Azzouni (1994), especially part I, §5.

44. Mistakes are a key ingredient in Burge's "anti-individualism."

45. This, incidentally, is one way that individuation conditions on the objects of mathematical thought can be infiltrated by tacit conventions.

turn, are (to some extent) conventional, in the sense of being historically contingent. In any case, empty singular numerical attitudes aren't (to repeat) anchored in a relationship to abstracta (or any other sort of object referred to), the existence of which dictate which formal systems are true (and false). How our ordinary numerical practices with small numbers become (over the course of millennia) normatively embedded in a practice with formal systems is a complex historical story, only some of which I've discussed elsewhere.[46]

Mathematical statements, therefore, have *truth-value inducers* that are the items that force mathematical practice to take the form it takes—in particular, that force mathematical statements to (indispensably) have the truth values they have. But there are no referents of mathematical language among these truth-value inducers.

There is more to say about the drawbacks of views—elsewhere called "externalist"[47]—with respect to language and thought. To do so now is to go far beyond the mathematical case. I will, at least, note this. Although it's natural, as I said at the outset of this section, to characterize singular thought as essentially requiring the objects they are (purportedly) about, this doesn't fit with ordinary intuitions. People, for example, don't think—after they have discovered that unicorns don't exist—that their (past and present) thoughts about unicorns have been discovered to be different in any way (apart from some of their truth values, of course). Nor did I think such a thing—many years ago—after I traumatically learned that Santa Claus doesn't exist.

1.7 Meinongian Moves

Let's turn to the other position that may be taken regarding numerical objects, that although such don't exist, they nevertheless have a robust ontological presence. It's a somewhat slippery matter exactly what the Meinongian position comes to (as held, say, by Parsons 1980; Routley 1980; Smith 2002; Zalta 1983, 1988; and others). I mean this in the following sense. Here's one (possible) position regarding mathematical objects. Such don't exist. Furthermore, they don't subsist, and (indeed) they have no sort of being whatsoever. In addition, they have no properties, and they cannot be referred to. Finally, statements like "2 + 2 = 4," and "2 + 2 = 5" may be true or false, but they aren't true or false because the terms appearing within them refer to objects, the properties of which determine those truth values. They are true or false for other reasons entirely.

As I understand any of the Meinongian positions, the view just sketched (and that I endorse) isn't any of those. Although almost all contemporary Meinongians do claim, of the objects that they deny existence to, that such don't exist "in any

---

46. See Jody Azzouni, *Tracking reason: Proof, consequence, and truth* (Oxford: Oxford University Press, 2006), especially chapter 6, and Jody Azzouni, "Why do informal proofs conform to formal norms?" *Foundations of Science* 14 (2009b), 9–26.

47. As in A. D. Smith, *The problem of perception* (Cambridge, Mass.: Harvard University Press, 2002). Or "Millian," with respect to names, as in the work of Salmon. This family of views, in any case, is very popular.

sense at all"—that is, they don't subsist, persist, and so on, that is, they don't have any "being" whatsoever,[48] it isn't true (on Meinongian views) that they don't have (some) properties and not others, and that one can't refer to them.[49] These latter claims establish the topic of what doesn't exist as nevertheless a legitimate (metaphysical) subject-matter. There is quite a bit to say about what doesn't exist in any sense at all, if such are particular items that have some properties, not others, are items we can (moreover) refer to, and finally, are the items in virtue of which the statements about them are true or false.

I have, in the past, come pretty close to describing this conglomeration of views as incoherent.[50] What I want to do now is dig a little deeper in a charitable way, to try to indicate what motivates such views. What does motivate them, I suggest, is the attempt to take really seriously the singular character of the thoughts in question. Part of what's involved in numerical thinking—so I have conceded—is the essential object-directedness of that thought. Thoughts of 1 are *about* 1; they are not *about* 2. Similarly, when Macbeth hallucinates a dagger, he has thoughts about *it*, not about something else (a unicorn, say) or about nothing at all. If we press the idea that Macbeth is having thoughts about nothing at all (and that thoughts of 1 are, similarly, thoughts about nothing at all), then we seem, in Smith's words (2002, 260) to have the result (e.g., in Macbeth's case), "that there is no *truth* at all as to the nature of the intentional object of which Macbeth was aware." That is (and this is the point of his objection), whatever truths about the dagger we are prone to accept have become utterly detached from any sort of correspondence to the content of Macbeth's hallucination. They are not about the contents of that hallucination (for they are not about anything). So, too, "1 + 1 = 2" isn't about 1 or 2 (for it isn't about anything). In pressing consistently and systematically for the genuine

48. Smith (2002, 240) stresses that "Meinongian objects" don't have "*any kind of being whatever.*" In saying this, he is both arguing that such was (at least at a certain stage in his thinking) Meinong's position, and that it's one that he himself endorses. Such objects are "intentional" objects, on Smith's view (2002, 241), also Edmund Husserl's (*Logical investigations* (1900), trans. J. N. Findlay [London: Routledge and Kegan Paul, 1970], 596) that he quotes with approval: "That the object is a 'merely intentional' one does not, of course, mean: it *exists*, albeit only in the *intentio* (and so as a real [*reelles*] constituent of it), or that some kind of shadow of it exists in it. Rather, it means: the intention, the intending [*Meinen*] of such an object exists, but the object *doesn't*." (I've given Smith's translation of the quotation, one which deviates slightly from Findlay's.) Similarly, Richard Routley (*Exploring Meinong's jungle and beyond: An investigation of noneism and the theory of items*, interim ed. Philosophy Department monograph 3 [Canberra: Research School of Social Sciences, Australian National University, 1980], 2) writes of such objects that they "do not exist; and in many cases they do not exist in any way at all, or have any form of being whatsoever."

49. For example, Routley (1980, 2) writes: "Non-existent objects are constituted in one way or another, and have more or less determinate natures, and thus they have properties. In fact they have properties of a range of sorts, sometimes quite ordinary properties, e.g. the oft-quoted golden mountain is golden." Smith (2002, 248) writes: "I shall term the 'Ontological Assumption' [following Richard Routley and Valerie Routley, "Rehabilitating Meinong's theory of objects," *Revue Internationale de Philosophie* 27 (1973), 224–54] the claim that it is not possible to make genuine reference to what does not exist, so that no statement, at the very least no true statement, can have a non-existent as its genuine subject." (Smith, of course, intends to deny the Ontological Assumption.) Terence Parsons (*Nonexistent objects* [New Haven, Conn.: Yale University Press, 1980], 1) writes (describing what Smith (2002, 248) takes to be the same position as the Ontological Assumption—to be similarly denied by Parsons) that, "[the Russellian rut is the view that] though there may be *kinds* of things that are nowhere exemplified (e.g., being a winged horse) there is no *particular* thing that fails to exist" (emphasis in original).

50. Azzouni (2004a), 55–56.

nonexistence of the objects corresponding to numerical thought we have (undesirably) lost the "aboutness" that's so crucial to that thought.

A related issue has been pressed against my views by Bueno and Zalta 2005 (297–98). They write: "Suppose that '2' refers to 2. Now . . . it follows from this that there is something to which '2' refers or that there is nothing to which '2' refers. Suppose Azzouni thinks the former. In this case, '2' refers to something, namely, the number 2 and so there is something which is the number 2. If so, then the resulting view is not nominalist."

They continue (298–99): "Alternatively, suppose Azzouni thinks it does not follow from the fact that '2' refers to 2 that '2' refers to something. If so, then on his view, '2' refers to 2 but '2' refers to nothing. But then he clearly has a nonstandard notion of reference. Note that we are not saying that the notion of reference requires the existence of an object to which we refer. But it does require that there be something to which we refer."

Finally (299), "Suppose that '2' does not refer to 2. In this case, '2' would either refer to nothing or else refer to some object other than 2. In the former case, '$\exists y(y = 2)$' would be false. . . . In the latter case, we would not be referring to the object that '2' is normally taken to refer to."

What should be realized is that the "aboutness" of singular thought has two aspects. One aspect is that the content of such thought corresponds to externalities. The second is that the content of such thought is essentially object-directed. Where the object that a thought is directed toward exists, these two aspects are assimilated into (are both aspect of) the referential relation. The externalities that such thought corresponds to (and in terms of which the thought is individuated) just are the objects to which that thought is directed. S sees an urn, and thinks: "That's an urn." The thought corresponds to the state of affairs regarding the urn.

This neat correspondence between language (thought) and the world vanishes when there is no object. S hallucinates an urn, and thinks: "That's an urn." In this case, the thought *parallels* the state of affairs with respect to S's state of mind (psychologically speaking)—but not via an object the "that's" is directed toward. There is no object that "that's" is directed toward; thus, although the content of that thought is essentially object-directed, and although the truth-value inducers—that determine the truth value of the thought—include the psychology of the individual having the experience, it's not the case that those inducers include the "object hallucinated" for there is no such thing (and, consequently, "it" has no properties).

To help characterize what's happening here (and to avoid the equivocations that, for example, the Bueno and Zalta quotations are involved in), we need to distinguish the two ways that a thought or a statement can be about something and, correspondingly, the two ways that a term can refer to what it refers to.[51] In ordinary language, we use the same word, "about," to describe a thought about Mickey Mouse as "about" Mickey Mouse, and a thought about Hillary Clinton as "about" Hillary Clinton. I'll make distinctions between these two ontologically different cases by introducing the terms "about^r" and "about^e," and the corresponding terms

---

51. This is a refinement of the discussion of this matter in Azzouni (2004a), 61–62.

"refer^r" and "refer^e." Quite simply, a thought or sentence is about^r something (and a term refers^r to something) if, respectively, what it is about exists and what the term refers to exists. Otherwise, it is about^e that something, and correspondingly, the term refers^e.

Turning to numerical thought, in describing numerical thought as about^e numbers, I thus indicate the essential object-related quality of that thought. Thoughts of $\underline{1}$ are about^e 1; $\underline{1}$ refers^e to 1. Thoughts of $\underline{2}$ are about^e 2; $\underline{2}$ refers^e to 2. In saying these things, the content of numerical thought (its "intentional" qualities, as it were) are acknowledged: what a thought is about^e is largely read off from its content.[52] To talk about aboutness or reference where the items exist, I say instead (for example) that "'Hillary Clinton' refers^r to Hillary Clinton," or (more generally) that talk of "people" is about^r people.

Three points should be made about the distinction being drawn here between two different uses of the ordinary notions of "about" and "refer." First, one way to contrast my view with the Meinongian one is this: the Meinongian position, as I read it, is that reference and aboutness are both relations on all their uses. Where the object a term refers to exists, then what I've called "reference^r" is a relation between a term and an object that exists. Where the object a term refers to doesn't exist, then what I've called "reference^r" is—for the Meinongian—a relation of the term to an object that doesn't exist. The Meinongian has no use for my notions refer^e and about^e. Rather, the Meinongian position is that a thought or statement about^r something that doesn't exist is about^r *something* that doesn't exist. On my view aboutness^r and reference^r are, respectively, relations between thought (statements) and things, and terms and things. Aboutness^e and reference^e aren't relations at all.

For me, therefore, the ordinary words "about" and "refer" are neutral between uses of them that indicate genuine relations between language and thought and the world, and pseudo-relations: items that have the appearance of relations but aren't.[53] As already noted, one indication of this is how often we often speak of the subject matter of something, or what it refers to, without any concern at all about the existence or nonexistence of such.[54] It also manifests in our practice of using "refer," in particular, sometimes as specifically indicating reference^r and as sometimes specifically indicating reference^e—where context usually indicates which is meant. I'll occasionally accent the contextual complexity of the ordinary words "about" and "refer," where valuable, by noting them like so: "refer$^{(r/e)}$," "about$^{(r/e)}$."

Second, although either notion, reference^r or reference^e, can be exemplified in a Tarskian theory of truth; the most valuable notion to so exemplify is the neutral

---

52. "Largely," because, as I repeat, our practices regarding what that content is about^e can (and do) involve conditions that go beyond the content itself, strictly speaking. This is not to introduce a kind of object that the content is actually about^r. See what follows.

53. In practice, we switch effortlessly back and forth—often without realizing it. The linguistic phenomenon is close to—unsurprisingly—our commissive and noncommissive uses of "exist." See Jody Azzouni, "Ontology and the word 'exist': Uneasy relations," *Philosophia Mathematica*, forthcoming (a) for details on "exist."

54. As in: "There are many books about fairies and the British gardens they supposedly live in." "Supposedly," here, can range from faint scepticism to sarcastic commentary, both about the fairies themselves and about where they (presumably) live. These doubting (ontological) attitudes don't (presumably) extend to British gardens, falling under the same word "about."

notion: reference. (See chapter 5.) Third, most philosophers deliberately use "refers," "about," and their cognates in an ontologically committing manner, in contrast to the ordinary use (a practice I followed, for example, in section 1.6). That is—using the terminology I've just introduced—they deliberately use *refer*[r] and *about*[r] instead of the ordinary person's *refer* and *about*.

Recall the quotation from Bueno and Zalta (2005, 299) repeated here: "Alternatively, suppose Azzouni thinks it does not follow from the fact that '2' refers to 2 that '2' refers to something. If so, then on his view, '2' refers to 2 but '2' refers to nothing. But then he clearly has a non-standard notion of reference. Note that we are not saying that the notion of reference requires the existence of an object to which we refer. But it does require that there be something to which we refer."

Applied against me, as noted, this passage commits sins of equivocation. It's true that if "2" refers[e] to 2 that "2" refers[e] to something. This is compatible with "2" referring[r] to nothing at all. (Nothing nonstandard here.) So, too, the notion of reference[e] doesn't require the existence of an object to which we refer[e]. But it does require that there be something to which we refer[e] (although not something to which we refer[r]). The first use of "something" in the sentence before this one is an ontologically innocent use of "something"—one that's compatible with a syntactic form that's relational, although one that's (metaphysically speaking) a pseudo-relation; the second (contrasting) use is ontologically loaded. The first use, therefore, doesn't indicate an object in any sense; correspondingly, it doesn't indicate that reference[e] is a metaphysical relation (a truism: not all syntactic relation-forms correspond to *actual* relations.)

Finally, let's return to the concern articulated by Smith (2002, 260): that if, when Macbeth hallucinates a dagger, we describe him as having thoughts about nothing at all, the result is that "there is no *truth* at all as to the nature of the intentional object of which Macbeth was aware." Recognizing that Macbeth is aware[e] of a dagger but not aware[r] of such only goes part of the way toward resolving this issue. We must add that although there are no truth makers that determine the truth of the thought Macbeth has, there are truth-value inducers, among them the psychological states that Macbeth is in during his hallucination.[55]

1.8 Concluding Remarks

I've argued in this chapter that my way of construing empty singular thought is defensible and sensitive both to the phenomenology of numerical thought (to the nature of its object-directed content) as well as to the factors that make that thought singular (that it's thought that isn't fully conceptualized).

In conclusion, I want (i) to comment further on some claims I've made about empty singular thought—in particular, empty singular numerical thought; (ii) to recapitulate some of the specialized terminology introduced in this section; and

---

55. "Among them," because other factors affect the truth-values of statements about the contents of Macbeth's hallucinations: he can be wrong about what he's hallucinating. See chapter 2.

(iii) to characterize a different way of broadening the notion of singular thought that (I argue) has drawbacks.

Let's start with the following objection. I've clearly described empty singular numerical thought as singular thought. Is that really a legitimate description of it? How can it be singular if there is no object that the thought is (actually) directed toward? Burge (in the epigraph to part I) describes a "singular capacity" as the enabling of a connection of "our thought to particulars in a singular way." Surely nothing like that is on offer in empty singular thought, as described here.

My response: I've suggested (along with Burge) that numerical thought is singular in the sense that it can't be reduced to "predicative, attributive capacities," nor is it to be understood as conceptual in a broader sense that involves deference to expert conceptualizations. I claimed, in fact, that the dictates of ordinary numerical practices (e.g., calculation), if anything, force constraints on the resulting expert conceptualizations, rather than the other way around.

The content of such thought is singular in a second sense because—psychologically speaking—it's necessarily object-directed. These two ways that thought is singular are knitted together in cases where a thought involves only reference^r—where all the referring expressions in the thought are to things that exist. For in that case the object-directed psychological states are linked to external objects that the thought is about. But this isn't the case with numerical thought or with empty singular thought in general: the truth-value inducers of such thought don't include the items that the referring^e items in such thought denote: there are no such things. The points, however, (i) that the truth values of numerical thoughts are determined by factors external to the thinker's conceptualizations, (ii) that what such thoughts are about is also not (fully) determined by the conceptualizations of the thinker, and last, (iii) that the content of such thought essentially requires thought of objects, all stand nevertheless.

Empty singular thought is psychologically indistinguishable from singular thought in general. Correspondingly, empty singular sentences employ exactly the same parts of speech that are used by singular sentences. Given, in addition, the first two points of the last paragraph, it would be unwise to try to assimilate such thought to predicative or fully conceptualized thought.

It's appropriate to review and illustrate again the terminology introduced in this chapter. Consider "Barack Obama is president of the United States (in 2009)," and "Mickey Mouse was invented by Walt Disney." "Barack Obama is president of the United States (in 2009)" is about Barack Obama; "Mickey Mouse was invented by Walt Disney" is about Mickey Mouse and Walt Disney. "Barack Obama is president of the United States (in 2009)" is about^r Barack Obama; "Mickey Mouse was invented by Walt Disney" is about^e Mickey Mouse and about^r Walt Disney. "Barack Obama" and "Mickey Mouse" refer, respectively, to Barack Obama and Mickey Mouse; "Barack Obama" refers^r to Barack Obama; "Mickey Mouse" refers^e to Mickey Mouse. I will also speak this way: Barack Obama exists (in 2009); Mickey Mouse doesn't exist. "Mickey Mouse" is a vacuous term; "Barack Obama" is a nonvacuous term. Sometimes, instead of the contrast "vacuous" and "nonvacuous," I instead use "empty" and "nonempty." These are meant to be synonyms. Of course, "Barack Obama is president of the United States" is a singular sentence (or singular thought), and "Mickey Mouse was invented by Walt Disney" is an empty singular sentence (or empty singular thought).

Finally, some recapitulations about truth, truth conditions, truth-value inducers, and truth makers. As I show in chapter 5, truth-conditional semantic theories of various sorts, when appropriately interpreted, are insensitive to matters of ontology—as they should be. Call the truth-value inducers of a sentence those aspects of the world (entities and relations among those entities) that, coupled with our truth-assertion practices, force a truth value on a sentence. Where at least some of the terms in a sentence are nonvacuous, included among the truth-value inducers are the relata of those nonvacuous terms and the relations among them. These may be called the truth makers of the sentence. However, where all the terms of a sentence are vacuous, it has no truth makers, only truth-value inducers.

Sometimes, we use "about" in a somewhat different way than the one(s) just described. When speaking about true sentences with vacuous terms, we think of them as speaking (albeit indirectly) "about" the real world. For example, we may think of sentences that are about^e fictional characters as—more broadly—really "about" our (collective) fictional practice. So, too, we may think of sentences that are about^e the contents of hallucinations as really "about" the psychological states of the hallucinators. More esoterically, some philosophers may want to think of applied mathematics indispensably coupled with an empirical subject matter as really "about" what they call the nominalistic content of the theory.[56]

In all these cases, I claim, this talk of "about" is better described as talk about the truth-value inducers of a sentence, or about a collection of such: the study of exactly how those truth-value inducers force the particular truth values on a sentence (or collection of such) that they force. As noted, such truth-value inducers bear both on the truth values of such statements or thoughts, and on what objects such statements or thoughts are about.

That statements containing only vacuous terms nevertheless have truth-value inducers (and truth values as a result)—although no truth makers—is a view that echoes aspects of older "coherence" views of truth. Such earlier approaches—according to their adherents—reject "correspondence": that the truth and falsity of statements turn on a correspondence between what the sentence says and the facts in the world involving the relata of the terms occurring in such statements. Traditional coherence views, however, tend to be global and exclusionary: *all* truths require coherence (with, say, other background truths); none involve correspondence. That's not the perspective taken here. There are truths—just as correspondence theories

---

56. Such commonly expressed views about so-called nominalistic content implicitly presuppose that there is a nominalistic way that the world is that cannot be expressed directly in our language but only in language that reflects the indispensable use of mathematics coupled with empirical doctrine. Although one can grant that "the world" contains no abstracta, and that the world is the way it is without such existing, it doesn't follow that anything like "nominalistic content" exists because it doesn't follow that anything language-like (or, for that matter, thought-like)—that could directly express that purported content—is coherent. See Jody Azzouni, "Evading truth commitments: The problem reanalyzed," *Logique et Analyse* 206 (2009c), 139–176, for details.

demand—that truly describe the state of affairs of the referents[r] of their terms. This isn't, however, the case with all truths.[57]

Dichotomies invariably have Procrustian drawbacks. A simple *de re/de dicto* (or corresponding singular/predicative) distinction distorts by either forcing such thought to be inappropriately involved with ontological commitments of one sort or another, or to be interpreted in a way strangely different (e.g., metalinguistically) from how we ordinarily understand it. I hope I've established the possibility of there being an overlooked option. Another way of approaching this problem area, however, that might be considered to facilitate a more sensible application of the singular category of thought and speech, is to "broaden" it by dropping the requirement of objects along with corresponding truth values.[58] In this way, hallucinogenic experience can continue to be treated as (broadly) singular without requiring objects as the target of the content of those experiences. This doesn't work if only because such statements can have truth values regardless of whether there is an object involved. (Even in the hallucinogenic case this is so: I can, in full knowledge of what is happening to me, point at the elf I'm hallucinating the presence of, and say truly: "That is an hallucination of an elf.") What's needed instead is the empty singular thought category: there are nonconceptual relations of the thought to something external, but they aren't necessarily to an object that's the reference[r] of the (in this case) not fully conceptualized thought. Burge is right to note how numerical thought, despite its being fully conceptualized, necessarily involves relations that aren't conceptualized; the mistake is to think that this—in turn—implies that numerical thought requires either genuine relata as its referential target, or the acknowledgment of such.

One last point about some of the literature concerned with this issue. Donnellan (1974) offers a construal of negative existentials, like "Pegasus doesn't exist," that preserves their singularity but doesn't introduce nonexistent objects. The trick is to couch the truth or falsity of such sentences in terms of the presence of a "block" in the history of the usage of the words in question (e.g., "Pegasus") where a block, for example, is such a usage-history ending in a storytelling.[59] One right idea motivating this strategy is to detach the truth of the negative existential containing "Pegasus" from a something to which "Pegasus" refers.[60] However, there are statements containing vacuous terms that must be accommodated in

---

57. There are other significant differences: ultimately, I reject claims about truth makers or truth-value inducers as bearing on a "theory of truth": I'm a truth deflationist (see Azzouni 2006). Another important difference is one of stress: coherence views focus on truths fitting in—according to one or another notion of coherence—with other truths. I instead focus on such truths being required by our current evidential and deductive approaches. The model I advocate for sentences with vacuous terms isn't a coherence model so much as it is an "indispensability" model.

58. I'm under the impression that Burge suggested something along these lines to me on December 3, 2007.

59. See his rule N (Keith Donnellan, "Speaking of nothing," *Philosophical Review* 83 [1974], 3–32, reprinted in *Naming, necessity, and natural kinds*, ed. Stephen P. Schwartz, [Ithaca, N.Y.: Cornell University Press, 1977], 239).

60. Donnellan (1974, 238) writes: "This means that in this case we are divorcing the truth conditions from meaning." I don't think, however, that this is the right way to characterize the suggestion; see my discussion of the relationship between truth-value inducers (and the truth values they induce in sentences) and truth conditions (as supplied by a semantic theory) in section 5.4.

addition to the negative existentials. There are true (and false) statements, for example, about^e Pegasus that change in truth value when "Pegasus" is replaced with "Hercules." The notion of empty singular thought is directed toward preserving the truth values of positive statements—for example, with respect to numerical, hallucinogenic, or fiction-directed thought. With respect to these cases, most philosophers concerned with statements and thoughts containing vacuous terms (Burge, Donnellan, Evans, Kripke, Salmon, etc.) instead either opt for (i) making such thought truth-valueless (mock), (ii) finding something real for such thoughts to be truly about, or (iii) acquiescing in one or another version of Meinongianism. I argue in this book that there is an unnoticed—and better—way to handle them.

Hallucinations

2.0 An Introduction for Browsers, Grazers, and Those People Who Like to Know What's Coming before It Shows Up

I start with a discussion of those aboutness intuitions that compel the sense many have that when we talk about something, we can do so in a "singular" way. Because such intuitions arise in cases where we also take ourselves to be talking about nothing at all (e.g., Pegasus) and are further coupled with truth-apt intuitions about the resulting statements, none of four possible characterizations of such empty terms has carried the day (among philosophers): each fails to satisfy one or more of the operative (and powerful) intuitions in play here. In section 2.2 I revisit the Meinongian approach, laying it out in fair detail before contrasting it with my (fifth) option, which breaks the connection between the truth-aptness of certain statements and what they apparently refer to. This is all preparatory background for the topic of hallucinations, which is the central topic of this chapter.

In section 2.3, I describe an experimental setting within which discourse about hallucinated objects occurs that's both truth-apt and evidentially crucial to scientific studies. Some details about the discourse in question are given: (i) that quantifiers ranging over hallucinated objects, the proper names attributed to those objects, and the demonstratives directed toward those objects are all standardly used; (ii) that properties are attributed to such things; and (iii) that identifications and distinctions are made among them.

In section 2.4, it's shown that indispensable to this discourse is quantification *into* language contexts governed by "*S* hallucinates that . . ." In section 2.5, I turn to the possibility of singular reference directed toward hallucinated objects. Evans (1982) mounts a sustained and sophisticated set of arguments that such isn't possible. I describe a condition he places on singular reference, the diversity condition (that he claims demonstrations of hallucinated objects cannot meet), and I show in section 2.6 that it's not a genuine requirement for singular reference. I show further (in section 2.7) that in any case the condition can be met by hallucinated objects. In an appropriate sense, hallucinated objects are both public objects, and suitable objects for scientific study.

In section 2.8, I return to a discussion of the pretence strategy: that when someone knowingly demonstrates an hallucinated object (for example), he is just pretending to do so and just pretending to utter truth-apt statements about that object. The primary result of this section is that pretence views are shown to violate the external discourse demand: that the statements directed toward hallucinated objects not only have to be pretence-truth-apt (truth-apt within the pretence), they also have to be truth-apt vis-à-vis statements outside of the pretence context. That is, they have evidential and deductive roles vis-à-vis other statements that in no way can be regarded as part of the hallucination pretence. It's shown that the pretence theorist cannot meet this challenge.

If hallucinatoric discourse is to be truth-apt, and meet the external discourse demand, it cannot be inconsistent. But the attribution of properties to hallucinated objects seems to invite just such inconsistency because an hallucinated object can both have attributed to it the property (say) of being on a table while it is also true that nothing at all is on the table. It's shown in section 2.9 that a distinction between the properties that hallucinated objects have and those that they present (to the hallucinator) solves this problem.

Just as properties are attributed to hallucinated objects, so, too, hallucinated objects are distinguished and identified. It's shown in section 2.10 how this is possible without there being—in any sense at all—objects to be identified and distinguished. In particular, the cogency of this practice cannot rest on an approach, popular among Meinongians, that identifies and distinguishes "nonexistent" objects on the basis of the properties they have and lack. On the view being developed in this book, there are no such objects, and consequently they have no properties. It's shown that a consistent identification and distinction practice is possible without it being metaphysically grounded in "real" distinctions and identifications among objects. In particular, it's shown that such a practice is possible—without it being metaphysically grounded in real objects (and their "individuation conditions")—that's not purely response-dependent. That is, it can be cogent for someone to be wrong about whether a particular object he is hallucinating is the same as another, without there being a metaphysical fact of the matter about this (because, after all, there are no such objects). To properly show all this, a general discussion of bivalence and "identity conditions" is required (and undertaken).

No philosophical study of hallucinations is complete without some discussion of the argument from hallucination. The argument seems to show that there is a perceptual veil between the perceiver and the objects she sees during ordinary acts of perception. Such a veil is taken by some philosophers to be established if the contents of hallucinatory experience can be positively characterized, and if such content is (in certain cases) indistinguishable from the ordinary perception of objects. In section 2.11, I show that although there are perfectly innocuous ways of positively characterizing hallucinatoric content, a version of a disjunctive characterization of experience (as hallucinatory or not) is nevertheless appropriate. Despite this, the possibility of shared "content" between an hallucination and an experience of real objects remains, although the existence of this particular kind of "highest common factor" is nevertheless neutral with respect to whether ordinary objects are "directly perceived." Reasons for thinking otherwise (on the basis of considerations arising from the argument from hallucination) are due to a kind of use/mention error. The remainder of the chapter contains elucidations and characterizes, in light of the case of hallucination, the appeal of the empty construal of singular thought directed toward things we see but that aren't there.

One terminological matter. In section 1.7, I distinguished between two uses of "about" and "refer," respectively, about^e and about^r, and refer^e and refer^r. I also claimed that the ordinary words "about" and "refer" are neutral between these (something I occasionally indicate with the locutions about$^{(r/e)}$ or refer$^{(r/e)}$.) As a result, I take myself as licensed to utilize the ordinary "about" and "refer" except when it's crucial to note ontological distinctions. Most of the time (in this section, for example) I utilize the ordinary "about" and "refer," naturally and intuitively, and expect that the philosophical reader to keep track—where pertinent—when ontology is involved when it isn't (when, say, aboutness^r is in play; when, instead, aboutness^e is), and when it doesn't matter. This is, after all, what the ordinary speaker does all the time.

2.1 Aboutness, Truth, Nonexistence

When we talk or think about something, we often do so in a *singular* way. To say (or think) that Bertrand Russell was born in 1872 is to say (or to think) something directly about *him*, and not something indirectly about him by means of some proposition or thought (quantifying over everything and containing an individuating description) that holds uniquely of him. This is the "aboutness" intuition— and it's very compelling. The intuition is that statements (or thoughts) like

(1) Bertrand Russell was born in 1872,

(2) He [demonstrating Bertrand Russell] was born in 1872,

(3) That man [demonstrating Bertrand Russell] was born in 1872,

are *about* Bertrand Russell in a sense quite distinguishable from

(4) Anyone who invented the theory of descriptions, co-wrote a three-volume work in mathematical logic published during 1910–13, and was the only one to do both of these things, was born in 1872.

Although (4) "denotes," "holds of," or "uniquely refers to" Bertrand Russell, it nevertheless isn't about Bertrand Russell in this intuitive sense. It quantifies over everything (it's about anyone who . . .); it uniquely describes Bertrand Russell via a general condition, a general condition—as it turns out—that holds of (and only of) Bertrand Russell.[1]

The aboutness intuition arises not only with the use of (most) names but also with definite descriptions—when used referentially (as opposed to attributively)[2]— and with many uses of demonstratives, pronouns, and so on. This intuition is the source of the widespread opposition to certain applications of Russell's (1905) theory of descriptions—specifically, to attempts to treat names or demonstratives as "implicit" or "disguised" definite descriptions. For Strawson (1956), for example, in "mentioning" or uttering a statement "about" something, one is "refer-ring," and to do that is to do something above and beyond using a definite description that happens to pick out an object uniquely, and that one's sentence is (therefore) true or false of.

The "majority view" in philosophical semantics is conservative about the relationship between sentences and the objects that make those sentences true: these objects must exist. There must be appropriate objects that determine the truth values for statements or thoughts that one utters or has in those cases. In the case of singular reference, one's "access" to the objects in question is achieved nonconcep-tually—by "acquaintance," "perception," an appropriate "causal" or "historical" relation, and so on. "That's an ugly urn," for example, is true or false because of the properties had by the urn that's singularly referred to via "that," contextual factors, and/or the perceptual powers of the speaker (and/or her audience). Similar for "Aristotle is a great philosopher" (with the addition of an historical referential chain), "the man over there drinking a martini is famous," and (said in a restaurant because of a voice one is hearing) "he is rather too loud."[3]

When (prima facie) there is no object referred to, as with "That's an ugly urn" (said while hallucinating an urn), or with "Frodo is shorter than Gandalf," the

---

1. No word of English captures the desired sense of "about" as so described; "about" as used above, therefore, is semi-technical language. (4) isn't about Bertrand Russell in this semi-technical sense (it's about everyone); (1), (2), and (3) are about Bertrand Russell. Noting that (4) uses a quantifier, that (1) doesn't, and that (2) and (3) operate referentially to indicate something (otherwise contextually available), helps convey the sense of "about" in play; noting that (4) "gets to" Bertrand Russell via concepts, that (1) "gets to" him by his name without concepts, and that the concepts utilized in (2) and (3) can be referentially idle (i.e., the items demonstrated can fail to fit the concepts) also helps to convey the idea.

2. Keith Donnellan, "Reference and definite descriptions," *Philosophical Review* 75 (1966) 281–304. Intui-tions perhaps scatter with respect to definite descriptions. The attributive usage "The tallest man in the world lives in the Andes," strikes my ear as a statement about the tallest man in the world, even though I have no idea who that is. This is because, intuitively, "The tallest man," is heard as a singular term and not as a quantifier governing a descrip-tive phrase. So, strictly speaking, "aboutness" intuitions are sustained both descriptionlessly via names, as well as by (what's presumably) fully functioning descriptive content. I won't make anything of this intuitive point in this book.

3. There are subtleties that aren't central to the concerns of this book. Nathan Salmon (e.g., "Nonexistence" [1998], in *Metaphysics, mathematics, and meaning* (Oxford: Oxford University Press 2005], 51) distinguishes between Millianism ("according to which the semantic contents of certain simple singular terms, including at least ordinary proper names and demonstratives, are simply their referents") and direct reference ("according to which the semantic content of a name or demonstrative is not given by any definite description").

majority tradition offers four maneuvers: (i) rejecting singularity for such propositions and thoughts, and characterizing them instead as disguised descriptions;[4] (ii) treating such thoughts or propositions as defective, gappy, or "mock" (they aren't genuine thoughts or propositions), and rejecting the claim that they are truth-apt;[5] (iii) isolating the discourse in question (e.g., fictional discourse) by introducing a pretence or fictional operator (e.g., "in the fictional world of —"), and restricting the thought or utterance in question only to occurrences within such operators (and as "true relative to —"); a more drastic alternative is to treat the discourse as one that's only pretendedly engaged in;[6] and (iv) denying the apparent datum that the items don't exist.[7]

No approach, based on strategies (i)–(iv)—neither an approach using one or another of these strategies alone, nor one that couples several together, nor one that helps itself to other tools from philosophical semantics (e.g., accommodating dissenting intuitions about what's said by such propositions with tools from pragmatics, and/or drawing a distinction between what the proposition says and what conditions determine its truth value)—has convinced even a significant minority of the majority tradition because of the pressure from four (sets of) powerful intuitions that operate destructively on the strategies.

First (Aboutness), there are the already mentioned aboutness intuitions (that drive the singular approach); these intuitions are equally present whether one speaks of real items or of fictions and hallucinations.[8] Contributing to the presence of singular intuitions even in the case of hallucinations or fictions is the purely epistemic fact that one often doesn't know whether the something that one is speaking of or thinking about is real.[9] These intuitions resist any solution

4. For example, W. V. O. Quine, "On what there is" (1953), in *From a logical point of view* (Cambridge, Mass.: Harvard University Press, 1980), 1–19—who applies the approach to all singular terms. Rewritings of the propositions as metalinguistic belong here as well.

5. For example, P. F. Strawson, "On referring" (1956), in *The philosophy of language*, 2nd ed., ed. A. P. Martinich (Oxford: Oxford University Press, 1990); Keith Donnellan, "Speaking of nothing," *Philosophical Review* 83 (1974): 3–32; reprinted in *Naming, necessity, and natural kinds*, ed. Stephen P. Schwartz (Ithaca, N.Y.: Cornell University Press, 1977) (page citations are to the latter), 234; Gareth Evans, *The varieties of reference* (Oxford: Oxford University Press, 1982), 45–46; and David Braun, "Empty names," *Noûs* 27 (1993), 443–69.

6. For example, David Lewis, "Truth in fiction" (1978), in *Philosophical papers* volume 1 (Oxford: Oxford University Press, 1983), 261–75, with respect to fictions; Evans (1982), chapter 10, urges a pretence view—partially on the grounds of the inadequacy of operator views—with respect to hallucinations and fictional discourse.

7. For example, Peter van Inwagen, "Creatures of fiction" (1977), in *Ontology, identity, and modality* (Cambridge: Cambridge University Press, 2001), 37–56; Salmon (1998); and Amie L. Thomasson, *Fiction and metaphysics* (Cambridge: Cambridge University Press, 1999)—all with respect to fictions.

8. Marga Reimer ("A 'Meinongian' solution to a Millian problem," *American Philosophical Quarterly* 38 [2001], 233–48) directs an objection to gappy approaches to the effect that such fail to preserve or to explain away such aboutness intuitions—what she calls "content intuitions"—that arise with empty names, such as "Vulcan." See David Braun, "Empty names, fictional names, mythical names," *Noûs* 39 (2005), 624, note 18, for a response.

9. Other cases where a person fails "to have a thought of the kind he supposes himself to have" (Evans 1982, 45) may motivate the model of thought failure to fictions and hallucinations. However, it's striking that the discovery that Santa Claus doesn't exist isn't (ever experienced as) the discovery that one was mistaken in the kinds of thoughts one was having; it's (always experienced as) a discovery that one was mistaken about what one was thinking about. The object *Santa Claus* is reclassified. When, however, one discovers that "Sarah" is actually twins, or that one's use of "here" is ill applied (because one has been unknowingly moving) or that sometimes "that vase" is a vase and sometimes a hologram, one does intuit the presence of a referential gap in one's thoughts or statements (that at least infirms their being truth-apt) instead of a reclassification of the "objects" talked about: the thought no longer seems to have been of anything. See section 2.12 for further discussion and comparison.

utilizing (i). They also resist solutions that attempt to recharacterize what such propositions are really about: concepts, for example.

Second (Normality), we have strong intuitions—rooted in how we talk and think about hallucinations and fictions—that propositions and thoughts about the nonexistent, Santa Claus, the elf I'm hallucinating, are ordinary ones. More strongly, they are of the same form and structure. As propositions, "Santa Claus is optimistic" differs not at all from "Barack Obama is optimistic." The only difference (intuitively) is that Barack Obama exists and that Santa Claus doesn't. Thus, statements about nonexistent entities don't seem to involve special psychological attitudes not involved otherwise. This makes the application of any strategy (i), (ii), or (iii) to fictional or hallucinatoric discourse intuitively *ad hoc*.

Third (Truth), and related to Normality—but deserving of special notice— we also have strong intuitions—also rooted in how we talk and think about hallucinations and fictions—about the specific truth values of many such propositions and thoughts.[10] This is what makes (ii) and (iii) implausible, because we not only take such propositions and thoughts to have specific truth values, but in addition we employ them unrestrictedly in our reasoning along with other statements.

Fourth (Nonexistence), we also have ordinary and straightforward "plain-speaking" intuitions (beliefs, if you will) that what makes fictions and hallucinations *fictions* and *hallucinations* is that there simply are no such objects in any sense at all. We reassure the victim of an hallucination that there is nothing there; in the case of Santa Claus and his elves, that it's all "made up," or that "there are no such things."[11] Importantly related to this third intuition are that things that don't exist don't have properties either. This is also plain-speaking. To attribute properties to something that doesn't exist invites the rejoinder "*what*, exactly, is it that doesn't have properties?"[12] This rather directly creates a problem for strategy (iv).

---

10. For example, "*That* is the hallucination of a dwarf, not the hallucination of a hobbit." "Mrs. Gamp . . . is the most fully developed of the masculine anti-women visible in all Dickens's novels" (from van Inwagen 1977, 41).

11. Peter van Inwagen ("Quantification and fictional discourse," in *Empty names, fiction and the puzzles of nonexistence*, ed. Anthony Everett and Thomas Hofweber [Stanford, Calif.: CSLI Publications, 2000], 246–47), while admitting that "everyone" is firmly convinced that such items don't exist, nevertheless refuses to read such sentences literally. As he puts it, "the non-existence of Holmes is not an ontological *datum*" (emphasis in original).

12. J. L. Austin (*Sense and sensibilia* [Oxford: Oxford University Press, 1962], 96, note 1) writes, "how could one possibly say, in the same breath, 'It must really have the qualities it seems to have', and 'It may not exist'? *What* must have the qualities it seems to have?'" Such intuitions also strongly arise in cases where someone wants to talk of (specific) objects that could have existed but that don't (e.g., the gnome in my garden). Again, the compelling rejoinder is: *what* might existed?

Note the intuitive singular flavor of this plain speaking: what *specific object* could you possibly be talking about? This is what makes such plain speaking nevertheless compatible with the intuition that although there aren't flying horses, there might have been; that is, "there might have been flying horses," is intuitively glossed as "there might have been creatures with such and such properties," whereas "Pegasus might have existed," is glossed singularly as: the (specific) creature Pegasus being spoken of might have existed. Here the challenge, "*what specific creature* Pegasus is being spoken of?" has intuitive force.

These four sets of intuitions (all arising from our ordinary discourse practices) rather directly undercut the four strategies available to majority tradition philosophers. To recapitulate: nonsingular construals of fictional and hallucinogenic statements and thoughts, even when they can be finessed into providing the right truth values,[13] don't respect the singular intuitions that hold as strongly of uses of "Pegasus" and "Zeus" as they do of "Bertrand Russell" and "Noam Chomsky." Mock or gappy approaches don't respect the intuitions that many of the things we say about nonexistent things are both meaningful and true. (More basically, they don't respect the intuition that the things we say about nonexistent things are about those things.) Isolating-discourse strategies contradict our ordinary practices of speaking (and thinking) truths about nonexistent things in the very same breath that we use to speak of what's real—as, for example, when we claim that Bertrand Russell was cleverer than Sherlock Holmes is, or that Abe Lincoln was taller than Frodo is. Finally, to claim that fictions, hallucinations, and the like actually exist (e.g., as abstracta of some sort) violates that "feeling for reality which ought to be preserved even in the most abstract studies."[14]

The lack of professional consensus on the four strategies sketched here, and the still living Meinongian approach—to be discussed in section 2.2—strongly suggest that the four intuitions are jointly inconsistent in their (prima facie) demands: something must go. That all four intuitions are so strongly held explains the intractability so visible in this subject area.

2.2 The Meinongian Minority Tradition

Despite (or perhaps because of) the scornful characterizations it sometimes receives,[15] the Meinongian minority tradition continues to have (many) adherents. I describe this tradition quite broadly as one that introduces objects

(*The Meinongian assumptions*)

   (i) that don't exist, but that
  (ii) nevertheless have properties, and
 (iii) are referred to by singular terms and/or fall within the range of one or another type of quantifier, and
 (iv) the properties of which determine the truth values of statements within which these singular terms, quantifiers, and perhaps other terms, occur.

---

13. Something that's recognized to be a severe problem all by itself. See, for example, van Inwagen (1977, 2000); Jody Azzouni, *Deflating existential consequence: A case for nominalism* (Oxford: Oxford University Press, 2004a), chapter 3; or the literature on Geach's Hob/Nob problem (discussed and cited in Nathan Salmon, "Mythical objects" (2002), in *Metaphysics, mathematics, and meaning* [Oxford: Oxford University Press, 2005], 91–107).

14. Bertrand Russell, *Introduction to mathematical philosophy* (London: Routledge, 1919), 169.

15. Choice quotes from Richard Routley and Valerie Routley ("Rehabilitating Meinong's theory of objects," *Revue Internationale de Philosophie* 27 [1973], 224): "the unspeakable Meinong," and "the horrors of Meinong's jungle."

Some caveats and amplifications. Let's start with the term "Meinongian." This adjective is used in quite different ways, and consequently some philosophers don't think of themselves as "Meinongian" because (for example) they take Meinongians to assert (although they deny) that there are circular squares. There are subtle textual questions about the interpretation of Meinong's original position.[16] In using "Meinongian," I intend only to label a rather broad family of positions that—at least with respect to the semantics of some terms—share essential characteristics. Van Inwagen (1977, 37) describes Meinongians as meaning to assert that "there *are*, there really *are*, certain objects that have . . . the attribute of nonexistence." This underestimates the range of pertinent Meinongian positions. The nonexistent objects in question are sometimes described as ones that don't exist but nevertheless are; sometimes the view is that they don't exist in any sense at all, and perhaps more strongly, that there *aren't* such objects. Technically speaking (that is), there is a broad range of (specific kinds of) quantifiers allowed (and sometimes all that's allowed) to range over the nonexistent (in contrast to the ordinary or "actualist" quantifier).[17] I've thus captured this aspect of the Meinongian position with the vanilla characterization that the objects don't exist, leaving further details—of how these objects are to be referred to—to the particulars of specific Meinongian positions.

Crucial to any Meinongian position, therefore, is (ii)–(iv): that such nonexisting objects and their properties play truth-maker roles. Such objects are referred to and/or quantified over (in one way or another),[18] and they and their properties are necessary to the truth conditions of statements about them. Such views thus respect Aboutness, Normality, and Truth.

The Meinongian, however, weasels around the fourth intuition Nonexistence by means of what looks like a technicality. The objects officially "don't exist" (this is the letter of Nonexistence); despite this, such nonexistent items play truth- and falsity-conferring roles for the statements about them. This is one

16. See, for example, A. D. Smith, *The problem of perception* (Cambridge, Mass.: Harvard University Press, 2002) for citations and for careful discussion; also see Charles Crittenden, *Unreality: The metaphysics of fictional objects* (Ithaca, N.Y.: Cornell University Press, 1991), 5, note 4. I should note that Roderick Chisholm, "Beyond being and nonbeing" (1972), in *Metaphysics: The big questions*, ed. Peter van Inwagen and Dean W. Zimmerman (Oxford: Blackwell Publishing, 2008), 40–50, is especially valuable.

17. Charles Parsons, "A plea for substitutional quantification" (1971a), in *Mathematics in philosophy: Selected essays* (Ithaca, N.Y.: Cornell University Press, 1983), 63–70 explores the relevance of substitutional quantification to *a* concept of existence, one on his view (65) close to Meinong's. Also see Charles Parsons, "Ontology and mathematics" (1971b), in *Mathematics in philosophy: Selected essays* (Ithaca, New York: Cornell University Press, 1983), 37–62. Terence Parsons, *Nonexistent objects* (New Haven, Conn.: Yale University Press, 1980); Edward N. Zalta, *Abstract objects: An introduction to axiomatic metaphysics* (Dordrecht: Reidel, 1983); and Edward N. Zalta, *Intensional logic and the metaphysics of intentionality* (Cambridge, Mass.: MIT Press, 1988) are also examples of philosophers who quantify (one way or another) over nonexistent objects. And there are many other Meinongians who do so.

18. Although Nathan Salmon ("Existence" [1987], in *Metaphysics, mathematics, and meaning* [Oxford: Oxford University Press, 2005], 9–49; 1998) thinks fictional objects exist, he also thinks that there might have been (and, as well, that there couldn't have been) objects that our terms (nevertheless) *do* refer to. Indeed, things that (only) might have existed or couldn't have existed (actually) *have* properties, even though there (actually) are no such objects (although, that is, one can't quantify—actualistically—over them). There are terms that designate such objects (he defines some); indeed, there are terms that directly refer to items that don't exist and that can't exist; there (actually) are terms that (actually) refer to items that there (actually) aren't.

source of the scorn directed by majoritarians toward minority Meinongian positions. A second (related) source of scorn is a denial (among some majoritarians) of the wiggle room the Meinongian needs between ontologically loaded concepts to make his position cogent.[19]

The fifth option. It may seem that in this and in the last section I've sketched all the response options possible in this problem area. I have not. Both Meinongians and their majoritarian opponents share a ontological/semantical assumption that statements (of various forms—e.g., involving singular terms) are true and false on the basis of the properties had by objects referred to by the singular terms appearing in those statements, or that fall within the range of one or another kind of quantifier appearing in those statements. This assumption structures many of the polemical (but deadlocked) moves and countermoves among the four majoritarian strategies and against the Meinongian.

In suggesting a fifth option that denies this common assumption, I'm not making the drastic move (suggested by some metaphysical nihilists) that metaphysics be exiled from truth altogether (from the conferring of truth and falsity on our statements)—that the "representational" powers of true (and false) sentences be denied. There are statements with truth values—for example, "protons have positive charge," "Hillary Clinton was alive in 1972"[20]—where the shared ontological/semantical assumption is exactly the right one. But the truth idiom doesn't require "correspondence," and where such is missing, it isn't the case that anything goes. There is still a determining relationship between the truths (and falsities) in question and aspects of the world. It's just that those determining aspects of the world (the truth-value inducers) aren't represented (referred to and/or quantified over) by terms in the statements in question. A concrete case, worked out in fair detail, is needed to see how this goes, and especially to convince sceptical readers that the resulting truths are not "free-floating" items.[21] I discuss the test case of hallucinatory thought and statement in the sections to come.

The problem of nonbeing. I'd first like to motivate the fifth option by noting that a special case of it is not unknown to philosophers. It's been suggested more than once that negative existentials, for example, "Pegasus doesn't exist," are true not because the somethings that words refer to (the word "Pegasus" in this case) lack the property existence but because such statements successfully describe occurring states of affairs—that, for example, no Pegasus is to be found among such. The question remains, of course, how these statements manage to

---

19. For example, by distinguishing between the predicate "exists" and the quantifier "there is." Alternatively, by assimilating the predicate "exists," and "there (actually) is," on the one hand, but distinguishing these from "there might have been," or "there can't be," on the other—and (crucially) allowing the latter quantifiers to range over possible and impossible objects that (nevertheless) actually have properties.

20. I'm not a presentist.

21. It's worth noting, however, that a systematic (book-length) attempt to show the independence of a truth-governed discourse from any metaphysical state of affairs (that its referential apparatus is to be related to) already exists. Crucial to this study (of mathematical discourse) is that it's shown that the metaphysics-free practice of mathematics is objective in the sense that truth values for mathematical statements are nevertheless (and for the most part) forced. See Jody Azzouni, *Metaphysical myths, mathematical practice: The ontology and epistemology of the exact science* (Cambridge: Cambridge University Press, 1994).

represent these states of affairs. In accord with the four intuitions, one would like to answer this question without reinterpreting such statements as covertly quotational—as meta-statements that certain words appearing within those very statements fail to refer[r]. So, too, one would like "Pegasus doesn't exist" to say something different from "Athena doesn't exist"; more generally, one would like to retain the singular quality of the statements, their being about, respectively, Pegasus and Athena.[22]

This is the old problem of nonbeing—with a singular twist—but the ordinary person's reaction to it is informative. The straightforward impression of singular negative existentials is that (i) they are fully meaningful, (ii) the objects described nevertheless don't exist, and yet (iii) these negative existentials are about those objects. Here is an important fact: when ordinary people are pressed about what they are talking about when they claim "Pegasus doesn't exist" (since there is no such object), many fall into a use/mention error, and describe the "idea" of Pegasus as the topic matter.[23] That is, they give up on the intuition that "Pegasus doesn't exist" is about Pegasus, in light of the nonexistence of Pegasus—although they don't give up on a subject matter (of some sort) for the sentence. This suggests that of the four powerful intuitions, Aboutness, Normality, Truth, and Nonexistence, it's Aboutness that should be challenged, or at least modified.[24] My aim is to do just that: to modify Aboutness in the case of singular statements such as "Pegasus doesn't exist," and "Pegasus is a mythical creature," although retaining the singular character of these statements. That is, despite modifying Aboutness, Normality is not to be rejected.

This may not seem possible. To call certain thoughts or statements singular may seem to non-negotiably entail that there must be objects involved. This impression—in the case of hallucinations—drives some philosophers to either the position of denying that the hallucinating victim is aware of anything at all or to embracing Meinongian objects as what the hallucinator is to be aware of. But as the last chapter indicated there is room for maneuver between the denial that a thought or statement is completely conceptualized (is purely descriptive) and the

22. Crittenden (1991, 73–74) neatly indicates the singular quality of these singular negative existentials by noting that "Sherlock Holmes doesn't exist" doesn't seem equivalent in meaning to "Nothing has all the properties ascribed to Sherlock Holmes (in the Sherlock Holmes stories)," because if the latter were false (if it turned out that something somewhere did have all those properties coincidentally), it wouldn't necessarily make the former statement false. We (intuitively) were making a claim about the (fictional character) Sherlock Holmes, and of course, that character doesn't exist even if some same-property bearing item (that we weren't talking about) does exist.

23. This isn't to go descriptive on the word "Pegasus": the use/mention error treats the concept as something the sentence is about, not something the meaning of the word "Pegasus" is analyzed in terms of. Otávio Bueno (personal communication) has pressed me on the question of why I describe the error as a use/mention error rather than a mistaken change in topic. Use/mention errors are mistaken changes in topic; more specifically, they are shifts from the intended topic of the thought or statement to aspects of the thought or statement itself. I later diagnose exactly the same kind of use/mention error to be at work in the argument from hallucination (and, although I don't discuss it, in the argument from illusion). See section 2.11.

24. Some nonphilosophers, I have to admit, describe the singular negative existential as about the imaginary Pegasus or the imaginary character. This isn't easy to interpret. On probing, it sometimes turns into a use/mention error (the character is what's on paper, or on film, etc.); sometimes it's revealed to be a folk version of a Meinongian strategy; and sometimes it's actually seen as a description of something the speaker thinks "exists," but that doesn't exist in "our" space and time.

assertion that such an item must therefore be about (some sort of) object. What's needed to recognize this (until now unrecognized) option in logical space is to notice that both the semantic and psychological factors that make perceptually directed thoughts (and statements) singular are operative regardless of whether one's thought and experience are directed toward real items or toward one's hallucinations. This point about the fifth option naturally invites the nomenclature *empty singular thought*. I now turn to a specific illustration, that of hallucination.

2.3 Talking about Hallucinations

I start by laying out some data that ratify the four powerful intuitions in the case of hallucination; I also want to indicate the (nature of the) indispensability of this way of talking.[25] Imagine, therefore, that one way of exploring brain function is by inducing powerful and continuous hallucinations in subjects by means of hallucinogens. The qualities of the hallucinations indicate locations of activity in the brain, the nature of those activities, and the sensitivity of those activities to external stimuli (priming), to episodic and other types of memory, and so on. This information, coupled with background knowledge of neurological function and specific facts about specific hallucinogens, contributes to evidence for and against various (neurological) hypotheses.[26]

In the experimental setting, a subject *S* sits in a totally darkened room while the hallucinogen takes effect. Once the lights go on, *S* sees and hears (seems to see and hear) many things. Although he knows that some of the objects he's seeing (seems to be seeing) aren't real, he often doesn't know which ones those are. Some of the props (desks, wands, etc.) are real, and some are hallucinations; some of the hobbits and other creatures are actors and some are hallucinations. *S* can't tell (by the intrinsic qualities of what he experiences—or seems to experience) even whether particulars items are partially hallucinations and partially not.[27] During the episode, *S* may be asked to answer questions or be requested to carry out certain tasks.

25. I deliberately choose the word "indispensability," with its echo of a major literature in philosophy of mathematics.

26. My thought experiment is just that: a thought experiment. But it's not that far from the study situation of hallucinations, as currently undertaken. For illustrations of brain imaging, attempts to correlate experiences with specific brain activation, and studies of the effects of chemicals, see Christian Plewnia, Felix Bischof, and Matthias Reimold, "Suppression of verbal hallucinations and changes in regional cerebral blood flow after intravenous lidocaine: A case report," *Progress in Neuro-Psychopharmacology and Biological Psychiatry* 31 (2007), 301–3; G. T. Stebbins, C. G. Goetz, M. C. Carrillo, K. J. Bangen, D. A. Turner, G. H. Gover, and J. D. E. Gabrieli, "Altered cortical visual processing in PD with hallucinations: An fMRI study," *Neurology* 63 (2004), 1409–16; Olaf Blanke, Stéphanie Ortigue, Theodor Landis, and Margitta Seeck, "Stimulating illusory own-body perceptions," *Nature* 419 (2002), 269–70; and Dirk De Ridder, Koen Van Laere, Patrick Dupont, Tomas Menovsky, and Paul Van de Heyning, "Visualizing out-of-body experience in the brain," *New England Journal of Medicine* 357 (2007), 1829–33. The literature is vast and growing. The tools of study are becoming more sophisticated as well. For an overview of the current (2008) situation, see André Aleman and Frank Larøi, *Hallucinations: The science of idiosyncratic perception* (Washington, D.C.: American Psychological Association, 2008).

27. The hobbit may be a real actor, but what he's wearing is sheer hallucination; similarly, a hobbit may be an entirely (visual) hallucination, although what he's uttering are (actually) real sounds from a (nearby) loudspeaker. An actor who is (actually) talking to himself, and looking up at the ceiling, may appear (to *S*) to be talking to a (much taller) wizard.

- What are the hobbits wearing?
- Are any of the hobbits you see today the same hobbits that you saw yesterday?
- Point to the hobbit with the bright red shoes, if there is one.
- Follow the hobbit with the bright red shoes around the room. Then close your eyes for two minutes, and after opening them again, continue following him around the room. How is he reacting to your following him?
- Are any of the hobbits laughing? Which ones?
- Can you hear what the hobbits are saying to each other?
- Can you tell the difference between the hobbits you see and the dwarves you see?
- Do you recognize any of the hobbits you see (for example, from movies or from pictures in fantasy books)?[28]

There are three significant observations to make about the (possibly quite extensive) discourse about these hallucinations that the experimenters and subjects (regularly) engage in and the contents of which are evidentially relevant to the experimenters' theorizing. I summarize them now, and then I motivate and defend them in the sections to follow.

(P1)   The ordinary language quantifiers,[29] the proper names hallucinated objects may be given,[30] and the demonstrative expressions are all standardly used. S's terms, therefore, indiscriminately refer to and/or quantify over hallucinated and real objects.[31]

(P2)   Properties are attributed to these things in a manner semantically indistinguishable from how such properties are attributed to real objects.[32] The hallucinated objects (along with what's real) are temporally and spatially indexed—both in terms of coordinates (to the extent that S can ordinarily do that)[33] and in their relations to other objects, both hallucinated and real.[34]

---

28. Although I've tried to acknowledge the possibility of a distinction between "seeing" and "seeming to see," it's unlikely that either the experimenters or S would bother to. Consider the following interview questions from Maurice M. Ohayon, "Prevalence of hallucinations and their pathological associations in the general population," *Psychiatry Research* 97 (2000), 155–56: "Have you ever seen things, objects or persons which other people can't see?" "Do you have the sense that you are outside of your body and watching yourself?" "Have you ever heard sounds, music or voices which other people can't hear?" My subsequent claims don't turn on issues of usage laziness.

29. "I see six hobbits today. That one by the door is wearing red shoes. Two of them are sitting at desks—there are a lot more desks today than yesterday—and the rest are anxiously milling around reading scrolls, or talking to one another. No one seems to have noticed that I'm here watching them. That wasn't true yesterday, when several friendly ones talked to me."

30. "That's Frodo—from the movies—at the desk. I don't recognize any of the other hobbits; I don't think I've seen any of them before." "That one's called Gailus. Although I've seen him off and on for several weeks, I never knew his name until yesterday—when several hobbits called him by name."

31. "There are only six hobbits here today. I'm not sure which ones are real and which aren't. I think the hobbit sitting at the desk is an actor. Oh!—both the desk and the hobbit suddenly vanished; so I guess neither of them was real." The ranges of ordinary-language quantifiers probably shift contextually "at the drop of a hat." The question, ultimately, is what to make of what's "in" such ranges when they include "nonexistent" entities—as they clearly do in these cases.

32. "Three of these hobbits are wearing red waistcoats, and two are wearing green ones."

33. "I saw Frodo walk through the door at two o'clock sharp."

34. "Frodo is over there, by the desk." "Samwise is playing with a baby unicorn less than a foot from me."

(P3)   The hallucinated objects are identified as the same or different from ones that are seen at other times and other places.[35]

(P1)–(P3) are prima facie characterizations of (many of the statements of) the discourse about S's hallucinations that he engages in with the experimenters. That discourse is indispensable in two senses. First, as indicated, the discourse is evidentially significant. I won't dwell further on this point in this chapter, but will largely take it for granted.[36] Second, this discourse cannot be paraphrased away or replaced with discourse of some other sort—at least it cannot be done so in a way that eliminates the crucial elements described by (P1)–(P3). This (second) important point is developed in the following sections.

2.4 Quantifying In

It's clear that all of this discourse about S's hallucinations is most naturally (third-person) couched in terms of what S (neutrally) sees: "S is seeing two hobbits that . . ." is the natural form for (third person) descriptions of his experiences. I choose the neutral construal of "S is seeing" because it isn't always correct to say that "he is hallucinating two hobbits that . . ." In some cases what's to be described is only partly his hallucination.[37] This neutral locution "S is seeing that . . . ," cannot be construed as adverbial, as descriptions of states or properties of S, but rather must be codified as involving a logically genuine relation (between S and what he sees or hallucinates); that is, what appears on the right side of the locution must be construed as open to quantification from outside that locution.[38] I'll illustrate this with respect to the phrase "S is hallucinating that . . ."—but it should be clear that the illustration can be developed using the neutral idiom instead. The point is that we need deductions of the following sort.[39]

(*Generalization*)

Every hobbit that S hallucinates either resembles some movie character in a movie that S has seen, or it resembles a hobbit in the calendar poster that S keeps by his bed.

---

35. For example, as in note 30.

36. See chapter 4, however, for extensive discussion of this.

37. The distinction between what S is "really" seeing and what he's hallucinating can be counterfactually construed, if one likes. What's part of the hallucination is what S wouldn't (seem to) see if he weren't drugged. What isn't part of the hallucination is what he would see in any case. Adopting such neutral terminology is not—all by itself, anyway—to claim that for S to "see" an actual hobbit or for him to "see" a qualitatively indistinguishable hallucination, is for him to "see" the same thing.

38. This is not to claim, however, that this logically genuine relation corresponds to a relation between S and a nonexistent object. The use of logically genuine relations, ones that admit quantification, are noncommittal (ontologically), and so there can be no such relation (in the world) because it requires something for S to be related to. These ontological matters have no impact on the use of logically genuine relations any more than they have an impact on the use of an (ontologically neutral) idiom of quantification. Recall the discussion of this in section 1.7.

39. This kind of reasoning (with respect to fictional characters) occurs in van Inwagen (2000).

And

> Gailus is a hobbit that S hallucinates (regularly) who doesn't resemble some movie character in a movie that S has seen.

Therefore:

> Gailus resembles a hobbit in the calendar poster that S keeps by his bed.[40]

Not only is quantification needed here (both to state *Generalization* and to draw inferences from it), but as noted (and as the illustration indicates) the quantifier in question must be outside the "S hallucinates" context, and yet governing a variable within that context. *Generalization* can't be stated if all the quantifiers governing hallucinated objects are forced to occur within an "S hallucinates" context. *Generalization*, it should be noted, is a third-person observation that S may not even have knowledge of (let alone hallucinate the contents of).

Consider the alternative:

> S hallucinates that every hobbit either resembles some movie character in a movie that S has seen, or it resembles a hobbit in the calendar poster that S keeps by his bed.

This fails to capture the appropriate generalization; it instead claims that S hallucinates of every hobbit that . . . It attributes the hallucination of a generalization to S, rather than stating a generalization about S and his hallucinations.

For S, speaking totally within the context of his experience, the use of an "existence predicate" or a "realness adjective" that operates contrastively against an ordinary language quantifier is quite natural—if not indispensable.[41] But given *Generalization*, and inferences drawn from it, such usages are invaluable in the third-person setting as well, to distinguish the items that S really sees from the ones he hallucinates. As just shown, this can't be done by judiciously keeping all (quantified) references to hallucinated objects within an "S hallucinates" context while allowing quantification into such contexts from outside only with respect to what's real. One thus has to fall back on a predicate or adjective to do the job (e.g., "S has realized that four of the hobbits he is seeing today aren't real").

One last observation. Evans (1982, 200)[42] writes: "If after it has been acknowledged on all sides that it seems to the hallucinator that he is confronting something . . . one says that it seems reasonable to the generality of mankind to suppose that the hallucinator is actually confronting something . . . then one is attempting to double-count the fact that has already been acknowledged."

---

40. Reductio is possible, of course. If—as far as the experimenters can gather—Gailus doesn't resemble any of the hobbits depicted in the calendar, the initial generalization can be (provisionally) overthrown.

41. For example, "There are six hobbits today, but only two of them are real" (or, "There are six hobbits today, but only two of them actually exist").

42. In the rest of this chapter, all references to Evans's work will be to his 1982 publication.

It should not be thought that this consideration motivates a restriction to only "notional" characterizations of what the hallucinator experiences, characterizations of the form "It seems to S that there is something that . . ." Let not, that is, the use of "actually" convey the impression that quantifying into such a characterization of hallucinatory experience has been ruled out. It cannot be ruled out—on pain of infirming hallucinatory discourse for evidential purposes.

2.5 Evans's Conditions on Singular Reference

For many philosophers—especially for those who have adopted Quine's criterion for ontological commitment (plus certain auxiliary claims about how that criterion is to be applied to natural languages)—the foregoing suffices for a commitment to such hallucinated objects. If such quantification cannot be brought entirely within an intentional context, and/or if the quantification in question can't be paraphrased away, that's it: we must take there to be such objects. But for other philosophers, quantifying over hallucinations is one thing; demonstrating them or giving them genuine (nondescriptive) names is quite another. Singular reference is special.

One way to argue, therefore, that quantification—even if indispensable for hallucinatory talk—is nevertheless ontologically "lightweight" is to argue that singular thoughts and statements about such "objects" aren't possible; that is, genuine demonstrations of hallucinated objects, and nondescriptive names of such, aren't possible. Perhaps this difference can motivate an ontological wedge between quantification over hallucinated objects and other "real" objects. Indeed, perhaps the "essentially private" nature of hallucinations can be brought to bear ontologically against them.

To this end, consider a claim Evans (143, note 1) makes. He writes that,

> the connection between demonstrative singular terms and perception comes out if we ask what is required in order to *understand* an utterance accompanied by one of these pointing gestures. It is necessary to perceive the object pointed out (to make it out), and to have the thought, about the object thus distinguished, that the speaker is saying of it that it is thus and so. . . . the central concept is not that of *making* a reference of such-and-such a kind, but that of *understanding* one. (emphasis in original)

Imagine, therefore, that S points at an elf he hallucinates, and that he calls it "Elrond." The experimenters are supposed to understand the remark; they are supposed to grasp the thought that S is having. But to grasp the thought in question, the experimenters have to make a judgment "about the right object."[43] This seems—to put it mildly—impossible to do without an object that they can see.

___
43. Evans, 332.

When we imagine, however, a case where S is pointing in a certain direction in which an experimenter is also looking, it's easy to think that a (real) object isn't needed. Instead, as Evans (332–33) puts the idea,

> even though there is no object, both speaker and hearer have information-based thoughts, and . . . communication and understanding can be seen to take place in virtue of a certain *correspondence* between the thoughts of the speaker and the hearer, depending on a correspondence in the ways in which they are based upon information. . . . [So] it makes sense to say that two people are focusing on the same place . . . even though there is nothing there.[44] (emphasis in original)

What's wrong with this line of thought—as Evans points out—is that much (if not most of the time) a useful "correspondence" between the thoughts of the speaker and the hearer is absent: invariably, the object referred to provides the needed identification between what speakers and hearers are thinking (and talking) about. That is, they are (usually) talking about the same thing even though their thinking about it, and the ways that they have gained access to that object, are quite different. One person may hear the object; another see it. One person may see it, and the other have only heard of it. One person may be sensitive to certain aspects of its visual appearance, and another sensitive to entirely different aspects of its visual appearance.[45] Evans (335) calls this the "argument from diversity." One way to read the point is that if one must require a certain sameness in the content of thought for statements about hallucinations to be successfully shared and for thoughts of such to be successfully understood, one has introduced an ad hoc restriction because sameness of thought is never otherwise an appropriate constraint.

What's instead required for singular thought, therefore, is that what's referred to be public in the following sense: It must be something that—as it were—can be reached by more than one cognitive route. Call this *the diversity condition*. I make two claims that I argue for in the next section. First, I claim that the diversity condition is false. We recognize no such demand on the "objects" that we can demonstrate and name (that is, that such must be approachable via more than one cognitive route). Such items can—as a matter of fact—be entirely private in nature. Second, and more surprisingly, the diversity condition is met by hallucinations. Hallucinations (despite universal philosophical opinion to the contrary) are not intrinsically private items, restricted—that is—to the subject having those hallucinations. I now go on to substantiate both of these important claims.

---

44. "The adjective 'information-based' is a term of art for Evans. The crucial issue is that information-based thoughts (Evans, 326–27) "commit the subject to the existence of something as their object." Think, therefore, of "information-based" as deriving necessarily from an object. "Object-dependent" thought (and speech) is another common locution used in the literature that amounts, for my purposes, to the same thing.

45. A nice illustration—Evans (337) writes that, "a speaker and a hearer may attend a party at which they circulate independently of one another. On the next day, the speaker may say 'Did you meet that Russian? He was extraordinarily drunk', and the hearer may understand him in virtue of retaining and invoking information acquired in quite separate episodes from those which gave rise to the speaker's information. This constitutes communication because, and only because, the same object was involved in both sets of episodes."

2.6 Entirely Private Demonstrations

We recognize that the causal powers of (certain) things can be so specific that our epistemic access to them is—consequently—narrow: we can only get to them like so, and in no other way. Coupled with this is the equally significant impression we rightfully have that our epistemic powers are limited, and limited in ways that we can't predict—especially with respect to objects that we haven't interacted with before. Last, we also recognize that the sensory powers of different individuals can vary—sometimes quite drastically.[46] Together these three working insights structure our ways of speech and thought to allow de facto private events—events that, in fact, can be experienced by one individual and by no others.

If I point at something that only I can see, and I describe it (correctly) as squarish, there is nothing that prevents such a speech act from being cogent and cogently understood by others. It's true, on the one hand, that I could not have learned to apply the term "squarish" except by the application of it (and similar words) to public objects and by being trained by others in my use of pointing gestures. This cannot prevent correct extensions of what I have learned to contexts where the public cannot follow. Should everyone except the speaker suddenly die, she would certainly be at a loss for words. But not because all her words had suddenly become meaningless.

It cannot be denied that if I point at something no one else can see, aspects of what I am thinking about (and gesturing toward) cannot be communicated to witnesses. There is a sense in which it's sometimes correct to say that they don't know what (in particular) I'm talking about. But to say, as Evans (73) does, that "nothing counts as understanding what the speaker said," is to speak in a decidedly exaggerated fashion. For one thing, people can know that I purport to point at something, that I take myself to see it, and that it has a shape that I'm describing. (Imagine one person looking through a keyhole and describing to another what he's seeing.)

To claim that there is a difference of principle between cases where the other person can possibly see what the first does (by changing places with him), and cases where the other person can't possibly see, is to bring in an irrelevant kind of verificationism. It's irrelevant because the verificationism in question is epistemic; one is attempting to make it do referential (semantic) work. One strong piece of evidence that the verificationism in question isn't relevant is the evident comprehensibility (for the folk) of fantasy stories where invisible beings can be seen (and heard) by only one (special) individual. Also relevant is the religious idea that a powerful supernatural being—such as God—could decide to reveal himself (through the senses) to only one designated person while others in the same locale continued to experience nothing unusual. Others doubting what the special experiencer in these cases may claim to be experiencing certainly makes good

---

46. This point is only strengthened by the twentieth-century development of instruments that can enhance what an instrumentally endowed individual can detect by means of his (enhanced) senses—for example, visual devices to enable someone to see infrared light.

epistemic sense: other people can quite reasonably doubt the claims of a special experiencer. In response, the special experiencer might successfully use other sources of evidence to prove that he really is experiencing what he claims to be experiencing. Imagine invisible beings—sorts of gremlins, say—that only one person can see, and how he might get others to realize that what he's seeing aren't hallucinations (by trapping one in a cage, say, so that others could see the results of the invisible being snarfing up food placed through the bars or hear the rattling and shaking of its banging against the bars). Imagine, for that matter, how a person—finding himself in a community of blind people without a concept of sight—might be able to prove that he has sensory access to things in a way they have not previously imagined.

Notice the point. A person might have resources for proving he really can see something others can't. Those resources will turn on him discovering other forms of epistemic access to the objects that he sees that others can subsequently exploit—for example, that the objects can be detected by the other senses, or that they can be seen under certain circumstances (in certain kinds of light) or by the traces they leave of what they have done. On the other hand, the person might fail to have such resources; there really is no way he can prove to others that he sees what he claims to see. This is a purely epistemic distinction, however, that has no echo (for us) in a line between language we can understand and language we can't.

Consider, however, the following counterclaim to what I've just written. "That is an *F*," is a public language expression. And—one might claim—for it to function correctly in public discourse, both speaker and audience must (be able to) perceive the target of "That."[47] It's a mistake (bordering on rudeness), when in the company of a blind person, after all, to use pointing gestures. Indeed it is, but the blind person (after all) can't see the *gestures*. In cases where the audience can see the gestures, but the object in question is invisible to them, pointing gestures might still be useful. Imagine (again) that one person can see an otherwise invisible animal. She might guide others to where the animal is (so they can attempt to trap it) by pointing even though she is the only one who can actually *see* it. If they understand that it's a kind of animal they're attempting to hunt, and they have a rough idea of its shape and size (as described by her), they have everything they need to understand the meaning of her pointing gestures. If the creature proves to be so wily and quiet and fast that what she does to indicate its location doesn't succeed in convincing others of what she claims, this doesn't transform her gestures, and the statements that accompany those gestures, into something others can't understand.

---

47. G. E. Moore, *Commonplace book 1919–53*, ed. Casimir Lewy (London: George Allen and Unwin, 1962), 158 (cited by Evans, 305, note 1): "Can we say 'that thing' = 'the thing at which I am pointing' or 'the thing to which this finger points' or 'the nearest thing to which this finger points'? No, because the prop[osition] is not understood unless the thing in question is *seen*" (emphasis in original).

Evans works hard to show that there are restrictions on our ordinary notion of understanding that are in accord with his views and not in accord with how I've argued above. Consider the following example (Evans, 307–8):

> *S* and *A* were in the habit of going hunting together in their youth. On one of their hunting trips, they saw a dazzlingly beautiful bird perched in a pine tree. Years later, *S* (the speaker) may advert to this incident, and say something like: "Do you remember that bird we saw years ago? I wonder whether it was shot." *A* (the audience) may not remember the episode. In order to jog his memory, *S* may say "Surely you remember; a hunting trip years ago; we saw, on a pine tree, a magnificent bird"; and *S* may be able to indicate a very similar bird, perhaps in a photograph, or in the wild. *A*, knowing *S* to be trustworthy, will believe all that he says, and will of course be prepared to bring his belief (which may become quite rich and detailed) to bear upon *S*'s original remark. But I do not think that he can be said to have understood the remark, as it was intended to be understood, until he *remembers* the bird—until the *right* information is retrieved. (emphasis in original)

It's true that in such a case, when *A* (finally) remembers, that it can be natural for him to say, "Oh, *now* I understand which bird you're talking about!" But Evans intends these intuitions to bear more (theoretical) weight than they can. His idea is that *A* can't understand *S*'s statement (or thought about the bird) as *singular* until his memory kicks in. Therefore, he is only thinking of the bird in a purely descriptive way: as "the bird that *S* says such and such about." But this isn't true about *A*, and it isn't what *A*'s exclamation of "understanding" which bird *S* was talking about indicates. Rather, *A* recognizes that he is supposed to activate his memory to tap a particular information route to the bird.[48] Failing to do so means that he can't use his memory to inform himself about that bird. But this isn't to fail to understand the remark "as it was intended to be understood": this is only to fail to manage the task that was asked him—to remember that bird.

For this example, and others like it, to do the work Evans needs, what must be shown is that the ordinary use of "understanding" indicates that when a statement or thought is singular, and the audience has no access to the object the thought is about, the audience in this ordinary sense of "understanding" doesn't understand the statement or thought. Instead, the audience must approximate understanding of the statement or thought via a conceptual proxy.[49] In this way, for example, Evans can be very quick with the case of hallucination: because there is no object, no one can understand singular statements about hallucinated objects—including the (knowing) hallucinator. This isn't true of the ordinary notion of understanding, and therefore Evans has unwittingly introduced a technical notion of "understanding" with a stipulated requirement: singular thought and speech are

---

48. *S* has asked of *A*, "Do you remember . . ."

49. Or by utilizing "quasi-understanding," as Evans (363) describes our "understanding" of much of what we say when pretending.

to be "understood" by a subject only when an information link to the objects singularly denoted are had by that subject.

It's striking that what ordinary speakers describing themselves as "not understanding" is never the proposition or thought but, instead, "what you're talking about." They never focus on the proposition (except when they find the proposition hard to parse) but always on the topic of the conversation. It might be thought that this is all that's needed to make Evans's case: after all, in cases like the bird example, the object can only be grasped not in a singular way but as such and such is described by someone. This isn't how the listener has to understand the statement, and it's usually not how the listener understands it. The listener presupposes that the speaker is fallible; thus, it's always open to the listener to reject (in part or in whole) the speaker's characterization of the object and instead use the speaker and what the speaker has said as itself a defeasible information link to the object described.[50] This is to grasp what the speaker has said in a singular way. Indeed, this is to engage in borrowing the speaker's singular terms and to henceforth use them (with understanding) oneself.[51]

A's failing to grasp which bird it is from memory, of course, doesn't mean that his grasp of the bird therefore isn't singular—that his grasp must be fully conceptual, for example, "the bird that A is talking about." For example, he might discover that he has a picture of that bird. He might realize that this is a picture of the bird (on the basis of collateral information, e.g., the time the picture was taken or his memo on the picture: "This is the most beautiful bird S and I have ever seen. S hasn't stopped talking about it for days"), and yet he might still have to stare at the picture for some time before his memory kicks in. Then he'll say: "Oh *that's* the bird S was talking about," even though—because of the picture—he's already got a singular thought about the bird. If he never remembers the episode (and doesn't have any access to the bird apart from S's memory of it), he still understands S's remarks perfectly well. When someone says, "You don't know which bird S is talking about," what's meant is the more specific, "You don't *remember* which bird S is talking about," but it wouldn't be thought (given the ordinary use of "understanding") that A doesn't understand as S meant his remark to be understood, singularly as "*that* bird was beautiful."

I have been speaking here of an "object" being the subject of conversation, but that isn't required. All that's necessary are not fully conceptualized thoughts and statements about[(r/e)] something. Notice: allowing the thoughts and statements in question to be open to correction while continuing to treat as fixed what they are about suffices for this.

50. Can everything the speaker says be wrong about something, and what that speaker has said still be a useful information link to the object? Yes, depending on what the listener knows about the speaker, and in particular, what the listener knows about what the speaker is (usually) wrong about, for example, that he regularly confuses lizards with birds.

51. This significant practice plays a major role in how we can talk about others' hallucinations singularly. See section 2.7.

I should add that these considerations don't—all by themselves—make cogent the idea of an "intrinsically private" language. They turn solely on the crucial fact that we successfully apply our words, and the other tools that we use to communicate to one another, beyond the cases where we have learned them; they also turn on the fact that our communication practices factor in quite naturally that individual epistemic powers can differ strikingly from one person to another. These aspects of our usage of words and gestures have not been extended unnaturally in the thought experiments described in this section.

My denial of Evans's diversity condition—as I said in the last section—although significant, doesn't bear on hallucinations because (so I claim), contrary to the cases of objects that de facto prove to be cognitively accessible to only one individual (and in perhaps only one way), hallucinations can be suitably public objects that other individuals (apart from the subject of the hallucinations) can have cognitive access to. I turn to establishing this claim in the next section.

2.7 The Public Nature of Hallucinations

Let's return to the experimental situation described in section 2.3. Imagine that the hallucinations that S experiences are ones that engage all his senses. In particular, the objects he hallucinates seem to be located physically in space in precisely in the same way that other objects are (until, let's say, they reveal themselves to be hallucinations by suddenly and inexplicably vanishing). He can focus on them the way he can focus on other objects, he can approach them to see them more clearly,[52] and he can reach out, touch them, and otherwise interact with them. In this way, he can determine additional details about them or discover that they are not as they appeared to him when he was farther away.[53] Even if he realizes that a particular object is an hallucinated one and that the experimenters can't see it, it can be cogent for him to point at it, should the experimenters ask him where the hobbit with the red waistcoat is now located.

Because of the nature of how the hallucinations that S experiences are infiltrated by priming cues, aspects of what he remembers, and other more purely neurological facts that the experimenters may have access to, it's possible for the experimenters to be able to predict—to some degree—the nature and location of S's hallucinations. Indeed, this may be a crucial way they both test and apply various correlations they have discovered between neurological (and neuropsychopharmacological) facts and aspects of S's hallucinations. Because of this, the initial space that was opened up in the last paragraph—between how S's hallucinations appear to him "on first glance" (as it were), and how they appear to him on closer

---

52. Smith (2002, 195), in arguing that in the case of hallucinations the subject is aware of something, writes: "This subject . . . can shift his attention from one to another part of his visual field, or from what he sees to what he is hearing; he can scrutinize objects more closely and can describe what he is aware of."

53. "Gailus's waistcoat has buttons with dragons etched on them. No—now that I've moved closer, I can see that these etchings are of dinosaurs, not dragons. I didn't expect dinosaurs."

inspection—is one that not only allows S to correct his own initial misapprehensions about what he's either seeing or hallucinating, but one that allows the experimenters to correct him as well. We see, therefore, that S can point to one of his hallucinations, and describe it as a hobbit drinking a martini, but then realize (or even have it pointed out to him by the experimenters) that in fact that's not the hallucination of a hobbit but one of Gimli the dwarf drinking mead out of a horn.

From the point of view of the experimenters, the situation is very like one in which someone, P, is wearing special sensory-enhancing glasses that enable him to see objects that only reflect wavelengths not visible to the human eye. If P is accompanied by others without such glasses, the latter may rely on background information about the scientific properties of those wavelengths and about the nature of the objects that can be seen with such glasses, to enable them not only to predict aspects of what P will see but to correct his initial impressions.

In S's case, of course, it isn't real objects that the background information enables the experimenters to predict the properties of but his "private" hallucinations. Nevertheless (just as in the case of P's experience with his sensory-enhancing glasses), the experimenters have cognitive access to S's actual hallucinatory experiences in a way obviously quite different from how S has access to them. This is all that's needed to show that Evans's argument from diversity can be satisfied in the case of hallucinations.

This point justifies the claim (P1) that not only are the ordinary language quantifiers used standardly in the experimental situation described in section 2.3, but the demonstrative expressions and proper names are used standardly as well. More specifically, the vindicated claim is that such singular terms can be (and are) legitimately used in a singular fashion. The allusion to Donnellan's (1966) thought experiment (about the man drinking a martini) indicates the appropriate route to vindication.

The first step is easy. This is that S's experiences with respect to his hallucinations are indistinguishable with respect both to what he perceives, and to how his verbal (and gestural) actions use what he perceives as a basis.[54] Psychologically speaking, it's the objects—real *and* irreal—that are both the sources of S's information and the truth- (and falsity-) supports for his claims about those objects. It's by making a closer inspection of both real and irreal objects that he can correct his initial claims about those objects.[55]

---

54. Notice the ontological power (but only psychologically speaking) of the hallucinatory experience, as described here. By assumption, everything that occurs in ordinary sensory circumstances that convinces us of the presence of an object is operative in these hallucinatory contexts as well: perceptual constancies and what Smith has called "the Anstoss"—both in conjunction with the rich sensory givens that accompany these. See Smith (2002), especially 224–25, 233–34. It's worth noting that it's these considerations that drive Smith to the view that hallucinated objects must be treated as Meinongian objects.

55. Evans (352, note 16) writes: "It needs to be stressed that the content of 'That little green man does not exist' cannot be represented descriptively. 'There is no little green man there' does not capture the force of '*That* little green man does not exist'. And a specification of the content does not involve *reference* to the information ('The little green man of whom *this* purports to be information . . .'); although someone who has understood and accepted the statement will know not to trust the information" (emphasis in original).

The second step is nearly as easy—given the public access that the experimenters have to *S*'s hallucinated objects. The means of cognitive access to *S*'s hallucinated objects on the part of the experimenters is quite different from *S*'s. They can't see what he sees. Nevertheless, that what he sees has location and sensory properties is entirely cogent to the experimenters, and *S* communicates these facts to them by demonstratives in a way that provides further information (for them) about what he's seeing. Furthermore, as I've indicated, the exchange of information between experimenters and *S* is potentially a two-way street. Not only can he correct them about misapprehensions they may have about the perceived properties of what he's pointing at, so can they (on the basis of background information that they have gathered) correct him. The mere fact that there is nothing there—one can provocatively say—for either *S* or the experimenters to be talking about does nothing to undercut all the standard demonstrative tools that ordinary speakers and their audiences have at their disposal.

Granting that the uses of demonstratives by *S* and the experimenters are standard singular ones doesn't yet seem to show the same is true of proper names. Even though the names (of these hallucinated objects) are used by the experimenters as well as by *S*, isn't it the case that such names—as used by the experimenters—are disguised descriptive names that the experimenters implicitly employ? Perhaps the point can be put this way. Even if the case that's been made—that *S*'s uses of names are singular—is successful, surely the experimenters' uses of these names defer (and defer explicitly) to *S*'s use. When speaking (or thinking) of Gimli, descriptions such as "The hallucinated object called 'Gimli' by *S*" are in place in the experimenters' thought about these objects.

No. It's true that the experimenters have learned these names from *S*, and it's because of this that they can apply them to the specific hallucinated objects *S* is aware of. But any description ("the hallucination of a dwarf that *S* has in such and such circumstances," "the hallucination of a hobbit that *S* calls 'Gailus'") (i) can fail to be precise enough to replace those names—if only because neither the experimenters nor *S* can fully predict the precise nature of *S*'s hallucinations, when such and such an hallucinated object may appear again, and so on; and (ii) can be recognized (in the fullness of time) to not correctly apply. Even the use of names within quotations in descriptions can prove to be incorrect in the fullness of time.[56]

The attempted strategy of the last paragraph is to characterize the experimenters' deference practices with proper names designating *S*'s hallucinated objects as what I called (in section 1.5) "conceptual deference." A body of (hallucinogenic) thought that's due to *S* is (on this view) being deferred to by the experimenters. But this mistakes the nature of the deference in question. The

---

56. The general point is that—to an unpredictable extent—*S*'s hallucinations can approximate the world in its unpredictability. (The world too, is both unpredictable and predictable.) Thus, whatever it is about the world that faults our attempts to cognitively reach objects within it by the use of descriptions can be similarly operative in the case of *S*'s hallucinations. The assumption of the successful replacement of uses of singular terms by *S* and by the experimenters to designate *S*'s hallucinated objects would imply the successful replacement of such uses tout court.

deference in question is to S's experiences of objects. The gap between S's thought about his experienced objects and those objects as experienced is exploited when it's pointed out that the properties attributed to S's hallucinated objects (either by S or by the experimenters) can be discovered to have been wrong. The hallucinated objects, that is, can take on "a life of their own"—acting in ways, and revealing aspects of themselves neither anticipated by the experimenters nor by S. S's hallucination experiences can sprint well beyond any conceptualizations (of the objects hallucinated) on the part of S or on the part of the experimenters. This is a crucial symptom of the terms used by the experimenters as names of (S's) hallucinated objects being singular in their use: S's experiences are experiences of hallucinated objects. These objects—as hallucinated by S—therefore, are the targets of the experimenters' claims and thinking and not S's thoughts about such things. We mistake the experimenters' thoughts and claims about "Gimli," "Frodo," and so on, if we attempt to reconstrue them as descriptive names.[57]

Some paragraphs back, I noted that the experimenters can't see what S sees. That could change. One might endeavor to design a device that would appropriately replicate the hallucinations of S for others. Sufficiently rich descriptions of S's past hallucinations, of the causal factors (e.g., priming cues) that affect them (and how), as well as the use of real-time feedback about what parts of S's brain are active (and how) when he's hallucinating, in addition to calculations of (optically relevant) differences in the positions of S and the experimenter wearing the device, would result in such a device being able to approximately situate S's hallucinations in the perceived space and time of others, as well as being able to approximate their visual content. Such a device would have to be tested and refined in light of S's descriptions of what he experiences; nevertheless it might eventually be used against (some of) S's claims. (In some cases, it would show that S was being insincere in his descriptions; in other cases, experimenters wouldn't be able to know.[58]) Such an item would make hallucinations public in pretty much the same way that holograms are. The experimenters—but only in this case—could themselves point at one of S's hallucinated objects because they could see them. (And this is how it would be described: "I can see what S sees.") Nevertheless, and this is crucial: no one would think (a) the status of such hallucinations had changed. They would still be regarded as S's hallucinations. (b) They would still be regarded as existing in no sense at all.

---

57. Notice the suitability of Evans's (268) singular characterizations of remembered objects—(both from S's point of view and from the experimenters' points of view) as applied to the relationship of S's later remembered descriptions of the objects he hallucinates:

> In the subject's choice of description, he can be regarded as aiming at something, namely the object from which he acquired, and of which he retains, information, and so there is room to speak of error here—with its consequence of ill-grounded thoughts—in a way which is completely absent in the case of descriptive thoughts.

This description also suits S's attempts to describes his hallucinated objects during the time he sees them.

58. We can, at times, recognize that someone's pain behavior and avowals are insincere. Background information could similarly reveal that S could not be hallucinating what he claimed to be seeing; this knowledge would have to be based on the hallucinated experiences of many individuals on which such a device would have been tested and refined.

A couple of caveats about this thought experiment. I'm not underestimating the computational—and other technical—difficulties of such a device.[59] The point is to notice how such a thought experiment illuminates the ways we take ourselves to be able to speak of hallucinations. In particular, there is no surface incoherence in these thought experiments of (say) the following sort: it's not possible for someone else to see S's hallucinations because (of course)—being hallucinations—they're (kind of by definition) private to S.

Second, notice that such a device would only have to work passably well for it to sustain discourse presupposing that wearers of the device were perceiving S's hallucinations. (Compare this to a case where someone who sees very much better than I do is attempting to point things out to me.) As Evans (179) notes, it isn't required that the experimenters' "information-link be functioning well—so long as it provides an effective route to the object." Indeed, such a device would be regarded as a tool to enable experimenters to see (to more or less accuracy) the hallucinations that S sees. What this seems to come to, of course, is instrumental access to someone else's hallucinations.

It's relevant—although I haven't dwelt on it—that the folk notion of hallucination allows for them to be seen by groups of people (e.g., induced wirelessly by a central computer in a group of people, or whatever). In fact, in folklore, a common idea is one where shared hallucinations can be localized to places. In such stories, demons (or vampires) can create an hallucination that anyone will experience when entering, say, a house. In such cases, people can independently circulate and nevertheless interact (in different ways) with the same hallucination (of, say, the vampire's servant). In these cases, in both folklore stories and in contemporary versions of such stories, there are several subjects, all of whom see the same things, and among whom pointing takes on (public) significance precisely because attention can be drawn to aspects of these public hallucinations that individuals might otherwise miss.

2.8 Isn't Everyone Just Pretending?

Consider a case where B has taken a recreational drug, he's having a bad hallucination-experience, and A knows this. (In the cute traditional language stemming from the late 1960s and early 1970s, "B is having a bad trip.") B is frightened of something he sees. A reassures him by pointing in the direction that he knows B's hallucination is (apparently) located and telling him that there is nothing there. A (so most people will think) isn't pointing at an hallucination, at something he can't see (at something that doesn't exist). He's pointing at a place, and saying of that place that there is nothing in it. Also notice this: he isn't pretending to be

---

59. I've implicitly restricted its concerns to vision alone. Even so, such a device is hardly to be considered an easy achievement. Off-hand, the best way to get such a thing going (if it's possible at all) would be to train it up on S himself—when he wasn't under the effect of hallucinogens ("That's not how I remember Elrond; his hair is a darker brown, and . . .").

pointing at an hallucination of B's. Both A and B (if B isn't too panicked to think clearly about this) recognize what's going on.

Not all cases are like this one. Imagine that S, when he realizes that a particular hobbit he has been staring at is an hallucination, triumphantly pointing at it, and saying, "*that* doesn't exist." Certainly the experimenters could note of his gesture in a certain direction that "there's nothing there." It seems in this case, however, that S isn't pointing at a place, and also that the experimenters realize this: they realize that he's pointing not at a place but at what he sees.

What many philosophers want to suggest that's instead going on in this second case, when S (in full knowledge of the fact that he's hallucinating) nevertheless points at something he sees, and when the experimenters also point (or when they "understand" S's gestures to be directed not at a place but at what he's seeing), is instead pretence or acting. S is pretending to be referring to something; S is pretending that his thought is *of* something. Indeed, S is pretending to be uttering statements that have truth values. More dramatically (but in accord with the singular use of the proper names and demonstratives in these contexts), S is only pretending to be having thoughts or making statements.[60] The experimenters are pretending as well, both with respect to their "understanding" (scare quotes) of S's remarks, and with respect to their own observations about Frodo, Gandalf, and the other things that S sees.

There are two problems with the pretence approach to hallucinations. One arises from the needs that statements about hallucinations are required to satisfy with respect to other discourse that's not (directly) about hallucinations; to meet those needs hallucination-discourse must really be truth-apt. But hallucination-discourse can't be truth-apt if it's pretence-construed. I call this the *external discourse demand* on hallucinogenic discourse; I regard the inability of pretence-construals of hallucination-discourse to meet the demand as fatal to those approaches.[61] The other issue is psychological. In what respects are claims of pretence genuine descriptions of the psychological states of both S and the experimenters? In no good respect—or so I argue. I take these issue up in reverse order.

---

60. See Evans, chapter 10. A strong influence on Evans's thinking, here, is work by Kendall L. Walton ("Pictures and make-believe," *Philosophical Review* 82 [1973], 283–319; "Fearing fictions," *Journal of Philosophy* 75 [1978], 5–27). Also see Kendall L. Walton, *Mimesis as make-believe* (Cambridge, Mass.: Harvard University Press, 1990).

61. The external discourse demand is a powerful broad tool for refuting various approaches to "empty names" precisely because, when it applies to a kind of discourse, it demands truth-aptness that goes beyond mere claims of nonexistence, for example, it isn't satisfied by an approach to, say, "Pegasus" that merely ratifies the claim that Pegasus doesn't exist. Most of the literature fails to meet it. Apart from what's been cited so far, see R. M. Sainsbury, *Reference without referents* (Oxford: Oxford University Press, 2005); Kenneth A. Taylor, "Emptiness without compromise: A referentialist semantics for empty names," in *Empty names, fiction and the puzzles of non-existence*, ed. Anthony Everett and Thomas Hofweber (Stanford, Calif.: CSLI Publications, 2000), 17–36; and Anthony Everett, "Referentialism and empty names," in *Empty names, fiction and the puzzles of non-existence*, ed. Anthony Everett and Thomas Hofweber (Stanford, Calif.: CSLI Publications, 2000), 37–60 for further examples of recent sophisticated work that doesn't respond to (or even acknowledge) the external discourse demand.

The psychological fact about *S* is this: his hallucinogenic experiences are indistinguishable from those he has with real objects.[62] Indeed, in the experimental setting, where his hallucinations begin and leave off is something he can only determine on the basis of background knowledge and contextual clues. This means that his psychological states and reactions—that underwrite his pointing and referring to hallucinated objects—are similarly indistinguishable from cases where he takes what he's gesturing at (and referring to) to be real. To this extent, therefore, it's inappropriate to describe *S* as engaged in "pretence." It might be countered that there is a wedge to be driven between the object-related experiences that *S* has—given his recognition that such things don't exist—and his intentions to refer. He has no intentions to refer (so it might be argued) because he knows there are no objects to refer to. So here is where pretence, on *S*'s part, comes in.

This misdescribes the situation, and for reasons we've seen before (section 1.4). There is no psychological wedge to be driven between the object-related experiences that *S* is having and his intentions to refer to such objects. The terms and demonstratives he uses are ones he intends to use (and succeeds in using) in ways he recognizes to be utterly standard. The ontological recognition that there are no objects involved stands apart from all this. When in the grip of an hallucination, one can try to calm oneself by saying, "None of this is real." In particular, one can—in an utterly standard way—point at something one is seeing, and say: "That *thing*'s not real."

If, however, *S* is standing in a room, and he's asked to point at something that he knows the experimenter can't see, he may experience the feeling that he is pretending that the experimenter can see what he can see. In point of fact, even this feeling of pretence is unlikely if only because *S* recognizes that the experimenter is trying to locate the position of what he (*S*) can see. Is he, therefore, really only pointing at the place the hallucination is apparently located—because that's all the experimenter can see? No, this is a misconstrual as well. The experimenter asks, "Where is the hobbit right now?" and *S* points at it. Compare the case to one of an actual animal that only *S* can see. In both cases, the fact that the experimenter can't see what *S* can see doesn't mean either (i) that the experimenter doesn't realize (in this case) exactly what *S* is pointing at, or (ii) that *S* can't be entirely cognizant of this fact.

Imagine a case where *S* faces a line-up of hobbits, where some of them are hallucinated objects and some of them are actors. "Which ones are real and which ones aren't?" the experimenter asks. *S* successively points at each hobbit he sees,

62. This is an assumption that's built into folk attitudes about hallucinations, and consequently, built into our speech and thought about such. But there is good evidence that what's sometimes called (in the psychological literature) "reality monitoring" involves "inferential processes"—where (as is common in this literature) the "inferences" aren't understood to be consciously accessible. Such processes, therefore, can degrade because of disease or injury; they can also be fooled in appropriately prepared circumstances (e.g., the Perky phenomenon). See R. P. Bentall, "The illusion of reality: A review and integration of psychological research on hallucinations," *Psychological Bulletin* 107:1 (1990), 82–95 for some discussion of the literature on this, especially pp. 88–89. Also see J. Barnes, L. Boubert, J. Harris, A. Lee, and A. S. David, "Reality monitoring and visual hallucinations in Parkinson's disease," *Neuropsychologia* 41 (2003), 565–74.

saying, "real, real, not real, not real, not real, real, not real, real," while the experimenter dutifully notes in which cases *S* has guessed correctly. It seems perfectly clear to the experimenters and to *S* what *he* is pointing at. (*S* hopes he is guessing correctly; he isn't hoping that in those cases where he's pointing at something unreal that he's actually pointing at a place—or at nothing at all.)

Suppose I'm hallucinating, and I know it. Can it be reasonable to say that I'm pretending to be pointing at an object? No. I'm aware that there's no object. I'm not pretending to be pointing at an object. I'm pointing at what I see. There is no pretence involved. I'm not (for example) only pretending to be pointing at what I'm not seeing. One can, that is, point at what isn't there. The performative aptness of pointing gestures doesn't place any ontological constraints on what's pointed at. Thus we can perfectly reasonably point at something, and ask: "Is that real, or just in my mind?" The other person can look in the direction of where I'm pointing and say, "Not real."[63]

More surprising, perhaps, is that pretence is an inappropriate description of what the experimenters are engaged in as well. An experimenter may ask *S* to pick up an hallucinated object and, using his hands, indicate to the experimenter exactly what the contours of the object in space are. In doing so, *S* may hallucinate the movement of the object from one location to another (as he carries it in his hands, say). In watching *S*'s gestures, the experimenter is trying to determine more precisely the contours of the hallucinated object that he (the experimenter) can't see. He isn't pretending to try to determine more precisely those contours. Nor is he pretending to be talking about what *S* is talking about; referential practice in this case—even on the part of the experimenter—is entirely standard. In saying this, I'm not suggesting that either *S* or the experimenter thinks there is an invisible, or hallucinated object to be indicated. They both recognize that there is nothing there. Nothing at all.

Compare this to the very different case where the experimenter pretends to be able to see the object that *S* can see. Or compare it to a game where two people pretend to see an object that doesn't exist (and which neither is hallucinating the presence of). These cases do involve genuine pretence, which isn't the case in the experimental situation. In the experimental situation, the experimenter is trying to get something right about what *S* sees. What *S* sees, however, is not merely sensory: his hallucinations are object-directed. They involve the experience (in the full sense of the word "experience") of something located in space and time So the experimenter's attempts to get those hallucinations right must be object-directed as well if those attempts are to succeed in capturing what *S* is experiencing. "Object-directed" experience doesn't require an object. Both *S* and the experimenters will continue to call what *S* sees "hallucinations." They both mean: there is nothing there. Nevertheless, just as we can attribute properties to what we take to exist in no sense at all, so can we point at such.[64]

---

63. Regardless, by the way, whether that person can see what I'm seeing or not. I make something of this shortly.

64. Of course this raises "aboutness" issues. How can the talk and gestures be about what doesn't exist? I touch on this later in this section and in section 2.10. Also recall the discussion of this at the end of section 1.7.

Notice that the argument of Evans—that I've been countering—doesn't (directly) deny that demonstrations of the nonexistent aren't possible. Rather, as described in section 2.5, Evans (143, note 1) is attempting to place the condition on apt demonstration that the object demonstrated be seen by the audience. If this condition isn't fulfilled—so he claims—no statement is achieved (nothing has been gestured at—with accompanying statement— that can be understood). Thus, it's only indirectly that the nonexistence of hallucinations prevents the demonstration of such. But the invisibility of the object demonstrated—generally—doesn't infirm demonstrations of it. To argue otherwise—as stated earlier—is to attempt to make a purely epistemic distinction (between what's seen and what's not seen) illegitimately do semantic work.

It's worth noting that the ontological condition Evans tries to place on what he calls "information-based" thought and speech, and the visibility condition that he's also placed on such, come apart in thought experiments about group halluci-nations. We find it (intuitively) cogent to ask, if we know we might (collectively) be the victims of a group hallucination: is that real? We are not asking one another: are we actually pretending to point at something?

In any case, Evans has a second argument that goes directly at the cogency of demonstrations of the nonexistent. The claim is the one discussed in section 2.5. S attributes a certain property to something he sees. In appreciating (the content of) his remark, and in regarding it as true, the experimenters—so Evans argues— must believe there to be something to which that property is to be attributed. Here is how Evans (329) puts the point:

> The inclusion of this or that property in such an appreciation of a remark is not an attempt to be faithful to the speaker's conception of the referent, but represents the hearer's view as to how things stand with a particular object. The only possible justification of the belief that, if what the speaker said is true, there is something which is $\phi_1, \ldots, \phi_n$ and F is that it follows from some belief of the form "The speaker is referring to a", together with a view as to how things stand with a.

It's clear that Evans (like most philosophers, I should add) sees the landscape of possibilities here as involving only three options: singular directed thought of an actual object, pure conceptualization (description) of what the speaker is thinking of, or pretence. Either one is attempting—by means of the replication of content—to be faithful to the speaker's conception of the referent, or one is repre-senting how things stand with a particular object that the speaker is referring to, or one is engaged in pretence.

There is another option. The experimenters are fully aware that S is halluci-nating. They are aware of what that means: object-directed experience (on the part of S) without a corresponding object. What this means, first of all, is that the experimenters' thinking isn't directed toward capturing S's conception of the referent[e]. As we've already seen, what S thinks and says about something he's hallucinating can be wrong.[65] Rather, the experimenters' understanding of S's remarks are directed toward characterizations of his *experience*. That experience—subjectively speaking—is of objects, and so their attempts to evaluate S's statements as true or false turn on whether the objects S experiences are best construed as having such and such properties and not whether S thinks or experiences them as having such and such properties.[66]

It's true, of course, that if there are no such objects (in any sense at all) then S's gestures and what S says, and what the experimenters say, about these objects can't be about[r] those objects. The truth-aptness of these remarks and the performative aptness of the gestures, of both S and the experimenters, can't turn on a correspondence between these truth-acts and the properties had by the objects designated[r] (for there are no objects designated[r]). There is a long distance from this sound point to the result that what must therefore be going on is "pretence." S's gestures and remarks about hallucinated objects, as well as those of the experimenters, are about[e] the hallucinated objects. The position I argue for in this book with respect to hallucinations (and with respect to abstracta and fictions) is that aboutness[e] so understood, when used to characterize (i) object-directed experience (whether to real objects or not) in a discourse context where there are (ii) sufficient constraints that make consistent a practice of truth-apt statements (and other truth-apt acts, such as pointing gestures) about[e] the objects the experience is directed toward, is sufficient to underwrite singular thought and statements about[e] those objects. One additional factor is always needed, however, to force this truth-apt practice to be taken seriously—to be, that is, a practice that cannot be sidelined from our other scientific beliefs and epistemic activities. This is that such a practice has an evidential and implicational role with respect to thought and statement outside the context of that practice (that there be an external discourse demand on that discourse-practice).

This is the other problem with the pretence construal of the discourse S and the experimenters engage in. The problem is that such discourse is required to be truth-apt if it is to play the evidential role for the scientific discourse it's needed for. One way to describe this evidential role is to note, as I've just said, that S and the experimenters are serious. What I mean is this: in pretence situations, within plays, for example, within fictions, and in games generally,[67] a distinction is drawn between what's true in the game and what's false in the game. Furthermore, what's true and what's false in the game may be due to facts outside the game. For example, in chess, that a piece is threatened has to do (in part) with the actual physical location of the pieces on the board; in a children's mud pie game, that a (mud) pie is "baking" may have to do with its location in the playground: it's "in" the "stove."[68] Crucial,

---

65. Thus it would be inaccurate to describe S's hallucinated objects as "response-dependent"—as ones with properties due entirely to S's construal of them.

66. Recall from section 2.4 that Gailus, for example, might resemble some character S has seen in a movie even though S doesn't realize that.

67. See Walton (1990).

68. Evans (354–55) characterizes these as "basic principles," an "incorporation principle," and a "recursive principle." These, together, generate the (infinite number of) statements that can be asserted within the game. He also discusses other possible principles needed to generate statements within the game.

however, to pretence is that the distinction—drawn between statements true-in-the-pretence and those false-in-the-pretence—has no bearing outside the pretence. In contrast, the distinction between those statements in the hallucination-discourse that are true-in-the-discourse and those that are false-in-the-discourse do bear outside that discourse. That a particular hobbit is wearing green and not blue, or that he resembles a famous actor but not another such actor may bear evidentially on one or another neurological theory.[69] Within the evidential situation with respect to certain theories (given certain correlations that have been established) such statements may imply important neurological claims that otherwise say nothing about hallucinations per se. In general, statements within the hallucination-discourse bear outside "the pretence" insofar as they have both deductive and evidential implications on statements that in no way are included in the "pretence," no matter how broadly "pretence" is construed. As mentioned, this is the external discourse demand, as it applies to hallucination-discourse, and a pretence-construal of hallucination-discourse can't meet it.[70]

One option remains for the pretence theorist. This is to allow pretence to infect (via implication- and confirmation-relations) the rest of our discourse—to accept "global pretence." For example, if a certain neurological view about brain function is implied (or confirmed) by certain hallucination-discourse, one takes it (instead) that such a view is only pretend-implied or pretend-confirmed by such. But then, one can only pretend-believe (pretend hold-true) the neurological view which—itself—isn't directly about hallucinations. In this way, the confirmation and implication relations that hallucination-discourse has to other discourses infect those other discourses with pretence by those very relations. Consequently, global-pretence views have very little to recommend them—especially because they violate the original motivation for a pretence construal of hallucination-discourse: to distinguish that discourse from other discourse that isn't pretence.

Summary. Pretence views have a prima facie plausibility specifically in regard to hallucinations. It does seem, during hallucination events, that should all parties know that there is nothing there, it would prevent any of them from singularly referring (with a "straight face," anyway) to the supposedly hallucinated objects. This seems especially compelling in the case of demonstratives, where (so it

69. Aleman and Larøi (2008, 160) describe a study that revealed that "in patients who hallucinated in color, activity was found in the color center, V4, whereas in the only patient who hallucinated in black and white, the activity was outside this region."

70. Actually, in my view, the problem is worse. Were the pretence theorist to succeed in meeting the constraint by perhaps inventing truth conditions for every indispensable statement about fictions (on the basis of a practice with pretended-true statements) so that such would be truth-apt, he would be open to the methodological charge that what's needed is more directly achieved by pursuing the approach of this book. One must weigh, that is, the costs of snapping the link between truth and ontology against the costs of a perspective that keeps that link in place, but where genuine truth conditions for a large number of indispensable statements must be built out of the materials of a systematic pretence practice that's intuitively inaccessible. I should note, of course, that Evans's particular strategies for providing truth conditions for statements about nonexistent entities handle only small classes of such—and not everything that's needed: singular negative existential statements on the one hand (10.4) and certain attitudes speakers manifest about fiction (10.3). He also honestly admits the limitations of his approaches (e.g., in Evans, 366, note 39).

seems) one must be pretending to be pointing—since one recognizes there to be nothing at all where one is pointing. But this plausibility turns on underdescribing possible cases of hallucination, and it evaporates when such cases are developed more fully. What's being overlooked is the involuntary nature of hallucinogenic experience (at least as construed in these thought experiments). The singular nature of one's pointing gestures require only that one's relevant psychological states are indistinguishable from when one is facing real objects—that one's recognition of the true ontological state of affairs makes no inroads into the psychological states that underwrite gesture and speech about what one sees. That this is so is indicated by thought experiments of group hallucinations: one can point and draw the attention of others to aspects of things that everyone recognizes don't exist. So, too, the hallucinator can make mistakes about his hallucinations and have those corrected. Thus, when compared to cases where genuine pretending is occurring, singular reference to and quantification over hallucinated objects prove to be psychologically (and referentially) disanalogous.

As I've argued, it's more significant that pretence construals of hallucination-discourse can't meet the external discourse demand. They can't respond to the fact that such discourse must be generally truth-apt (it must be truth-apt outside the pretence) and that this is precisely for the same reasons that other forms of discourse must be truth apt: because hallucination-discourse is deductively and evidentially brought to bear on discourse that isn't taken to be pretence. If this latter point weren't true, the psychological distortions introduced in speaking of hallucination-discourse as a "pretence" could be—perhaps—treated as the introduction of a specialized terminology that generalizes how pretence occurs in ordinary life. The real motivation in calling such discourse (and accompanying thought) pretence is that one is allowing that one isn't really taking that discourse to be truth-apt (otherwise, why bother with all the pretence apparatus?). This motivation is the one damaged fatally by the external discourse demand on hallucination-discourse (a demand placed on such discourse by scientific discourse in general) that it—despite having no ontological ambitions—be genuinely truth-apt.[71]

The bottom line is this: the factors that pressure speech and thought to be truth-apt, and to be about^e objects, are entirely distinct from anyone's ontological evaluation of those objects. This might be thought to motivate Meinongianism: we need to talk about^r objects that we nevertheless recognize not to exist. But this is to miss the point. The point, recall, is that the factors that pressure speech and thought to be truth-apt and to be about$^{(r/e)}$ objects are distinct from any ontological

---

71. It's striking that there is no discussion of the confirmational and implicational relations of hallucination-discourse to other scientific results anywhere in Evans (1982). Of course, scientific studies of hallucination didn't really take off until various brain-imaging techniques had reached a certain sophisticated level—roughly in the 1990s. As an illustration, contrast the two review articles Bentall (1990) and Nico J. Diederich, Christopher G. Goetz, and Glenn T. Stebbins, "Repeated visual hallucinations in Parkinson's disease as disturbed external/internal perceptions: Focused review and a new integrative model," *Movement Disorders* 20:2 (2005), 130–14. It's worth noting, in Evans's defense (as noted in note 70) that he does endeavor to construct truth-conditions (and appropriate truth values) for certain restricted classes of statements. The concern with negative existentials has been of wide concern in the literature; but this literature has not followed suit with respect to a recognition of the widespread (truth-apt) use of other kinds of statements about nonexistent entities.

evaluation of those objects. To need to talk about something isn't thereby to impose on it—in some roundabout indirect way—some ontological status or other.

2.9 Properties Presented and Had by Hallucinated Objects

Even though pretence has been ruled out as a suitable method of reconstruing discourse about S's hallucinated objects, there is still enormous pressure on the idea that S's descriptions of hallucinated objects should be taken at face value, as truthfully attributing the same properties to hallucinated objects that real objects have. As stated, (P2), here repeated, "Properties are attributed to these things in a manner semantically indistinguishable from how such properties are attributed to real objects. The hallucinated objects (along with what's real) are temporally and spatially indexed—both in terms of coordinates (to the extent that S can ordinarily do that) and in their relations to other objects, both hallucinated and real," is open to the straightforward attribution of the same properties to hallucinated objects as to real ones. Although this is required in certain cases, for example, the hobbits that S hallucinates are ones he (currently) can't distinguish from the actors dressed up as hobbits, it could be extended to the wearing of waistcoats, as well as to being located in certain places or to the having of certain relations with real objects (e.g., sitting at desks). But here's a plausible sounding reason to strenuously object to directly attributing such properties to hallucinated objects. Whatever a hallucinated object may be doing, it seems wrong to claim that it's "wearing" a waistcoat, that it has gold coins in its pocket, or that it's waving a jeweled stick around. The problem isn't just that nonexistent objects don't have properties; it's that waving around a jeweled stick (on anybody's view) is to do something physical, and even those philosophers who think hallucinated objects exist (in some sense or other) don't think they do anything physical.

It's important to understand clearly, given the metaphysical background assumed in this book, what the requirements are for property attributions to non-existent objects. One cannot set aside the fact that there are no nonexistent objects, and that therefore they don't have properties. This is because the Meinongian (or most contemporary Meinongians) can be legitimately pressed with the objection that since hallucinated objects aren't physical, they can't be doing anything physical. This Meinongian, that is, has the real problem of determining, even of objects that exist "in no sense at all," what properties these things really have.[72] But this is not true of the view that there are truth-apt statements with terms that don't refer^r. With respect to such statements, the project becomes one of trying to make sense of an indispensable practice of truth-apt statement-making and accompanying truth-apt thought. The pertinent question therefore is

72. Recall, for example, the quotations in section 1.6, note 49.

this: what sorts of truth-apt statements and thoughts are needed? The provisional answer being investigated is this: truth-apt statements and thoughts of the form "Frodo is wearing a waistcoat" are being considered on the grounds that S routinely makes comparisons like this: "All the hobbits are wearing waistcoats today," when some of the items he's seeing are actors wearing waistcoats and some of the items are hallucinated objects (that appear to him to be wearing waistcoats).

An important terminological point about the forthcoming discussion: It's fallout from any such set of indispensable truths, that one has the capacity to make truth-based attributions of properties to objects that we otherwise recognize not to exist (and that we recognize, therefore, to have no properties). Consider, for example, the proposed truth that "All the hobbits are wearing waistcoats today." Suppose that all the "hobbits" in question are hallucinated objects; then the statement has no truth makers but only truth-value inducers—in this case, the psychological state(s) of S during his hallucinations and other background facts about hobbit talk. If one of the hobbits were an actor, the truth "that hobbit is wearing a waistcoat" would have as its truth makers the actor, his waistcoat, and his wearing the latter. Nevertheless, in both cases, we can speak of all the hobbits wearing waistcoats, and read off a truth-based attribution of a property to the hallucinated hobbits on the basis of the truths (and not on the basis of the objects, since there aren't any). This truth-based attribution of properties to hallucinated objects—a recognized *façon de parler*—is needed to avoid extensive circumlocution, so I'll be employing it in what follows (e.g., in the first sentence of the next paragraph).[73] Another piece of valuable terminology is this: we can describe the properties attributed to nonexistent entities as themselves *truth-based properties*.

To return to the issue at hand, it may seem innocuous to extend the meaning of "wearing a waistcoat" so that it applies veridically to an actual object only if that object is really wearing a waistcoat and applies veridically to an hallucinated object only if the latter appears to be wearing a waistcoat. But this isn't innocuous—it leads to contradictions.

If S hallucinates an actor talking to Gandalf, whereas (in reality) the actor is merely looking up toward the ceiling and mumbling to himself, it's problematic to say that the actor is talking to Gandalf, an hallucinated object (something that's implied by the "truth" that Gandalf, an hallucinated object, is talking to the actor). The point isn't that the "talking" between the actor and Gandalf is relative to S's hallucination; the point is that we are skirting (if not falling into) contradiction with the pair of remarks: "The actor is talking to Gandalf," and "The actor is mouthing meaningless words in the direction of the ceiling."

A solution to this (that I'm not going to explore) is to avoid contradiction by tampering in various ways with the implicit prima facie "logic" of statements

---

73. The truth-based attribution of properties to nonexistent objects is needed to avoid otherwise engaging in semantic ascent—describing instead true statements or thoughts. For example, I write later in this section, "First, on this reconstrual, hallucinated objects still have plenty of . . . properties." Instead, what would have to be written is this: "First, on this reconstrual, there are still plenty of true statements of the form . . .," where a lengthy description of a kind of statement would then have to be given.

about hallucinations—to deny, for example, that "Gandalf is talking to an actor" implies that "the actor is talking to Gandalf." The problem with such a family of solutions is that they must be invented piecemeal, and therefore they are both arduous to execute and arduous to evaluate the success of.[74]

A better solution[75] is to distinguish between the properties and relations that hallucinated objects and real objects have, and the ones that they only "present" to a hallucinator. For example, it's correct to say that a particular hallucinated object, Gailus, is an hallucination of S's, that the properties he presents to S are due (in part) to S's memory of a calendar that he keeps by his bed, and that the properties he presents to S can be affected by (various) priming cues. It's not true that Gailus is a hobbit, that he wears a waistcoat, or that he resembles the hobbits, pictures of which S has. It is true that he presents (to S) the property of being a hobbit, that he presents (to S) the property of wearing a waistcoat, and that he presents (to S) the relation of resembling the hobbits, pictures of which S has.

Two points. First, on this reconstrual, hallucinated objects still have plenty of truth-based properties; indeed, for something to present as such and such to someone *is* for it to have the property of presenting to someone as such and such. Second, to reconstrue property attributions to Gailus in this fashion still allows the needed quantification over hallucinated objects (as described in section 2.4), and, indeed, it still allows the mistaken attributions that are such a crucial part of singular reference to hallucinated objects. Consider the earlier described distinction between S mistaking a hobbit drinking a martini for Gimli drinking mead from a horn. This is now to be described as S mistaking which properties that hallucinated object presents to him. The hallucinated object seems (to S) to present the property of being a hobbit drinking a martini; in fact, it's presenting to him the property of Gimli drinking mead from a horn.

"Presents property P to S" is obviously coined (and specialized) terminology. Such specialized language is needed because ordinary English—and all natural languages, I suspect—employ various "appearance" words, such as "appears," "seems to," "seems like," "looks like," and so on, that are subtle and complex.[76] In particular, such terms are often employed to indicate an epistemic dimension, to indicate—that is—that the speaker means to place in doubt how the experience is being interpreted by the experiencer or to indicate that the experiencer himself is in doubt. Sometimes the very same terms are employed to indicate an ontological position—for example, that what the experiencer is experiencing doesn't exist (whether he realizes it or not). Such complex idioms are employed because of the conflict between two needs: to describe the experiencer's experience "from inside" or subjectively, and at the same time to register a judgment on the experience or interpretation of that experience by the experiencer, for example, that the experiencer

74. Another problem is that we need the logic we use to be one that's operative across all the sciences. See section 4.7.

75. Following van Inwagen (1977, 2000), with respect to fictions. Similar distinctions, with respect to fiction, are made by Kripke in unpublished work, by Salmon, by Thomasson, by Zalta, and by a number of other philosophers.

76. See Austin (1962), chapter 4, for some discussion of this.

is wrong (in some way or other).[77] Context is often (implicitly) employed to determine exactly what is being said or implied by a particular usage. It's no insult to these subtle idioms, I think, to circumvent them with specialized terminology that unambiguously provides what's needed to be expressed at this juncture.

The "presents to *S*" locution I've adopted is valuable because we no longer have to claim (simultaneously and inconsistently) that the actor is talking to Gandalf and that the actor is mouthing meaningless words in the direction of the ceiling. Gandalf presents (to *S*) as bearing the relation of talking to someone, but of course, Gandalf isn't (actually) talking to anyone.[78]

I have made it clear that "an object o (real or not) presenting to *S* a property or relation *P*" involves a relation to a hallucinator. This enables us to capture the possibility of an object (real or hallucinated) presenting differing properties or relations to more than one hallucinator. It also allows the relations of presenting particular properties and relations to be to more than one individual. Instead of an object (real or hallucinated) presenting a property or relation to *S*, it may be presenting such to a group of individuals who are all hallucinating the same thing.

What about the attribution of temporal and spatial attributions to *S*'s hallucinated objects? Should they be treated as presentations to *S* of temporal and spatial properties of those hallucinations, as has been suggested with the other properties they otherwise share with real objects? Let's take up spatiality first. Consider *S*'s experience of Frodo standing by the door. We do want to say, simultaneously, that there is nothing by the door; there is nothing in the place where *S* (seems to) see Frodo. This motivates treating experienced spatial relations as relations that hallucinations present to hallucinators, but that they don't have: Frodo presents (to *S*) the relation of standing by to the door—more generally, Frodo presents (to *S*) the relation of being at to certain places at certain times. He doesn't actually have any spatial properties or relations; Frodo doesn't have a location. There are never places where the hallucinated object Frodo is (actually) at. So for the same reasons (avoiding contradiction) that invite us to avoid saying that Frodo bears such and such relations to real objects, we are also invited to avoid saying that he's anywhere in space.

What about temporal properties, or the treatment of Frodo as having (or presenting) this property at a time and that property at a different time? I repeat the methodological point that to answer these questions isn't to answer questions in metaphysics: despite appearances, no questions of the form, "what properties do hallucinated objects actually have and which ones do they actually only present?" are being raised. Rather, a kind of indispensable discourse is being investigated,

---

77. This can also be done from a first-person perspective. People sometimes later know that some of the things they saw weren't real. And so, it can be said, "I *thought* there was a pink elephant over there, but I was hallucinating," or "A pink elephant *appeared* to be dancing on the table, but—of course—I hallucinated the entire episode."

78. I'm here characterizing the properties and relations of hallucinated objects as ones presented to an hallucinator. This isn't to say, however, that only the hallucinator can see them, as the thought experiment at the end of section 2.7 indicated. "Presents property *P* to S" being relative to S makes *S* the source of the hallucination in much the way that an author is the source of a novel that she's written.

and it's being considered how such a discourse is to be rendered consistent with the rest of our discourse. Thus, in particular, no project of arguing for (or against) the idea that hallucinated objects are actually types or abstracta (of some sort) is on the table. The concern is only the avoidance of contradiction (coupled with the requirement that the resulting statements respect the external discourse demand). No contradiction arises, however, in describing hallucinated objects as presenting such and such (spatial and other) properties at one time, and presenting such and such properties at other times; no contradiction arises, for that matter, in attributions of their having certain properties at certain times and not at other times. Temporality, per se, raises no issues.[79]

We do, however, need to verify that the replacement of certain properties with the presentation of those properties creates no problems with the kinds of generalizations that the experimenters may find valuable. Consider, for example, *Generalization*, here repeated,

> Every hobbit that S hallucinates either resembles some movie character in a movie that S has seen, or it resembles a hobbit in the calendar poster that S keeps by his bed.

This must be replaced with

> Every hobbit that S hallucinates either presents (to S) the relation of resembling some movie character in a movie that S has seen, or it presents (to S) the relation of resembling a hobbit in the calendar poster that S keeps by his bed.[80]

Is this generalization as valuable as the original one? Consider the rest of the inference as presented in section 2.4:

> Gailus is a hobbit that S hallucinates (regularly) who doesn't resemble some movie character in a movie that S has seen.

Therefore,

> Gailus resembles a hobbit in the calendar poster that S keeps by his bed.

These are to be rewritten like so:

> Gailus is a hobbit that S hallucinates (regularly) who never presents (to S) the property of resembling some movie character in a movie that S has seen.

79. When in a Meinongian frame of mind, there is a strong temptation to argue that hallucinated objects are either in space and time, or neither in space nor in time: how can such objects be in time but not in space? If the contours of a kind of talk is all that's at issue, however, this possibility is straightforward and natural.

80. No doubt, talk of "movie characters" and "hobbits in calendar posters" will require a similar distinction between the properties had by such characters, and those that they are only "depicted" as having, or similar language. I'm taking this as understood.

Therefore,

> Gailus presents (to S) the property of resembling a hobbit in the calendar poster that S keeps by his bed.

Systematic replacement of a property P with the relation R, where the latter is "presents-P to," should, therefore, leave unaffected all the needed inferences and confirmation relations. Notice that the modified generalization makes graphic that an hallucinated object's "presenting a property to S" can't be glossed simply as that property being something that it "appears to S" that the object has. Gailus presents (to S) the property of resembling a hobbit in the calendar poster that S keeps by his bed not necessarily because it appears to S as if he resembles such a hobbit. S may not recollect this fact or even be aware of it. It may be something that only the experimenters have realized about how the hallucinated objects S sees are affected by his other experiences. That something is relative to S doesn't mean that it's therefore subjectively transparent to S—even when the something in question are the relations or properties that an hallucination presents to S!

Nor should we demand that presenting a property or relation be something dispositionally connected to how things appear to S—on the grounds that if the resemblance is pointed out to S, he will see it. The latter might not be true either; S might be particularly bad at (consciously) recognizing resemblances between hallucinated objects and the real objects that he's seen—the memories of which nevertheless operate as subpersonal priming cues.[81]

One last related issue. Some philosophers may suggest that instead of the layered set of properties that hallucinations are to have and to present, it's more suitable to introduce explicitly "S hallucinates . . ." contexts that ascriptions of presented properties are to instead occur strictly within, like the following: "There is something such that S hallucinates of it that it is wearing a waistcoat." In this way, one can still quantify into such a context, as required by *Generalization*, and the other generalizations that might be needed (as described in section 2.4).

There are several points to make about this suggestion. First, as mentioned earlier, this alternative approach should not be motivated by the thought that the introduction of intentional contexts in this fashion is a more accurate construal of the "metaphysical facts," that is, that in binding the presented properties of halluci-nated objects within an intentional context, one is acknowledging that such are not properties of anything, but instead are only as S hallucinates things to be. After all, as the considerations of section 2.4 showed, one still has to quantify into such a context—to say in effect that "there is an object such that S hallucinates it to be," and such quantification is therefore officially distinct from how S hallucinates things to be. That is, the metaphysical facts (the true state of affairs) must be represented in any case by an acknowledgment that such quantifications, even though they occur outside any such intentional context, are nevertheless ontologically idle, and

---

81. See Barnes et al. (2003), 565, where some of the literature describing these kinds of confusions in "reality monitoring," is reviewed.

this is also true of the truth-based properties (presented or had) that are "attributed" to the objects in question. As I mentioned earlier, once one is clear about the metaphysical state of affairs, there is only the issue of the best way to codify our descriptions of S's hallucinatory experience so that appropriate generalizations involving them (that the scientific study of hallucinations requires) can be expressed.

With respect to that issue, the introduction of intentional contexts may be an acceptable alternative to locutions that attribute the presentation (relative to hallucinators) of properties and relations to hallucinated objects—but (notoriously) such contexts introduce logical complications that it may be desirable to avoid. Such a complication arises from the cognitive access (discussed in section 2.7) of the experimenters to the properties presented by S's hallucinations—even to the extent of those experimenters being accurately described as seeing S's hallucinations. Another is the possibility of group or shared hallucinations. Descriptions of these possibilities must be handled by the introduction of additional intentional contexts (for each individual other than S), and concomitant rules governing the intentional contexts that allow appropriate inferences from the content appearing in one intentional context to that appearing in another. Perhaps, therefore, it's just cleaner to adopt the layered system of truth-based properties presented and had, where it's simply presumed that the properties presented by hallucinations, although relative to the hallucinators, are nevertheless (in principle) public.

Another problem is raised by the demands of *Generalization*, and related generalizations, is that such generalizations may involve the comparison of presented properties with the actual properties of other objects. If the presented properties are to appear only within intentional contexts, this also creates complications. As discussed earlier in this section, the presented properties of hallucinated objects can be relational ones that S isn't aware of; an hallucinated object may present as looking exactly like S's grandfather (from a photograph that S no longer consciously remembers seeing). Indeed, under such and such (neurologically specified) circumstances, similar content may often be hallucinated. It's thus correct to say that the hallucinated object presents as resembling S's grandfather; but not that S is hallucinating him as resembling his grandfather. This is simply to replicate the point that people can be wrong or unaware of aspects of the content of their hallucinations. If so, intentional contexts appear to be the wrong tools to describe that content.

2.10 Identity Conditions among Hallucinated Objects

(P3), given in 2.3, states that

> The hallucinated objects are identified as the same or different from ones that are seen at other times and other places.

But there are no such objects. What, then, is the basis for such identifications? How is the identification practice supposed to be cogent if there are no objects to ground these identifications—to make sense of when we should say they are to be identical with themselves and distinct from one another? I'm quoting Quine (1953, 4), who once wrote of possible objects: "But what sense can be found in talking of entities which cannot meaningfully be said to be identical with themselves and distinct from one another?" His demand, clearly, was meant to be one that applied to entity-talk of all sorts.

On a later occasion, Kripke (1972, 43) wrote: "Really, adequate necessary and sufficient conditions for identity which do not beg the question are very rare in any case. Mathematics is the only case I really know of where they are given even *within* a possible world, to tell the truth. I don't know of such conditions for identity of material objects over time, or for people" (emphasis in original).

What are "*adequate* necessary and sufficient conditions for identity" supposed to be? That's not obvious. What is it that we want (so often) to know? (What's our problem?) On a still later occasion, Lewis (1986, 193) illuminatingly urged us not to think of these concerns in terms of "identity":

> Is it ever so that an F is identical to a G? That is, is it ever so that the same thing is an F, and also a G? More simply, is it ever so that an F is a G? The identity drops out. Thus it is a good question whether a river is something you can bathe in twice; or whether a restaurant is something that can continue to exist through a simultaneous change in ownership and location and name; or whether numbers are von Neumann ordinals; or whether there is something that all charged particles have in common; or whether there could be a time traveller who meets his younger self; or whether there was ever a genuine nation that included both Austria and Hungary. All of these questions could be stated in terms of identity—harmlessly, unless that way of stating the questions confused us about where to seek for answers.

These are the sorts of questions we (sometimes) want to answer, classify them however you like. But if what's hoped for are general conditions that supply for any F (or for a class of objects F) whether or not that F is a G, for an arbitrary G, we have no such conditions *for anything*.

Kripke writes of "adequate" conditions—that he knows of—only being "given" in the case of mathematics. That's instructive. Certainly, necessary and sufficient conditions for a kind of mathematical "object" are regularly given in terms of other "objects." For example, the classical line is linearly ordered. This enables the provision of a neat "identity condition" for real numbers: a real number F is a real number G if and only if $F \leq G$ and $F \geq G$. This doesn't, of course, tell us what to think about whether a real number F is identical to one or another particular set G. Indeed, there is apparently more than one perfectly good answer to that question. Kripke's "adequate necessary and sufficient conditions" in the case of mathematics are adequate only relative to the practice of mathematics—more particularly, to specific needs in specific cases. Mathematical practice doesn't require—for mathematical objects—(and doesn't have) sets of "identity conditions" that tell us in every possible case, with respect to a mathematical object (or a class of such), whether it is a G (whether they are G's), for arbitrary G.

What, then, makes a set of necessary and sufficient conditions for identity inadequate? Presumably this: we require (for one or another reason) specific adjudication regarding the possibility of identity for an F and for a G (or for F's and G's), but we are at a loss (for one or another reason) as to how to go about it given the necessary and sufficient conditions we have. So, consider an F, a person at time t_1, and persons G and H at subsequent time t_2, where the F enjoys psychological continuity and psychological connectedness to both the G and the H because he has "split into" them.[82] For one or another reason, we want there to be a definite answer to the question which item, the G or the H (if anything), the F is the same person as.[83]

The point I'm making is small but crucial: whether "identity" conditions—for a particular kind of F—are "adequate" or not has nothing to do with how far-ranging they are, or how many different kinds of things they adjudicate the identity of F with respect to. Rather, it has to do with background metaphysical assumptions, as well as to aspects of the discourse-practice that "F" occurs in. In the case of person splittings, we (at a particular time) possess a certain "self-regarding" attitude toward later person-stages only if we think of them as stages of the same person that we (at that particular time) are. So we want to know—even in bizarre thought experiments where we imagine ourselves (amoeba-like) as splitting into psychologically identical successor persons—which of those persons, if any, we are the same person as. In mathematics, on the other hand, it matters for various computational purposes that we have conditions that individuate real numbers from one another; it doesn't matter if we have such conditions for real numbers and sets. Or, it matters in the latter case only after a certain identification between (some) sets and the real numbers has been stipulated.

The foregoing would have been philosophically uncontroversial, I suspect, except for a certain complication stemming from an adherence to classical logic. For any discourse governed by classical logic, there seems to be a constraint on the scope and range of identity conditions just as there is a similar constraint on all predications. This is that for *any* F and for *any* G, either F is G or it's not the case that F is G. Or, alternatively, for anything F, either it's a G or it's not the case that it's a G. We seem to take—that is—an F's being a G (or it's not being a G) to be a fact regardless of whether we have any idea which is the case, or any idea which could be the case, or any idea how we could establish a case, or even when we haven't any idea what could possibly bear on which is the case. Call this the "bivalence constraint"; it's one due (as I've said) to our adopted classical logic.[84]

82. See Derek Parfitt, "Personal identity," *Philosophical Review* 80:1 (1971), 3–27, and related literature.

83. Or, less naturally (but more accurately), we want to know of person-stage F, which person-stages—if any—G and/or H, it's a stage of the same person as.

84. See W. V. O. Quine, "What price bivalence?" in *Theories and things* (Cambridge, Mass.: Harvard University Press, 1981), 31–37; see J. Azzouni and O. Bueno, "On what it takes for there to be no fact of the matter," *Noûs* 42:4 (2008), 753–69.

It seems—to some—that the bivalence constraint conflicts with the evident fact that (often) there is no fact of the matter about particular identity claims. No answer is—even in principle—metaphysically motivated in many cases. Indeed, this is more broadly the case with many (if not most) statements we can easily formulate. Often, although we accept *A or it is not the case that A*, for arbitrary *A*, we recognize in many specific cases that there is nothing—metaphysically speaking—that makes one or the other (even in principle) the case. Vagueness in this sense is ubiquitous. Is that man bald or not? There are no facts, either about how we actually use the word "bald," or about the distribution of the hair on his head, that determine an answer. Is that a heap or not? Again, there are neither facts about how we use the word "heap," nor facts about piles of pebbles, that determine an answer. This isn't to say that we couldn't (at least in many cases) stipulate an answer: we could. But it would be dishonest to say that lurking behind our practice with applying the word "heap," or located somewhere in the organization of a heap of pebbles—or supervenient on the union of both a practice of "heap"-applications to pile of pebbles and those piles of pebbles themselves are facts of the matter that neatly divide all piles of pebbles into heaps and nonheaps of such.

I argue elsewhere[85] that the answers to some of these questions are metaphysical "don't cares." It doesn't matter to us that there isn't an answer to be had—that a neat division of cases isn't available. Where it does matter, but there are no facts to determine an answer, we (in practice) do stipulate an answer or endow someone officially with the authority to stipulate an answer, when needed—if the latter will do. Much of what happens in the evolution of legal concepts (for example) should be seen as those endowed with the appropriate authority so legislating on matters of vagueness. To add to the epistemic complications, there are also cases where there actually are metaphysically determined answers, but we can't tell ahead of time that this is so. This is because there being answers may be due to there being facts that can be brought to bear on the situations in a way we didn't see coming ahead of time, or because practical discourse needs evolve in such a way as to enable certain facts to bear on such questions.

For these reasons, a practical solution as to how we're to speak with respect to vagueness—thus broadly construed—that retains the bivalence constraint (that for all statements *A*, expressible in our language, *A or it is not the case that A*[86]) is to invoke a broadly used epistemic idiom of ignorance. We say that one or the other of a bivalent option is true, but that "it's not known" or that "we don't know" which. However, in invoking this ignorance idiom, no burden is being undertaken of presuming there really is a fact of the matter toward which ignorance is being expressed.[87]

---

85. Jody Azzouni, *Knowledge and reference in empirical science* (London: Routledge, 2000a), part IV, §6.

86. And, for every *o* and every F, that either F*o* or ¬F*o*.

87. In contrast to, say, the Epistemicism of Timothy Williamson, *Vagueness* (London: Routledge, 1994), where arguments are offered that in thought experiments, of pebbles being removed one by one from heaps, there actually *are* (metaphysically speaking) specific individual-pebble-removing events, whereupon a heap of pebbles then becomes a nonheap—and this is whether we've actually (arbitrarily) stipulated such points of change or not. Williamson's position is misdescribed by the label "Epistemicism," I think, since the position requires a metaphysical assumption about there being sharp lines in the world that match our word usage, metaphysical assumptions about the specification of our usage of the word "heap" (that goes beyond any facts about our usage of the word, and beyond, more generally, any facts about us), or both.

Rather, the ignorance idiom is a broad verbal tool that encompasses the three kinds of cases just mentioned: those where we think one or the other (A or $\neg A$) is the case (but we honestly don't know which), cases where nothing, in particular, determines which is the case,[88] and cases where we don't know which of the first two situations is the case. We describe ourselves as "ignorant," regardless. Call this claim about how we self-ascribe ignorance to ourselves *the broad ignorance claim*. It's (so I say) our use of the broad ignorance idiom ("don't know") that enables our use of classical bivalence to fit compatible with the large number of "no fact" cases that are generated by vaguely applicable terms.[89]

It might be thought that expressions of ignorance—contrary to what I've just stated—themselves presuppose one or another factuality condition. If there is no fact of the matter about whether A or $\neg A$, then it isn't that one doesn't know whether one or the other is the case because there isn't anything *to* know. This counter to my view deserves extended discussion; three points about it can be made now to indicate the substantial obstacles it faces. The first is that ordinary-language expressions of ignorance, in any case, are too frail for mounting a sophisticated claim of this sort. Precisely because it's often impossible to distinguish cases of nonfactuality from cases where there is factuality, but we have no epistemic access to those facts, it's natural (and typical) to indicate one's presence in either situation with the same epistemic idiom. Second, it's quite hard to see how to even state constraints on idioms of ignorance—to tighten them up—so that they aren't to apply to cases where there are no "facts" to be known. One can't merely say, for example, that someone P is ignorant of whether A or $\neg A$, but only when either A or $\neg A$ "is the case" or "is actually the case" (or something like that). "Is the case" and "is actually the case" need content that goes beyond the bivalence constraint itself, and it's hardly obvious how that's to be done. Third, a family of drastic solutions, of course, is to either (i) give up the bivalence constraint (i.e., change the logic), or (ii) draft the truth idiom into enabling a factualism/nonfactualism distinction. Neither is easy or obvious if only because both the logic and the truth idiom already have central indispensable roles that don't nicely mesh with attempts to use them to enable a distinction between facts and nonfacts.[90]

One last point about this should be stressed. This is that the foregoing suggestion regarding the ignorance idiom—the broad ignorance claim—provides a concomitant

---

88. Care is needed in laying out exactly how a nonfactualism claim (within the classical setting—subject to the bivalence constraint) can be cogently formulated. I indicate a little about this issue shortly—see the second point made in the paragraph following the one this note is appended to.

I should add that "heap" thought experiments are particularly graphic ways of pressing intuitions of factlessness against the apparent (classical logic) assumption that one or the other of a disjunctive claim is true. In particular, the removal of one pebble from a pile of such seems insufficient to determine a change from "heap" to "not a heap." Resistance to the claim that such a change can responsibly be a matter of mere (subsequent) stipulation is undermined by a view—like the one being pressed in this book—that refuses to treat *every* truth as metaphysically grounded. For that matter, resistance to the claim that A or $\neg A$ can be literally true without there being a "fact of the matter" according to which it is true, is undermined by the very same kind of view.

89. The broad ignorance claim makes its first appearance in Azzouni (2000a), part IV, §6, although I don't there use this nomenclature.

90. See sections 4.7, 4.8, and 4.9 for further discussion of the third point. Azzouni and Bueno (2008) also give details about the second point and (ii) of the third.

reading of *A or ¬A* (and, for that matter, concomitant readings of [*A or ¬A*] *is true*, and *A is true or ¬A is true*) on which they are not to be interpreted as automatically stating something to the effect that one of the two, *A* or *¬A*, is the case—in some "metaphysical sense" or something like that. Rather, the second point about it being hard to formulate a distinction between a fact of the matter being in place (and underwriting the disjunction *A or ¬A*), and there being no such fact, can be used to place an interpretation on that formulation that doesn't treat it as committed to "there being a fact of the matter," in some metaphysically rich sense.

My recommendation, one that's in accord with the general tenor of this book, is to capture "nonfactualism," when present, in some other way entirely. For example, the distinction between cases where there is "a fact of the matter" about *A or ¬A* holding, or none such, can be drawn not at the sentential level (e.g., not in terms of a kind of truth holding of sentences), but rather at the level of the term. If the quantifiers or singular terms occurring in the sentence *A* refer to nothing real, then *A or ¬A* is to be read nonfactually; otherwise, it need not be so read. The foregoing is an illustration of one way of marking out nonfactualist cases against a general factualist background (all within a context in which the bivalence constraint holds). I'm not denying that there may be other ways of doing this.[91]

So I read the state of play with respect to "identity conditions" as follows: "adequate identity conditions" are ones that adjudicate disputed cases of identity in those cases where adjudication is specifically needed. When, otherwise, the metaphysical facts come up short, and no arbitrary stipulation is in place—or naturally adopted—or when such facts are in place, but we haven't access to them, we describe ourselves as not knowing which (of either *A* or *¬A*) is the case.

Returning to the subject matter of this chapter: with hallucinations, of course, metaphysical constraints (due to what terms refer to) on what's truly said and falsely said are nonexistent in any case. Still operative, however, is the demand that any identification of an F (an hallucination or a type of hallucination) with a G be coherent—that is, be consistent with the other truths about hallucinations we accept (and, more broadly, with all the other truths we accept). That is, as discussed in section 2.9, one thing to be surely avoided is contradiction: to identify an F with a G, and yet to deny that identification as well.

Given the general aim of characterizing the content of the hallucinator's experience, the identification of the appearances of two hallucinated objects as appearances of the same hallucinated object—when it occurs—is usually a response-dependent matter based on the qualities that such hallucinated objects

---

91. See Azzouni and Bueno (2008) for discussion. I should add that the major problem with factual/nonfactual distinctions is that they aren't fine-grained enough. They are designed to apply at the sentential/propositional level; but the problem is that even if our vocabulary items are so separable—for example into the ontologically robust (e.g., physical items and their relations) and those that aren't (fictional entities)—sentences and thoughts involving these are a potpourri of such items. For example, "Walt Disney invented Mickey Mouse," "the number of cats is the same as the number of dogs," and so on. I've instead employed talk of truth makers and truth-value inducers, as above, to capture how ontological variation among terms affects sentences and thoughts. Incidentally, the same problem not only bedevils attempts to draw a factual/nonfactual distinction among sentences or propositions; it also bedevils pluralist views of truth. See section 4.9.

present (to the hallucinator).[92] Indeed, in the literature, such identifications often aren't of particular hallucinated objects. Type classifications in terms of kinds of content suffice. The same tune is heard over and over; a particular metallic flavor is experienced (again and again), the same unpleasant odor, a visualization of Jesus, or (more primitively) colors and patterns of various sorts. In these cases, type classification in terms of presented qualities captures all the identity that's needed to be posited.[93]

S's particular hallucinations—as described in the foregoing—are a different matter. Here, the thought experiment turns not on pure sensory repetition but on the presentation of particular objects with the accompanying aspects of such transcending their sensory accompaniments. I am, of course, alluding to the hallucination of perceptual constancies and other aspects of our object-directed experience that so clearly go beyond sheer sensory qualities (the sense data) presented in experience. Here, at least in principle, the question of how an hallucinated object is to be reidentified over time becomes cogent. On what grounds can S (and the experimenters) say that he is seeing a particular hallucinated object again?

To a very large extent, at least in the experimental setting as described in section 2.3, S's identifications of hallucinated objects that he experiences at different times are—as I've mentioned—largely (although not entirely) response-dependent *on S*. More accurately, two hallucination events are (most of the time) to be taken as of the same hallucinated object when they present to S as the same object. But when is that? Any answer should be parasitic on how the same thing happens with real objects precisely because the thought experiment in question treats hallucinatory experience as similarly parasitic on our experiences with real

92. "I see people who are not there. I see people in the street with clipboards, sometimes it's the same person turning up, little fat chap, looks like Mickey Rooney." This remark (of "a person with visual hallucinations associated with schizophrenia") is quoted by Daniel Collerton, Elaine Perry, and Ian McKeith, "Why people see things that are not there: A novel perception and attention deficit model for recurrent complex visual hallucinations," *Behavioral and Brain Sciences* 28 (2005), 737.

93. It's worth noting that a sharp distinction between sensory hallucinations, and hallucinated objects—the latter being where type sortals like tunes, or persons, apply—emerged very early in neurological studies. For example, Wilder Penfield and Phenor Perot ("The brain's record of auditory and visual experience," *Brain* 86 [1963], 690), write:

There is a sharp functional frontier between the sensory and the interpretative areas. . . . In the visual cortex . . . the electrode may elicit lights, stars, or coloured flashes moving about. In the auditory cortex a ringing, humming or rumbling may result.
    But then, if the electrode is moved only a few millimetres away into the neighboring cortex around these sensory areas, a response of a totally different order of neuronal organization may result. There is no longer a sound but a voice, no longer a rumbling but music. Visual flashes of coloured lights give way to a scene, or the sudden appearance of a familiar person.

Collerton et al. (2005), 738, relying on the same distinction—but restricted to visual hallucinations—write: "We will also primarily deal with complex, or formed, hallucinations of people, animals, and objects. Classically, these are differentiated from simple hallucinations of dots, lines, flashes, and amorphous shapes, as well as from panoramic hallucinations of landscapes." Also, see Collerton et al. (2005), 739, which suggests that each type of hallucination ("simple" and "complex") "has a single primary cause . . . and that these causes are separable within the visual system."

objects. That is, S judges (experiences) an hallucinated object to be the same as another the way he so judges (experiences) any object to be the same as another: because of how it appears to him, because of how he perceives it to move through space and over time, and because of the apparent successor relations that later hallucinated objects seem to have to earlier ones. For example, if an hallucinated hobbit looks just like one he's seen before, if it responds to the same name he used earlier, and if it presents the appropriate psychological continuity to the previously hallucinated hobbit, S will experience what he sees to be the same (hallucinated) hobbit. Indeed, as he watches the hallucinated hobbit move about the room, he naturally and automatically identifies the object he hallucinates with the object he has hallucinated only seconds earlier (he takes them as one object that he's hallucinating the movement of).

These identifications are part of the content of S's experiences, and so they can prove to be just as useful for theoretical purposes as the attribution of properties to S's hallucinated objects. Indeed, it can prove neurologically significant that such and such an object—one that S recognizes to be the *same* object—is repeatedly hallucinated by S.

The needed qualification "for the most part," in describing these identifications as response-dependent, arises for the same reasons we've seen it arise before. S can be wrong in so many ways about the objects he's identified as the same. He may discover that what he's taking to be Frodo is actually Gimli in disguise; as noted earlier, the experimenters may be able to warn him that this is the case. He may discover that what he is taking to be Frodo—an hallucinated object that he dealt with yesterday—is today an actor disguised as the hallucinated Frodo. These shouldn't be identified, as S will admit once he realizes the true state of affairs.

I should note that in denying—as I just have—that a real object can ever be identified with an hallucinated object, I'm neither relying (solely) on the fact that S wouldn't accept such a claim, nor am I making an essentialist (or an a priori) point that of course, no nonexistent object could be (or is) any actual object.[94] Rather, the aim (again) is simply the flat-footed and ordinary one of avoiding contradictions in indispensable hallucinatory discourse.

These claims about when and how hallucinated objects are to be identified with other hallucinated objects may strike some philosophers as problematical insofar as there doesn't seem to be any grounding in "reality" as to when such should be taken to be the case. What on Earth, therefore, decides the correctness of S's claims about the hallucinated objects? Isn't it all rather arbitrary? Well, it's true that there isn't any grounding in reality as to when one hallucinated object is the same as another. For that matter, there isn't any grounding in reality as to what properties hallucinated objects have. Nor is there grounding in anything else (metaphysically speaking) that's referred[e] to by the terms appearing in hallucinogenic discourse. There are no such objects, and so such have no properties, and aren't to be identified (nor not identified) with one another. That doesn't mean, however, that we can't have truths and falsities about[e] such things; that doesn't mean that such truths and

---

94. Pace Smith (2002), chapter 10, and a number of other philosophers, for that matter.

falsities can't be about^e when such are to be identified with one another and when not. Such truths and falsities, interestingly, cannot be arbitrarily stipulated—at least not if we want the resulting discourse to be evidentially valuable. As we've seen, the point of the discourse is to capture (without reference^r) the content of S's experiences, and to do so in a way that's responsible to the psychoneurological facts that underwrite those experiences. And as we've seen, both the experimenters and S can be wrong about claims made within this discourse. This is what makes cogent the singular character of such empty statements and thoughts.

Evans (332–33) offers a challenge to singular thought and statement with respect to hallucinations that's in the neighborhood of the foregoing concerns about the cogency of ascriptions of identity between hallucinated objects; but it's in regard to S and the experimenters talking about—as they supposedly do—the same objects. The question can be put this way: given that the experimenters are talking about what S sees, how do they manage to talk about the right objects? Here's another good way to put the issue: if there are no objects that S sees, then how are the experimenters' thoughts and experience to match up with S's experience and thought? Or (yet another way to put it): if there are no objects involved, then how are the "virtual objects"—that are the content of S's experience and thought—to match up with the "virtual objects" that are the contents of the experimenters' experience and thoughts? This is a problem that can be posed against the very coherence of the idea of "group hallucinations" that's come up several times already. If an hallucination is just virtual, if—to avoid the use/mention conflations I've indulged in the last few lines—there are just the contents of the various hallucinators' experiences and thoughts, and if these contents cannot have a equivalence relation imposed on them by virtue of their similarity in the minds of the experimenters and S (and their "being about^e the same things" can't therefore be defined in terms of that equivalence relation), then what are the grounds on which certain object-directed contents are to be characterized as of the same objects? There are, after all, no objects to so unify them as being about those objects. Saying that the objects in question are ones that the experiences and thoughts are about^e doesn't help because aboutness^e isn't a relation to anything. We want the thoughts and experiences of the hallucinators to be about^e the same things; but we haven't any resources—any things—to enable this.

To continue the objection: on the singular picture, information—or perhaps pseudo-information—is supposedly being shared by a number of people. That is, they are communicating with each other about something referred to in common—a common subject matter. The natural thought (in standard circumstances) involves finding that common object of discourse via the origin of this shared information. As Evans (336) puts it, "the statement of the conditions for communication must make some reference to the origin or pedigree of the information upon which speaker and hearer respectively base their thoughts."

He continues, "The natural suggestion in filling this gap, is once again Russellian in its implications. This is to say that the information of the speaker and hearer must derive (in ways which typically produce) knowledge *from the same object*" (emphasis in original).

So Evans has posed a challenge. Either an (actual) object "unifies" the thought of the experimenters and S, or similarity of the thoughts directed toward hallucinations (on the part of the experimenters and S) does it. But there is no object; and the thoughts cannot be (in general) regarded as similar. The response to Evans is to recognize that the hallucinatory discourse engaged by the experimenters takes the object-directed experience of S's as a given of any description of the content of that experience. That is, it stipulates an agreement in reference[e] (in aboutness[e]) between terms as utilized by the experimenters and as utilized by S: they refer[e] to the objects that are the objects of S's hallucinatoric experience. Exactly how (and when) does this stipulation occur? When the experimenters undertake to describe, name, and demonstrate the items that S sees—more accurately, when they choose to engage singularly with S in a dialogue about what he sees.

In doing so, they are stipulating their terms to co-refer[e] with S's, and therefore they are treating the object-directed nature of the content of S's thought as coherent enough for co-reference[e]—as a practice—to operate in terms of. In a similar way, a mathematician, who has axiomatically invented a new set of mathematical objects may invite me to talk to him about his new objects. In doing so, I'm assuming his axioms are coherent enough to support a discourse that can allow me to wonder what is and isn't true of such and such an object. Failure is always possible. In the case of S, the object-directedness of his hallucinatory experience could prove to not allow much by way of identification of hallucinated objects—even from one moment to the next. There might not be much sense in questions of whether this or that seen now by S is the same as that or this seen even seconds earlier. Dreams are similar. Some dreams allow a fairly coherent description of this, as presented in the dream being one thing, and that, also presented in the dream, as being another. But not all dreams are so referentially[e] friendly. If the content of a dream doesn't allow successful distinctive naming of presented things, then co-reference[e]—as when two friends talk about one of their dreams and refer[e] to the objects dreamt of—won't work either. So, too, if S's hallucinations are disordered enough to fail to be object-directed (psychologically speaking), then the experimenters may be able to fall back on types of things seen, as a way of capturing the content of his hallucinations. In that case, names and demonstratives will not occur in the discourse. Singular discourse requires a certain "coherence" in someone's experience if that experience is to allow her object-directed psychological mechanisms to engage with it.

The next question is, given that S's hallucinatoric experience is appropriately coherent, whether stipulations of the sort that I've attributed to the experimenters can enable a successful singular truth-apt discourse-practice about[e] the nonexistent subject-matter. I've tried to show in the foregoing sections of this chapter that the answer to this question is definitely *Yes*. Contradiction can (of course) be avoided; but that's a minimal requirement. The situation—interestingly—is strikingly similar to the utilization of theoretical terms in the science generally. In the S thought-experiment, the terms (about[e] hallucinated objects) are to track S's experiences, and more broadly, S's neurological states. They are to enable generalizations that underwrite predictions of what S will experience under such and such circumstances. If technical developments are favorable, it may even be possible for the experimenters to see—in a relatively respectable sense—what S sees. All of this is possible via a coordination between the content of S's experience and what the hallucination-discourse allows the experimenters (and S) to say about[e] that content. In addition, an appropriate (and crucial) *fallibility* emerges: The experimenters (and S) can be wrong with respect to their descriptions of the non-existent hallucinated objects. In standard singular reference to real objects, what's true (and false) of the objects spoken and thought of transcends our thoughts and speech about such; the same is true of hallucinated objects. And, all this is possible without reference to objects. Evan's challenge, therefore, can be met.

2.11 The Argument from Hallucination and Disjunctivism: Some Observations

A chapter on hallucination would not be complete, perhaps, without some discussion of the famed argument from hallucination.[95] So, too, some remarks about disjunctivism may seem in order. In the second case, my aim is not to engage in a full-blooded discussion of the various forms of disjunctionism: that would be a digression (as well as impossible, given the burgeoning body of literature). My goal is, instead, to make some points about how one particular form of disjunctivism should be presented. I take up this observation about this form of disjunctivism first because I use it to craft a formulation of the position that I apply in my discussion of the argument from hallucination.

I start, therefore, with Snowdon's original formulation of the disjunctivist premise.[96] Snowdon (1980–81, 159) offers the following formulation of his version of a disjunctive characterization of how things can looks to S—one based on a modification of a formulation due to Hinton (1967): "it looks to S as if there is

---

95. My thanks to Tim Crane for criticisms of a quite different earlier version of this section, criticisms that motivated a substantial rewrite.

96. Adrian Haddock and Fiona Macpherson ("Introduction: Varieties of disjunctivism," in *Disjunctivism: Perception, action, knowledge*, ed. Adrian Haddock and Fiona Macpherson [Oxford: Oxford University Press, 2008], 1–24) distinguish three versions of disjunctivism in theories of perception. The particular version of disjunctivism championed by Paul Snowdon ("Perception, vision, and causation," *Proceedings of the Aristotelian Society* 81 [1980–81]: 175–92; reprinted in *Vision and mind: Selected readings in the philosophy of perception*, ed. Alva Noë and Evan Thompson [Cambridge, Mass.: MIT Press, 2002], 151–66; citations are to the reprint), and that I focus on, is "experiential disjunctivism," a "metaphysical disjunctivism" (Alex Byrne and Heather Logue, "Either/Or," in *Disjunctivism: Perception, action, knowledge*, ed. Adrian Haddock and Fiona Macpherson [Oxford: Oxford University Press, 2008], 1–24.) to the effect that there are two distinguishable psychological states (L-states) that one is respectively in, when seeing a public object, on the one hand, and when one is not seeing such a public object, but instead is phenomenologically experiencing something introspectively indistinguishable from the first experience. The first L-state is understood to be one that "involves the surrounding objects" (Snowdon 1980–81, 161) or is one that's partially constituted by the external objects that are seen; the second is not so constituted: it is "intrinsically independent of surrounding objects" (Snowdon 1980–81, 161). This distinction between L-states needs refinement: it may be that because of priming effects (for example) the second sort of L-state isn't to be characterized as intrinsically independent of surrounding objects, although it is independent of the object the subject takes himself to see. Investigating this issue lies apart from the aims of this section. I should also add that in the passages I've quoted, Snowdon doesn't speak explicitly of "L-states" but instead of "states of affairs" that make the looks ascriptions true.

an F; (there is something which looks to S to be F) $\lor$ (it is to S as if there is something which looks to him (S) to be F)." As Snowdon's (1980–81, 152) allusion to Quine's distinction between the notional and the relational indicates, the crucial difference between the disjuncts in this formulation is one between quantifying into a "looks to S" context, and not so quantifying in: there being an object such that it seems to S that the object in question is . . . , and it seeming to S that there is an object such that the object in question is. . . . But, as was argued in section 2.4, purely notional construals of hallucinated experience are unsuitable as tools to characterize hallucinatory states: they are unsuitable as characterizations of most psychological states, for that matter. They are (in particular) evidentially useless to psychoneurological studies.[97] So Snowdon's formulation won't do as it stands. If we simply rewrite the second disjunct to allow quantifying in, we get a useless redundancy: "it looks to S as if there is an F; (there is something which looks to S to be F) $\lor$ (there is something which looks to S to be F)."

Snowdon's purpose is to characterize distinctive looks-to-S-states (L-states); this formulation obviously won't do that. Here's a supplementation that (I'll show) can do the job Snowdon needs:

it looks to S as if there is an F:
    [DIJ] (there is something that exists which looks to S to be F) $\lor$ (there is something that doesn't exist which looks to S to be F).[98]

This reformulation uses an existence predicate, one that's taken not to include hallucinated objects within its extension (since such don't exist). [DIJ], therefore, isn't a redundant disjunction. Furthermore, this new formulation is as useful for Snowdon's purposes as his original one was: if the clause "(there is something which looks to S to be F)" successfully characterizes an L-state that intrinsically involves objects, then because the new formulation contains the same clause, with the additional claim that such objects exist, it also so characterizes an L-state.[99] The second clause, with the important rider that the objects so quantified over don't exist, therefore, does *not* characterize the second L-state in terms of objects in the environment of the subject. This is what Snowdon requires of his second disjunct.

Both disjuncts of [DIJ] involve quantifications into what—as a matter of their form—are relations. As noted in section 2.9, with respect to the contrast between aboutness[e] and aboutness[r] (and more generally, with respect to the predication of properties to existent or to nonexistent objects), and despite surface syntactic appearances, a genuine relation isn't characterized by the second disjunct of [DIJ]. To attribute the quality of being a hobbit (or the quality of presenting a hobbit) to an hallucinated object is a truth-based mode of speech that

97. Recall the discussion of the external discourse demand in section 2.8.
98. My replacing Snowdon's semicolon with a colon, moving the disjunction to another line, and the label "DIJ" are purely typographical changes.
99. Presumably, Snowdon (1980–81) understands quantifying into a "looks to S" context to be one that's ontologically committing. If so quantifying in doesn't so ontologically commit, then an additional rider that supplies the ontological commitment is required.

doesn't require there (really) being an hallucinated object that presents itself as a hobbit; it's nevertheless an indispensable way of speaking. So, too, to say that there is something (that doesn't exist) which looks to S to be F is no more to commit oneself to something looking to S as being F than the previous locution involved a commitment to something presenting itself as a hobbit. Treating "it looks to S as if there is an F" disjunctively really is required. Only thus will it be made clear that there is an ontological requirement that's in place in the first disjunct but not in the second.

In this way—provided the phrase "which looks to S to be F" characterizes (for appropriate F) sensory experience—that some sensory experiences (but not others) are relations to mind-independent objects is honored by [DIJ] in the most direct way possible: by—in the first disjunct—quantification over such mind-independent objects. Such is not true of hallucinatory experience (as described by the second disjunct) of [DIJ].[100]

I turn now to a very brief discussion of the issue of the "content" of hallucinations. As I illustrate later in this section (and in chapter 4), current empirical studies of hallucination require there to be in place intrinsic characterizations of the contents of hallucinations, and not merely characterizations of their content in terms of relations to indiscriminable "veridical" perceptions. Furthermore, current empirical studies of hallucination also require the cogency of comparisons between the content of hallucinatory experience and nonhallucinatory experience. I want, therefore, to indicate the various ways that [DIJ] allows "content" to be shared between hallucinatoric and veridical experience without so allowing ontological commitments to be shared.

To begin with, if we imagine the hallucination of an object that looks F to S, exactly as some actual object could, we have the following shared content between the two (possible) states of S:

It looks to S as if there is an F.

That is, the purportedly shared content is captured by [DIJ] as a whole. It can be argued, however, that this isn't a characterization of shared content because this statement is glossed by [DIJ] as a disjunction. However, the shared content can be characterized nondisjunctively:

There is something which looks to S to be F.

Or, still better,

---

100. A caveat. I've deliberately used coy language in describing what [DIJ] does, for example, that "this new formulation is as useful for Snowdon's purposes as his original one was." This is because I'm dubious about whether [DIJ] (or Snowdon's original formulation) should be taken as describing distinct L-states. This is not a matter that can be explored further in this book. Suffice it to say now, however, that the disjunctivism that's surely captured by [DIJ] is "ontological disjunctivism," a disjunctivism that distinguishes between *characterizations* of psychological states, where such characterizations differ in the entities they describe as involved, one way or another, in the states they describe.

> Something looks F.[101]

That is, when we eliminate ontological characterizations—ones of existence or nonexistence—what's left is the shared content that some item looks to be *F*.

Perhaps, however, this isn't quite right. When I'm looking right at something in ordinary circumstances, the content of my experience (one might say) isn't that it *looks* F, it's that it *is* F:

> Something is F.

This won't create a problem with the presentation/having distinction established in section 2.9. We might say that sometimes an object turns out not to be F (because it's G). Then we fall back on an epistemic idiom: it *looked* F; but so saying isn't to redescribe the original content as only about what something looked like. It's to epistemically hedge oneself: the original content was: something is F. But then I learned that it wasn't an F. We say this by saying: it looked F. Thus the original content still is: it is F. So, too, sometimes an object turns out not be F (because it doesn't exist). Then we say, well, it *looked* F. Again, though the (nonexistent) object has turned out only to present as F (and not to be F), that isn't the content of our experience. The content wasn't: it presents as F. The content was: it is F.[102]

Regardless of whether this is right, shared content is to be—notice—cashed out not in terms of an experience having such and such qualities, but in terms of an object looking in such and such a way. Thus far, my content-claims are in accord with Smith (2002, 224–25) when he criticizes the no-content view of hallucinations as follows:

> Not only is the subject apparently entertaining a demonstrative thought, but the object of this thought is, phenomenologically, *present bodily*, as Husserl would put it. To say simply that our subject is not aware of *anything* is surely to under-describe this situation dramatically. Perhaps we can make sense of there being "mock thoughts," but can there really be such a thing as mock sensory awareness? Perhaps there can be "an illusion of understanding," but can there be an illusion of awareness? . . . In particular, we need to be able to account for the *perceptual attention* that may well be present in hallucination. . . .. But if so, what else can we say other than that the subject is, as the Argument requires, aware of a non-normal object? (emphasis in original)

Smith (ultimately) draws a Meinongian conclusion from his considerations: the non-normal object in question is a Meinongian object. I'll shortly argue we don't have to do *that*. But we certainly must keep distinct two different ways that we might characterize the content of hallucinatory experiences: (i) the subject attending to objects (of his hallucination) and, (ii) the subject attending to his internal

---

101. Shared content, thus described, can also be couched in a singular way, for example: *That looks F*, or *Gimli looks F*.

102. Recall the earlier discussion of this epistemic use of these idioms in section 2.9.

experience. Whether it's possible (or not) for a subject to ever attend to his internal experience(s) is somewhat debatable.[103] Regardless of the outcome of that particular debate, there is no reason to think that someone hallucinating, even someone who *knows* he is hallucinating, is—by virtue of that alone—attending in any way to qualities of his internal experience instead of to the objects that he sees. *S* is—in the experimental situation—certainly doing nothing that should be described as the contemplation of his own experiences. He's attending to what he sees. What he sees may not exist, but that doesn't mean he's attending to something else entirely: his sensory impressions, qualities of his experience, or something like that.[104]

A similar slide (the exact same slide, actually) is familiar in the case of empty names. Recall the discussion of this in the general introduction: Instead of Pegasus, one suggests that the topic is the word "Pegasus" or the idea of Pegasus—in short, one or another psychological/verbal vehicle about Pegasus. But neither of these is the subject matter of sentences or thoughts about Pegasus, in any case. No more so are perceptual vehicles such as sensory impressions, the qualities of one's experience, and so on, the objects of awareness in the case of hallucinatory experience. The subject matter of such an experience is the nonexistent items seen; not the experiences of such.

In the case of hallucination, the slide from characterizations of the content of such in terms of (nonexistent) objects being such and so, to characterizations of the properties of hallucinatory experience is often motivated by the felt need for truth makers. If the objects seen aren't real, they can't be the "content" of hallucinatory experience because the content of an experience determines truth and falsity, and nothing at all can't be the basis of the truth and falsity of statements about those experiences. But hallucinatory experience itself (so the thought goes) is certainly real. Therefore, that hallucinatory experience must be the basis of what's true and false about what an hallucinating subject experiences; so the content of such experience must be in terms of the experience itself to enable that experience to function as a truth maker.

---

103. See Gilbert Harman, "The intrinsic quality of experience" (1990), in *Reasoning, meaning, and mind* (Oxford: Oxford University Press, 1999), 244–61.

104. Notice that we capture the claim that *S* is aware of something, and that nothing is there, by saying that there is something he is aware of and that it doesn't exist. The quantifier, "there is" isn't indicating a Meinongian object; rather, it's ontologically neutral. Thus, to say that he is aware of an object is to describe his psychological state (and its content) in a way that's compatible with: there is nothing there. The latter denial uses an ontologically loaded "there is"; the previous quantifier (there is something he's aware of) remains neutral. What makes this intuitively confusing is a tendency to read both quantifiers the same way—both as ontologically committing or neither as. An additional problem is that—in English (and in all natural languages, I suspect)—no term indicates ontological commitment in a context-free way. (See Azzouni [2004a], chapter 4; Jody Azzouni, "Ontological commitment in the vernacular," *Noûs* 41 [2007], 204–26; and Jody Azzouni, "Ontology and the word 'exist': Uneasy relations," *Philosophia Mathematica*, forthcoming (a) on this.) What's so confusing in this case is that we must switch the ontological roles of the two quantifiers within the same sentence ("There is something he is aware of but there is nothing there"): as noted, there is pressure to read a term repeated in a sentence in the same way. This is one reason why the word "exists" is so useful: it can be used contrastively (as ontologically committing) against a neutral "there is" precisely because it avoids a repetition of the same word. But our intuitive need to fall back on the locution: "He's aware of something, but it doesn't exist," to get the point across (about *S* and what he sees) seductively invites a Meinongian interpretation: There is an object—a Meinongian hallucinated object that *S* is aware of—and *it's* one that doesn't exist. Ordinary language is quite treacherous in this area. We can't simply dismiss the intuitions ordinary language usage generates (it's methodologically daft to throw away evidence—pace Braun [2005], 612–13): we simply have to analyze usage fully enough to see exactly how and why the intuitions in question take the form they do.

It's exactly at this point that a threat to naive realism will be felt. If we correspondingly shift the awareness of the experiencer (in the case of hallucination) from the nonexistent objects and their presumed properties to the experiencer's own experience, then we seem forced to treat the awareness of the experiencer (in the case of "veridical perception") to be directed toward his own experience as well (since the phenomenology of the experience is indistinguishable in both cases). Then we have an experiencer (in the case of ordinary perception) being aware not of the objects in the world that he sees—and as naive realism would have it—but instead only of aspects of his own experience.[105]

Right here we see the motivation to boldly cut the Gordian knot: (i) deny content to hallucinatory experience altogether, or (ii) deny sameness of content to introspectively indiscriminable experiences. Correspondingly, deny the experiencer's own grasp of what he seems to be aware of (in the hallucinatory case). Nothing this drastic is called for if we simply refuse to allow a shift in the description of the content of hallucinatory experience from (nonexistent) objects being what the experiencer is aware of to his own experience being what the experiencer is aware of.[106]

Notice that, on my view, although hallucinatory experience has positive content, and that content can be characterized in ways in which it's correct to say that it's shared with the content of (appropriately similar) ordinary perceptual events, it's not correct to say that there is a same thing that's seen in cases of hallucination and in "indiscriminable" ordinary perceptions. During ordinary perceptual events, what's seen are actual objects. In hallucinations, such are not seen. Thus the threat to naive realism is averted.[107]

One last observation about the sort of content I'm attributing to hallucinatory experience, and that I claim the psychological sciences require. McDowell (1986, 167, note 57) writes that "Cognitive science manages to find content in the interior as it conceives that; but it does so by situating cognitive space (on its conception) in the world, not by considering things from the point of view of cognitive space."

I don't find this remark to be entirely transparent; but on the most obvious reading (which admittedly, may not be what McDowell intends), it's simply not true of the science. I'll illustrate the point briefly by means of contemporary studies of hallucination—by showing that characterizations of the "internal content" of such hallucinations is indispensable to studies of hallucinations. Bentall

105. It's worth noting that M. G. F. Martin, "On being alienated," in *Perceptual experience*, ed. Tamar Szabó Gendler and John Hawthorne (Oxford: Oxford University Press, 2006), 373–79, after quoting Smith's "incredulity" that hallucinatory experience could be of nothing at all, shifts the topic explicitly to the question of whether the experience itself can be characterized positively. This in turn motivates a discussion of the self-awareness of one's own states. All of this, or so I've been claiming, is the proverbial red herring, due to a kind of use/mention slip.

106. Having said this, there is—of course—a perfectly innocuous way of attributing properties to a subject's experience by way of what they are experiences of. This is to go adverbial: to speak of the hallucination of a purple man as a purple-man-hallucination. But doing this, of course, is not (or shouldn't be) to claim that thereby one is genuinely characterizing aspects of "experience" that the experiencer can be taken—in a substantial nonpleonastic sense—to be aware of.

107. I'm not, by the way, committing myself to naive realism, direct realism, or any of these other "isms" in the theory of perception. I'm simply denying the relevance of certain traditional (and still influential) arguments to the issue.

(1990) explains hallucinations as due to an impairment in "reality monitoring," the ability to discriminate between real and imagined events. The influence of this cognitive model is due to its being based on an experimental approach to discovering exactly wherein the supposed "impairment" is located. For our purposes, the point is that such discoveries are couched both in terms of subpersonal mechanisms (e.g., stress and emotional arousal disrupting "normal encoding processes that bind source-specifying cues to the memory"), and in terms of heuristic or strategic cues that individuals (automatically) apply to the content they are experiencing.[108] The latter allows Bentall (2000, 2003) to hypothesize that an explanation for how culture seems to affect the content of hallucinations is that source-monitoring judgments are influenced by background plausibility assumptions. There is, as well, a great deal of evidence that external stimulation suppresses hallucination. The source-monitoring hypothesis can explain this in terms of the strength of one's perception of one's surroundings. If these are "degraded" because of poor vision, more liberal criteria for assuming that perceived events are real will be presumed and therefore internally generated cognitive events will be attributed to an external source.[109]

It's fairly obvious that both the hypotheses put forward and the experimental literature that these hypotheses have given rise to are couched—by no accident—in language that attributes intrinsic content to hallucinatory experience. It's important to be able to characterize that content in a way that's compatible with at least some versions of disjunctivism and in a way that doesn't commit those scientists who attribute such content to hallucinatory experience to thereby commit themselves to the items seen[e] during hallucinations.[110]

108. Aleman and Larøi (2008), 121. "Source monitoring" following M. K. Johnson, S. Hashtroudi, and D. S. Lindsay, "Source monitoring," *Psychological Bulletin* 114 (1993), 3–28, is the implementation of the abilities a subject has to attribute origins to memories, knowledge, and beliefs. The working assumption in this area of study is that it's not intrinsic to one's experience of perceived events whether they are generated by the mind or generated by items outside oneself.

109. In my discussion, I've largely adopted the language of Aleman and Larøi (2008). I should stress that despite its voluntary sounding tone, it's not being suggested that individuals make conscious decisions about how stringent their criteria are to be. Rather, these "assumptions," "presuppositions," and "decisions" are all subpersonal, and their results, that is, hallucinations, are experienced as involuntary.

110. It's worth stressing that Bentall's theory indispensably requiring intrinsic characterizations of hallucinations is hardly eccentric to him. It's endemic to the field. Indeed, the specific content of hallucinations, and how it varies across cultures and across syndromes, is recognized as driving much of the research in this area. See Aleman and Larøi (2008), 179. Also, Collerton et al. (2005), 742, write, summarizing the literature on this:

> Hallucinations of people tend to be more common than are those of animals. Images of objects such as tables or cars are the least frequent. Unrecognised images are hallucinated as frequently as or more so than familiar ones. . . . There is often a stereotyped or repetitive quality to the images. Commonly, the same image repeats itself on different occasions, though over time, many patients will experience a range of hallucinatory images. There is generally movement, although this is often stereotyped and restricted. The images rarely interact with or respond to the environment. The image is usually whole and sharply focused. It is normal sized or unusually small with a normal or unusually vivid colour. If there is distortion, this is usually of the face with a consistent exaggeration of the mouth and eye areas.

Finally, when Collerton et al. (2005), 745, place requirements on what a "good general model" should account for, they include that: "it needs to account for the phenomenology of [recurrent complex visual hallucinations]: for the frequency of hallucinations of people and animals; for their abrupt onset and offset, and their movement; for temporal and situational regularities where they exist; and last, for their extinction with eye closure."

I conclude this section with an explicit application of the lessons of this chapter to the argument from hallucination. One version of the argument goes like this.[111] Given a case c where a subject S sees an object o, and sees that it has certain properties P, it's possible for there to be a case c' that is subjectively indistinguishable from c, where in place of o there is nothing at all. In describing c' as subjectively indistinguishable from c (for S), it's being claimed that it's not possible for S to tell that he is not in c by introspection alone.[112]

The argument from hallucination relies crucially on three premises, all of which have been challenged (by one philosopher or another). The first (the awareness premise) is that in case c', S sees (is aware of) *something*, something immaterial. "Immaterial," here, is operating as a foil for what S can see in c: the object o. There is no object o in case c'; what S sees (what S is aware of), which he finds introspectively indistinguishable from o, is the immaterial something that he sees. The second premise (the generalizing premise) is that what S sees (is aware of), in c', is the same kind of thing that he sees (is aware of) in c. Furthermore (the conflict premise), if S sees (is aware of) in c what he sees (is aware of) in c', then he doesn't see (isn't aware of) the object o.

Byrne and Logue (2008, 63) note: "On the usual diagnosis, the argument is unsound because the [awareness premise] is false . . . one may hallucinate a red tomato, even though one sees nothing at all." They add, however, of the awareness premise, that although it "is widely thought to be false, in both its illusory and hallucinatory versions, there is at least a case to be made for the hallucinatory version," and then they drop a note to Smith (2002, 195).

Let's pursue the considerations that Smith raises and see what the foregoing discussion in this book allows us to make of them. Smith (2002, 195) writes:

> The claim that a hallucinating person is aware of *nothing whatever* seems initially preposterous. Consider your present perceptual state: you are certainly aware of something. Now consider the possible hallucinatory course of experience that is qualitatively identical to your present one. It would, for such a subject, be subjectively *exactly* as it is for you now. This subject, if asked to report on what he was aware of, would reply just as you would now. This subject too can shift his attention from one to another part of his visual field, or from what he sees to what he is hearing; he can scrutinize objects more closely and can describe what he is aware of. Such reports would not be merely make-believe. Does the subject not say what he does because he is aware of things possessing a manifest phenomenal character? Here Broad's question comes back with full force: if such a hallucinating subject is not aware of anything, why does he say that he sees a page of print, as opposed to a motor-car or nothing at all?

---

111. See Byrne and Logue (2008). Also see Smith (2002), 193, and the pages that follow.

112. Refinements and elucidations are possible. See Byrne and Logue (2008), 58. I forgo these details because they aren't pertinent to the points I need to make. Notice, though, that the temporal spread of c and c' may have to be sharply defined.

Like the many philosophers Byrne and Logue allude to, I also reject the awareness premise; but I also want to bring to bear tools that dislodge the intuitions that Smith (in the above quotation, and as quoted earlier, (224)) uses against those who reject that premise. There is nothing, no object—not even a Meinongian one—in view when Macbeth hallucinates a dagger. But he is aware of *something*, one protests. Yes, but this is awareness[e], not awareness[r]. Indeed, the content of his experience is characterizable in ways indistinguishable from the experience of a Macbeth in an introspectively indistinguishable situation, where his experience is "veridical."

But if there are no objects that he is aware[r] of, what makes statements about what he's seeing true or false? His experience "makes" such statements true and false, just as the phenomenology indicates. (Or, more accurately, the psychological states that determine that experience is what "makes" such statements true and false.) But this experience is not a truth maker of statements that describe[e] the contents of that experience. No more are the objects he experiences[e] truth makers. There are no truth makers for statements about Macbeth's hallucinations. Rather, his experience (the psychological states he's in) are the truth-value inducers of the true (and false) statements about his hallucinations, for example, that Macbeth is seeing[e] a dagger (and not seeing[e] a cat).

Finally, it must be stressed yet one more time that the awareness premise involves an illegitimate slide from Macbeth's awareness[e] of a dagger to his awareness[r] of something mind-dependent (a sense datum, an immaterial something, etc.). He is aware[r] of nothing, although there are many truths about what he is aware[e] of, just as the true statement "Pegasus was worshiped by the ancient Greeks," is about[r] nothing at all, even though it's simultaneously about[e] Pegasus.

2.12 Two Loose Ends: Failures of Thought and Total (Reality-Free) Hallucinations

(I) A distinctive aspect of Evans's (1982) study is the exposure of a surprising kind of liability that thought, statement—and more generally experience—is open to. This is that, despite appearances—despite how it seems to the speaker (or thinker)—a thought (apparently) directed toward something can fail to be a genuine thought precisely because the something in question doesn't exist. In denying Evans's claim that this sort of liability holds with respect to hallucinatory thought and speech (and experience), I don't want to further claim that in general "information-based thought" is not open to these kinds of liabilities. That is, I don't adhere "to a conception of the mind as a repository whose contents are unmistakably accessible to us"—Evans (199)—nor do I think ordinary intuitions about the contents of one's own mind adheres to any such view. Attempted thought can indeed fail: there can be something we direct our thinking toward, but due to untoward circumstances we don't succeed in having a coherent thought. Although hallucinations needn't be (and aren't) this kind of case, pace Evans, other kinds of cases do arise. For example:[113]

---

113. These are all drawn, one way or another, from Evans (1982).

(i)   I'm thinking of Alice—"someone" I've met; in fact, I've met twins (that I don't know are twins) who jointly are the sources of my thoughts about "Alice." Sometimes I've been in the presence of one, and sometimes in the presence of the other; and this was the case even on the first day I met "Alice." (The twins like tricking the people they meet right from the start.) I think, on occasion, that "Alice is pretty." Such occasions, perhaps, are not ones on which I've successfully entertained a coherent thought. When apprised of the real situation, I would redescribe myself as regarding both of them as pretty; but I would still admit that there is a problem in describing accurately what it was I had thought before (when still under the misapprehension that the twins were one person).

(ii)   Unbeknownst to me, as I walk—on various occasions—past what I take to be the same lamp, sometimes it's a real lamp that I see, and sometime it's a hologram. I nevertheless speak of "that lamp in the guestroom" but there isn't one thing I'm (successfully) talking about. My thoughts directed towards "that lamp" fail to be coherent.

(iii)   [114] I'm lying in a bed, thinking "how quiet it is here." But I don't realize that the bed is on oiled wheels, and actually moving along a track rather quickly. My use of "here" misfires; there is no "here" that I've succeed in thinking of.

(iv)   [115] I'm trying to think of a particular object—an animal in the distant brush that I'm tracking with my eyes. But there are several identical-looking animals moving in that brush, and I fail—without realizing it—to continuously focus on only one. My thought, "what a clever animal that is," fails. I have "no thought," in the words of Evans.

Notice, in sharp contrast to the hallucination cases that I've discussed, that the thought and statement failures attributed to the attempted thoughts and statements in these cases are intuitively right: we recognize that the thoughts in question are of nothing, that they fail; at least we do so once the true state of affairs is described. But it's very striking (and, I think, significant) that intuition doesn't accept a corresponding failure of thought in cases of hallucinations or fictions, for example, a child's discovery that there is no Santa Claus. Ordinary intuitions seem responsive only to the acceptance of a failure in thought and statement when uniqueness lapses and not when existence does. Since the suitability—indeed, the truth-aptness—of a discourse doesn't turn on the metaphysics of whether or not terms in that discourse refer[r], these intuitions aren't methodologically untrustworthy.

(II) I've largely concerned myself in this chapter with a case—the experimental setting of section 2.4—where the hallucinations being studied are relatively well behaved with respect to the objective order of things. That is, the hallucinated objects present themselves as having properties that—for the most part—operate coherently within the space-time frame of reality. (I've allowed hallucinated objects to suddenly vanish—as a way for S to become definitive that the object he's seeing is an hallucinated one.) But of course, such generally good

114. Evans, 6.3.
115. Evans, 175–76.

behavior on the part of hallucinations needn't be the case. My point has been, where it is present that the hallucinatory discourse shared by the experimenters and S must take a certain form. But hallucinations can be quite disordered—and in that case there may be no easy way to describe them as occurring in the framework of objective order; indeed, it will be quite undesirable to so describe them if that doesn't respect the content of the hallucinator's experience.[116] What properties such hallucinated objects present themselves as having must be described differently: they are not presented as in (current) space and time but perhaps as "relived memories" or something like that. In some cases they may simply have to be described as sensorily presented—any attempt to characterize them as objects, or as objects located somewhere or other, fails.

The systematic hallucinations of a disembodied brain in a vat (in sceptical thought experiments) are yet another matter entirely. Here it's appropriate to describe not only the objects the brain (seems to) see as hallucinated but the spatial and temporal frame of such objects is hallucinated as well.[117] It's an interesting question whether the brain's use of—in its thought—"here" misfire as Evans (153)[118] suggests, or if instead it should be seen as successfully referring^e to an hallucinated "here." Such a view about a possible use of "here" would correspond to the singular referring^e to hallucinated objects described in this chapter. I actually think this is the right perspective; I won't argue for it now. "Here," and perhaps "now" as well, are terms that can successfully be about^e an hallucinated here and even an hallucinated now.

2.13 Concluding Remarks

The temptation to treat hallucinatory experience as contentless has its ultimate source in views that object-dependent thought and experience must be incomplete—not genuine—if there are no objects targeted. Thus the motives for the view are ultimately semantic—turning on a certain program for how the semantics of demonstratives, genuine names, and the thoughts corresponding to sentences utilizing such things must be. No wonder, therefore, that such a view fits so badly not only with the insights of mere introspection but, more ominously, with the research assumptions of the psychological sciences. This provides more motivation for the empty singular view of demonstratives and names—a view that provides a way out of what would otherwise be a deadlock between the demands of semantics and the demands of the psychological sciences.

Still, some may be unsatisfied. Even if the external discourse demand shows that we must treat the content of hallucinations in a truth-apt way, why doesn't

116. The hallucinations induced during the surgical operations described by Penfield and Perot (1963) look this way. Usually, the patient remains aware of the surgical setting and the individuals located there and describes the induced hallucinations as "like a dream." On the other hand, some out-of-body experiences aren't "like dreams" at all. The person really experiences him- or herself as floating above his or her body, that is, as located in a specific place in the objective order.

117. Well, at least the spatial frame is hallucinated. The temporal frame may or may not have to be treated as hallucinated. I'll be leaving aside explicit discussion of the temporal wrinkle in what follows.

118. Also see John McDowell, "Singular thought and inner space," in *Subject, thought, and context*, ed. Philip Pettit and John McDowell (Oxford: Oxford University Press, 1986), 137–68.

this prove the Meinongian (or the realist) to be right? After all, on my view, about-ness[e] isn't a relation. So we still have the problem of getting what the statement says (about[e]) the hallucinated object to correspond to the content of that hallucination. How can a statement about[e] an hallucinated object be true (match how the object is) or be false (fail to match how the object is)?[119]

Nothing can be easier. I am, let's say, a highly skilled artist. (Suppose, for illustration's sake, that my name is Goya.) I have a series of nightmares involving strange, frightening nonexistent beings. I paint those beings accurately. Doing so requires the content of my paintings to parallel the content of my dreams, including how those dreams depict such nonexistent beings to be individuated from one another. A less skilled artist (than I am) would get the dreams wrong. All of this makes entire sense without the need to posit—in any way—objects that are what my dreams are about (that the images in my dreams are to refer to).

Similarly in the case of S's hallucinations and what he says (and others say) about[e] their content, a parallel is called for between the statements in question and the experiences. Such a parallel isn't co-reference[r]. Fine (an irritated opponent might say), it's not co-reference[r]. What *is* it, then? It's a correlation between the content of one's (perceptual) experience and the content of sentences. Such a correlation, in the case where one is seeing objects, occurs by the term picking out what the person sees (where "what" is an ontologically innocent phrase indicating[e] via an aspect of the content in question). But the mechanism for doing so, we might imagine, occurs by the term (in a sentence) deferring reference[(r/e)] to perception. If so, the deference will take place even if perception fails (i.e., even if hallucination occurs). Like the case of the nightmares, where the artist "draws what he sees," what that artist has drawn is no more of anything than what he dreamed was. Nevertheless, the nightmares and the paintings are about[e] the same nightmare objects because the artist has deliberately correlated their content. Exactly the same is true in the case where S (and others) talk about[e] the objects in his hallucinations. The content of the talk is deliberately (stipulated) to be correlated with S's experiences.[120] This correlation, of course, takes place off-stage as far as the semantics of the sentences (their quantifiers, and their empty singular terms) are concerned. That should be no surprise if language (in this case) defers reference[r] (and reference[e]) to perception.[121]

The Meinongian wants there to be hallucinated (and nightmare) objects; but such things are referentially idle. I've already explained how co-reference[e] and aboutness[e] can occur without bringing those things into the picture.

119. Recollect Smith's (2002, 260) worry about there being "no *truth* at all as to the nature of the intentional object of which Macbeth was aware," discussed in section 1.7.

120. Notice that the correlation of content doesn't require a perfect correlation of the content of the sentences about hallucinated objects with that experience. Nor is such required in the case of the artist. The artist may paint one of his nightmare beings as doing something different from how that being acted in his dreams. Co-reference[e] relies on a correlation; but it isn't required that the contents in question be parallel in *every* respect. (In what respects can such correlations of content differ and yet still be regarded as involving co-reference[e]? To some extent, the matter is arbitrary—but it does turn on (it's parasitic on) the ordinary ways we categorize the appearances of objects we see as appearances of the same object. Recall the discussion of this in section 2.10.)

121. See chapter 5 for further discussion.

Fictions

3.0 An Overview for Browsers, Grazers, and People Who Need to Know What's Coming ahead of Time

Fictional discourse is subtle because truth-apt discourse containing fictional (vacuous) terms is built on a practice of fictional utterances that are not truth-apt. I thus distinguish fiction-internal statements from fiction-external statements. I then describe the drawbacks of paraphrase and pretence approaches to fiction-external statements (they can't handle the quantificational structure required of fiction-external statements—that quantification into fictional contexts is needed—nor can they handle the external discourse demand). I also describe a distinction between a fictional object being depicted as such and so in a work of fiction, and it's actually being such-and-so. In section 3.2, I compare my approach of characterizing fictional beings as having the property of being depicted in fictional works as such-and-so with van Inwagen's ascription relation. I then provide arguments that establish that fictional names are (empty) singular rather than descriptive.

In section 3.3 I turn to questions of identity and nonidentity statements about[e] fictional objects (both transepisodically: within fictions; and transtextually: across fictions). The degree to which such identity claims are arbitrary and open to alternative ways of construing characters as identical is explored. The degree of arbitrariness is far greater than most philosophers who discuss fictional entities (e.g., Parsons, Thomasson, Zalta) recognize. Nevertheless, it's shown that the arbitrariness of "identity conditions" comports successfully with an otherwise consistent practice of using truth-apt fiction-external statements. (In this respect, fictional discourse resembles mathematical discourse which also enjoys a striking amount of arbitrariness in how abstracta may or may not be identified with one another.)

3.1 Truth and Falsity Simpliciter

We knowingly use some names as the names of characters in literary fictions ("Anna Karenina," "Sherlock Holmes," "Jacob Horner"), some names as the names of fictional characters that have appeared on film or on television or in animation ("Mickey Mouse," "Lassie," "Cole Turner"), and some as names of characters that have appeared in both literary fictions and in movies and/or on television ("Sherlock Holmes," "Lassie," "Scrooge"). There are also the names we recognize to be "mythical names" of characters that we know some people to have once believed in ("Zeus," "Hercules," "Eden"), and some that we recognize to be myths that (very likely) no one ever believed in, right from beginning of their inception into public mythology ("Santa Claus," "Paul Bunyan," "Kilroy"). Some of these characters have also appeared in literary fictions, as well as in movies and on television ("Santa Claus," "Paul Bunyan," "Hercules"). Finally, not all the names that appear in literary fictions, movies and television are "fictional" ones—some real people are presented in fictions, and their names, when used in the fictions, refer[r] to them nevertheless.

I don't mean to claim that I've covered every sort of empty name in the previous paragraph. There are also those names of comic book characters ("Spider-Man," "Brenda Lee"), some of which have appeared in other media, such as film, and some of which haven't. Different perhaps, but equally empty, are those names that—despite their coiners hoping otherwise—are empty because whatever it was they were supposed to refer[r] to failed to exist ("Vulcan," "Bigfoot").[1] I'll call the above described class of names "empty names" or "fictional names."[2] I'll similarly describe myths, literary fictions, film, and so on, under the general labels "fictions" or "fictional works."

---

1. Names are ubiquitous in fictionalizing; demonstratives are not. But demonstrations—of fictional creatures—can occur. It's quite natural to point at a character in an animated feature—say, one in which Mickey Mouse suddenly appears—and delightedly say, *"That's* Mickey Mouse." Compare pointing at someone real seen on the television, and saying, *"That's* the president of the United States." Both demonstrations seem to be standard ones that are directed at the persons named and/or described, and not at the distribution of light and dark on the television screen. It looks like the limited role of demonstratives in fiction has more to do with the nature of the medium—that it's composed of sentences, and nothing visual that one can point at—than it has to do with anything specific to demonstratives and in contrast to names. Were a form of storytelling to develop that involved holograms (projected into one's living room) acting out their story, one could easily find oneself pointing at one or another hologram character and saying things about them. Nevertheless, I'll focus entirely on (singular) names in this chapter.

2. David Braun, "Empty names, fictional names, mythical names," *Noûs* 39 (2005), 620, note 3, objects to the term "empty name" because "it suggests that non-referring names are empty of meaning." I don't hear that implication in the terminology in question; in any case, I'm largely neutral in this book about issues of meaning. I've also wrenched terminology a bit by including names from mythology among what I call "fictional names."

Pretence-construing all uses of fictional names is very tempting; but it won't work. To show this, let's start with the observation that the sentences utilized—in both performed and in written fictions—aren't truth-apt.[3] The actors, in film and on stage, aren't held responsible for misleading the audience about the personal histories of the characters they depict or the ordinary facts of their lives as they say them to be. Remarkably, this is even true of films (excluding documentaries) where the phrase "This film is based on true events" appears on screen. That phrase, more than anything else, seems to provide a license for deviating (sometimes greatly) from those true events. Similarly, when a novelist writes the sentence, "It was a cold day in March. Robert had nonetheless resolved to travel north," she is in "storytelling mode." She is "as if" stating facts. She is engaged in an official form of "pretence."[4] Call the statements utilized in fictions, in this truth-aptless way, "fiction-internal statements."

Here are some examples.

(1)   James Bond, with two double bourbons inside him, sat in the final departure lounge of Miami Airport and thought about life and death.[5]

(2)   The following Tale was found among the papers of the late Diedrich Knickerbocker, an old gentleman of New York, who was very curious in the Dutch history of the province, and the manners of the descendants from its primitive settlers.[6]

3. As noted by Alvin Plantinga, *The nature of necessity* (Oxford: Oxford University Press, 1974), 159–63; J. O. Urmson, "Fiction," *American Philosophical Quarterly* 13 (1976), 153–57; and Peter van Inwagen, "Creatures of fiction" (1977), in *Ontology, identity, and modality* (Cambridge: Cambridge University Press, 2001), 41–42. Harry Deutsch ("Making up stories," in *Empty names, fiction and the puzzles of non-existence*, ed. Anthony Everett and Thomas Hofweber [Stanford, Calif.: CSLI Publications, 2000], 154–55), by contrast, claims that fictional passages (e.g., the opening pages of Fitzgerald's *Tender Is the Night*) truthfully describe objects in the "fictional plenitude." This is a bizarre view: fiction isn't involved in straight description at all, because fictional passages aren't presented as truth-apt (they're fictionally presented as truth-apt). Passages in written fictions are meant—of course—to look as if they're describing some past, present, or future state of affairs (that's what writing fiction is all about); but surely Deutsch's suggestion doesn't even match the fictional pretence with respect to visual fictions—for example, plays and movies. The pretence, in those cases, is enacted right in front of us: The actors point at one another, and pretend to attribute things to one another (among other things). It seems peculiar to say that what actors say when they point at one another is true of other items in the fictional plenitude. Deutsch has mischaracterized the "speech acts" involved in the various fictional practices.

4. Two complications. First, the sentences in a fiction not being truth-apt still seems to make cogent a fiction being attacked on the grounds that it fails to present a certain group of people "fairly," that is, truthfully. Because these sorts of charges are common, there may be ways of making sense of the idea that fictionalizing involves the presentation of "truths" by the author (e.g., by a "subtext" or perhaps by Gricean implicatures). In what follows, I set this topic aside. (See, however, David Lewis, "Postscripts to 'Truth in Fiction,'" in *Philosophical papers*, vol. 1 [Oxford: Oxford University Press, 1983], 276.) Second, a writer of fiction is "telling a story." To describe this as a "pretence," and thus assimilate it to the way that children playing a game is considered a "pretence," is sloppy categorizing. Nevertheless, the assimilation is common, and I'll sometimes acquiesce in this way of talking (as I already have earlier). The central point, however, is that the statements that occur in a fiction are not seen by cogent consumers of fiction as truth-apt. (Crazy people and/or philosophers, of course, are always a different matter.) Charles Crittenden (*Unreality: The metaphysics of fictional objects* [Ithaca, N.Y.: Cornell University Press, 1991], 49–51) makes a big deal of the psychological mismatch between real cases of pretence, and the very different storytelling practices we engage in. Nevertheless, and despite what he seems to think, sloppy terminology isn't fatal to what the pretence theorist is after: "Pretence" can instead be seen as specialized terminology that the pretence theorist has inducted for a general description of the claim that storytelling isn't truth-apt. It's the non–truth-aptness of fictional discourse that's crucial to the "pretence" position, and not whether the word "pretence" is misused.

5. Ian Fleming, *Goldfinger* (1959; 10th printing, London: Pan Books, 1961), 7.

6. Washington Irving, *Rip van Winkel and The legend of sleepy hollow* (1820; rpt., New York: Penguin Books, 1995), 1.

(3) The fire in my study smokes. It is not merely that the Bursar buys green wood; something is amiss with the chimney. Sometimes it smokes so much that I feel like those Jesuit missionaries who used to fling themselves on the floor in the longhouses of the Canadian Indians, because only within six inches of the floor could one breathe the air without tearing the lungs.[7]

It's not as if some instances of these statements, for example, "The fire in my study smokes," can't be truth-apt in other contexts. It's that none of these instances are truth-apt because of the particular kind of "speech-act" that's being engaged in by the writer. Actual truth and falsity is irrelevant. The fictional narrative (3) succeeds whether or not there actually were Jesuit missionaries who flung themselves on the floor in the longhouses of some Canadian Indians so that they could breathe. Similarly, there could actually have been a "Diedrich Knickerbocker" who was interested in the early history of New York. None of this matters. It's not that fictionalizing of all sorts involves the production of falsehoods; it's that truth and falsity aren't the point of the storytelling practice to begin with. Thus, even if the name "George W. Bush," appears in a fiction, and even if in such fictions the name "George W. Bush" is understood to refer to a former president of the United States, it's not the case that the statements occurring in that fiction are therefore truth-apt. Even if the sentence "George W. Bush was president of the United States in 2001," occurs in a fiction, it doesn't follow that the instance of the sentence—as it occurs in that fiction—is truth-apt. For one thing, it may be flanked by false storytelling statements. But the crucial point to stress again is not that falsehoods usually occur in storytelling contexts; it's that a story is being told and that the occurrence of such an event (a movie taking place, a short story being read, etc.) disarms the relevance of the possible truth-aptness of the statements that are used during such events.[8]

As has been noticed by philosophers, however, there is a kind of pretended truth-aptness that distinguishes the fiction-internal statements within each fiction. "Diedrich Knickerbocker is an old gentleman of New York," is pretended-true in Irving's fiction; "The scrupulous accuracy of Diedrich Knickerbocker's work should be questioned," is pretended-false (and pretended argued against) in that same fiction. "Zeus can throw lightning bolts," is pretended-true when contemporary nonbelievers present or enact Greek myths about Zeus; "Zeus can create an ocean storm at will," may be pretended-false in those same presentations or enactments. Such fiction-internal statements shouldn't be restricted to statements that actually occur in a literary fiction; they should include content from the visual depictions that occur in film, animation, and television.[9]

---

7. Robertson Davies, "Revelation from a smoky fire" (1982), in *A gathering of ghost stories* (New York: Penguin Books, 1995), 10.

8. This doesn't make inappropriate one's asking "did that really happen?" during a movie. This is a question about what one can say—later and truthfully—outside storytelling contexts.

9. There are subtleties in the details of how visual depictions—or the sentential vehicles corresponding to them—are to be treated as pretended-true; further analysis would be a digression.

The fiction-internal statements of a fiction aren't exhaustively divided into those pretended-true and those pretended-false. Any fiction necessarily leaves many things (perhaps most things) about characters, events, and so on, both unstated and unshown. We can extend the fiction-internal statements of a fiction, beyond what's explicitly stated or shown in that fiction, to include these unstated things that are pretended-implied by what's explicitly said or shown. So, for example, we can take it that it has been pretended-implied by (1) that James Bond first drank one double bourbon and then another (rather than having drunk them simultaneously, one in each hand, or having ingested the double bourbons via a hypodermic needle). We can similarly take it as pretended-implied by (2) that "It's not the case that Diedrich Knickerbocker is an old gentleman of London." The fiction-internal statements of a fiction can be regarded as closed under the pretended implication relation of that fiction, using its explicitly stated fiction-internal statements as a base.[10] In this way, we may say that "Sherlock Holmes lived on 221B Baker Street," is pretended-true in the Conan Doyle stories, even if that very sentence doesn't appear in any of Conan Doyle's fiction, but is only pretended-implied by sentences that do appear in that fiction; so, too, "Sherlock Holmes lives on Park Avenue South, in New York," is pretended-false.[11]

I'm not going to concern myself with further niceties regarding the right way to construe pretended truth-aptness, as it arises among fiction-internal statements, for example, the official introduction of operators such as *pretended-true* and *pretended-false* and their properties. My concern, rather, is with statements about[e] fictional objects that seem to be true and false simpliciter—despite their nonexistent topic matter. As many philosophers have noted,[12] there are many statements that both use fictional names and that involve quantifications over fictional creatures but that appear to be very different from the fiction-internal statements that either explicitly occur in or during a fiction or that are pretended-implied by the explicitly occurring fiction-internal statements of that fiction. In contrast to fiction-internal statements, these "fiction-external statements" seem to be truth-apt in exactly the same way that other truth-apt statements are.

10. I've relativized pretended-implication to fictions, just as pretended-truth and pretended-falsity have been so relativized, because the "implications" licensed by a particular fiction can be quite nonstandard and idiosyncratic. Perhaps "implication" isn't even the right word. I'm not only alluding to the evident inconsistencies most fictions involve; I'm speaking of the deliberate wrenchings of "logic" that also occur in a great deal of fictional work. I'm not claiming, in any case, that closure of the pretended-true and pretended-false statements of a fiction under its "implication-relation" will always result in something well defined. Pretences can be—and often are—very sloppy in what they come to.

11. In Jody Azzouni, *Deflating existential consequence: A case for nominalism* (Oxford: Oxford University Press, 2004a), 90, where I deny the truth of "Sherlock Holmes lived in London in the late 19th century," I'm indicating explicitly that statements made within fictions, or perhaps more accurately during fictions—and those pretend-implied by such—aren't truth-apt. That doesn't mean, of course, that corresponding statements about the content of those fictions, for example, "Sherlock Holmes is depicted in the fiction of Conan Doyle as living in London in the late 19th century," aren't truth-apt. See what's forthcoming. Pace Gideon Rosen, "Review of 'Deflating existential consequence: A case for nominalism,'" *Journal of Philosophy* 103 (2006), 314, it's important not to confuse fiction-internal statements from what I shortly call fiction-external statements.

12. Among others, van Inwagen (1977), 41–42; Crittenden (1991), 94–98; Amie L. Thomasson, *Fiction and metaphysics* (Cambridge: Cambridge University Press, 1999), 97–99.

Among such fiction-external statements are the negative existentials: "Zeus doesn't exist," "Sherlock Holmes doesn't exist," and so on. Were these (and the various truth-functional compositions of them, e.g., negations of them) the only fiction-external statements involving empty names that seemed to be true or false simpliciter, a number of approaches for handling them that are already in the literature[13] would be promising. There is the metalinguistic approach, treating such statements as—contrary to appearances—describing certain concepts as uninstantiated; there is the possibility that names not only contribute their referents to the semantics of the sentences they appear in but also contribute whether or not they have referents[r]. And a number of theorists think that taking such negative existentials to be only pretended-true will work.[14] Such approaches presume that all empty names make the same contribution to the truth values of all the statements they appear in. Thus, "Pegasus doesn't exist," and "Sherlock Holmes doesn't exist," can both be regarded as true (or pretended-true) on similar grounds: the subject term contributes exactly the same thing—whatever that is—to the semantics of the sentences in question.[15]

The immediate issue facing any such broad-stroke solution to the problem of negative existentials is that such don't admit of a needed generalization to the class of fiction-external statements that seem to be about fictional creatures, and that seem to be true (or false) simpliciter. This class of statements goes well beyond the negative existentials. To begin with, there are those statements that closely track the content of fiction-internal statements. For example,

(4)   James Bond is depicted in the first paragraph of the novel *Goldfinger* as having had two double bourbons and as contemplating life and death.

(5)   Diedrich Knickerbocker is portrayed in the fiction of Washington Irving as having died and as having had an interest in early New York.

(6)   The narrator of the short story "Revelation from a Smoky Fire" is depicted as presenting himself as believing that his study has a defective chimney.

---

13. For example, Keith Donnellan, "Speaking of nothing," *Philosophical Review* 83 (1974), 3–32, reprinted in *Naming, necessity, and natural kinds*, ed. Stephen P. Schwartz (Ithaca, N.Y.: Cornell University Press, 1977), 216–44, page citations are to the latter; Gareth Evans, *The varieties of reference* (Oxford: Oxford University Press, 1982); R. M. Sainsbury, *Reference without referents* (Oxford: Oxford University Press, 2005).

14. See Fred Kroon, "Negative existentials," in *Empty names, fiction and the puzzles of non-existence*, ed. Anthony Everett and Thomas Hofweber (Stanford, Calif.: CSLI Publications, 2000), 95–116; and Kendall L. Walton, "Existence as metaphor?" in *Empty names, fiction and the puzzles of nonexistence*, ed. Anthony Everett and Thomas Hofweber (Stanford, Calif.: CSLI Publications, 2000), 235–47. Also see Evans (1982), and a criticism of his approach by Michael Dummett, "Existence," in *The seas of language* (Oxford: Oxford University Press, 1993), 277–307.

15. A problem looms, however. the apparently different subject matters of different negative existentials. A form of this problem is the apparent co-referentiality of some empty names ("Santa Claus," "Father Christmas,") and not others. See David Braun, "Empty names," *Noûs* 27 (1993), 443–69; Anthony Everett, "Referentialism and empty names," in *Empty names, fiction and the puzzles of non-existence*, ed. Anthony Everett and Thomas Hofweber (Stanford, Calif.: CSLI Publications, 2000), 37–60; Kenneth A. Taylor, "Emptiness without compromise: A referentialist semantics for empty names," in *Empty names, fiction and the puzzles of non-existence*, ed. Anthony Everett and Thomas Hofweber (Stanford, Calif.: CSLI Publications, 2000), 17–36, for discussion. The issue I concern myself with—in the text following the sentence this note is appended to—somewhat includes this problem as a special case. But see section 3.3 for further discussion.

So, too, "Hamlet is a prince," may be pretended-true, but "Hamlet is portrayed as a prince in Shakespeare's play *Hamlet*," seems to be true simpliciter. False, and indeed false simpliciter, is "Hamlet is portrayed as a ghost in Shakespeare's play *Hamlet*," although this is true simpliciter of another character portrayed in *Hamlet*. Also true simpliciter are: "Hamlet appears in *Hamlet* and *Rosencrantz and Guildenstern Are Dead*," "Mr. Pickwick is a fictional character," and "Emma Woodhouse was created by Jane Austen."[16] True simpliciter is "Pegasus is the winged horse of Greek mythology"; false simpliciter is "Zeus is the winged horse of Greek mythology."[17] Still other illustrations are: "Mrs. Sarah Gamp . . . is the most fully developed of the masculine anti-women visible in all Dickens's novels,"[18] "The most famous detective, living or dead, fictional or real, is Sherlock Holmes," "Although Sherlock Holmes does not exist, his personality, as depicted in Conan Doyle's short stories, was based on someone real that Conan Doyle knew well."[19]

It's important to note that fictional names operate in an entirely normal fashion vis-à-vis quantification. For example, from "Mr. Pickwick is a fictional character," it follows that "There are fictional characters."[20] And quite intricate deductions—using quantification over fictional objects from outside "according-to-the story" operators—occur with respect to fictional characters. Thus,[21] from "There is a fictional character who, for every novel, either appears in that novel or is a model for a character who does," it follows that "If no character appears in every novel, then some character is modeled on another character." The first statement is implied by "Sancho Panza serves as a model for at least one character in every novel except for the novel *Don Quixote*."

It's also worth noting that quantification over fictional characters, and the use of fictional names, occur naturally in tandem with both quantification over real things, and the use of nonfictional names. For example, "In William Gaddis's *Recognitions*, Hemingway is depicted as being present at the bar of a restaurant where Otto and Esme, and other fictional characters, are having dinner," and, "Whenever a fictional character is depicted as talking to a real person in a novel, that real person needn't be depicted as speaking in the way that he or she really did in life."

Van Inwagen (2000) claims that the ineliminability of quantifications over fictional entities in various (indispensable) deductions requires an ontological

16. These examples are due to Thomasson (1999), 95.

17. These examples are due to Terence Parsons (*Nonexistent objects* [New Haven, Conn.: Yale University Press, 1980], 37).

18. Sylvia Bank Manning, *Dickens as satirist* (New Haven: Yale University Press, 1971), 79. Cited by van Inwagen (1977), 41.

19. Everett (2000), 38, calls (4), (5), and (6), and other sentences like them, "metafictional" (as many philosophers do), and distinguishes them from sentences like "Sherlock Holmes doesn't exist," which he doesn't describe as metafictional but instead as "nonfictional" because they "talk only about the real world and not about fictional or mythic worlds."

20. Some may be tempted to treat any sentence—just by virtue of containing a fictional name—as inducing an intentional context. Parsons (1980), 33–35, quashes any such view by showing that co-referential(°) substitutions for fictional names are as legitimate as they are in standard extensional contexts, and that existential generalization from such names seems normal as well.

21. Peter van Inwagen, "Quantification and fictional discourse," in *Empty names, fiction and the puzzles of nonexistence*, ed. Anthony Everett and Thomas Hofweber (Stanford, Calif.: CSLI Publications, 2000), 243–44.

commitment to those fictional objects. There is some distance between that conclusion and the premise of the indispensability of such deductions. For my purposes, the concern is only with whether such deductions require the truth-aptness of the statements involved, despite their containing fictional names, and their quantifying over fictional creatures. One strategy for avoiding the indispensability of the truth-aptness of such statements in such deductions is by circumventing the need for statements involving quantification (and the naming of) fictional entities altogether. The paraphrase strategy is one of providing alternative statements that don't name or quantify over fictional entities, but that can nevertheless still serve in the roles for which these fiction-external statements are otherwise needed. That is, the paraphrases must replicate the needed truth-values of the original statements, and they must sustain the same implication (and evidential) relations that the original statements sustain. I'm going to presume that attempts to circumvent the apparent reference to fictional objects (by names and by quantification) via paraphrase won't work. That is, I presume there are no systematic ways of finding suitable replacements of such statements with others that either (i) quantify over or name only ontologically acceptable items such as statements appearing on pages, or more generally, various real artifacts such as films, stories, and so on, or perhaps the content of such; or that (ii) quantify over or name ontologically unacceptable items only within an intensional context such as "In fiction such and such it is depicted that—." The burden—by now—should be firmly on the shoulders of anyone who still thinks paraphrases of this sort have a chance. Too much discussion of the evident drawbacks of extant candidate paraphrases has occurred in the literature over too long a period. I know of no promising options.[22]

Leaving such statements referentially fiction-laden but treating them—despite being fiction-external—as only pseudo-truth-apt remains an option. This option initially looks worse than it is because it's so often accompanied (by way of justification) with the sloppy word "pretence." It's psychologically false, however, to suggest that in claiming "Mr. Pickwick is a fictional character," or "Emma Woodhouse was created by Jane Austen," that one is only pretending (even in some extended sense) to say something true the way one evidently is when claiming—while enacting a fiction—that "Sherlock Holmes lives on 221B Baker Street," or that "Pegasus

---

22. See van Inwagen (1977); Parsons (1980), 32–37; and Thomasson (1999), 94–97, for good discussions of the ways that various paraphrase attempts fail and for further citations. Also see Azzouni (2004a), chapter 3, especially 67–71. It's worth noting that Quine—at least—regarded such paraphrasing as acceptable only because he regarded fiction-external statements about fictional objects as "don't cares": he failed to recognize their indispensability to science. (This indispensability is something I illustrate later in this section.) It's also worth noting that most philosophers who regard paraphrase as so failing draw the conclusion that the quantifications in question require either Meinongian objects or actual objects that one must be therefore committed to. I draw neither conclusion. See Azzouni (2004a), or, better (since this book is presumably more accessible), see chapter 5.

I should add that my knowing of no promising options doesn't mean that I'm unaware of *new* unpromising options (or the possibility of inventing such). Here's an unpromising option, borrowed from my 2004a, chapter 2: paraphrase any statement S that contains undesirable empty names with

S* All the implications of S without empty names are true.

Consider, however, the two statements: "The Greeks worshiped Zeus," and "The Greeks worshiped Thor." These have, as implications, exactly the same statements that lack the respective words "Zeus" and "Thor." I forgo further attempts at patching this "semantic ascent" approach to paraphrase, and finding counterexamples to the patches.

was captured by Bellerophron." One can still, nevertheless, cogently claim of fiction-external statements that such are only pseudo-true and pseudo-false, and correspondingly, that such are only involved in pseudo-implications. One might argue this on the grounds, for example, that because "Mr. Pickwick" doesn't refer^r, nothing true (or false) can be said using that name. In short, examples of fictional quantification in deductions, and more generally, all the examples of what seem to be true (and false) fiction-external statements—although fatal to the paraphrase strategy—make no direct inroads against a more radical view that treats apparent truth-aptness (and apparent truth-preserving deduction based on such apparent truth-aptness) as entirely pseudo in nature. Further arguments about whether such pseudo-deductive practices are a species of "pretence" or not are only—in my view—so much trafficking with red herrings. The hard polemical work is done by the placing of a reference^r condition on the terms occurring in truth-apt statements, such as: if such statements are genuinely truth-apt, and if they are used in deductions that are genuine, then the names must refer^r (and the quantifications involved have to be ordinary objectual quantifications over real objects). So the argument must go: such isn't the case with fictional "objects," items that don't exist; therefore the apparent truth-aptness of fiction-external statements is only pseudo-truth-aptness, and the deductions engaged with such involve only pseudo-implications.

What ultimately sinks this whole line of thought—pseudo-construing the truth-aptness of fiction-external statements, and pseudo-construing the deductions that include them as steps—is an important requirement on any characterization of fiction-external statements. This is the previously described (in section 2.8) external discourse demand. Statements like, "Hamlet appears in *Hamlet* and *Rosencrantz and Guildenstern Are Dead*," "Emma Woodhouse was created by Jane Austen," and the many statements like them, state facts that empirically confirm statements that aren't about fictions in any sense. That is, fiction-external statements, when coupled with other statements that aren't about fictions, will imply (for example) biographical and psychological facts about the creators of those fictions. The popularity (or unpopularity) of such fictional objects, how depictions of them evolve over time, what other uses they are put to by subsequent writers and readers, and so on, will empirically confirm sociological generalizations of various sorts. These statements—the ones that are empirically confirmed and that aren't about fictions—are truths and falsities simpliciter, both in the sense that such statements are ordinarily asserted as statements we believe, and in the sense that they, in turn, are used both in further inferences to and as confirming (or disconfirming) evidence for still other statements.

An illustration is helpful. I first observe (again) that the names and quantifiers that appear in these truth-apt statements are ones that must—at least some of the time—operate outside the context of intensional "fictional" operators. Thus, that Sherlock Holmes is depicted in the Conan Doyle stories as living at 221B Baker Street should not—strictly speaking—be described as a metafictional statement.[23] Although such statements are true or false only because of the way that various fictional works are, and not because of how fictional characters are (since there are

---

23. Pace Everett (2000), 38; Taylor (2000), 32.

no such characters), nevertheless—as with hallucinated objects—statements about[e] fictional characters cannot be uniformly regimented like so:

(7)   In the Conan Doyle fictions, it is depicted like so: Sherlock Holmes lives at 221B Baker Street.

To illustrate this claim graphically, and to illustrate a confirmation of a sociological generalization that isn't about fictions, imagine that there is a (bad) movie called *The Hound of Brooklyn Heights*, and:

(8)   In the movie *The Hound of Brooklyn Heights*, it is depicted like so: Sherlock Holmes lives in New York City.

A comparison can be made:

(9)   Sherlock Holmes is depicted in Conan Doyle's fiction as living in London; but he is depicted in the movie *The Hound of Brooklyn Heights* as living in New York.

There could also be a generalization of (9) that's true, such as:

(10)   For any fictional character depicted in a short story as living in London, there is a movie such that he or she is depicted as living in New York.

(10) involves quantification into such depiction contexts and over fictional entities. Despite this, we may find that (10) helps confirm a sociological fact:

(11)   During the 1930s, New Yorkers watched more movies than anyone in any other geographic group in the United States; film producers were sensitive to this demographic fact.

This may provide evidence for:

(12)   During the 1930s, New Yorkers had more discretionary income than any other geographic group in the United States.[24]

---

24. By no means am I attempting genuine sociology by exhibiting this illustrative string of reasoning. But real examples take exactly the same form as my illustration. For examples of how the descriptions of contents of fictions or paintings are utilized to draw conclusions about historical facts, see Fernand Braudel, *Civilization and capitalism: 15th–18th century. Volume 1: The structures of everyday life: The limits of the possible* (New York: Harper & Row, 1981), *Civilization and capitalism: 15th–18th century. Volume 2: The wheels of commerce* (New York: Harper & Row, 1982), and *Civilization and capitalism: 15th–18th century. Volume 3: The perspective of the world* (New York: Harper & Row, 1984). Also see Robert Darton, "Peasants tell tales: The meaning of Mother Goose," in *The great cat massacre and other episodes in French cultural history* (New York: Random House, 1984), 8–72. There are numerous other examples. Crucial to these examples is that their confirmatory value turns on quantifications over the unreal things that are depicted in visual and verbal fictions, that in tandem with nonfictional facts imply or confirm other facts or generalizations.

(7)–(12) illustrate how statements about[e] fictional characters may indispensably provide evidence for or against generalizations having nothing (directly) to do with fiction. The statements in this chain of reasoning cannot be reformulated so that the quantifiers in the statements involved all occur within the scope of fiction operators (of one sort or another). Nor can the force of such confirmations be captured by the idea that false or pretended-true statements can nevertheless be used in science in a confirmatory role. Therefore, to be depicted in such and such a way in a fiction must often involve the attribution of truth-based properties—for example, Being-depicted-as—to fictional things; and because of the possibility of real objects appearing in fictions as well, being depicted in such and such a way must (in principle) also be attributable to real things. Depiction in a fiction, therefore, cannot be construed as a kind of statement operator to be applied only to whole sentences.[25]

Because of the foregoing, to treat fiction-external statements as only "pseudo-true" and "pseudo-false" is to invite the threat of global pseudolatry—an epidemic of fake truth-aptness that must be taken to extend quite beyond the domain of the strictly fictional. Alternatively, should we treat pseudo-truth-aptness along with genuinely true statements as together sustaining genuine (valid) deductive (and confirmatory) relations to nonfictional statements, the special way in which fiction-external statements are supposed to be only pseudo-truth-apt is lost.

I won't say that the pretence theorist is left without resources for a response to the external discourse demand. I *will* say that the options remaining to that theorist are rather unappealing. One move is to bite the bullet: to claim that when pseudo-true statements are used in reasoning together with genuinely true statements, the results are nevertheless validity- and confirmation-preserving. That is, pseudo-truth is indistinguishable from actual truth as far as deduction is concerned, and pseudo-confirmation is similarly indistinguishable from actual confirmation. As just noted, one then legitimately wonders in what sense such statements should be described as pseudo-true (and why the corresponding notions of implication and confirmation that they sustain are only pseudo-implication and pseudo-confirmation).[26]

Another option is to try to show that fiction-external discourse, although not truth-apt, nevertheless has other properties that allow its statements to appear in tandem in reasoning along with nonfictional statements. For example, borrowing

25. As in, for example, David Lewis, "Truth in fiction" (1978), in *Philosophical papers* volume 1 (Oxford: Oxford University Press, 1983), 261–75. Lewis's approach is an attempt to codify "metafictional statements" within a possible-worlds framework (e.g., "In such and such fiction . . ."). But, as we've seen, fiction-external truths are subject both to the external discourse demand and to the need to take a form wherein quantification into such intentional contexts is allowed. Lewis's approach can't handle these demands. Neither, as has been argued in this section, can pretence views.

26. Part (but only part) of the problem is that the demands on truth and falsity—and notions dependent on such, like implication—are quite minimal. (See Jody Azzouni, *Tracking reason: Proof, consequence, and truth* [Oxford: Oxford University Press, 2006] on this.) This leaves very little wiggle room for notions of pseudo-truth, and notions—like pseudo-implication—based on such. If pseudo-truth is appropriately related to assertion (i.e., by Tarski biconditionals), and it supports deduction, it becomes indistinguishable from the real thing. Here the proponent of pseudo-truth faces the same problem faced by the "truth-pluralist"—that a careful analysis of the role of the truth idiom rules out truth-pluralism. I say more about this in sections 4.8 and 4.9.

a page from Field's nominalist project (1980), one might try to show that fiction-external discourse is "conservative"—that all deductions of statements that aren't about fictions but involve fiction-external statements as steps can be replaced by deductions that yield the same conclusions but don't involve fiction-external statements as steps. There are already good reasons to believe that such a result isn't true of mathematical discourse.[27] There is even less reason to think such an approach would be valuable for truth-apt fictional discourse because fiction-external statements aren't utilized only in strict deductions of nonfictional statements. As illustrated, fiction-external statements are also used to provide confirmatory and disconfirmatory evidence for sociological and psychological nonfictional generalizations.

Two last linked observations to round out this section. Consider fictional-character comparatives, such as "Sherlock Holmes is smarter than Mickey Mouse." Such do seem to be pseudo-true or pretended-true. But they aren't pretended-true by virtue of specific fictions.[28] One first thinks of handling this by positing a systematic pretence practice that extends over all fictions,[29] or by a fiction operator that similarly extends—in some way—over the entire domain of what's talked about in any fiction. This won't work as a general strategy because the class of fictions is so unruly. Someone somewhere might have (just composed) a story or cartoon in which Mickey Mouse is depicted as smarter than Sherlock Holmes. I suggest, alternatively, that one should deny that any fiction-internal pretence is being engaged in when one draws comparisons such as this one. Instead, the ordinary truth-apt fiction-external statement—corresponding to what would have been such a pretended-true statement—should be characterized as one that's an abbreviation for something that's explicit about the fictions involved, for example,

(13)   Sherlock Holmes, as he is depicted in the Conan Doyle stories, is smarter than Mickey Mouse, as he is depicted in (such and such) Disney cartoons.

Such an analysis naturally extends to comparatives between fictional characters and real ones:

27. See Jody Azzouni, "Evading truth commitments: The problem reanalyzed," *Logique et Analyse* 206 (2009c), 9–26. Notice what the project comes to, as applied to fictional discourse. One gives up the project of paraphrasing away fiction-external sentences: the project of replacing them with ontologically innocuous paraphrases that nevertheless yield—in deductions—the same nonfiction conclusions as fiction-external sentences. Instead, one turns directly to the deductions themselves, and plies the strategy of modifying those so that alternative deductions— that imply the same statements needed but within which fiction-external sentences don't appear—may be constructed. Failure of the paraphrase strategy, directed toward fiction-external sentences doesn't automatically imply failure of the paraphrase strategy when directed at entire deductions. What does indicate that failure of the former makes failure of the latter likely is that any global replacement of deductions containing fiction-external statements must be systematic. This does seem to suggest that each fiction-external statement must be replaced (in each deduction) with something else that does the same job but that doesn't quantify over or name fictional objects.

28. I'm presuming that Sherlock Holmes and Mickey Mouse don't appear in the same fictions. That may not be correct, in which case another example may be chosen, or (more radically) fictional characters can simply be invented for which the point being made here is true.

29. Lewis (1983), 276, following Kendall L. Walton, "Fearing fictions," *Journal of Philosophy* 75 (1978) 5–27.

(14)   Sherlock Holmes, as he is depicted in the Conan Doyle stories, is smarter than
George W. Bush (actually) is.

The comparison is between Sherlock Holmes, as he is depicted in a set of stories, and George W. Bush: "is smarter than" doesn't fall within the scope of the depiction of Sherlock Holmes. (14) cannot be reconstrued as:

(15)   As depicted in the Conan Doyle stories: Sherlock Holmes is smarter than
George W. Bush (actually) is.

This is because George W. Bush does not appear in any Conan Doyle stories.[30] In general, these comparisons require the use of fictional names outside the context of fictional operators or pretence operators, such as "It is pretended that —A—," or "In such and such stories, A is depicted as —." They also require treating being-depicted-as-intelligent-in-Conan-Doyle-stories, being-depicted-in-such-and-such-Disney-cartoons-as-a-talking-mouse, and so on, as various kinds of properties to be applied to both real and fictional creatures.[31]

The second observation is this. Consider a sentence such as

(16)   There are fictional mice that talk.[32]

This seems to be truth-apt and, indeed, true. However, it doesn't explicitly refer to any specific fictions. Coupled with:

---

30. Notice that the use of an actuality operator within the scope of a fiction operator that would indicate that the comparison is to be between Bush's intelligence as it actually is (and not as it's depicted in the fiction) won't do. Bush doesn't appear in the fiction.

31. Comparatives like (14) are a little complicated. I'll sketch some observations about them in this note. Presupposed is not only that it makes sense to compare "amounts" or "degrees" of intelligence, as in "Bill Clinton is more intelligent than George W. Bush is," but that it makes sense to compare "degrees" of intelligence had by individuals as they are depicted in different works, for example, "George W. Bush, as he's depicted in the *New York Post*, is more intelligent than he is, as he's depicted in the *New York Times*," or "George W. Bush, as he is depicted in the *New York Post*, is every bit as intelligent as Bill Clinton is, as the latter is depicted in the *New York Times*." This amounts to the comparison of the degrees of two different predicates, both as applied to George W. Bush in the first case: the degree of his intelligence-as-depicted-in-the-*New-York-Post* is being compared to the degree of his intelligence-as-depicted-in-the-*New-York-Times*, and similarly for George W. Bush and Bill Clinton, in the second case. Finally, not only can we compare two different predicates of this sort as applied to two different (actual) persons, we can even make such comparisons between two different creatures that don't exist. For example, we can compare Sherlock Holmes's intelligence-as-depicted-in-Conan-Doyle's-stories with Mickey Mouse's intelligence-as-depicted-in-Disney-cartoons. One last point about this. Each new fictional work—each new work containing depictions (whether fictional or nonfictional)—generates a new but finite set of predicates as described earlier in this note. How we engage in comparisons using them involves an extension of our understanding of how we effect such comparisons generally. So there are no learnability issues that need arise on this picture. Another approach would be to try to treat these comparatives as operating on relations between properties, individuals, and depicting works, for example (intelligence, George Bush, the *New York Post*) is of higher degree than (intelligence, George Bush, the *New York Times*). My purpose in this note has not been, of course, to present, attempt to develop, or adjudicate among general semantic analyses of comparatives of this sort; it's only been to show that comparisons of degrees of depicted properties of fictional characters raise no new or special difficulties.

32. I used this sentence as an example in Azzouni (2004a).

(17)   Fictional mice are mice,

it seems to invite:

(18)   There are mice that talk.

(18) is an undesirable result. To prevent it, we can deny (17), that fictional mice are mice. But then what work is the adjective "fictional" doing in (16)? One tempting suggestion is that (16) is a lazy locution, standing in for:

(19)   There are fictions in which mice are depicted as talking.

But this doesn't say what (16) says. (19) tells us that there are fictions in which mice are depicted as talking; what (16) tells us is that there are certain items— "fictional mice" (e.g., Mickey Mouse) that talk. We need, instead:

(20)   There are objects which are depicted in fictions as mice and as talking.

That is, "fictional mice" can be treated as a lazy locution, but for an implicit "depicted in fictions as ——." An alternative with a different scope for "depicted in fictions as ——" is:

(21)   There are objects which are depicted in fictions as mice, and these objects talk,

where the talking of the fictional mice is attributed to them, but not as what's depicted of them. It seems, however, that it's (20) and not (21) that's usually meant by an utterance of (16).

3.2 Singular Reference in the Context of Fiction

Thus far, fictional discourse has been revealed to be both similar to and dissimilar from hallucinatoric discourse—at least that form of hallucinatoric discourse that was described in chapter 2. There is a natural role for a concept of "pretence"—if broadly construed—in fictions; there really isn't any such natural role for pretence in the case of hallucinations. Correspondingly, there is also a possible role in fictions for a form of pseudo-truth-aptness, and corresponding pseudo-notions, such as pseudo-implication. Again, none of these seem to be valuable for hallucinatoric discourse.

Once, however, fiction-internal statements are clearly distinguished from fiction-external ones, it becomes clear that fiction-external statements, including those that closely track the content of fiction-internal statements, bear the same truth-apt and deductive burdens as statements in hallucinatoric discourse do. Although many fiction-external statements correspond to the pretended-true and pretended-false statements of fictional works, they are genuinely truth-apt for the same reasons that the statements of hallucinatoric discourse must be truth-apt—because of the external discourse demand. And, because of the indispensability of quantification into fictional contexts, there is a distinction to be made between the truth-based properties directly attributed to fictional creatures, such as "being created by Ian Fleming," and those truth-based properties such fictional creatures are only depicted as having in one or another fictional work, for example, "having drunk two double bourbons in an airport." For that matter, many—although not all—fictional creatures are depicted as existing in one or another fictional work. More accurately, given any fictional work, some fictional creatures are depicted in it as existing, some are depicted in it as not existing, and the vast majority are depicted in it neither way.

Being depicted in such and such a way in fictional works are truth-based properties not only to be attributed to fictional creatures; real objects appear in fictional works and are depicted in such and such ways as well. Van Inwagen's (1977) corresponding three-place ascription relation $A(x,y,z)$, where x is a placeholder for properties, y a placeholder for fictional characters, and z a placeholder for specific fictions—for example, A(fatness, Mrs. Gamp, *Martin Chuzzlewit*)—is similar in some ways to my notion of being depicted in such and such a way by a fictional work. But van Inwagen's "ascription relation" officially isn't to apply to real objects that appear in fictional works.[33] His reason for this restriction seems to be that sometimes, when speaking of "Napoleon" in the context of Tolstoy's *War and Peace*, we are speaking not of the actual Napoleon but of a creature of fiction. Van Inwagen regards creatures of fiction as really existing. Even so, nothing I've described in van Inwagen's position forces the name "Napoleon," as it appears in *War and Peace*, to refer to a fictional creature. Perhaps the worry is a potential violation of the principle of the identity of indiscernibles—but Napoleon is depicted in *War and Peace* (in some ways) not as he was in real life. No violation of the principle of identity of indiscernibles occurs by virtue of how someone is depicted to be, should that conflict with how he or she actually is, or even just conflict with how he or she is depicted to be in other fiction (or nonfiction, for that matter). I therefore see no reason for restricting "being depicted in fiction" only to fictional entities.[34]

One way to describe the difference between my "depiction" and van Inwagen's "ascription" is that I understand "depiction" as something that fictional works do. Thus fictional works do the same thing with respect to both fictional and real creatures: make pretended-true and pretended-false statements about[e] and about[f] them. Furthermore, for Napoleon (for example) to be depicted in such and such ways in Tolstoy's *War and Peace* is by virtue of that depiction to have various truth-based properties.[35] Because fictional creatures don't exist, although

33. Van Inwagen (1977), 51.

34. As noted in chapter 2, the same sort of truth-based attributions may be necessary when describing real objects that appear in someone's hallucinations. A real object—a real object seen during the course of an hallucination—can be nevertheless hallucinated as presenting properties and relations it doesn't have.

35. Two points: I am not a presentist. Apart from this, the properties that Napoleon acquires by virtue of Tolstoy writing *War and Peace* are similar to relational properties, such as being such and such millions of miles away from Pluto. They are not properties "intrinsic" to Napoleon, whatever "intrinsic" properties turn out to be. The properties that Napoleon acquires by virtue of Tolstoy's writing *War and Peace* are a species of what were once called *Cambridge properties*.

Napoleon being depicted in *War and Peace* is a genuine relation between something real (Napoleon) and something else that's real (*War and Peace*), this is not the case with Pierre Bezukhov and *War and Peace*, since the latter is a fictional creature.[36]

Another way that I claim fictional discourse to be very like hallucinatoric discourse is in the occurrence of empty singular names within it. It's very tempting, however, to treat names—as they appear in fictions—as purely conceptual, as short for definite descriptions. One reason for this temptation is the philosophical tradition. It's terribly common and somewhat natural to gloss singular negative existentials,

- Sherlock Holmes doesn't exist,
- Pegasus doesn't exist,

that apparently have names of mythological and fictional characters, by one or another kind of replacement negative existential that uses a descriptive phrase in place of the name, such as:

- The detective portrayed in Doyle's fiction doesn't exist,
- The flying horse of Greek mythology doesn't exist.

Do empty names—despite referring to nothing at all—nevertheless function nondescriptively?[37] Recollect the symptoms of a name functioning in a singular manner. One symptom is the mechanism by which that name refers, for example, by virtue of one's direct—nondescriptive—access to the object, for example, perceptually (as opposed to a description that one relies on). Another related symptom is the possibility of any definite description in one's possession that one takes to apply to what one takes the name to apply to in fact failing to so apply: the descriptions available to a person using a name don't determine what the name

---

36. Peter van Inwagen, "Fiction and metaphysics," *Philosophy and Literature* 7 (1983) 67–77, and van Inwagen (2000) distinguish between those properties a fictional object is depicted as having in a fiction—those they "hold"—and those properties they actually have. In neither his 1983 nor his 2000 publications does he officially relativize the notion of holding to specific fictions. The problem isn't that a fictional item may hold property P relative to one fiction and property ¬P relative to another fiction; after all, a fictional item may hold property P relative to one fiction and property ¬P relative to that very same fiction. The problem is that because characters may change so much when depicted in different fictions, too much information is lost if one treats a fictional character as holding properties simpliciter, as opposed to relative to one or another fiction. After all, in describing fictional characters, it is usually how they are depicted in one or another fiction that's relevant to the sociological and historical facts that such facts about the contents of fictions imply.

37. A common methodological argument for an affirmative answer to this question is to claim that it's appropriate to semantics to provide a uniform theory for *all* names—fictional or otherwise. Such arguments from requirements on the simple uniformity of theory are always risky because of the way they ignore the fact that empirical reality hasn't any corresponding simplicity aspirations. But these arguments are especially risky in the context of a special science—like semantics. Special sciences are often required to have jagged edges. A better argument for the claim is that the semantics of names shouldn't be infiltrated by epistemology: that we often don't know whether a name is empty or not, and that names (and propositions expressed using them) should operate independently of that ignorance. But this very view has been challenged by Evans (1982), and in any case, it looks like the begging of the question against, say, direct reference views, or "referentialism," as it's called by some philosophers (e.g., Everett 2000).

refers to. More broadly put, it can be that how one conceptualizes what a name applies to comes apart from what, in fact, that name applies to.

The description of the symptoms of singularity given in the previous paragraph seems to traffic heavily in ontological considerations—that one's access to the object differs in its mechanisms from one's descriptive conceptualizations of it. We have already seen in chapter 2 that these symptoms of singularity can be present even without an object for a name to refer to. Hallucinations, however, are a peculiar form of interaction with the nonexistent: one's perceptual tools are all functioning as if to present an object even though there isn't one there. Given that one's verbal and gestural repertoire is based foundationally on one's perceptual experiences and capacities, it might be thought that although the notion of empty singular thought and speech is therefore cogent in the context of hallucination, it isn't in the case of fictions, where nothing is perceptually amiss. This would be a second motivation for treating names—in a fictional context—as "descriptive names."

Some philosophers nevertheless suggest that something akin to a "baptismal ceremony" occurs with respect to fictional characters. Thomasson (1999, 47) writes:

> Although there can be no direct pointing at a fictional character on the other side of the room, the textual foundation of the character serves as the means whereby a quasi-indexical reference to the character can be made by means of which that very fictional object can be baptized by author or readers. Something counting as a baptismal ceremony can be performed by means of writing the words of the text or it can be merely recorded in the text, or (if the character is named later, for example by readers), it can remain unrecorded in the text.[38]

Thomasson means this suggestion to respond not only to the claim that fictional objects can't be dubbed and that "causal-historical" theories of reference are incompatible with any view on which fictional terms refer but also to the position that "reference by description must be the primary means of referring to fictional characters."[39] This doesn't seem to be an adequate response to descriptive construals of names in fiction—at least it doesn't seem to be adequate with respect to written fictions. There is too much by way of description that seems to be available, including (most important) access to the very depiction relation that the fictional character is involved in by virtue of that character appearing in a fiction. Indeed, this even seems to be true of televised and filmic fictional characters. Even though one can lack descriptions of filmic and televised characters in just the same way that one can lack descriptions of the people one sees in real life, and even though one may experience the latter kinds of characters as being named by pointing gestures of one's own or even by other fictional characters, there still seems to be plenty of description available, for example, "Jack is the suspicious

---

38. A similar view is attributed by Thomasson to Zalta, on the basis of then-unpublished work of the latter.
39. Thomasson (1999), 158, note 6 to chapter 4.

bearded character who collects dog leashes in the movie *The Hound of Brooklyn Heights*." Such a corresponding real-life description ("the suspicious bearded man I just met who collects dog leashes") may fail if only because either the man just met doesn't collect dog leashes or because someone else also just met also suspiciously collects dog leashes and is bearded.

This apparently firmer epistemic grasp of the descriptions of fictional characters is something of an illusion, however. Thought experiments that are parasitical on real-life thought experiments (that show that one's grasp of what a name refers to doesn't turn on one's conceptual grasp of the object) can similarly show that one's grasp of what a fictional name refers to doesn't turn on one's conceptualizations of the fictional object. For example, a fictional film or TV show may be about twins. One may confuse them, and one's resulting descriptions can be falsified, even though one has perceptual access to each individual twin via the correct application of those characters' names. Indeed, one may find that one's initial descriptions of how a fictional character is depicted can turn out wrong—the character wasn't really depicted in such and such a way but only *appeared* to be depicted in that way. (The character was depicted as appearing in such and such a way but wasn't depicted as actually that way.) Nevertheless, one's ability to talk about the character, using its name, is unimpeded by one's descriptions of that character being wrong. Fiction has the reputation of being able to imitate life; but this—if true—means that the ways that life can trick us by its real objects going beyond our conceptualizations of what those objects are like can also occur with fictional objects.

The same points apply to written fictions. Here, too, one's description of how characters are depicted can prove—in time—to be false. More striking is the experience of an author who talks about her characters to her friends. During the writing of any fictional work, characters usually change—sometimes drastically. Of course, what's written in any fiction is only pretended-true and pretended-false; the point is—during the process of writing a fiction—what's pretended-true and pretended-false can undergo changes. But what changes along with changes in what's pretended-true and pretended-false are the corresponding true and false simpliciter statements about how such characters are depicted in the (developing) fiction. So even the author's conceptualizations of the characters don't (semantically) constrain her use of the fictional names she applies to her characters.

It's true, however, that once a fiction is published, televised, or otherwise publicized, definite descriptions become available that can be taken to co-refer with the names occurring in those fictions. An institutional codification of what's true and false of a character (at least as it's depicted in such and such fictions) can and usually docs take place. This looks quite disanalogous to the hallucinatory case, where no such codification of any description need ever occur.

Indeed, what seems to be at work is something I denied to be at work in section 1.5 with respect to numerical thought. This is that our use of fictional names seems to operate subject to a deference practice to what may be called a body of thought, or a cultural pretended-true and pretended-false practice with respect to fictional characters. When anyone makes claims about Mickey Mouse, he or she can be corrected on the basis of what's pretended-true according to the various Disney products. This doesn't make Disney the final authority with respect to the truths and falsities simpliciter regarding Mickey Mouse. After all, if Disney studios releases cartoons that depict Mickey Mouse quite differently from how he had been depicted earlier, it still remains true (or false) that Mickey Mouse was depicted as such and so in this or that cartoon. If someone else depicts Mickey Mouse in some other way entirely, it's true simpliciter that Mickey Mouse is depicted in such and such a way in that work. The author(s) are in control of how a fictional work depicts a fictional character—what's true and false simpliciter about how that fictional character is depicted in that work—up until and only up until that work is published or otherwise becomes public.

It's a mistake, however, to suggest that official public thought about fictional objects is what the use of fictional names defers to; it's the fictional practice itself that the use of fictional names defers to. Consideration of this point will provide yet another route to the claim that fictional names are empty singular terms, rather than conceptual (but deferential to "publicly held" descriptions). The tool to show this is a variation of a popular modal argument[40] that's widely taken to show that names don't (semantically) involve conceptual content. A typical illustration is that although it's true that

(22) It's possible that Mark Twain wasn't the author of *Huckleberry Finn*,

it isn't true that

(23) It's possible that Mark Twain wasn't Samuel Clemens.

In this way it's taken to be shown that (many) names operate—semantically speaking—independently of (many) definite descriptions that co-refer with them. Although Mark Twain was, in fact, the author of *Huckleberry Finn*, he needn't have been.

Consider, now, a description such as

(24) Sherlock Holmes is depicted in Conan Doyle's short stories as living at 221B Baker Street.

It's true that Conan Doyle could have written his stories differently; thus:

(25) It's possible that Sherlock Holmes is depicted in Conan Doyle's short stories as living at 223B Baker Street.

In describing this possibility, we aren't engaged in imagining a possible world in which Sherlock Holmes lives at 223B Baker Street. There is no Sherlock Holmes, and so this is an undesirable way to try to imagine the possible world

---

40. See Saul Kripke, *Naming and necessity* (Cambridge, Mass.: Harvard University Press, 1972).

in question. If anything, we are imagining a possible world in which Conan Doyle varied his stories so that (24) isn't true at that world. The deference, therefore, isn't to a body of (actual) thought about fictions; it's to a fictional practice that could have varied just as anything else about the world could have varied. As a result, although fictional names may in fact be fixed[41] in their reference by various official codified descriptions of fictional characters, that leaves their (empty) singular status untouched.[42]

3.3 Identity and Nonidentity in Fiction

Fictional characters, and more generally fictional objects, are routinely identified and distinguished both within fictions ("transepisodically") and across fictions ("transtextually"—as Thomasson (1999, 57) puts it). Recognizing the reappearances of characters from earlier scenes of a fiction (or from other fictions) is an essential part of the activity of enjoying fiction. In later episodes of a written fiction—indeed in subsequent sentences of such a work—some fictional objects are invariably depicted as the same as others depicted earlier. Transtextual borrowings of fictional characters—and, more rarely, borrowings of other sorts of fictional objects—from other fictional works are also routine, and "conniving" readers (and viewers) understand and appreciate when this is being done. Not only are literary characters transplanted from written fictions to film and television; transplantation also occurs when an author writes a sequel to his or her own work, when an author writes a sequel to another author's earlier fictional work, or when fictional characters of earlier works are ironically or satirically depicted in later work.

I've clearly been speaking of what's pretended-true and pretended-false; but the transtextual borrowing of characters isn't something that's usually pretended-true *in* subsequent fictional works. For example, it's usually not pretended-true in Sherlock Holmes movies that the detective, Sherlock Holmes, is the same character as the Sherlock Holmes depicted in Conan Doyle's short stories.[43] Nevertheless, it does seem that there is a pretence operative that Sherlock Holmes as-depicted-in-such-and-such-movies is the same character as Sherlock Holmes as-depicted-in-Conan-Doyle's-stories. Perhaps the solution is this: there are the pretended-true (and pretended-false) statements that are in, or that are pretended-implied by statements in, the fiction itself (that "constitute" the fiction); but there

41. See Kripke (1972).

42. There is some controversy about whether modal arguments of this sort really do show that names "lack sense." Indeed, there are powerful thought experiments that seem to show that sometimes it is public descriptions of some sort—ones not necessarily available to the speaker—that ground some usages of names. See Gareth Evans, "The causal theory of names" (1973), in *Collected papers* (Oxford: Oxford University Press, 1985), 1–24 on this. My purpose has not been to contribute, one way or the other, to this debate. Instead, my aim has simply been to show that arguments for the singular construal of (some uses of) names are neutral about the ontological status of those names—that is, they are neutral with respect to the question of whether those names, on those uses, refer[e] or not.

43. It can be so pretended-true of course. A filmic Sherlock Holmes could complain to Watson about how he's been depicted in the short stories that Watson has been writing under the pseudonym "A. Conan Doyle."

are, apart from those, the statements that must also be pretended-true (and pre-tended-false) by appropriately cognizant consumers of that fiction—for example, those who are aware that Sherlock Holmes is a detective depicted in Conan Doyle stories (or that Spider-Man is a character depicted in comic books). In this way the scope of the pretence engaged in by readers and viewers can be reasonably expanded somewhat beyond the scope of the statements pretended-true and pre-tended-false in the fictions themselves.[44] We can call these pretences *transtextual pretences*.

As in the earlier sections of this chapter, my concern isn't so much with the pretended-true and pretended-false statements that are essential to fictional prac-tice, but rather with the fiction-external statements corresponding to them that are (and must be) true and false simpliciter. Such truths (and falsehoods) seem not only to identify fictional characters transepisodically (within one fictional work); there is also a literary practice of criticism that includes the comparisons of fictional characters as those same characters are depicted in different fictions. These sorts of fiction-external statements about the identities and nonidentities of fictional characters raise issues of "identity conditions" both for those philos-ophers who take fictional terms to refer[r]—either to real objects, such as abstracta, or to Meinongian objects—and for those fictional nominalists (like myself) who think fictional terms refer[r] to nothing at all: exactly what kinds of identity condi-tions—if any—should govern the terms of fiction-external discourse? This ques-tion, shared by fictional realists, fictional Meinongians, and fictional nominalists alike, is seen by fictional Meinongians and fictional realists as linked to a more fundamental metaphysical question: what kind of identity conditions govern fic-tional *objects*? Meinongians and realists also face a related robust metaphysical question: how exactly do the names and descriptions occurring in different fictions successfully refer[r] to the same fictional objects when they do so? A con-straint on answers to these questions is that they must sustain the needed identi-fications and distinctions among fictional objects that occur in fiction-external discourse.

Let's first take up questions of the identification of and nonidentification of fictional objects as such attributions occur within fictional works. It does some-times happen that someone fictionally introduced as named such and such, and as doing so and so, is fictionally revealed to also be such and such*, and as doing so and so*.[45] Most of the time, however, fictional objects that are introduced in a fiction using distinct language—as such and such people, so and so objects, and

---

44. Two points. First, notice (again) that talk of "pretence," because of its misfit with the psychological nature of the aesthetic appreciation of fictions, is creating subtle tensions. One does better by talking about non–truth-apt "platforms," that various aspects of the fiction rely upon. If I were writing a book that was more directly concerned with the aesthetics of fiction, this is the direction in which I would develop the points I've just sketched out. Second, I don't think this extended approach, to what consumers of fictions take to be pretended-true and pretended-false, should be extended to the analysis of comparatives (discussed in section 3.1) such as "Sherlock Holmes is smarter than Mickey Mouse." These go quite beyond what a viewer or reader needs to pretend-true (and pretend-false) to fully enjoy a fiction.

45. E.g., as in Orczy's *The Scarlet Pimpernel*.

so on—remain depicted as distinct. Fictional characters being introduced as having distinct names, or as having distinct properties, activates a default fictional convention: *those characters are distinct*. That is, such characters are introduced in a fiction as distinct only because nothing in the fiction treats them as identical. In these cases, it's by sheer virtue of two fictional objects having different properties attributed to them (or, in visual fictions, fictional objects visually exhibiting different properties), or having different names attributed to them, that viewers and readers are fictionally invited to presume that they are distinct. To fool the reader by introducing two objects, described as having different properties (or having them so look), and then revealing later that they are the same (e.g., in a fairy tale where objects—a rock, a tree, a mop—can turn out to be the same object, a wand, variously disguised) is recognized as a literary trick that exploits an expectation built on a fictional convention. As I've been stressing, this point applies to visual fictions as well. For any object can turn out to be identified with another (by the visual depiction, say, of there being an illusion or successful disguise that the viewer is induced to experience along with—some of the—fooled characters); normally, it's just by virtue of two objects being distinguished visually in space or by their backgrounds—their depicted locations—that the objects are depicted as being distinct.

The reidentification of fictional objects over the subsequent episodes of a book or a movie is enabled by the very same tools that are used to introduce the fictional objects in the first place. In conventionally written fictions, a fictional object from an earlier episode is depicted as having reappeared by a repeated use of an earlier introduced name of the object and/or by a repeated use of an earlier description of it[46]; in film or television, the same thing is done by a reoccurrence of similar visualizations—for example, the same actor, what appears to be the same objects against the same background, and so on.

I called it a fictional convention that fictional objects, depicted as having different names, or described as having differing properties, are default-depicted as distinct unless the fictional work makes the contrary explicit. Despite the phrase "fictional convention," it should be realized that some such presumption

---

46. In a sophisticated work, such as William Gaddis, *The recognitions* (New York: Penguin Books, 1955), one recognizes the presence of the fictional character Wyatt in different episodes of that novel sometimes by the author's (or another character's) use of his name, sometimes by the fact that he's described by the author or by other characters as wearing the same clothes or as looking as he did in an earlier scene—described with the same phrase, "piercing green eyes"—or as possessing the same objects (a golden bull, a coconut) that he had acquired in earlier scenes, or even by verbal peculiarities, tics, or obsessional ideas in dialogue that the character had manifested earlier. It's important to stress the "unless otherwise stated presume they're the same" convention at work in fiction when the same descriptions, names, and so on, show up in later episodes: to write at one point that, "John looked longingly at the last apple remaining in the fruit bowl," and then to return to John in a later scene with: "John was still at the kitchen table. He gazed down at the apple in his hand with awe and love," is to invoke the default assumption that the fictional apple is depicted to be the same one from the earlier scene. Unless, of course, the fictional work (later) indicates otherwise. Notice that the descriptive elements used in this fashion are nearly never uniquely depicting (e.g., lots of people have "piercing green eyes"). But the convention is that those descriptive elements have been associated with such and such a character in this particular fictional work, and with no other character (unless, of course, the convention is being deliberately flouted).

on storytelling is a relatively necessary one. Without it, a fictional work would need to explicitly list named and described objects and officially distinguish them; readers and viewers would have to wait for evidence of such an explicit stipulation before being able to pretend-true that the objects depicted are indeed distinct.[47]

The foregoing may seem to justify the thought that principles of individuation are possible for fictional objects on the basis of the properties they either actually have or are depicted as having. There is a small industry in metaphysics concerned with the question of "bare particulars"—with the question of whether an object is more than (or something else apart from) its properties, and so, with the question of whether two objects can agree in all of their properties, be (that is) only "numerically distinct."[48] Regardless of how that complicated and subtle metaphysical question sorts out for what's real, the content of a pretended-true depiction of fictional objects as two often only invokes numerical distinctness and nothing else. Because of this (as I'll illustrate in a moment), there are serious obstacles for those who claim that fiction has a genuine ontology of fictional objects that obey real individuation conditions.

Consider, first, a sufficient condition that Thomasson (1999, 63) offers for fictional characters x and y to be identical:

1. x and y appear in the same literary work.
2. x and y are ascribed exactly the same properties in the literary work.

This sufficient condition is open to counterexamples. Consider the following flash-fiction piece.[49] "Once upon a time there were two iron balls one mile apart from one another. Nothing else existed. The End."[50] The two fictional iron balls satisfy Thomasson's sufficient condition: they appear in the same literary work, and they are ascribed exactly the same properties in that work. But they are not identical, or so it would seem. It's open to Thomasson to claim that, in this story anyway, it's one fictional object that's been—fictionally—falsely described as two. But this is a fairly unappealing option, at least because it's so evidently ad hoc. Call this challenge to Thomasson's sufficient condition, *the problem of the underdescription of fictional objects.*

47. If a literature was replete with stories in which apparently different characters very often turned out to be the same one, the default convention I've described would disappear, to be replaced with perennially distrustful readers. There are some novels that invite just this response, of course.

48. See, for example, E. B. Allaire, "Bare particulars," *Philosophical Studies* 14(1963), 1–18; E. B. Allaire, "Another look at bare particulars," *Philosophical Studies* 16 (1965), 16–21; V. C. Chappell, "Particulars re-clothed," *Philosophical Studies* 15 (1964), 60–64; and J. P. Moreland, "Theories of individuation: A reconsideration of bare particulars," *Pacific Philosophical Quarterly* 79 (1998), 51–63; among others.

49. Due to Max Black, "The identity of indiscernables" (1952), in *Problems of analysis* (Ithaca, N.Y.: Cornell University Press, 1954), 204–16, who anticipated the currently popular genre.

50. A variation: *Once upon a time there were sixteen sisters. They didn't get along. Things ended badly for all of them. The end.* There are fiction journals that have published stories rather like this one. I call this particular story, by the way, "Sixteen Sisters." I'm hoping to publish it soon. (Outside of this note, I mean.)

A number of philosophers (Parsons 1980; Zalta 1983) individuate fictional objects by sets of properties that such are taken to uniquely instantiate.[51] These views also face counterexamples due to the problem of the underdescription of fictional objects. A fictional character may be depicted in a fiction as having two dogs; but the dogs may always be described in that fiction in a plural way: "Rover and Spot jumped up and down joyfully. He leashed them, and took them out for their daily walk."[52] The dogs are depicted in the fiction as being two by virtue of the plural references to them and their being given distinct names. (There needn't even be names given in the fiction, of course, but just plural references to them.) A possible response by fictional realists and Meinongians is to allow that fictional objects, when depicted as distinct from one another, really have distinct properties despite such not being indicated in any way by a fiction. This response, of course, requires sheer arbitrariness in the attribution of these additional properties to fictional objects, or a systematic ambiguity in what fictional objects are referred to by the terms in the fiction indicating these underdescribed objects, or the postulation of radically "incomplete" objects. Philosophers have adopted such positions, but it's necessary to be aware of burden of proof issues when evaluating them. There is nothing in fictional practice—nothing about how descriptions and names are pretendedly used, nothing about how such are used in the corresponding fictional-external statements—that points toward such metaphysical completions of fictional objects being the items fictional terms refer to, or that indicates that there is a systematic referential ambiguity in fictional terms. Only an already in-place metaphysical demand that fictional terms and quantifiers must refer can drive one to even contemplate such possibilities.[53]

Notice that a similar point can be made about the fictional depiction of a number of objects being present. We can be told that a specific number of somethings are present during such and such an episode of a fiction, without ever being told any further details that can be used to distinguish them from one another: "There were seventeen apples left in the fruit bowl; all of them were green and tart-looking." "The Earth groaned under the weight of fourteen billion, thirty nine thousand, two hundred and seventy three humans, all of whom wanted

51. On Parsons's view, there is a unique object correlated with every set of (nuclear) properties; x and y are identical iff x and y have the same nuclear properties. On Zalta's view, x and y are identical iff they encode the same properties. For both Zalta and Parsons, these conditions are supposed to apply to fictional objects. My forthcoming objection will be seen to apply regardless of what "nuclear" properties come to, or what "encoding" requires; so I omit details.

52. These examples, incidentally, provide yet another indication that fictional names are singular.

53. Two points. First, here is one way that the pretended-true and the pretended-false markedly differ from the true and the false simpliciter—at least in the context of a classical logic. There is no apparent gap between how objects are known to be depicted in fictions and what properties they have in addition. This is a fact that Parsons (1980) acknowledges and incorporates in his Meinongian picture: Meinongian objects are incomplete on his view. This should make him loath to adopt this arbitrary completion solution to the problem of the underdescription of fictional objects. Second, many philosophers—specifically concerned with fictional reference—invoke direct reference or representationalism or some such other semantic doctrine as an assumption of their approach. To do so is to legislate that fictional terms must refer[r]. The only question then remaining is: to what do they refer[r]? One point to be made in this book is that no such ontological assumption is needed for semantics, in general, let alone for an analysis of the semantics of fictional terms. See chapter 5.

to eat regularly." "Sixty-one dogs trudged slowly along the road, wagging their tails." Nothing more need be said in a fiction to further distinguish these fictional objects so depicted—these unnamed fictional objects so depicted.

The problem of the underdescription of fictional objects powerfully indicates that fictional realists and Meinongians are—metaphysically speaking—on the wrong track. The fictional practice itself openly acknowledges—by virtue of various fictional conventions, especially those that allow bare-bones acknowledgments of otherwise unnamed and underdescribed fictional things as the same or different—that there are no such things. The author, much of time, stipulates the presence of fictional objects for fictional pretence; his ability to do so—stipulating that nineteen cats are in the room (say) and choosing to say nothing more about them for the rest of the novel—exhibits that metaphysically speaking there is nothing the author is (really) speaking of, nor that others are speaking of when they say that his novel depicts, in one scene, nineteen cats sitting comfortably in a room.

In dismissing the metaphysically robust question of identity conditions (either necessary ones or sufficient ones) for fictional objects, by no means am I suggesting that anything goes in fictional discourse with respect to how characters should be identified or distinguished from one another. Drawing attention to the problem of the underdescription of fictional objects is only meant to achieve two things. First, to draw attention to the somewhat unnoticed fact that fictions are often richly populated with numerous characters that are depicted as distinct but that are described or named in no other further fashion. Second, to show how this first fact undercuts the impression that something akin to individuation conditions for objects is relevant to the fictional process. Individuation conditions require the use of descriptive conditions (of some sort)—at least in principle—for distinguishing objects. Those are precisely what can go utterly missing in fiction, and as a result, it's not only unlikely that necessary and sufficient "individuation conditions" for fictional objects are available,[54] but that any general conditions—necessary or sufficient—are available, even in principle.

To repeat: to suggest all this isn't to suggest that anything goes at all with respect to identity and difference talk within fictional discourse. After all, most of the fictional characters that we care about come both with names and with a rich set of specific depicted properties that we can talk about. With respect to these characters, we are successful (in a local way) with our talk of identifying them with, and distinguishing them from, other characters—transepisodically and transtextually. Let's turn now to probing our practice of transtextually identifying fictional objects.

The first point to stress (again) is that despite conversations, especially among avid moviegoers who also read, that routinely involve comparisons of the same characters as they are depicted in different fictions, it's true that people engage in such conversations competently without knowing anything systematic about "identity conditions"—if any—governing characters as depicted in different

54. As Thomasson (1999) concedes.

fictional works. That may not be much of a surprise. People, after all, are particularly bad about knowing anything systematic about the "identity conditions"—if any—governing the real things that they identify, say, over time. It's striking, as Kripke notes (see section 2.10), that philosophers haven't done much better in their studies of the "identity conditions" of various kinds of objects.

But in saying that people don't know anything systematic about when one is faced with one character as opposed to two, it's not being suggested that specific well-defined applications of identity and difference talk (restricted to small sets of fictional works and/or characters) are difficult. They're not: if two people in a conversation count a filmic version of *The Hound of the Baskervilles* as overlapping in its characters (e.g., Sherlock Holmes, Watson) with Conan Doyle's novel of the same name, then even if the sets of characters don't fully overlap, they will have no trouble pooling the characters from both fictional works, identifying the ones that should be identified, and counting up a total. Broaden the scope of the discussion a little, however, and the applications of identity and difference can be brought to break down. There are lots of easy thought experiments about possible fictional works that can be designed that will raise identity puzzles about the characters. Mrs. Laura Lyons is a fairly minor character in Conan Doyle's novel *The Hound of the Baskervilles*. If there is a quite different-looking character in the filmic version of *The Hound of the Baskervilles* with the name "Mrs. Laura Lyons," or if there are two—twins—that are the actual villains, and that Sherlock Holmes has to expose as twins and as villains, these characters may or may not be identified with the Mrs. Laura Lyons of the book. Different people may regard the identity question differently: most, I hope, will recognize that there is no real fact of the matter whether the filmic character is to be identified with a character depicted in a written fiction.[55] It should be noted that although it's a transtextual convention that the use of the same distinctive names ("Sherlock Holmes," "Clark Kent") is a primary tool that an author uses to indicate that he or she has borrowed a particular (already depicted) character, in satire—and in other fictional works—the names are often changed,[56] despite the characters still obviously being transtextually identical—at least to knowledgeable consumers of the subsequent fictional works.

It's clear, I think, why people are comfortable engaging in such transtextual identifications (and nonidentifications) of fictional characters despite lacking a systematic or global set of conditions governing such. They are comfortable for exactly the same reasons they are comfortable reidentifying each other over time despite lacking a systematic or global set of same-person-as conditions. They reidentify persons by means of a narrow set of cues (physical appearance, psychological similarities, symptoms of psychological continuity, background indicators, e.g., going by the same name, living in the same places, moving slowly from one part of a room to another), and any of us would be quickly bewildered were

55. Of course, this discussion hasn't even raised the possibility of the fictionalization of the various thought experiments about the fusing and splitting of people, so that puzzles about personal identity can compound questions about when one is faced with a depiction of one character or of several over the course of the episodes of a book.

56. As in the case, for example, of "Frankenstein's monster."

the sorts of bizarre personal identity puzzle thought experiments that philosophers like to think up to become common phenomena. Exactly the same narrow set of cues are used in fictions to invite the reader or viewer to reidentify a character transtextually (and, of course, transepisodically). As long as things don't get too weird in the fictions in question, these cue-dependent faculties suffice for a comfortable practice of transtextually identifying characters.

But a philosophically sophisticated question can be raised about the transtextual identifications of fictional characters. It seems clearly essential to the appreciation of a fictional work that one successfully individuate the characters in it along the lines that the fictional work dictates. One will enjoy a Sherlock Holmes story only in a rather peculiar and oblique sense if one systematically thinks of Sherlock Holmes and Watson as the same character—despite what the novel officially pretends. But, despite our tendency to naturally transtextually identify characters, exactly how essential are such transtextual identifications of fictional characters to how we talk about fictional works? Could we get by without them? No, Thomasson thinks. She writes (1999, 67) that

> it is quite important to understanding our literary traditions to recognize how a single character like Sherlock Holmes may reappear in many different works of the same series, or a character like Gudrun may develop over the course of different D. H. Lawrence novels. Similarly, many literary works would not be comprehensible at all if we could not take them to include the well-known characters of other works. Stoppard's *Rosencrantz and Guildenstern are Dead* makes little sense if we do not see that these are the same Rosencrantz and Guildenstern from *Hamlet*, and Fielding's *Joseph Andrews* would lose much of its humor were he inventing a new young maid rather than poking fun at the character of Richardson's invention.

Unfortunately, this very much overstates what the data of our literary tradition shows about the transtextual identifications of fictional objects. In particular, it does show that to understand the many Sherlock Holmes works that arose because of Conan Doyle stories, is to understand that the character depicted as "Sherlock Holmes" in these later works is transtextually pretended to be the same character as the character "Sherlock Holmes" as he was depicted in the Conan Doyle stories. So, too, *Rosencrantz and Guildenstern Are Dead* makes little sense unless one appreciates that Rosencrantz and Guildenstern are (in that particular piece) depicted as the same characters as the same-named ones in *Hamlet*. But there is a major metaphysical leap from how the identities of fictional characters are depicted or transtextually pretended to be to what they (metaphysically speaking) actually are.

Once this point sinks in, it should be obvious that "it's clearly essential to the appreciation of a fictional work that one successfully individuate the characters in it along the lines that the fictional work dictates," is an overstatement, too. What seems to be essential is only that one recognize what identities and differences among the fictional characters are depicted or transtextually pretended to be; it's another question whether those fictional characters are or aren't as so identified.

At this juncture, fictional realists and fictional Meinongians must travel a different road from the one that fictional nominalists can take. Fictional nominalists aren't worried about the "real" identities and differences among fictional characters. They are only concerned with making identity and difference talk consistent with the evidential and deductive burdens that external-fiction discourse shoulders. How essential, they ask, is transtextual identity and difference talk to the evidential and deductive role that fiction-external discourse has? Fictional realists and fictional Meinongians, however, are concerned with metaphysics, with the in-principle identity conditions that govern fictional objects.

It's unfortunate for fictional realists and Meinongians that there is an intrinsic looseness to the question of how fictional objects should be "individuated." Part of the reason for this looseness is the background fact that there is a troubling looseness to identity questions in general.[57] Much more important for our purposes is the immediate issue that nothing in the fictional practice forces any particular metaphysical conclusions about how such objects should be individuated. The reasons for this are twofold. First, as just stressed, most of the properties attributed to fictional objects are attributed to them by virtue of how they are depicted in fictional works. These are genuine property attributions in one sense. Consider the statement that Sherlock Holmes is depicted in *The Hound of the Baskervilles* as being a great detective. I've argued that this statement is true simpliciter; in any case, on the view that Sherlock Holmes is a something, a property of being depicted in such and such a way is attributed to that something. But the content of this attribution is restricted only to depicted content. In particular, as those focused on the "intentional" nature of such content stress, from so and so being depicted in such and such a way, nothing follows about how so and so really is (apart, of course, from the already mentioned fact that so and so is depicted as such and such). That Watson and Holmes are *depicted* as distinct characters doesn't force the conclusion that they *are* distinct characters. The issue, metaphysically speaking, should remind one of related issues surrounding Kant's thing-in-itself. If we only have access to how things-in-themselves appear, then we haven't any access to how they (it?) are. That, among other things, leaves us at a loss should we want to individuate "the" thing-in-itself—suggest there are at least fifty of them, for example.

I say, therefore, that the fictional realist and the Meinongian realist have no way out of this epistemological bind. They can only invoke depicted properties—plus some general logical principles about identity and suchlike—to try to force the particular individuation conditions that they want. But there is a massive disconnect between how objects are depicted and how they are—in particular how they are depicted to be numbered and how they are actually numbered. As a result, there is a massive disconnect between what fictional and Meinongian realists can take themselves to know about fictional objects, and therefore what conclusions they can draw about what fictional objects are like.

---

57. Recall the quotation from Kripke (1972) at the beginning of section 2.10, and then think of all the literature on identity issues with respect to persons, physical objects, over time, across space, across possible worlds, and so on.

The fictional nominalist, by striking contrast, is in a far better position. This is because he can adopt exactly the ways of speaking of identity and difference that ordinary people use when they individuate fictional objects transepisodically and transtextually—provided only that the practice of doing so remains cogent. The fictional nominalist reasons this way: how we talk (how we are psychologically inclined to talk) about the identities and differences of fictional objects is, by virtue of the mere fact that this is how we talk and are psychologically inclined to talk, convenient. There is no fact of the matter about how these objects really are individuated, and therefore convenience and ease dominate as the relevant (as the only) considerations governing such talk because there are no (actual) fictional objects to make additional demands on how we should talk about them.

I now want to make several linked claims about the transtextual identification of fictional objects. The first is that the practice allows quite a bit of arbitrariness in how it can be done. (Remember: quite a bit of arbitrariness isn't: anything goes.) We often can identify—or choose not to—fictional characters: different people can make different choices, and the same people make different choices at different times. The second point is that this arbitrariness has limitations due to the purposes that such talk is put to, and due to the difficulties alternative ways of talking may create. The third point is that none of the arbitrariness allowed in the practice affects the cogency of that practice.

I'll start my presentation of these three points by first criticizing a necessary condition on the transtextual identification of fictional objects urged by Thomasson (1999, 6):

> Suppose that a student happens on two literary figures remarkably similar to each other; both, for example, are said to be maids, warding off attempts at seduction, and so on. Under what conditions would we say that these are works about one and the same fictional character? It seems that we would say that the two works are about the same character only if we have reason to believe that the works derived from a common origin—if, for example, one work is the sequel to the other, or if both are developments of the same original myth.

The necessary condition on offer thus seems to be that there be real-world causation (influence) of the fictional works either on one another or from an earlier common origin on both of them.[58] Two points should be made. First, as a matter of the sheer metaphysics of fictional objects, there doesn't seem to be any metaphysical reason such a necessary condition should hold. Thomasson describes fictional objects as "dependent" on the fictional works that they appear in. But this isn't to give an argument; it's only to make her necessary condition a matter of definition. Second, contrary to Thomasson's claim, this doesn't seem to be a requirement on how we speak about fictional objects. In studies of mythology, for example, there are identifications of mythological figures as the same ones

---

58. The details of this necessary condition are spelled out in Thomasson (1999), 67–68.

depicted in different depictions, despite the absence (or awareness of the need for) a careful study of whether there are common influences underlying these different depictions.[59] It may simply be convenient to describe two depictions as of the same character, regardless of whether there is a sociological net of influences that includes both depictions.

One important factor, in whether it's convenient or not to so identify two characters depicted in two different depictions, is the nature of background theories about the sources of such. Thomasson's necessary condition fits nicely with a sociological picture on which fictionalizing—and mythmaking—operate entirely through public influences, where storytellers borrow stories from earlier storytellers. A rather different picture is this: Jung has the view that there is a collective unconscious that we all share (hence the adjective "collective"), and that it's the source of the various myths and myth-like creatures that populate our dreams, mythology, and storytelling. Also crucial to his view is that the contents of the various myths play important causal roles in the psychological significance of the myths—for example, that one's focus on, say, *THE MINO-TAUR* is (actually) a focus on a particular aspect of one's own personality, an aspect of one's own personality that one shares with all others in the human species. The view is wrong (I think); but my point in bringing it up is to show the sensitivity of our practice of identifying fictional characters to background sociological and psychological assumptions. If something in the neighborhood of Jung's theory were true, it would be sensible to identify, say, *THE MINO-TAUR* across dreams, myths, and so on—regardless of whether Thomasson's necessary condition were satisfied—because such a figure would play a certain causal role more easily described by indicating its reappearance in such and such a myth, rather than by invoking comparisons of different characters that resemble one another.

The point is this: if our descriptions—of how fictional characters influence fictional work, and influence us more broadly, and how fictional characters are influenced by other fictional works, and are more broadly influenced—are evidentially and deductively indispensable, then such descriptions will be easier to state and use if we reduce the number of fictional characters that we are talking about (and that are similar) by coalescing them into identical characters in accord with the machinations of those influences. This makes natural the unification of the various Sherlock Holmes of films, cartoons, and written fictions as depictions of a single character.

One thing that motivates—but doesn't require—transtextual identifications, therefore, are the things we need to say, things that are indispensably about[e]

---

59. For example, there are many stories about Zeus and the other Greek gods. These stories are not the result of mutual influences; rather, they are a result of assimilations—stories about gods from different worship traditions that were pooled together under a single name by subsequent believers (and storytellers). There is massive sociological evidence in Greek mythology that this is what happened during the long oral tradition: the gods often have several names, several different stories describing their births, different geographic locations that they are associated with, and so on.

fictional characters. As an illustration of this phenomenon, let's consider the possibility of systematically restricting the identifications of characters to within fictional works and try to get a sense of the added difficulty created in expressing what we need to say.[60] We stipulate, that is, that characters within two different fictional works are, by definition, different characters. Can we redescribe all the things we need to say about fictional characters without invoking transtextual identities across fictional works? One piece of apparatus we need is the notion of a doppelgänger. Instead of claiming that the Sherlock Holmes of film and the Sherlock Holmes of the Conan Doyle stories are the same character, we instead say that they are doppelgängers—that one is a fictional copy of the other. We employ the idealization that characters occurring within fictional works can be organized into equivalence classes of doppelgängers.[61] Now consider some of the things we'd like to say. We'd like to say:

> Hamlet appears in *Hamlet* and *Rosencrantz and Guildenstern Are Dead*.

Instead we now say,

> Hamlet appears in *Hamlet* and a doppelgänger of his appears in *Rosencrantz and Guildenstern Are Dead*.

We (might) want to say:

> There is a fictional character who, for every novel, either appears in that novel or is a model for a character who does.

Now we say instead,

> There is an equivalence class of fictional doppelgängers E such that, for every novel, there is a character from E that either appears in that novel, or is a model for a character who does.

We want to say,

> Sherlock Holmes is more famous than any real detective.

---

60. This is an inquiry into some constraints on how we can say what we need to say due to language; it's leaving aside the additional object-directed psychological propensities that make reidentifications of fictional objects transtextually, and transepisodically, so automatic.

61. This is a massive idealization if only because fiction, in general, is unruly: there are often no facts of the matter about whether two characters are doppelgängers, just as there are often no facts of the matter about whether two characters from two different fictional works are to be (pretended) identical. We stipulate that copying induces a transitive, symmetric, and reflexive relation among all fictional objects that are copies and are copied, with degenerate equivalence classes containing only one fictional character when that character isn't a copy of another character, and no character is a copy of it.

This is a little more difficult. Strictly speaking, we can't say that a particular character Sherlock *Holmes* is famous because, after all, not only is there no unique Sherlock Holmes with respect to Conan Doyle's stories (since there are many stories), but some people know of the Sherlock Holmes from such and such a movie, others know of a different Sherlock Holmes from a different movie, and so on. Worse, all these people talk about these different characters under the impression that they're all talking about the same one. This makes it hard to single out any particular doppelgänger, for example, the one from the first Conan Doyle story, as *the* Sherlock Holmes doppelgänger that's famous. Perhaps we've got to credit the entire group of them with fame like so:

> The equivalence class of fictional doppelgängers of Sherlock-Holmes-in-*The-Hound-of-the-Baskervilles* is more famous than any real detective.[62]

Some will protest, it isn't an equivalence class of characters that's famous. (Most people have never even *heard* of an equivalence class.) But consider "Nicolas Bourbaki"[63]—the group of mathematicians who all published under the same name. In describing Bourbaki as famous, we knowing ones mean that the group of mathematicians is so famous; if someone knows of Bourbaki and thinks it's a person, he is simply mistaken. Similarly, we must describe those people who speak of the character Sherlock Holmes as either involved in an error or as speaking lazily. The same point holds of

> Hercules was more popular among the ancient Greeks than Theseus was,

and indeed, for any relation, "worshipping," "admiring," "imitating," that consumers of fiction are described as bearing to a transtextual fictional character. All such must be redescribed in terms of a relationship to one or more equivalence classes of doppelgängers. Everyone who thinks in terms of transtextual characters—everyone who speaks of fictional and mythological figures, as it turns out—must be described as laboring under an error. In noting this, I'm not criticizing the suggestion; I'm not denying that so describing people as systematically mistaken, and the concomitant rewriting of statements about transtextual characters in terms of characters restricted only to single fictional works (and equivalence classes of such) can be successfully implemented. I think it can be—at least I'm not aware of any recalcitrant examples. There are philosophers who think that attributing a systematic referential error of this sort to (most) speakers to make a theory work is a prima facie methodological infirmity of any such theory; I'm not one of those philosophers because I'm not particularly moved by what sound like a priori methodological considerations. Leaving aside our object-directed psychological proclivities to transtextually identify depictions as of the same characters given

---

62. I chose Sherlock-Holmes-from-*The-Hound-of-the-Baskervilles* arbitrarily. Any doppelgänger from the equivalence class would do equally well.

63. See P. Halmos, "Nicolas Bourbaki," *Scientific American* 196 (1957), 88–99.

the presence of certain content (which are very powerful and should not be over-looked in any evaluation of the practicality of a reform in how we speak), only this point can be made in favor of retaining reference[e] to transtextual fictional characters: it's always easier to speak of a single being than a crowd of such that are deemed similar in such and such ways. The same point is operative in many cases: it's easier to speak of the same person than of person-stages that are appropriately related in such and such ways, of rocks rather than so-related rock-stages; it's easier to say that Humphrey might have won an election because he did so win an election in a possible world than it is to say that Humphrey might have won an election because a counterpart—similar in such and such ways—did win an election; it's easier to speak of Sherlock Holmes than it is to speak of various Sherlock Holmes doppelgängers. For that matter, it's easier to speak of a (whole) person doing such and such and so and so than to speak of an arm, related in such and such ways to a leg, as doing so and so, and the leg correspondingly doing this and that. When a collection of what we could describe as distinct objects act in certain coordinated ways, it's easier to talk of them as one thing, and coalesce the distinct actions of those objects into a single action of the one containing thing. But just because it's easier to speak in one way than in another doesn't mean it's impossible to do otherwise—and perhaps we should do otherwise if other considerations (metaphysical ones, for example) dictate this as an appropriate choice.

However, the fact that people think of depictions of certain fictional characters transtextually as depictions of the same fictional character really is a good reason to imitate that identification practice with respect to the statements about fictional characters that are deemed true and false simpliciter. This is because these statements are meant to describe the fictional practice in a way that best enables satisfaction of the external discourse demand. Similarity of content in fictional works (e.g., all being about[e] "Sherlock Holmes") indicates that those works have overlapping causal powers precisely because psychological responses to fiction turn not only on the content of those fictions but on the very transtextual identities that are transtextually pretended in the appreciation of such fictions. Necessarily included, therefore, in an explanation of the influence of a body of fictional work is that it's often taken to be fictional work about[e] the same (fictional) person, for example, Sherlock Holmes. That fictional characters depicted in one work are perceived as the same as those depicted in other works codes a particular kind of influence. Just as we best capture fictional content by attributing properties directly to fictional characters (as popular, as influencing the behavior of real people in various ways based on the properties attributed to those characters, and so on), we also best capture that content by replicating the identities and differences among such characters as they are perceived.

With a clear conscience, fictional nominalists can fashion identity and difference talk with respect to fictional objects to match the ways that it's pretended in the fictional practice because only they owe no metaphysical debts; only they think that nothing that's claimed about[e] the identities or differences among fictional objects must track the identities or differences of actual objects that (metaphysically speaking) themselves have no allegiances to the ways it's convenient for us to describe them.

One last point about the contrast between the fictional nominalist's characterization of the grounds of talk of identity and difference (in, broadly speaking, the psychology of the practice of fiction) and the fictional Meinongian's and fictional realist's grounding of such in metaphysical facts about fictional objects. How people think of fictional characters as identical or different is affected by contextual factors that realists and Meinongians have no right to take seriously. For example, whether a depicted fictional character is transtextually identified with a fictional character depicted in another fictional work often depends on what else is known to be going on—fictionally speaking. Suppose there were one fictional superhero, Superman, that had been invented at a time. Suppose that subsequently another superhero was introduced with a different name, but with similar powers, the ability to fly, x-ray vision, as well as a secret identity, but (say) depicted as lacking some of Superman's other depicted powers. It might be felt that such a creation was the same character under another name.[64] In a different context, however (ours), where there are many fictional superheroes, many of whom fly, have secret identities, and so on, it would be (and is) felt otherwise. If talk of transtextual identities and differences among characters is meant to help track palpable influences of fictional works on one another, this result is no surprise. In a context where there aren't many fictional superheroes, an inference to a specific kind of influence is almost unavoidable; in a context with many such superheroes, the idea of this kind of fictional character "is in the air" and influences can't be traced to specific previous fictional works. This kind of contextual latitude in whether we are to say that a fictional character is the same as another or not is expected on a view that takes fictional discourse to be empty. It's a problem, however, for any view that takes fictional objects to be metaphysically real—because then their intrinsic properties should be what's dictating when they are and aren't the same as other fictional objects; whether lines of influence among fictional works can be traced or not should be irrelevant.[65]

Noting that real lines of influence matter to our transtextual identifications of characters explains why the author's intentions, although taken very seriously with respect to whether a character is to be transtextually identified with another, aren't definitive. Authors often categorically show that a character depicted is to be identified with another by the use of the same name and the same descriptions or by allusions to descriptive content in the earlier work, and so on. They may also simply assert the claim. An author's transtextual fiat carries authority in part because the author, in mentioning or utilizing the

---

64. In this kind of case, if the author claimed that the character was a version of Superman, that would clinch the identification; if the author claimed he wasn't, that might absolve the character of transtextual identity with Superman—even if (in the two cases considered) there were no differences in the content of the author's fictional works about the character.

65. I am presupposing the idea—discussed elsewhere—that there must be an (epistemic) gap between the properties attributed to real objects, and their (actual) properties; in turn, I'm presupposing that our ways of speaking of having been wrong about such objects isn't to be merely a convenient *façon de parler* imposed on a set of terms, but has to do instead with the somethings that the terms refer to. See Azzouni (2004a), part II; also see the appendix to the general introduction of this book.

details of the earlier work, exhibits the influences crucial to motivating us to transtextually identify characters. But also crucial are our object-directed psychological tendencies to treat the appearance of something as the reappearance of something else only if certain cues occur. Absent these cues, the author can claim all he wants about transtextual identities: we won't transtextually identify the characters. On the other hand, if these cues are present, we will identify the characters transtextually, even if the author claims otherwise.[66] An author can deny that her character is the fictional Tarzan of the Edgar Rice Burroughs novels; nevertheless, a court could find against her if her character is similar enough to Burroughs's Tarzan. On the other hand, should I write a story about a frog, where nothing about that frog reflects anything of Sherlock Holmes as he is depicted in stories and film (e.g., the frog shows no particular nonfroglike qualities of mind—it's just an ordinary frog who dies at the hands of someone French at the end of the story), my claim that the frog is Sherlock Holmes (and even if the narrator in my story calls the frog "Sherlock Holmes") would be denied.

In practice, we usually require rather a lot of the content of fictional works to overlap if certain characters in them are to be treated as depicted in both such fictions. But nothing more precise can be said about how far content can differ in a fiction—how differently a character can be depicted in two fictions and yet still be described as the same character depicted in both such fictions. This actually turns entirely on the ingenuity of an author—and often on his or her rhetorical skills: that is, what he or she can get away with (what viewers and readers will allow that author to get away with, perhaps because they've been charmed by the narrator's voice).[67]

Let's turn now to the third point I promised to establish, that the arbitrariness of these transtextual identifications doesn't make the set of fiction-external statements incoherent. The worry is this. Sometimes, I've suggested, such identifications are made, and sometimes they're not. Why shouldn't this kind of latitude introduce discrepancies that impact on, in particular, what follows from fiction-external statements? If it did, then the ability of fiction-external statements to meet the external discourse demand would be impaired.

---

66. Thomasson (1999), 56, denies this. Fred Jones, purely coincidentally, writes up a Pamela with depicted properties identical to those of Richardson's or Fielding's Pamela. Thomasson stipulates that Jones's Pamela would not be identified as the same character as Richardson's and Fielding's Pamela. That's not true. (Thomasson underdescribes the possible backgrounds for such cases.) For example, imagine that Jones's book became a bestseller, and only much later was it discovered that Jones knew nothing of the earlier Pamela works. The critical literature would continue to identify (and compare) the characters anyway. (Academic inertia—intellectual inertia in general, for that matter—should never be underestimated.) Even if the coincidence were known from the beginning, but Pamela—the character—became as famous as Sherlock Holmes, it wouldn't matter that Jones's Pamela was entirely independent of Richardson's and Fielding's Pamela. (In this case we would have a contemporary version of the sorts of assimilations of characters that occurred with the Greek gods.) People would speak of such a character (in film, for example) as identical to earlier ones. It would be an interesting fact—when people heard about it—that Jones's invention of his Pamela was independent of Richardson's and Fielding's Pamelas, but that wouldn't be enough to halt the sociological momentum of the transtextual assimilation. (In this case it's rather important that the characters—despite the massive amount of sheer coincidence—have been given the same name.)

67. For example, Calvino's narrator Qfwfq, in his *Cosmicomics*.

A comparison with how exactly the same issue arises in mathematics is profitable. There, too, identity conditions seem to be given that are—at best—only locally applicable. Globally speaking, it seems that different identity conditions are possible, and in practice, sometimes one, sometimes another, is chosen. Why doesn't this create problems in mathematics? For example, number theory introduces ways of distinguishing the counting numbers from one another and, indeed, provides a canonical notation of numerals that—in principle—provides a decision procedure for distinguishing one number, when named in that notation, from another. But no such in-principle ways of distinguishing the counting numbers from other objects is supplied by number theory; in addition, other ways of describing counting numbers, for example, using integrals, or empirical descriptions, aren't adjudicated—even in principle—by numeral notation. Number theory neither affirms nor denies that 9 is the number of planets; it neither affirms nor denies that 2 is Julius Caesar. Nor need it do so.

We normally treat the number 2 as distinct from all other objects—we stipulate it as so distinct is the right way to put it, and indeed, we normally treat the number 2 as distinct even from other mathematical objects, except when we find it suitable to stipulate an identification of it with such. After the invention of set theory, it became appealing to identify the counting numbers in one way or another with a sequence of sets. Such set-theoretical presentations of the foundations of classical analysis are continuous with an already existing (and widespread) practice in mathematics of identifying kinds of mathematical objects with other kinds of mathematical objects to exploit the theorems true of the first sort of object in the context of the second kind of object. What this really comes to is an identification of (some of) the referents[e] of terms across languages—more precisely—an identification of (some of) the referents[e] of terms across (informal) mathematical languages. But these identifications are ultimately arbitrary in the sense that, precisely speaking, there is no fact of the matter about which set (if any) the number 2 is, nor need there be any such fact—as far as purely mathematical purposes are concerned.

Why doesn't this latitude in "identity conditions" cause problems? The reasons are twofold. Consider the identification of the counting numbers with one or another progression of sets. The requirement is that such an identification conserve the theorems of number theory: it cannot be that a theorem of number theory is falsified by a purported identification. Identifications that violate this condition are simply disallowed. Second, the identification is, anyway, in principle dispensable. We could just as easily say that the set-theoretic progression of objects aren't numbers but are just like numbers in the relevant respect (forms of the same theorems are true of both). What's crucial isn't the identification: in a way all that saves us is ink. Instead of writing 1, 2, 3, . . . , 1*, 2*, 3*, . . . , we avoid asterisks by identifying terminology and thus the objects referred[e] to as the same numbers. There is no difference in the resulting theorems or in the application of the mathematics if we say either that we have built a set-theoretical superstructure around the actual numbers or we say that we have a set-theoretical superstructure within which a set of objects similar to numbers with respect to certain of their properties (the number-theoretical ones) have been found. Either way of deducing theorems, or of applying empirically the resulting superstructure yields identical results.[68]

Returning to the case of external-fiction discourse, it's clear that in many respects the allowing of the same fictional objects to be depicted in more than one fictional work is similar to the identification of mathematical objects across mathematical systems that's just been described. In particular, the fact that there is more than one way that people, in practice, do it, is harmless with respect to the external discourse demand. Fiction-externally describing two characters depicted in two different works as the same character or describing them as different characters that are doppelgängers transtextually pretended to be the same character, in no way affects the historical or sociological generalizations that follow from or are confirmed (or disconfirmed) by statements presupposing such characterizations. What's crucial to the external-discourse demand, as it applies to fiction-external statements, is the tracing of the influences on and sociological effects of literary characters and using statements about them in turn as evidence for sociological and historical facts. But these uses are insensitive to whether the Sherlock Holmes of the Conan Doyle stories is the same character as the Sherlock Holmes of such and such films or whether these are instead just doppelgängers, a pair of distinct characters, where one is depicted as the same as the other. In particular, therefore, it has no negative effect if we sometimes speak of Sherlock Holmes as depicted in one story or as in another as the same characters or as a pair of doppelgängers.[69]

Let's turn, finally, to an issue that Thomasson (1999, 79–80) thinks that those who want to deny that fictional objects exist cannot handle. This is the question of how someone's thoughts—involving quite different content—are nevertheless to be taken to be thoughts of the same fictional object. I am thinking of King Lear, let's say. Let's also say that I (on a different occasion) think of the father of Cordelia. How—if there are no fictional objects—is it to be made sense of that my thought of King Lear is to be a thought of "the same object" as my thought of the father of Cordelia? One natural approach is to attempt the identifications on the basis of the same thought-content occurring in both thoughts. Thomasson (1999, 79–80) writes—raising an objection to "the content theory" similar to one raised by Evans (1982, e.g., 70–71)—and discussed in section 2.10—that

---

68. As noted, this is a widespread aspect of mathematical practice—and it motivates, among certain philosophers, structuralist views of mathematical ontology. See Michael D. Resnik, *Mathematics as a science of patterns* (Oxford: Oxford University Press, 1997). Also see Jody Azzouni, *Metaphysical myths, mathematical practice: The ontology and epistemology of the exact science* (Cambridge: Cambridge University Press, 1994), part II, for further discussion of the mathematical case. I should also note that views that attempt to identify mathematical objects with one or another kind of empirically real object implicitly rely on the cogency of doing so being compatible with the "identity conditions" of mathematics—so far as they are made explicit in mathematical practice.

69. Literary criticism allows either. Sometimes, one contrasts the Sherlock Holmes of one fiction with that of a later one. The contrast between the two characters may be significant. In other cases, all the Sherlock Holmes may be assimilated (nearly enough) to compare them to some other fictional detective. Notice that what drives these distinctions and identifications is ease of expression (and what's psychologically natural). We can slice the characters differently, and make the same points.

The content theory can analyze the fact that in [the case where I'm thinking of either of Bill Clinton or of the father of Chelsea] we have two intentional acts, two conceptions, and one object, by explaining that these two acts have different contents . . . but these contents pick out one and the same object, namely Bill Clinton. . . . In the [case of King Lear] we want just as much to be able to say that the two acts are about the same object. The trouble with the latter pair of acts is that according to the content theory these also exhibit the first feature of intentionality: The object of these acts does not exist. . . . So our ability to explain that these two thoughts are about the same thing, namely King Lear, is lost, for it seems that the content theory can only tell us that there is no object in either case.

The challenge, as Thomasson (1999, 80) puts it, is to "unify" thoughts containing the content "King Lear" and those containing the content "the father of Cordelia." Psychological content hasn't the resources for doing this simply because our use of fictional terms is—as discussed earlier—a deferential practice. Fictional names and descriptions are taken to co-refer^e relative to a fictional practice (that the individual may, in fact be wrong about). What must be regarded as true simpliciter about fictional objects includes various fiction-external statements that track the pretended-true identifications of certain names and/or descriptions of fictional objects as co-referring^e. The singular nature of fictional names, in particular, is due on the one hand to what those names refer^e and co-refer^e to not being determined by descriptions (content) that the individual user has, nor even (as noted earlier in this section) necessarily being determined by descriptions that occur in the fictional works that are deferred to.

Thomasson seems to deduce directly from the inability of content theories (ones that draw their resources only from the psychological states of individual users) to explain how thoughts directed toward fictional objects can be treated as about the same "objects" and about different ones, the conclusion that real fictional objects are required for this purpose. She notes that (84) "We can, however, have two acts with qualitatively identical contents—attributing the very same properties to the object, invoking the same background individuative principles and background beliefs about the properties of the object, and ascribing sameness to the objects in question—that are nevertheless about *different* fictional objects" (emphasis in original), and concludes (84) that "What this seems to show is that, even in the case of fictional characters, the identity of the object is transcendent in relation to any finite set of contents about that object—that there is some real metaphysical identity of fictional characters apart from their individuation for consciousness."

This leaves entirely out of account the possibility that what's "transcendent," what provides identity and difference among fictional objects—where that's to be had—is a publicly available practice of literature, mythology, or whatever. In fiction or in known mythology, it's a practice of fictional pretense, with names and with descriptions, that provides the identifications that external-fiction statements track when they truthfully indicate which fictional characters are identical with which.[70] On the other hand, where a body of mythology—involving empty terms—is genuinely believed, it's a (worship) practice involved with a body of beliefs that provides the identifications needed. Pretence on the part of an individual user isn't crucial to explaining co-reference[e] of empty terms. Deference to a public practice with names and descriptions is the decisive element.[71]

It's worth noting that "deference," as I've been using it, is to be understood as a genuine psychological state that consumers of fiction are to be in when their thoughts about Lear, Sherlock Holmes, and other characters, refer[e] to those characters.[72] If, while daydreaming, I coincidentally imagine a character like Lear—if my thought content during that daydream is indistinguishable from my thoughts of Lear on other occasions—that daydream isn't about[e] Lear exactly because I'm failing to defer the reference[e] of my thought to *Lear*, the fictional character. Deference, in this sense, doesn't have to be a conscious act; the deference in question doesn't have to be directed toward a specific text. If I'm reading Shakespeare's *King Lear*, in doing so (if, that is, I'm really reading it), I'm engaged in a deference practice in just the same way as when I defer to the locally public usage of names when I repeat gossip I've heard about "Saul" to others who know him. But I can think about the character Lear independently of Shakespeare's play: in particular, I can decide to place Lear—that very character—in my own play.

It's a sticky question, and one I won't pursue, whether—when I'm thinking of King Lear—the deference involved in that thought being about[e] King Lear should be regarded as part of the "content" of that thought. In some sense, it need not be: it may only be presupposed, given as it were, that the thought is about[e] King Lear. (It's rarely part of the thought that a name-token contained—as it were—in that thought defers in such and such a way to such and such a public referential practice involving other name-tokens, so that the token used is to be a token of the same name-type as other name-tokens used.)

3.4 Some Final Observations about the Ontology of Fictional Discourse

A complexity of fictional discourse is that when one is engaged in it, the sentences one produces aren't truth-apt. When one—broadly speaking—talks about that practice, one does produce a discourse that's truth-apt. The latter discourse, however, is required to refer[e] to the various products of the fictional practice, including (most notably) nonexistent fictional objects. It's the appearance of fictional terms in both truth-apt and non–truth-apt discourse about and in fiction that tempts philosophers to various extreme positions, such as the positing of one or another kind of ontologically robust fictional object on the one hand, or the attempt to render all discourse involving fictional terms non–truth-apt, on the other. Keeping the

---

70. In the language used earlier in this book, the fictional pretence practice constitutes the truth-value inducers of the external-fiction truths (and falsehoods).

71. Here I find myself in accord with remarks found in Taylor (2000), 26–27.

72. What follows responds to concerns raised in Thomasson (1999).

non–truth-apt/truth-apt subtlety of (different kinds of) fictional discourse in the forefront of the analysis enables the possibility of a view that—I think—best captures all aspects of our fictional practices, both as they play out internally and externally (with respect to other kinds of discourse).

As the preceding paragraph amply indicates, I've presumed throughout this chapter that fictional objects don't exist, and I've tried to show how our fictional practice is cogent despite that assumption; in particular, I've shown how truth-apt fiction-external statements are possible even when the terms occurring in those statements are empty. It's important to realize that I haven't argued explicitly for the claim that fictional objects don't exist. In particular, the looseness I've described as operative in how fictional objects are to be identified and distinguished isn't part of my brief against the existence of fictional objects.[73]

I have arguments against the existence of fictional objects, and I've presented those arguments elsewhere.[74] What they come to, briefly, is that for something to exist is for the attribution of properties to it to be independent of our very property-attribution practices themselves, in short, for our property-attribution practices to be open to a kind of failure because they don't match the properties that such objects actually have. Truth-apt fictional discourse lacks the required independence. As I've said, I've not been explicit about those arguments here, apart from some discussion of them in the appendix to the general introduction.

Rather, I've relied on something else. I've taken the burden of proof to be on those who believe that fictional discourse requires either a Meinongian or a realist ontology. Indeed, it seems that the literature more or less recognizes that the burden of proof does fall on Meinongians and realists, for philosophers like van Inwagen, Thomasson, and Parsons have assumed the burden and pressed positive arguments for why there must be Meinongian or real objects for fictional terms to refer to. I've endeavored to rebut those arguments in this chapter, to show that our understanding of fictional practices and our understanding of the evidential and deductive role of fiction-external statements are (indeed) impeded should we adopt a Meinongian or a realist view.

Another reason to think the burden of proof is squarely on the shoulders of fictional Meinongians and realists is that the ordinary person regularly denies that fictional objects—such as Sherlock Holmes, Mickey Mouse, Santa Claus—exist. Philosophers, such as van Inwagen, Parsons, Thomasson, and others, try to deny this. The arguments they run rely, implicitly or explicitly, on the assumption that the use of the particular quantifier commits the ordinary person to something (either real or Meinongian, depending on the particular philosopher). But this is wrong, and in addition no ordinary person thinks the use of "there is," as above, is ontologically committing. I've already discussed this at length elsewhere,[75] although I will revisit the issue somewhat in chapter 5.

---

73. Substantial argument is needed to show that the absence of precise "individuation conditions" for a kind of object bears one way or the other on the ontological status of that kind of thing. I don't pursue this topic any further in this book.

74. Azzouni (2004a).

75. See Jody Azzouni, "Ontological commitment in the vernacular," *Noûs* 41 (2007), 204–26.

Conclusion to Part I

It's a natural question: why is there empty singular thought and speech? Broadly speaking, an answer isn't hard to give. Let's start with the following pair of notions. A language seems to contain terms that individuate objects. We speak of "that vase," this chair," and so on; we distinguish between the chair and the book on the chair, rather than coalescing them into a single object (a "chairbook"). Call this *the linguistic individuation of objects*. Our vocabulary contains terms that hold of objects that are individuated—both in their extension in space and in their life over time, as for example, "apple." The objects referred to are distinguished from other objects (of the same or different kinds) in such a way that—at least in principle—we can count them.[1]

We also experience or perceive—in a relatively automatic and involuntary way—objects as identified and as distinguished from one another and from their backgrounds. Our perceptual capacities subpersonally exploit cues—some that we're conscious of, and some that we're not—so that, based on light patterns, how things feel, and so on, we simply perceive (we "experience") *this* as different from *that*. Objects are perceptually individuated, in space and across time. They are

---

1. Quine often talks about this. See, for example, "Speaking of objects" (1958) in *Ontological relativity and other essays* (New York: Columbia University Press, 1969), 1–25, or *Word and object* (Cambridge, Mass.: MIT Press, 1960). There are also various (ancient) metaphysical puzzles—for example, of the statue/clay sort—associated with the "individuation conditions" of vocabulary items. Some terms—"mass terms"—don't individuate in a way that allows counting. Although formal logic seems to comport fairly nicely with ordinary language terms that allow—at least in principle—the counting of their referents, this isn't true of mass terms. There is, understandably, a large literature on these topics.

experienced as continuing over time (as we watch them move, say),[2] and they are experienced as extending so far (and no farther) in space. Again, apples come to mind. Call this *the perceptual individuation of objects*.

As recently as the last century, it was popular for philosophers to regard the perceptual individuation of objects—to a greater or lesser degree—as parasitic on the linguistic individuation of objects.[3] One motivation for this family of doctrines runs way back: the impression that we don't "directly" perceive objects, but instead only patterns of sense data, percepts, or whatever. How those patterns (e.g., of sense data) are therefore organized by us into objects has to be a matter of our (habitual) imposition: We quickly "infer," in some sense of "infer," the objectification of what we experience sensorily. The strongest support for this turned on a misanalysis of the ways the perceptual individuation of objects often gets it wrong, how it often imposes an organization of objects on something that isn't organized into objects in that fashion at all:[4] the *mechanism* by which this happens was not treated as involving automatic subpersonal stratagems, but instead as involving something rather like conscious reasoning—thus, the use of "habitual" some sentences back.

The lesson of recent developmental psychology, vision science, and related areas, however, is this: our perceptual capacities generate the experiences we have of objects in a way that's largely independent of (and indeed, immune to) causal effects from the linguistic individuation of objects. In saying this, I do not claim—or at least I don't need to claim—that the development of our sensory capacities takes place without any causal input from our acquisition of language. If this strong thesis were true, the ways we perceive objects and perceive them to be individuated from one another would be matters we would experience the same way regardless of whether we had acquired language.

In point of fact, however, something like this strong thesis does seem to be largely true. That is, the psychological literature seems to show—both in studies of normal cognitive development, and in studies of those unfortunate humans who (largely) fail to acquire language—that our perceptual interactions with the environment are developmentally independent of language acquisition (and, crucially, developmentally independent of the specifics of the language acquired). Indeed, it seems to proceed independently of much of our otherwise parallel cognitive development. Thus, how we (perceptually) experience objects to be distinguished from one another (to be laid out in space and time) seems independent of what we know (or think) or say about those objects. How the world chunks into objects—perceptually speaking—is involuntarily experienced as given to us. Someone may have no idea what a typewriter or a book is; nevertheless, he or she will have no trouble distinguishing it—as an object—from other objects.[5]

2. Pace Hume.

3. The popularity of these views extended well beyond philosophy, of course.

4. I'm thinking primarily of movies and photographs. But early thinkers took keen note of reflections in mirrors and paintings—especially (I imagine) the breathtakingly realistic paintings of the Renaissance.

5. The hallucination literature—focused as it is on cases where perception dramatically fails to accord with what's otherwise normally seen—nevertheless ratifies the presence of subpersonal mechanisms determining the individuation of what's seen. Even where the plausible hypothesis seems operative that hallucinations are occurring

The points I go on to make about singular thought and speech and empty singular thought and speech don't require the strong independence thesis with respect to the perceptual and the linguistic individuation of objects, although I think that thesis is true. As far as the role of what's perceived (by the utterer and his audience) in the semantics of singular thought and speech is concerned, such is compatible with the developmental facts about the perceptual individuation of objects involving causal vectors from the language that a child simultaneously acquires. All that's required is that the (resulting) fully functioning adult experience the perceptual individuation of objects as—in practice—independent of the linguistic individuation of objects; indeed, the adult's experience should be that (as far as she can tell) the linguistic individuation of objects rests almost entirely on an already in-place perceptual individuation of objects that she shares with those she communicates with.[6] It's this that enables adults to rely so unthinkingly on demonstrations (plus some use of vocabulary) to indicate what they are talking about—even to an audience of children.

"That is ugly" is sometimes experienced as a remark that makes sense because of a lazily unexpressed sortal ("That chair is . . . ," "That vase is . . ."). Just as often, "words fail us"—especially when face to face with contemporary sculpture—and in those cases, we let our (shared) perceptual individuation of objects take over when we say, "That's ugly," and have no possible sortal in mind.

Some of our singular verbal practices, therefore, nestle securely within the shared perceptual individuation of objects. That the perceptual individuation of objects is shared species-wide greatly diminishes the scope for ambiguity in demonstrative gestures. This is something unnoticed by philosophers (influenced by Wittgenstein, among others) who are still in the grip of the earlier picture that treats the perceptual individuation of objects as—in adult practice—parasitical on the linguistic individuation of objects. To the contrary, we constantly and successfully demonstrate what it is we want to say something about.

Empty singular expressions exist because of the simple fact that involuntary and subpersonal perceptual processes rely on cues and exploit factors that don't unvaryingly co-occur with the ways that objects are, and are—in fact—chunked

---

because filtering mechanisms (that enable an individual to distinguish between imaginings and what he's perceiving) have broken down, those hallucinations are nevertheless fairly conservative in how they are individuated from one another.

6. In point of fact, the perceptual individuation of objects is quite rigid and immune to a person's desire to individuate objects differently because—as already noted—the mechanisms by which that person is brought to experience objects is almost entirely subpersonal (and involuntary). The linguistic individuation of objects, on the other hand, despite largely resting on the antecedent perceptual individuation of objects, and despite being due to an antecedently acquired language that as a result imparts a lot of terminological inertia, is nevertheless capable of undergoing serious mutation because of those individuals intent on changing how they speak. Philosophers (e.g., Eli Hirsch, *Dividing reality* [Oxford: Oxford University Press, 1993]) who contemplate various weirdly defined objects such as the item that's my chair until noon and is Paris for the rest of the day, or unusual objects with detached moving parts, such as the mereological sum of my chair and the floor of my apartment, and so on, are exploiting just this flexibility in the linguistic individuation of things. It's significant how, even if an individual can be brought to talk in these new ways, no one can bring himself to perceive objects this way—despite whatever he says to try to talk himself into so-seeing things.

in the world.[7] As we are apt to put it: our senses can be fooled. Indeed, crucial to the discovery of the mechanisms (the cues) by which we are impelled to experience a scene as involving such and such objects, engaged in such and such activities, is the discovery of the ways that we can be brought to perceive objects as present when they aren't.[8]

From this point of view, singular thought and speech directed toward what exists and empty singular thought and speech are aspects of language that naturally arise together. Specifically (focusing on one way that singular thought and speech arise), our demonstrative practices involve locutions that are provided with truth values based on the dictates of something nonverbal: how things are perceived by us. In turn, what we think about, when we think about what we perceive, is what's given to us (presented and individuated) by our perceptual faculties.

The subject matter of our demonstrations is given by what we experience. What we experience, in turn, needn't be of anything real. It could have been[9] that our language was such that we would take our utterances (and thoughts) to fail Evansesquely if our perceptual experiences correspondingly failed to present real objects for those utterances and thoughts to be about. But that isn't the language we actually have. One can ask why. A straightforward answer (and one that generalizes to the context of professional science) is that we want to continue talking and saying truth-apt things, even if we know that what we are talking about doesn't exist.[10] Indeed, we would go on talking, and saying things that were important— that explained why we did what we did, and didn't do what we didn't do—regardless of whether what we were talking about existed or didn't exist. Part of the reason for this is that indispensable evidence for why someone does (or doesn't) do what she does (or doesn't do) are characterizations from her first-person point of view; such characterizations are insensitive to whether what's being talked about is real or not.

Consequently, it's never the fact that our thought is aimed at something or is (internally) about something that makes it really about that something. Aboutness

---

7. I mean: the way that objects are chunked in the world at the level at which we experience them. I'm relying, for the moment, on the fact that the world—at the level at which we interact with it, anyway—chunks into distinguishable items that operate (causally speaking) independently of one another. Evolutionarily speaking, it was valuable for us to perceive the tiger running toward us through the trees as an object distinct from those trees, and indeed to perceive those trees as objects distinct from one another and from the landscape, generally. In this sense, the perceptual individuation of objects can correspond or fail to correspond to the individuation of the objects with which we interact. Whether how (macro-)objects are individuated in the world—at this level of description—can (ultimately) be given a sustained and systematic metaphysical characterization is an issue I can't discuss any further in this book. See, however, Jody Azzouni, "Individuation, causal relations and Quine," in *Meaning*, ed. Mark Richard (Oxford: Blackwell Publishing, 2003), 197–219.

8. Film and photographs, for example, exploit some—but not all—of the cues that we (subpersonally) rely on to experience objects as being thus and so. However one wants to individuate the "objects" that are actually present during a movie, one won't do it in terms of the objects that the movie seems to present. (What's actually present is a movie screen and a lot of light.)

9. In the sense of "We can imagine that . . ."; not in the sense of: it could have really gone this way instead of the way it did go.

10. It has always been (and still is) important to us to understand other humans; this is possible only if we can describe not only how they're right in what they perceive about the world, but how they're wrong.

intuitions—in the case of demonstratives, but more generally as well—arise from an automatic deference practice: our verbal practices are self-recognized to defer to what we perceive. But what they defer to provides ontologically neutral products: what we see may not exist. And, as far as our psychological grasp of what we are perceiving and saying is concerned, that doesn't matter. This in turn creates the illusion that the teleological feel of intentionality is accompanied by real teleological "powers": when we talk about something, there must be something (real or not) that we are talking about.[11]

I've touched on another point that should be more loudly stated. It's one thing for the psychological mechanisms by which we demonstrate objects and talk about them to be insensitive to ontology. It's quite another for the resulting kind of talk to be indispensable. Just because the (subpersonal) mechanisms by which our talk defers to what we perceive induces a tendency to talk a certain way—to treat our conversations about what we discover not to exist to nevertheless be truth-apt conversations, but about things we now sanguinely describe as nonexistent—doesn't mean that such a tendency should continue to be honored. Perhaps we should regiment our discourse to fit the dictates that Evans and other philosophers have (mistakenly) suggested our verbal practices already fit: speech-acts fail when they depend on gestures that turn out to be directed at nothing at all.

Here is where broader issues about the requirements on truth-apt discourse intrude (i.e., the external discourse demand). As a first pass, it must be noted that we must describe—however we can—the evidence we have that supports our claims. One crucial kind of evidence, as already noted, that we take very seriously in ordinary life and in the psychological and sociological sciences as well is how things appear to people. If it seems to S that such and such exists (although such and such doesn't really exist) then our explanations of why S does this and not that must take account of it seeming to S that such and such a thing exists.

At this point, what looks like a somewhat technical issue arises—that the language we use to formulate our truth-apt claims must take a certain form. "Must" should be understood in a qualified way: I'm not prepared to say what form any language must—in principle—take. It's clear, however, that the languages that we are required to use—if we are to understand what we are saying, and what we are saying to one another—must (broadly speaking) take a predicate/object form and

---

11. Does this lead to a veil of perception: percepts that are the actual relata of our demonstrative gestures and that only (if we are lucky) correspond to real objects? There is no reason what I've said should so lead. If there is nothing there, then there is nothing there that one is pointing at. One isn't consequently pointing at one's own percepts. The tempting view (that one is pointing during hallucinations at one's own percepts) becomes overwhelming if one thinks that the truth of one's pointing gestures requires something for one to be pointing at that one's remarks are about. Meinongianism is a result of the same temptation. No—the right view is this. One is pointing at nothing at all; there is nothing there. However, one is having an experience that makes one's pointing gestures cogent, and that makes what one says true-apt. This isn't, however, because what one says is about what one is pointing at. (I talk further about this shortly.) To dismiss the threat of the veil of perception, one need only reject the idea that what someone is pointing at when pointing at a real dog and what he is pointing at when he's pointing at an indistinguishable hallucinated dog is the same thing. Because he's not pointing to his percepts in either case, this is easy to do. In the first case he's pointing at a dog; in the second case (alas) he's pointing at nothing at all. Nothing at all isn't the same thing as a dog.

involve (various kinds of) quantification. Given this restriction on languages, however (and it's a significant one), it seems that to talk about how things seem to S doesn't allow descriptions purely of the form: *It seems to S that . . .*, but instead requires talk that—as it's put—quantifies over nonexistent objects from *outside* any such "It seems . . ." context.

This constraint—at least in the case of hallucinations—dovetails nicely with our method (the only method available) for understanding a subject S when he describes his hallucinations. To understand S is—at least in part—to see how things look from his perspective. To be able to predict what he will do and why, we must replicate in our understanding what sorts of objects are being presented to him and what properties those objects are perceived by him to have.[12] To do so, however, is to quantify over—and more generally—to refer^e to what isn't there.

The intrusion of indispensable talk about nothing at all (to put the point in an arch way) arises for somewhat different reasons in the case of fictional discourse, and different reasons again in the case of mathematics. In the latter case, linguistic factors seem to be the primary ones driving quantification over the nonexistent: given that we are restricted to languages of—broadly speaking—predicate/object form, we need such languages to be deductively tractable, to be successfully applicable in the sciences, and to enable the representation of phenomena we can represent in no other way. Such languages invariably and necessarily quantify over more than what's really there (more, that is, than the actual targets of the study-discourse). One reason (but not the only reason) is that predicate/object languages that reify properties and relations (that treat relations and properties as things to be quantified over, and talked about^e) are deductively more tractable than ones that leave the "logical form" of such relations and properties as relations and properties.[13]

In the fictional case, I think, something different yet again is going on. Systematic entertainment institutions of "pretence" are in place (literature, film, etc.), institutions wherein all forms of language (including singular forms like demonstratives and names) are "pretendedly" exploited. However, what we might (broadly speaking) describe as the institutional facts about fictions are a crucial part of our social world, and consequently they play a causal role in how that world operates. Therefore, these institutional facts are crucial in evidential arguments. But because of the systematic exploitation of singular forms of language in pretence (e.g., the widespread naming of fictional characters), as we saw in chapter 3, truth-apt statements about those institutions cannot be couched in forms like: *It is pretended in such and such fictional institution that . . .* , or anything similarly innocuous.

12. Presupposed here is something unavoidable in any case: descriptions from the first-person perspective are not foreign to science (pace Daniel Dennett, *Consciousness explained* [Boston: Little, Brown, 1991], 71; Thomas Nagel, *The view from nowhere* [Oxford: Oxford University Press, 1986], 7). How could they be if science encompasses, as it does, psychology, sociology, and even instrumental interactions with the cosmos meant (in part) to describe how our neighborhood in the cosmos is like and different from other neighborhoods in the cosmos?

13. I've talked about this in more detail elsewhere. See, for example, Jody Azzouni, *Deflating existential consequence: A case for nominalism* (Oxford: Oxford University Press, 2004a), chapter 3, and Jody Azzouni, "Evading truth commitments: The problem reanalyzed," *Logique et Analyse* 206 (2009c), 139–176.

It might have been thought (and actually is thought by most philosophers, past and present) that to say what is true about things in the world requires only sentences, statements, propositions (whatever), containing terms that only refer^r to those things and that only attribute properties (and relations) to those things that they actually have. It might have been correspondingly thought (and actually is thought by most philosophers, past and present) that our thinking about the world similarly tracks actual objects by containing concepts that refer^r to and only to those things and that attribute (when correct) properties and relations that actually hold of what is thought about. In reality, however, thought and speech often successfully match aspects of the world—and enable true thought and speech about the world—in a far more indirect way. True thought and speech corresponds to the way the world is, but it (often) doesn't do so by directly attributing properties and relations to (real) things in the world.[14]

For example, we get S's experience descriptively correct—sometimes—not by describing the objects that his experience is of because (sometimes) those experiences aren't of anything at all. In such cases, our statements correspondingly aren't about his experience; they're about^e what those experiences are of. Aboutness^e, though, isn't a tricky or clever way of being about something unreal (that Meinongians posit); it's not (as I indicated in 1.7) a genuine relation at all. Nevertheless, statements about^e the content of S's experience are true and evidentially relevant to S's actions and psychology, and more deeply, evidentially relevant to his neurophysiology.

But how? some may wonder. How are we able to construct truths that are relevant to S's experience without those truths being about^r the contents of that experience (without, in fact, those truths being about^r anything at all)? Nothing is easier. If S's experiences were of actual objects, all that would change in the corresponding true descriptions would be that the truths in question actually refer^r to those objects. Because S's experiences (in the case under discussion), however, are (ontologically) of nothing at all, the corresponding truths are similarly about^r nothing at all. They manage, however, to be pertinent to S's experience via the indirect route just described. They are constructed by "correctly" describing how things seem to S, not by correctly describing how those things are but by giving a descriptive form that would have fit things that would have existed (i.e., if S's experiences had been veridical).[15]

This may seem to invite a parasitical construal of these statements: they are "as if" pretence-statements, written (ontologically speaking) as if S's experience is veridical. This is correct as a description of how we are able to write and say

---

14. Notice the point: I am definitely *not* making the claim that true statements cannot have terms within them that refer^r to items in the world and that such statements cannot attribute to those items properties and relations that they (actually) have. True statements (and thoughts) are complicated and come (ontologically speaking) in all sorts of shapes and sizes. For example, some of their terms refer^r; but some only refer^e.

15. I am not saying that there are possible objects, by the way. I am describing how certain verbal utterances are regarded as truth-apt. They are so regarded on the basis of how other statements (of the same form) would have been evaluated under such and such different circumstances. We can understand how to do this without there being possible objects, possible worlds, or anything in the neighborhood of those doctrines positing such.

such sentences; but it's not correct (and cannot be correct) as a description of the "logical form" of such sentences. This is because such sentences are not of the form (and cannot be of the form): *It is pretended that there are objects such that S experiences them as* . . . So, too, these sentences cannot be sentences that we only pretend to be truth-apt. We need them to actually *be* truth-apt.

The foregoing points show the inadequacy of a number of alternative approaches to sentences (and thoughts) within which empty terms occur. Sainsbury (2005) is an elegant application of negative free logic to the problem of empty terms.[16] Utilizing it, however, provides no way of underwriting any truths containing empty terms other than nonexistence claims.[17] This—in light of the external discourse demand—is unacceptable.

Taylor (2000, 33–35) introduces the idea of pseudo-assertion, where an utterance of "Santa Claus isn't coming tonight" is a pseudo-expression of a statement that replaces "Santa Claus" with descriptive content (during a pragmatic process that's psychologically executed by the utterer), for example, "No jolly, white-bearded, red-suited fellow, who lives at the North Pole and delivers toys via a reindeer-drawn sled is coming tonight." The latter, on Taylor's view, is a fully determinate proposition, in contrast to the former. This kind of view, like pretence views, cannot handle the deductive and confirmatory burden that truth-apt statements using empty terms undertake by virtue of the external discourse demand. Apart from this (and unlike pretence views), Taylor's reconstruction in addition suffers from its systematic replacement of names with psychologically available descriptive content (what he calls "conceptions"). Therefore, his replacement pseudo-assertions aren't responsive to the phenomena—described in 3.2—that make fictional and mythological names empty singular ones: our practice of correcting ourselves in virtue of our recognition that our descriptive content associated with Santa Claus isn't true of Santa Claus. (We mistakenly think he is depicted as having a red beard when in fact the mythological practice depicts him with a white beard.) Not only does Taylor's approach fail to handle the deductive and confirmatory roles of empty singular statements and thoughts, it fails to handle the representational role as well. That is, the pseudo-asserted truths don't line up well with what we take to be the actual truths about fictional and mythological entities, and they can't handle the evidential and deductive jobs that those truths have.

I've been describing (in a general way) the results of chapter 2 (and chapters 1 and 3, for that matter). Nevertheless, this may all seem to be a little too much like magic. We need sentences to be about the perceived "objects" of *S*'s experiences, but because there are no objects to have such sentences about[r], we pretend that the sentences we say are about[e] those objects.[18] But we can't say—for what

---

16. Inspiration for the approach is due to Tyler Burge, "Truth and singular terms," *Noûs* 8 (1974), 309–25.

17. R. M. Sainsbury (*Reference without referents* [Oxford: Oxford University Press, 2005], 73) notes in passing problems with sentences such as "Homer believes in Pegasus," and "Tom is drawing Pegasus," and asserts by way of defense of his approach that "problems of this kind affect all theories."

18. I leave aside the point that talk of pretence is awkward in contexts where our psychological responses are largely involuntary.

look like technical reasons (having to do with the fact that the sentences in question have to actually be truth-apt)—that the sentences we so utter are pretences, and so we don't say that. Furthermore, our semantics can't treat the sentences as—whisper, whisper—pretences; in fact, nothing we say or do can so treat the sentences. Talk of pretence only comes up in philosophical settings, rather like this one where it's noted, not that such sentences are pretences (since they're not allowed to be) but only that we can successfully construct such sentences that are truth-apt but not about[r] what they seem to be about[r] (because there isn't anything for them to be about[r]).

Well, yes, that's exactly how the practice goes. And (surprise, surprise) it's a perfectly consistent and far-reaching practice. Furthermore, there's no alternative. The pretence-theorists want us to just admit that in some sense of "pretence" it's all pretence—more particularly, they want the pretence-aspects of the practice to show up explicitly and contrastingly somewhere in that practice, for example, in the semantics of the sentences or in some way that we fail to treat these sentences as truth-apt. But these are impossible requests.[19]

By contrast, Meinongians and realists grasp a different part of this (very complicated) stick. They focus on the fact just described that we can't treat our way of speaking—semantically (or in terms of how we treat the resulting truth-apt statements)—as a pretence or as truly about nothing at all; they draw the conclusion that therefore we must treat such sentences as truly about[r] "Meinongian objects" or real objects. That doesn't follow either. That we have to speak a certain way—and that we have to frame our semantic theories a certain way—simply says nothing about what our resulting ontological commitments must be. A metaphysical invocation of objects of any sort needn't arise. Pretence theorists, I think, have the right picture of our verbal practices (in these areas); they simply underestimate what can be done to change them. (Or they misrepresent the forms those practices actually take.) Meinongians and realists, on the other hand, are guilty of a (admittedly subtle) non sequitur. No argument exists that takes us from the ways that a verbal practice must be to either what there is or even to what that verbal practice commits its users to take there to be. By the way (and some philosophers will see how this point is related to the foregoing) the ontological argument doesn't work either—even if existence *is* a predicate.

---

19. I leave aside the global pretence option. My approach can make distinctions, between genuine pretence and genuine truth-aptness, that the global-pretence theorist has no access to.

LANGUAGES WITH AND WITHOUT ONTOLOGY

Must not dragons have some *mode of being,* exist in some universe of discourse? To [this] rhetorical question it is sufficient to reply with another: What, *beyond the fact that it can be referred to,* is said of something when it is said to have some mode of being or to exist in a universe of discourse? The alleged modes and universes are so admirably suited to perform their function that they are not above suspicion of having been invented for the purpose.

—Richard Cartwright (1960, 30)

Introduction to Part II

Each chapter of part I studied a different area of discourse in fair detail. The aim is to show that an ontologically neutral construal of singular idioms—when applied to domains of discourse that we antecedently take to be about what doesn't exist—is fruitful and plausible despite the widespread perception that singular idioms semantically require ontology. Apart from the shared ontologically neutral perspective, there is a second significant methodological assumption at work: the external discourse demand. Our talk about fictions, hallucination, and (of course) mathematical abstracta cannot be treated in isolation from the rest of our discourse. This is because such talk bears evidentially and deductively elsewhere in our science, and it also bears on our ordinary beliefs.

Part II contains two chapters that aren't unified in this way, either with each other or with the previous chapters. The aim of chapter 4 is to present a picture of science, scientific languages, and truth in accord with the methodological assumptions of part I. Chapter 5, on the other hand, is meant to overthrow the widespread assumption that ontological commitments are crucial to semantics in general, and to the semantics of singular idioms in particular. The motivation for chapter 5 should be clear already. I use the rest of this introduction, therefore, to motivate the set of topics that chapter 4 addresses.

Let's start with the obvious fact that we have ever so many kinds of discourse that differ strikingly in subject matter and (correspondingly) in the nature of their vocabulary. Quite broadly speaking, there is (for example) moral discourse, mathematical discourse, scientific discourse, commonsense discourse, and fictional discourse. A closer look shows that speaking of each of these as discourses is still too coarse-grained: these "discourses" also splinter into many distinct subdiscourses with distinct subject matters and correspondingly distinct vocabularies. The many scientific discourses, for example, splinter into subdisciplines: chemistry, biology, physics, sociology, psychology; these, too, splinter into subsubdisciplines—ones that differ strikingly in subject matter, in the regularities that are used, in the tools deployed, and so on. (This is most obvious in physics, biology, and the psychological sciences.) Even more strikingly, a particular scientific subsubdiscipline may itself employ many different "models" to study a phenomenon, where such models themselves differ in mathematical structure, apparent ontology, and so on. So, too, mathematics has numerous subbranches that differ not only in subject matter, vocabulary, and characteristic methods of proof, but even in the logics deployed. Specialization in the sciences has been incredibly successful: the explosion in knowledge has been accompanied, however, by an explosion of subdisciplines and applications of doctrine to such subdisciplines that differ in their approaches, for example, utilize different "idealizations," languages, instruments, and different domains of quantification.

Now modestly add to this welter of differing doctrines, Quine's criterion for ontological commitment—that indispensable quantification brings with it ontological commitment—as well as a companion constraint on singular idioms that such operate successfully only when directed toward what exists. The result—pretty straightforwardly—is ontological pluralism: such discourses must differ in what they're ontologically committed to. The reasoning that leads to this conclusion is a version of the Quine-Putnam indispensability thesis coupled with the recognition that a unified discourse (and accompanying unified metaphysics)—even when restricted to the sciences—isn't an option.[1]

One striking development in late twentieth-century (analytic) philosophy and—consequently—in early twenty-first century (analytic) philosophy is the emergence of a stunningly large number of pluralist philosophical views. Metaphysical pluralisms, for example, have become very common: the world (we're told) is a variegated metaphysical structure (where "structure," when applied in a worldwide fashion, is empty of content) that locally varies in the kinds of things that there are, in the regularities that govern all these many kinds of things, and in the ways that such things (and their regularities) can be studied.[2]

Specific to philosophy of science has been a corresponding demise of general studies of science and scientific method, and their replacement by specialized

1. Also excluded as options are the various species of fictionalism: attempts to render the discourses in question as either false or as not even truth-apt. I indicated in earlier chapters that pretence approaches to indispensable discourse face problems because of the external discourse demand. For further discussion of the Quine-Putnam indispensability thesis, and the drawbacks of fictionalist responses to it, see Jody Azzouni, "Evading truth commitments: The problem reanalyzed," *Logique et Analyse* 206 (2009c), 139–176.

2. *The dappled world*, the title of Nancy Cartwright's 1999 book (Cambridge: Cambridge University Press), nicely conveys the kind of metaphysical pluralism that has become so popular. A somewhat neglected anticipation of the current embrace of pluralist metaphysics is Nelson Goodman, *Ways of worldmaking* (Indianapolis, Ind.: Hackett, 1978).

subdomains in philosophy of science: philosophy of biology, philosophy of chemistry, philosophy of quantum physics, philosophy of general relativity, philosophy of psychology, philosophy of vision science, and so on.[3] Part of the motivation for this, no doubt, is the increasing specialization of the empirical sciences themselves; part of it surely is the background pluralist assumption that scientific method—and the accompanying philosophical issues it raises—have been empirically revealed to be philosophical studies of scientific method(s) specific to scientific subdisciplines with no (or little) unifying structural tissue.

Of course, a thoroughgoing unity of science doctrine (with respect to metaphysics, laws, and even epistemology) was never truly on the table if only because of the indispensability of abstracta in science—and, indeed, because of such abstracta (e.g., properties) various metaphysical pluralisms are in many ways of ancient vintage. But nominalism was still a hope—one that was seen by many to have been dashed along with other attempts at the unification of our collective ontological commitments.

Equally dramatic, if not more so, has been the emergence of pluralist philosophical views directed toward the very framework-concepts of discourse—I mean here the notions of truth, existence, and logic: our various discourses, various pluralists claim, not only differ in ontology, they differ as well (and more fundamentally) in the notions of truth and existence that are in play.[4] They even differ (or so some philosophers say) in the logics that are employed. A picture of our current weltanschauung is emerging from this welter of (sometimes quite technical) views: it's a fabric (a "dappled" fabric) of doctrine that serves different needs and connects to a world that is itself unified in name only.

I won't say that the foregoing discussion has provided all the motivations at work for these numerous pluralist doctrines. One must also include Wittgensteinian influences as well as the many philosophical views that attempt to erase borders between moral and factive discourse. Apart from this, no doubt, there are broader intellectual, cultural, and even political factors that have played a major role (perhaps the major role) in making pluralist doctrines such natural ones for so many contemporary philosophers to adopt.

(*Sigh.*) I find myself, alas, tilting against this mob of pluralist views (one against the many, as it were). In a sense that I'll endeavor to make clear, I am an antipluralist. Once upon a time, a very very long time ago (when logical positivists—many with German accents—roamed these United States), various unification views were in vogue. Once one separated cognitively significant discourse from the other stuff (e.g., excluded modes of verbal recreation like poetry), and once one recognized that such discourse was meant to describe the (one) world, one faced the question of how the sciences (that were so describing this one world)

3. These titles alone don't do a very good job of indicating the range of subdisciplines that have emerged in contemporary philosophy of science; they should be accompanied by citation records.

4. One issue I leave aside is this: if notions of existence and truth are pluralized this apparently undercuts the cogency of the previously discussed metaphysical pluralism. I don't claim, of course, that the various pluralisms amount to a grand (and consistent) philosophical pluralist framework.

were being unified—how, despite appearances, these various sciences really involved only one ontology (that given by what is in the world—and, according to most in those days, described by physics) and one set of laws. Doctrines of reductionism (of various sorts) coupled with implicit ontological unifications (e.g., via a hierarchy of structured compositions of objects out of ones lower in the hierarchy) that scaled up in tandem with a corresponding hierarchy of sciences (physics, chemistry, biology, etc.) was seen as the way to go.

Were I a recidivist, (intellectual) life would be easy for me. I would live out my life in the (intellectual) past and pettily carp about the new pluralist views (or ignore them); I would publish short articles about how one or another specific objection to various unification approaches fails on one or another narrow technical ground; and I would spend the rest of my time publishing nostalgic intellectual history. This would be a good life, one peacefully dedicated, as it were, to intellectual punctuation (pun intended). Unfortunately, my hope isn't to return to an earlier set of (positivist-inspired) views but to move past contemporary pluralist doctrines—and fictionalist doctrines, for that matter—to something new. This calls for a lot of work.

In chapter 4, I indicate how I hope to accomplish some of this work. Key to my strategy are the two methodological assumptions that I earlier described as operative in chapters 1–3. The first is this: if one rejects Quine's criterion and the companion ontological doctrine about singular idioms, the inference from discourses that vary in their quantificational (and singular) commitments to a concomitant variation in ontological commitments is denied. Pluralism in doctrine—all by itself—no longer implies anything metaphysical.

The second is the external discourse demand. Contemporary pluralisms, especially in their framework-concept forms (e.g., with respect to truth and logic), misrepresent the relationships among discourses by treating those discourses as if they operate entirely in isolation from one another. The reality is that not only are such doctrines brought to bear on one another evidentially and deductively (as the external discourse demand indicates), but that it's a (philosophically misleading) myth that the statements we employ to represent the world can be neatly segregated into such distinguishable discourses to begin with. The reality is that—at best—all that can be segregated are vocabulary items. The statements we use to represent what the world is like, that we use as evidence and that we use in deductions, are motley constructions with vocabulary from everywhere.[5]

I ply both methodological assumptions in chapter 4 to, on one hand, sketch a new view of science, scientific discourse, our discourse (more broadly), and how that discourse can be taken to relate to what there is. On the other hand, I use these assumptions to rebut various pluralist doctrines. I can't, however, undertake everything needed in this chapter. For example, chapters 1–3 show how to avoid ontological commitments with respect to certain forms of discourse, ones that we

---

5. In fact, to describe the vocabulary items themselves as segregatable is itself a myth, too. The vocabulary items we actually use are themselves strange mixtures from more than one discourse. I cannot discuss this any further now, or in this book.

antecedently take to have as subject matters items that don't exist. But that's not true of scientific doctrine generally. The pluralism of doctrine in science isn't—one would think—to be handled by simply denying ontological commitment tout court to scientific discourse. I indicate some of what needs to be said about this issue in chapter 4, specifically in section 4.6.[6] My primary aim, however, is to explain exactly how—without there being quantifier commitments in common—different scientific discourses can nevertheless deductively and evidentially bear on one another as required by the external discourse demand. Explaining how this is possible is one of the two primary aims of chapter 4. As mentioned, the other is to undercut pluralist views about truth and logic; to this end, the external discourse demand is brought against those views in sections 4.7–4.9.

One last point. The first several sections of chapter 4 are dedicated to an overview (and refutation) of certain forms of strong reductionism and of supervenience approaches to the unification of scientific theories. Some philosophers will be understandably impatient: why are we going over all this (old) stuff? Well, one reason is that this (old) stuff isn't entirely dead. Supervenience in particular, in one form or another, is very much alive and flourishing—both in philosophy of science, and more generally, in metaphysics. Second, and more important, *that* a philosophical doctrine is false is almost never of interest. What's of interest is *why* it's false. It should be no surprise that my reasons for denying that these approaches will work differ from other attacks on the approaches found in the literature. I claim that what sinks these approaches is precisely fallout from the rejection of Quine's criterion: that differing domains of scientific theories contain items that we recognize not to exist (in any sense at all)—despite their quantificational indispensability.

---

6. I say more of what needs to be said in Jody Azzouni, "A new characterization of scientific theories," *Synthese*, forthcoming (c).

Scientific Languages, Ontology, and Truth

4.0 An Overview for Browsers, Grazers, and Those Who Need to Know What the Future Brings before It Brings It

My aim in this chapter is to illustrate the impact of the existence of evidentially and deductively indispensable truth-apt statements (that nevertheless don't refer to anything real) on broader issues in philosophy of science. To this end, I'll illustrate how the standard picture of the ontology of a science—as given by the domain of discourse of that science—must be modified, and I'll sketch the alternative picture that's needed.

I begin by broad-stroking a picture of scientific theories and scientific knowledge gathering. Such theories (even within disciplines such as "physics" or "chemistry") have specialized unshared vocabularies that demand (when such theories are construed semantically) specialized discourse-domains. In general, such discourse-domains have only oblique relationships to the actual ontology of the subject matters being studied (as those are recognized by scientific practitioners). Compatibly with this view of science, I describe a version of minimal physicalism: that (i) there is a set of physical laws that applies to everything that there is, and that (ii) any thing (that exists) is an aggregate of items from a certain set of such that are referred to in certain physical theories. Minimal physicalism is open to empirical refutation. I should stress that I'm not committing myself to minimal physicalism; my aim, rather—as noted—is to show its compatibility with the view of scientific theories that I am committed to. In particular, it's an empirical possibility that there is no set of laws that apply to everything there is. I should also add that "law" should not be given a particularly heavy reading: everything I have to say in this chapter is compatible with a reading of the word that amounts to: general regularity.

In section 4.2, I begin undertaking the question of how statements utilizing such specialized vocabularies (and taken as referring^r and referring^e to specialized entities) are nevertheless successfully brought to bear on statements in other specialties that involve quite different vocabularies. To prepare for this, I provide a somewhat "potted" history of classical positivistic (and postpostivistic) views about scientific laws, physicalism, and strong reduction, and describe how successor supervenience views arose from the perceived failures of the earlier views. In turn (in section 4.3), I show that supervenience forms of physicalism ("token physicalism") also fail because of the specialized nonexistent entities that terms in scientific theories refer^e to.

The question of how statements from different scientific theories are brought to bear on one another is, therefore, still a live problem. I show that the primary tools for enabling the evidential and deductive crossing of vocabulary barriers are gross correlational regularities. (The reader has already seen examples of such items in chapter 2, but I didn't so label them at that point.) Gross correlational regularities are empirically established correlations that contain the vocabulary of one specialized scientific subspecialty (or another) in their antecedents and the vocabulary of a different specialized scientific subspecialty in their consequents. In section 4.4, I give one illustration of a class of such regularities (correlations between genotypes and phenotypes) and describe the general properties of such regularities. In section 4.5, I describe a second class of such regularities, correlations between neurological states, events, and so on, and psychological states, events, and so on. Section 4.6 characterizes the logical form that some of these regularities take.

With the descriptions of gross correlational regularities in place, the external discourse demand is pressed into service to refute certain versions of logical pluralism (in section 4.7) and truth pluralism (in sections 4.8 and 4.9). I show that the demands of an indispensable truth idiom, which is needed for the deductive application (from one area of science to another) of evidence, and of scientific regularities and laws (i) require that such a notion of truth be uniformly applicable to *all* our statements (and, thus, that pluralist approaches to truth are inadequate), and (ii) require that such a notion of truth not be conceptually wedded—as in certain metaphysically robust versions of correspondence truth—to ontology.

I also show a version of (i) with respect to what may be described as the logic governing the role of deduction in the applications of scientific generalization and in bringing evidence to bear on such: this logic, as well, must be uniformly applicable (and so, pluralist approaches to logic will also be shown to be inadequate). All of this may be described as the unveiling of the epistemic and metaphysical machinery that's operative behind the external discourse demand that has played such a prominent role in the foregoing chapters of this book.[1]

4.1 Scientific Languages, Their Domains of Discourse, Ontology, and Minimal Physicalism

The point of this section is to give a general description of my picture of scientific languages and scientific knowledge gathering (and to indicate some of the arguments for it).[2] In so doing, I prepare the ground for discussions in later sections of "strong reductionism," "supervenience," the "logical form" of scientific generalizations, and the existence of what I call *gross correlational regularities*—scientific regularities that are motivated by ontological assumptions but that must be empirically established rather than deduced from background theories.

In this section, I illustrate how what we take to be real (what we presuppose there to be) in our study of scientific subject areas is only obliquely related to the contents of the "domains of discourse" of the scientific languages that we use to describe those scientific subject areas.

Scientific studies always involve taxonomies of subject areas embodied in changing collections of terms (that is, embodied in changing interconnected collections of predicates and constants to be used in characterizations of evidence and regularities) that are contained in languages L_s. The "domains of discourse" (domains for short) of such collections of terms of such languages L_s can be described in the standard first-order way: as what the quantifiers of any such L_s range over, as what the constant terms (the names) of L_s refer to, and as what the predicate terms of L_s hold of.[3]

Although scientific studies, using scientific languages, are directed toward the study of (various kinds of) objects, or more accurately, are directed toward a range of (sometimes quite specific) phenomena (e.g., a certain family of insects, the calls of prairie dogs, the materials and events occurring in the Earth associated with earthquakes, volcanoes, the movement of landmasses, and so on, how plant life on other planets is likely to vary according to the class of star that those planets orbit, changes induced in certain sorts of solid materials under certain sorts of stresses and pressures, the flow at certain speeds of liquids with certain properties, and so on), there is no assumption that the actual ontology of that

---

1. Otávio Bueno (personal communication) has pressed me on why I treat scientific theories as linguistic entities rather than as models—as so many contemporary philosophers of science insist on doing. The primary reason is that pace van Frassen, Suppe, and others, I regard the distinction between scientific theories as linguistic entities and as models as one "without a difference." In particular, as the reader will see, many of the insights proponents of the "semantic conception" of scientific theories credit themselves with (and indeed, deservedly so) are nevertheless easily transferred to an approach that treats scientific theories as linguistic entities. See Jody Azzouni, "A new characterization of scientific theories," *Synthese*, forthcoming (c) for further details.

2. Further details—with examples from the sciences—may be found in part I of Jody Azzouni, *Knowledge and reference in empirical science* (London: Routledge, 2000a; paperback edition with important corrections, 2004). Also see part II of Jody Azzouni, *Deflating existential consequence: A case for nominalism* (Oxford: Oxford University Press, 2004a), and Azzouni forthcoming (c).

3. I make no real distinction, here and in what follows, between a "theory" and a "language."

range of phenomena (the sorts of things actually being studied) has to be identified with the "objects" in the domains of the various languages, L_s, that are brought to bear in these studies.

Sometimes the domain of such a language genuinely overlaps with the real ontology of a subject area; usually such a domain contains much else—the referents of mathematical terms, for example. More surprisingly, it may fail to contain some or all of the real objects that are (actually) being studied.[4] Finally, when a domain of discourse of a scientific language L_s does contain something related to what's really out there (and being studied), the items in the domain are often idealized in various fashions.

Such idealizations can be quite dramatic—both in the properties attributed to the objects, and in how those objects are distinguished and identified. For example, it may be understood that actual physical objects appear in a domain of discourse of a theory; but they may appear there as point masses, or as topologically defined continua.[5] There isn't anything, I think, that can (or should) be said in general about the nature of the overlap (if any) between the domain of a scientific language L_s and the actual ontology of (or that underlies, i.e., involves the truth-value inducers of) the phenomena being studied.

My describing scientific studies as—generally—implemented by the use of many scientific languages is deliberate. For current purposes, it's best to understand "language" fairly narrowly—to make the word amenable to first-order idealizations. But in doing so, especially when it comes to the physical sciences, the terminological result is that what we must describe as brought to bear on a subject area is therefore not a single language—not a single "theory"—but a family of such. Complementing this fact is that often, scientific laws—Newton's second law is an excellent example—are schemata-laws.[6]

---

4. Arguably, certain subdisciplines of linguistics—for example, the study of syntax or phonology—have ontologies (have truth-value inducers) that can be characterized physiologically, or perhaps more specifically, neurophysiologically. But the domains of the languages these syntactic theories are couched in contain—and sometimes only contain—Platonistic types.

5. I should note that there is no difference—no methodological difference—between saying that a real object appears as a point-mass (in the domain of a theory) and saying that the theory (having in its domain only purely mathematical objects, point-masses—among other things) is applied to real objects to yield results that hold of those real objects but only insofar as their not being point-masses can be, to a degree and in a context, disregarded. Everything else one should want to say can be adjusted to accommodate either way of speaking. (This kind of looseness of identity has arisen before—in the case of the embeddings of mathematical theories in other such mathematical theories. Recall the discussion of this in section 3.3.)

6. It's especially important to recognize the schemata nature of Newton's law F = ma; otherwise one will be misled by the many guises that "forces" take in various applications of this law. One may even indulge in Wittgensteinian extremes by describing the concept of "force" as affected by "property-dragging"—claiming, that is, that the concept of force really isn't the "same thing" as it appears in different physical applications, for example, in statics, or in the various theories of fluid mechanics, or the various theories of subatomic particles. One may thus claim that the way that the concept of "force" mutates to fit various applications isn't theory governed; instead, it meanders and transforms—in a theory-independent way—under the differing pressures of different applications. See Mark Wilson, *Wandering significance: An essay on conceptual behavior* (Oxford: Oxford University Press, 2006) for an example of this kind of mischaracterization. Pace Wilson, the notion of force (both in Newton's hands, and after) is one of the most successful theory-governed concepts of all time. The extensions of the notion of force—in new applications—have been due almost entirely to successful theory-mediated embeddings of that notion (and the laws governing it) within new mathematical theories that yield extremely useful applications. Force is definitely not a family concept—it's not like "game." Distinction are to be made,

Consider, for example, the collisions of billiard balls or other relatively spherical objects. It would be naive to think that this is a topic area to be studied by one (physical) theory. There is no such single "theory." Rather, there are theories describing "billiard balls" where such are internally structured only in such and such ways, collide only in such and such ways (e.g., only in pairs, and/ or only at certain low velocities, and/or generating no internal temperature changes, and/or generating only small internal deformations of such and such sorts, etc.). Real spherical objects—of one sort or another—that hurtle toward one another and collide (actual billiard balls, made of such and such materials, rolling toward one another on such and such surfaces, and otherwise constrained in special ways; actual subatomic particles of such and such sorts, colliding under such and such specified circumstances) are studied only indirectly by the construction of mathematical "collision models" that replicate, more or less well, aspects of the behavior of these real things.

There are many different sorts of mathematical "collision models" of various degrees of physical and mathematical complexity that—despite that complexity—nevertheless involve numerous constraints on (simplifications of) the internal structure of the colliding objects, the medium of their movements, and the nature of their contact with one another. Mathematically speaking, the class of such models is entirely open-ended—there can be no a priori (or axiomatizable) set of constraints on what sort of mathematics is to be included in the apparatus of such a model. Therefore, the class of all mathematical "collision models" isn't well defined and isn't properly described as a physical theory. Corresponding to this is that the collisions of spherical—and nearly spherical—objects can't itself be a proper subject area for one branch of physics but only for a number of them.

This (toy) example illustrates an important lesson in how little the individuation of scientific theories—even the individuation of scientific theories within narrow subspecialties—can have to do with the individuation of kinds of objects (as we understand those objects to really be like). Real events and objects are rarely, if ever, to be fully described within the rubric of one scientific theory—regardless of how broadly such a theory is to be understood. Instead, a subject area—a collection of objects engaged in one or another kind of event—is approached by a variety of descriptive approximations of those objects and events (via mathematical ersatz) that take account of (to varying degrees) the complex aspects of the behavior of those objects by bringing in additional science and (often) by using ever more complex mathematics. In some cases, the descriptive approximations can be ordered in their levels of complexity: an increasing physical

---

of course, between the various fundamental forces (with their particular force laws), various derived forces of one sort or another, the latter often combined with pseudo-forces (like centrifugal forces, Coriolis forces; the inclusion, in the external forces acting on a fluid "particle," of the net gains and losses when rapidly moving real molecules exit and enter that "particle," etc.). Acknowledgment of these—ultimately metaphysical—distinctions among forces is eons away, however, from any (Wittgensteinian) thesis of the sort Wilson hopes to impound the concept of force into illustrating.

accuracy corresponds to the increasing complexity of the additional mathematics that's included as part of the toolkit of the model.[7] Other times—because of the sheer intractability of the mathematics or the complexity of the phenomena under study—different aspects of the behavior of the phenomena cannot be treated in a series of theories of increasing complexity (and corresponding accuracy), but only by concomitant approaches that take account of different aspects of that phenomenon (and, therefore, each of which can only be applied in a narrow range of special circumstances, where what they leave out or treat in a simplified way has correspondingly little empirical effect).[8]

This is why it's important to note—contrary to the popular (but gruesome) characterization of science or scientific terms (or "natural-kind" terms) as "carving nature at its joints"—that scientific subject areas aren't particularly distinguished or delineated ontologically; at least, they aren't for the most part. Rather, they are delineated by the range and scope of a (then currently available) tractable set of tools, specifically instrumental ones, and by in addition a kind of conceptual tractability: access to a set of mathematically exploitable regularities, couched in one or another language of that study area, that can be brought to bear on the phenomenon (although often only under special circumstances). Thus, methodologically well-defined scientific studies are often irregular and jagged from a purely ontological point of view: what's naturally included (or excluded)—ontologically speaking—isn't particularly natural. The (then current) degree of tractability of instrumental and conceptual tools, in turn, may or may not be related to aspects of the actual items being studied.[9]

The ontology of the sciences—the objects, and their machinations, that we study—although only obliquely visible through the lenses of the discourse-domains of the languages of the sciences, are not otherwise unavailable to scrutiny. We are often quite good at recognizing the objects that exist—tables, books, ourselves, animal cells, viruses, molecules, stars, and also (instances of) water, gold, mercury, and so on—even if these things must be described from the vantage point of theories and languages that characterize them as in various relations to things that don't exist and/or as bearing properties that they (strictly speaking) don't have. It isn't possible, however, to formulate languages—at least it's not possible to formulate languages that are particularly useful—that describe such things but that don't also bind these things via descriptions to other things that don't exist. That's why—in a nutshell—the domains of scientific languages, generally, only obliquely reflect our actual ontological commitments.

This picture of scientific languages and their discourse-domains is compatible with a version of physicalism that regards everything there is as "composed"—as

7. For example, by adding additional terms to differential equations. Because solving such equations involves integration techniques, even small changes in the differential equations can translate to massive increases in the complexity of the methods (of the sophistication of the mathematics) needed—even when the methods are not directed toward explicitly solving the equations (something usually impossible) but just to the extraction of useful information from such equations without providing solutions for them.

8. Similar examples may easily be found in economics or ecology.

9. A case where ontological factors do bear: chemical methods affect the electromagnetic relations among and within the molecules of substances. They don't affect the strong forces that govern the nuclei of atoms. Thus chemical methods can be found for transforming iron and oxygen into iron oxide, but not ones that can transform wood into gold.

amounting to nothing more than what is composed, or that are the "aggregates"—of the physical items that are the target study items of (certain branches of) physics. According to such a physicalism, that's all there is. This isn't to say, of course, that characterizations of what there is as they occur in current (fundamental) physics are either complete or even—as far as they go—right. Rather, the physicalism being described is programmatic. It's also (as I've just indicated in the preceding paragraph) not to say that the descriptions of these things in the language of physics—more precisely, what the terms of the languages of fundamental physics refer to—is all and only what there is. Apart from the fact that the macro-objects (composed of the items studied in such fundamental physical theories) don't directly appear in those theories, the terms of such theories also indispensably refer to mathematical objects.

I'm going to call *minimal physicalism* the joint commitment to, first, that there is a set of physical laws that apply to everything that there is, and, second, that any thing (that exists) is an aggregate of items from a certain set of items referred to in certain physical theories.

Having stated minimal physicalism, I need to give a couple of caveats. On the first condition: many physical laws and regularities are specialized, and recognized as specialized. But the hope is that there are general, exceptionless laws that apply to everything. (This, of course, is a hope open to being dashed empirically.) On the second condition: (i) any physical theory, as noted, refers to a great deal more than what exists, abstracta for example. But some (fundamental) theories are taken to refer to—among much else—items that both exist and that are fundamental precisely in the sense of being the elements that everything (else) is composed of. (ii) Where coherent, "aggregates" may be composed of single fundamental physical items.

I need to stress again the point of presenting minimal physicalism. It's to show that the forthcoming rejections of reductionist and supervenience approaches to the unification of scientific theories (and scientific ontology) doesn't lead—as many philosophers presume—all by itself to a demise of a substantial physicalist position. Having said that, I'm not—at this time—committing myself to minimal physicalism, but I do take it very seriously, think it's defensible, and in any case will use it in comparisons with the other kinds of physicalisms that philosophers have committed themselves to. I should also note that with the demise of Quinean approaches to ontology, how serious ontologists are to read the ontology of the physical sciences off of the truths (and, more broadly, off of the practices) of those sciences is no longer a philosophically trivial technical matter of reading off commitments from quantifiers of appropriately regimented scientific theories.[10]

Despite taking the sciences to study what may, broadly speaking, be regarded as the objects and events belonging to a physicalist ontology (despite, that is, minimal physicalism), scientific practice dictates that the "language of science" must splinter into numerous languages that only somewhat overlap in their domains and only somewhat overlap in their terminology. The varying domains of these languages contain different kinds of items (most of which don't exist, or don't exist as they're so described). Couched in such languages, therefore, are various generalizations and

---

10. For further discussion of these issues, see Azzouni (2004a).

regularities that utilize highly specialized vocabularies. This is especially true of the physical sciences—the sciences that philosophers are quite prone to describe as if they all occur within the rubric of one "physicalistic" language.

Given this picture, the following question becomes pressing. How is it that the resulting scientific evidence and generalizations can be brought so widely to bear on one another? Given, say, that one theory is housed in a language L_s with one domain, how is it to be brought to bear on statements housed in another language L_{s*} with an entirely different domain? Another way to put this important question is this. Given that scientific studies are so specific in the subject area studied, the specialized tools utilized, the tightly applicable conceptualizations brought to bear, and the languages within which scientific specialists write and speak, how is it that science (as a whole) nevertheless manifests so much deductive and evidential "holism?" (How is it that scientific results and data are brought so widely to bear on other scientific studies that are so far away from the specific language locales where they were originally spawned?) Answering this question properly is one of the aims of this chapter, and it's taken up explicitly in section 4.4. As a preliminary, however, it's necessary to present in moderate detail an older view of scientific law and illustrate earlier attempts to answer this question via the tool of strong reductions and via the tool of supervenience. This is undertaken in the next two sections.

4.2 Scientific Regularities, Laws, and Strong Reductions

The old (positivistic) characterization of the form of scientific laws and regularities is that such laws and regularities take the general forms: $(x)(Px \rightarrow Qx)$ or (x) $(Px \leftrightarrow Qx)$.[11] It's crucial to the old view that the variable x appearing after P and after Q is the same one, and therefore, that the variable following P and the one following Q range over the same domain. This syntactic model seems to characterize some regularities found in the sciences, for example, *every electron has negative charge, copper conducts electricity, sugar dissolves in water; water, at such and such ranges of temperature and pressure, is liquid.* These, provided the mass terms that appear are appropriately regimented, seem to take the required form $(x)(Px \rightarrow Qx)$.[12] Call this the standard (postivistic) model of a law.

11. See, for example, Carl G. Hempel, "Studies in the logic of confirmation," in *Aspects of scientific explanation and other essays in the philosophy of science* (New York: Macmillan, 1965), 3–46; or Nelson Goodman, *Fact, fiction, and forecast*, 4th ed. (Cambridge, Mass.: Harvard University Press, 1983).

12. But with a closer look, it becomes clear that some (most) of these examples don't fit the model. Consider "Copper conducts electricity." This is fairly silly as a characterization of a real law if only because "conducting electricity" must be cashed out in several subdisciplines of physics (and branches of engineering) in a number of different ways, involving the use of rather different domains; this results—syntactically speaking—in a much more complicated law or set of laws. It would be a fascinating matter to illustrate all this at length, but that would be a digression. Suffice it to note that the content of the generalization is hardly to be captured by the fact that pieces of copper wire manifest such and such properties (e.g., when used with batteries). Similar remarks apply to the other examples. The positivistic hope, of course, was that any successful science is captured in its (theoretical) content by its being construed as a complex set of such generalizations.

The standard (postivistic) model of a law, coupled with the subsidiary assumption that such laws and regularities are derived from or subsumed under one another via their deductive relations, and that the same is true of how they are empirically applied, provided (for at least two generations of philosophers) a relatively unified paradigm of scientific law that raised a correspondingly unified set of philosophical problems to which a continuing community of philosophers of science could attend. (It provided, as it were, a unified paradigm, in Kuhn's several senses of the word.) We have seen nothing like it in philosophy since its demise.

Confirmation and disconfirmation, for example, were characterized syntactically in terms of universal instantiations: $(x)(Px \rightarrow Qx)$ is confirmed by Pa & Qa[13]; it's disconfirmed by Pa & $\neg$Qa. More generally, scientific explanation itself was characterized as tracking deductive relations among statements (the "covering law" model of explanation). Numerous technical problems accompanied both the standard model and attempts to extend that model beyond the cases it was originally applied to: the raven paradox, the new riddle of induction (grue), questions about degrees of confirmation (and disconfirmation), the accommodation of statistical regularities, the problem of true generalizations with empty antecedents, the distinction between lawlike and accidental generalizations, the insensitivity of deductive models of explanation to the apparent asymmetry of explanation, the insensitivity of deductive models of confirmation to the apparently time-sensitive nature of scientific confirmation (e.g., the avoidance of after-the-fact confirmations of theories), and so on.[14]

One other complication in extending the model is the apparent fact that scientific practice seems to introduce many regularities—even laws—that clash with the anaphoric role of the variable x in the standard model of a law: the regularities (instead) seem to cross domains of discourse. *All water is H_2O; musical hallucinations are associated with hyperperfusion in the right temporal cortex and in the right inferior frontal cortex;*[15] *upon reversal of the anode polarity the ions*

13. Actually it's confirmed either by $\neg$Pa or by Qa (the raven paradox).

14. The literature is beautiful and vast. See the works of Hempel, Carnap, Popper, and many of their students; anthologies like H. Feigl and M. Brodbeck, eds., *Readings in the philosophy of science* (New York: Appleton-Century-Crofts, 1953), or Baruch Brody, ed., *Readings in the philosophy of science* (Englewood Cliffs, N.J.: Prentice Hall, 1970). Also helpful for filling out the picture are Ernst Nagel, *The structure of science* (New York: Harcourt, Brace & World, 1961); Goodman (1983); and Bas. C. van Fraassen, *The scientific image* (Oxford: Oxford University Press, 1980) (the latter because he contrasts and motivates his position with respect to the previous literature).

I should note one other striking problem. This is that almost all scientific regularities involve exceptions that cannot be cleanly characterized; that is, the exceptions to the regularities cannot be anticipated ahead of time (they involve "ceteris paribus clauses"). If such exceptions could be cleanly characterized, we could replace the P in a ceteris paribus law $(x)(Px \rightarrow Qx)$ with an appropriately qualified P*, and in that way provide an exceptionless generalization. Notice that the problem—in part—is a problem of expressibility: the hedged regularity can't be written down. (At least, it can't be written down in a formal language or, for that matter, in an appropriately mathematized one. Using the words "etc.," or "and so on," only indicates the open-endedness of the regularity; they don't provide suitable devices that deductions can take account of—because each regularity is open-ended in its own way.) Many of the scientific laws indispensable to science cannot (similarly) be written down. This is one reason for the corresponding indispensability of the truth idiom, as utilized in blind truth-ascriptions. See chapters 1 and 2 of Azzouni (2004a) for further discussion of this. I discuss blind truth-ascriptions, and give other reasons for their indispensability, in section 4.8.

15. Kazuhiro Shinosaki et al. "Desynchronization in the right auditory cortex during musical hallucinations: A MEG study," *Psychogeriatrics* 3 (2003), 91.

migrate to the anode and tube walls, recombining with charges there, and the current goes to zero.[16]

The standard model of a (scientific) law allows only a narrow range of responses to this problem. In part, this is because the domain of discourse is simultaneously treated—by proponents of that model—ontologically, as containing all and only what the best science takes there to be (at a time). As a result, attempts to "unify" the sciences—to eliminate the different domains of discourse of the different scientific languages—become intertwined with various broader metaphysical reductive programs, such as versions of "physicalism." "Strong physicalism"—as I call the doctrine—isn't merely the claim that all objects, events, and states are physical. This latter claim is restricted to a characterization of the contents of the domain of discourse of the appropriately unified sciences. Strong physicalism adds to this requirement on the domain of discourse one or another requirement on the predicates or the properties suitably present in the sciences: these, it was thought, should only be those of—or definable from—the fundamental science. In turn, for most philosophers concerned with this topic, that fundamental science was taken to be "physics." For ease of presentation, therefore, and despite the discussion of scientific languages in section 4.1 that so strongly militates against it, I'll now acquiesce in this way of speaking of one fundamental science: physics, with one domain of discourse, with a proprietary set of predicates, and with the concomitant talk of other "special sciences" as having their own differing proprietary sets of predicates.[17]

---

16. John D. Ryder, "Electron tubes," in *Encyclopedia of physics*, ed. Rita G. Lerner and George L. Trigg (New York: VCH Publishers, 1991), 319. There is terminology in this last regularity that must be spelled out a little more fully before the regularity can be regarded as—more or less—linguistically self-standing. But doing so will not eliminate the intermeshing of "micro-" and "macro-" terminology. It should not be thought that the appropriate way with these regularities is to treat them not as laws but as "mere" regularities, items to be derived from laws of the appropriate form. One point to make is this: that's usually not possible because the hedged regularities of the special sciences, in general, cannot be deducible from those of fundamental physics (if the latter are exceptionless laws). This hasn't been widely recognized—but the impossibility arises simply from the fact that unless the hedges can be incorporated into a predicate, deduction fails because (as noted in the second paragraph of note 14) the specialized regularity can't be written down in a form that admits its deduction from something exceptionless. (For some details on how such regularities are—with the help of scientific theories—empirically established, see Azzouni 2000a.) A second point to make is this: focusing just on (exceptionless) laws would eliminate from philosophical concern nearly all of the regularities that science actually utilizes—both theoretically and in applications—in physics and elsewhere.

17. Usually accompanying this perspective is an additional assumption that fundamental physics—so described—also provides the "natural kinds" or natural properties of the universe, and that these and only these (and not the properties described in the special sciences) should be represented as the real properties of the real objects of the universe as revealed by science. I won't be dwelling much on these latter concerns; in particular, I'll avoid pronouncing on issues (for example) about disjunctive kinds not being genuine kinds, and thus on the concern that such disjunctions either can't appear in genuine laws or that they can't be used to provide genuine explanations. (See, e.g., Jerry A. Fodor, "Special sciences, or the disunity of sciences as a working hypothesis" [1974], in *Representations* [Cambridge, Mass.: MIT Press, 1981], 127–45; Jaegwon Kim, "Multiple realization and the metaphysics of reduction" (1993a), in *Supervenience and mind: Selected philosophical essays* [Cambridge, Mass.: Cambridge University Press, 1993].) I'll also sidestep demarcation issues—as I've already been doing—regarding laws and mere regularities, as well as other hotly contested topics about natural kinds as those topics bear on such concerns. See Azzouni (2000a) for a (metaphysically deflated) take on much of this.

Given this concern with the unification of the *terminologies* of the sciences, it's not surprising that one early approach to "reduction" (often called "strong reduction," or "type-type" reduction) is modeled on a similar (but successful) practice already widespread in mathematics. The terms—and regularities—of a (special) science are to be "reduced" to that of an "underlying" (more fundamental) science (and ultimately to physics) via the introduction of what have come to be called by some philosophers "bridge laws."[18] P and Q are to be replaced, respectively, with predicates P* and Q* (definable from the terms of that underlying science) so that a generalization $(x)(Px \rightarrow Qx)$ with a quantifier that ranges over one domain can be replaced by $(y)(P*y \rightarrow Q*y)$, using a quantifier that ranges over a different domain. Similarly, number theory can be embedded in a branch of set theory, and the quantifiers ranging over numbers replaced by ones that range over sets. The needed shift in domain is invisible in the foregoing notation, despite my alphabetic switch in variables (but that could be changed with subscripts).

The result of these definitional reductions of the terms of a "special science" to those of a more fundamental science (and ultimately to physics) was therefore supposed to be accompanied by a corresponding reduction in the laws and regularities of the special science to those of the fundamental science (and ultimately to physics) just as the various branches of classical mathematics—their specialized terminology and theorems—were (successfully) so reduced to set theory.[19]

Purported examples of such (promised) strong reductions in terminology, accompanied by corresponding reductions of the laws and regularities, are thermodynamics, for example, contained macro-sized amounts of gases governed by regularities described in terms of pressure, temperature, density, and so on, as reduced to statistical mechanics, for example, to collisions of molecules described in terms of their micro-properties; events characterized in terms of mental items of various sorts as reduced to events described in terms of various functionally relevant biological/physical items occurring within humans ("psychoneural type-physicalism"); chemical transformations and relations of chemical kinds as reduced to physical changes (in configurations) of atoms bearing various kinds of bonding relations to one another; diseases characterized in terms of macro-symptoms manifested by various animals or their organs, as reduced to various physiological events described at—or near—the cellular level that are induced

18. See Nagel (1961), especially chapter 11, 352–66; see Fodor (1974).

19. I'm focusing on strong reductions as they relate to relations between less and more fundamental "special sciences" (e.g., molecular biology and chemistry) and between those and (fundamental) physics. See J. G. Kemeny and P. Oppenheim, "On reduction," *Philosophical Studies* 7 (1956), 6–19; Paul Oppenheim and Hilary Putnam, "Unity of science as a working hypothesis," in *Minnesota studies in the philosophy of science*, volume 2, ed. Herbert Feigl, Michael Scriven, and Grover Maxwell (Minneapolis: University of Minnesota Press, 1958), 3–36; and the more recent Robert Causey, "Attribute identities in microreductions," *Journal of Philosophy* 69 (1972), 407–22. The reductions to be studied were taken both by proponents and opponents to include "reductions" between physical theories and successor physical theories (e.g., Newtonian physics and special relativity). See, for example, P. K. Feyerabend, "Explanation, reduction, and empiricism," in *Minnesota Studies in the philosophy of science*, volume 3, ed. Herbert Feigl and Grover Maxwell (Minneapolis: University of Minnesota Press, 1962), 28–97; Clark Glymour, "On some patterns of reduction," *Philosophy of Science* 37 (1970), 340–53; Larry Sklar, "Types of inter-theoretic reduction," *British Journal for the Philosophy of Science* 18 (1967), 109–24.

by bacteria, viruses, described in such and such ways, for example, genetically, *and so on.*[20]

Although, as noted, mathematics contains numerous such embeddings of mathematical theories in other mathematical theories—ones that are successfully implemented by just such strong "reductions" (definitions)—this isn't true of the empirical sciences, where such are rare enough to be practically nonexistent. The primary reason for the difference is that—usually—the needed terms P* and Q* are simply not definable in the language of the "underlying sciences." Chairs, or squirrels, for example, may be taken to be "aggregates" composed only of the items described in fundamental physics. Such a compositional assumption offers no way of defining the predicates "chair" or "squirrel," so that "chair" can be replaced by "so-and-so many molecules arranged in such and such a fashion."[21] A common way of putting this widely applicable point is that such a definition would require an infinite disjunction of predicates from the underlying science. This is described as the "multiple-realizability" problem.[22]

It's worth noting that multiple realizability is only an in-principle problem: if a special science predicate in fact corresponds to an infinite disjunction of fundamental science predicates, then the possibility of definition is only ruled out by the termino-logical absence of "et cetera" from the formal languages that philosophers are presupposing as normatively operative in the sciences. Of course, this invites the idea that perhaps the needed infinite disjunctions could be introduced definitionally

---

20. A vigorous debate has occurred over whether classical Mendelian genetics is in the process of being (strongly) reduced to molecular biology; most philosophers—it must be said—think that it isn't being so reduced. See, for example, Philip Kitcher, "1953 and all that: A tale of two sciences," *Philosophical Review* 93 (1984), 335–73; Alexander Rosen-berg, *The structure of biological science* (Cambridge: Cambridge University Press, 1985); and C. Kenneth Waters, "Why the antireductionist consensus won't survive the case of classical Mendelian genetics," *PSA 1990*, Philosophy of Science Association, 1 (1990), 125–39. Further citations to the literature may be found in the last item mentioned. With respect to psychological predicates and neuronal ones, Kim (1993a, 309–10) notes that it's "virtually uncontested" that the Feigl and Smart psychoneural "type physicalism" has been refuted, and cites as textual examples of philosophers believing such, passages from Geoffrey Hellman and Frank Thompson, "Physicalism: Ontology, determination, and reduction," *Journal of Philosophy* 72 (1975), 551–64; Ernest Lepore and Barry Loewer, "More on making mind matter," *Philosophical Topics* 17 (1989), 175–92; and Ned Block, "Can the mind change the world?" in *Meaning and method: Essays in honor of Hilary Putnam*, ed. George Boolos (Cambridge: Cambridge University Press, 1990), 137–70. Note 8 of Kim (1993a, 311) provides a substantial list of additional philosophers with the same view.

21. Note the point being made: it isn't a worry—or not exactly a worry—about how items in the domain of the special science are to be assimilated to those in the reducing science. That part, at least as far as the issues raised thus far are concerned, is easy. A squirrel just is such and such a conglomeration of molecules. The problem is that special-ized laws that apply to squirrels need the squirrel-conglomerations of molecules to be more specified than that.

22. See Kim (1993a). Kim credits Hilary Putnam, "The nature of mental states" (1967), in *Mind, language and reality: Philosophical papers*, vol. 2 (Cambridge: Cambridge University Press, 1975), 429–40, for first injecting mul-tiple realizability concerns into discussions of the mind-body problem, and credits Fodor (1974) for developing the ar-gument further. Multiple realizability, however, has been widely recognized to affect candidate strong reductions of all sorts. It should also be noted that even when the needed definitions of terminology are available, as in the case of the thermodynamical properties of gases, the hoped-for corresponding deduction of the laws and regularities of the science (to be reduced) from those of the underlying science, might nevertheless not be available. This is because the underlying science might be deductively intractable (either because of deductive complexity or because of our ignorance of the empirical details), and the needed regularities of the overlying science therefore are "deducible" only under highly constrained (idealized) conditions (e.g., with respect to the "reduction" of thermodynamics to statistical mechanics, the molecules must be treated as simplified thus and so; their contact forces must be idealized as acting in this and that way, the container walls treated as if . . ., their movements as if . . . , etc.). For detailed discussion, see Azzouni (2000a), part I, §3. I return to this point toward the end of this section.

if more powerful languages (ones that look more like English) are presupposed instead.[23] The problem, however, is that no scientific practitioner has any idea what the infinite disjunctions in question would look like. Strong reductions—utilizing definitions—can matter to scientists (and to scientific practice) only if the definitions in question can be explicitly exhibited. Indeed, strong reductions are valuable in mathematics precisely because (and only because) such definitions are explicitly exhibited and explicitly used. In a subtle way, therefore, attention to multiple realizability issues misfocuses the philosophical understanding of the relationships between different scientific languages and theories and how those relationships matter to the science.

It's an illustration of the point of the last paragraph that the ways the laws of a fundamental scientific theory (of one or another branch of physics, say) are brought to bear on squirrels or chairs (or anything else not directly described by the scientific theory in question) don't involve anything even in the ballpark of strong reductions. Rather, in certain contexts a chair or a squirrel can be treated—nearly enough—as a simplified object (such as a homogenous solid sphere, say), and only then can (certain) physical laws be brought to directly apply to it. (E.g., the chair is orbiting the Earth, or it's supporting a small stack of books, or it's twirling symmetrically on one of its legs in a vacuum under uniform gravitational forces, or . . .)

One of the principles of minimal physicalism is that (certain) physical laws apply to everything there is.[24] Such a claim is compatible with such laws not applying directly to anything, but only via various mediating tools such as the "idealizing" of the descriptions of the things in question in various ways. However, as long as such idealizing descriptions can be shown to be restricted to various sorts of "complexity-limiting" ones, the minimal physicalistic claim that there are (some) laws of physics that apply tout court isn't threatened by the ubiquitous use of such idealizations.[25] As noted, minimal physicalism is compatible with the general impossibility of strong "reductions of" the predicates of various scientific theories to the predicates of other scientific theories; it's also compatible with a denial that the domains of discourse of the various "special sciences" are the same as or reducible to those of certain designated theories of fundamental physics. Notice that failures of strong reduction are not to be expected only with respect to the "special sciences"; such failures are also numerous within (with respect to the various theories of) physics itself. I detail this point a little later in this section.

I've already indicated that targeting multiple realizability as the obstacle to strong reductions, rather than targeting the various forms of (mathematical and empirical) intractability that scientific theories labor under, can lead to a serious underestimation of the feasibility of (some versions of) strong reduction. Kim (2005, 55–56) sees multiple realizability as only leading to "reducibility to multiple

23. It also invites the metaphysical postulation of such a definitional "reduction"—of the corresponding properties—as actually existing but as being inexpressible in the language. I won't discuss these options any further.

24. Fodor (1974), 127, stresses that a commitment to the "generality" of physics needn't be accompanied with a commitment to "strong reductionism."

25. Pace Nancy Cartwright, *How the laws of physics lie* (Oxford: Oxford University Press, 1983).

reduction bases, not to irreducibility." Even more strongly, he suggests that (68): "The standard view, as I understand it, is that chemistry and macrophysics are reducible, and in fact have already been substantially reduced, to particle physics via quantum mechanics."[26]

This is naive. The reason has already (essentially) been given: the various "areas" of macro-physics require serious fundamental idealizations; only given such idealizations will the phenomena studied be theoretically (and mathematically) tractable. In particular, fluid dynamics and rational continuum mechanics indispensably use numerous concepts (arising from various physical continuity and differentiability conditions) that presuppose the substances studied to be nongranular and smooth—apart from other "approximation" assumptions. The resulting physical theory must be applied to the phenomena in an autonomous way— relatively independently of more fundamental science (e.g., quantum mechanics and particle physics)—and, correspondingly, without there being any possibility at all of the deduction of such from particle physics (via quantum mechanics). This is both because of the massive mathematical intractability of the latter, and because the specialized concepts of these branches of macro-physics are wedded so thoroughly to particular applications of the mathematics of analysis and topology.[27]

It's also a remarkable underestimation of the situation in chemistry to say the subject has been "substantially" reduced to "particle physics via quantum mechanics." What *is* true is that the elements, and many chemical substances, have been successfully described using (various) physical molecular models of atoms that depict such items and their parts as being in various (spatial) configurations. This is hardly to have reduced chemistry to particle physics via quantum mechanics. Almost every (actual) atom and molecule is theoretically intractable—should direct applications of quantum theory (and related physical theories) to predict its configurations and interactions be attempted. Consequently, chemically relevant notions like "bonding" are open-ended notions not definable from underlying predicates of particle physics (however the latter set of predicates is construed—e.g., as belonging to which fundamental physical theory, in particular). It shouldn't be overlooked that a strong reduction of one scientific field to another—even local

---

26. That the view is "standard"—presumably among philosophers (of science)—doesn't sound right to me, if only because a number of substantial difficulties with the model, raised in the 1960s and 1970s, are recognized to have never been satisfactorily resolved. See, for example, Glymour (1970); Dudley Shapere, "Notes towards a post-positivistic interpretation of science," in *The legacy of logical positivism*, ed. P. Achinstein and S. Barker (Baltimore, Md.: Johns Hopkins University Press, 1971), 115–60; Sklar (1967).

27. See, for example, C. Truesdell, *A first course in rational continuum mechanics*, 2nd ed. (San Diego: Academic Press, 1991), and C. Truesdell and K. R. Rajagopal, *An introduction to the mechanics of fluids* (Berlin: Birkhäuser, 2000). G. K. Batchelor, *An introduction to fluid dynamics* (Cambridge: Cambridge University Press, 1967) starts with a useful discussion of the underlying molecular facts about fluids to indicate why the idealizations indispensably required for successful fluid dynamics are successful (and in what contexts—roughly speaking—they can be relied on). To be recommended highly is Lawrence E. Malvern, *Introduction to the mechanics of a continuous solid* (Upper Saddle River, N.J.: Prentice Hall, 1969), especially (for philosophers) the introduction. My thanks to George Smith for drawing my attention to this book.

It should be added that one searches in vain even for "quantum mechanical" definitions of the subject matters described here: for example, solids, liquids, gases. Often a (macro-) kind of thing is best "defined" this way: it's a kind of thing that such and such a specialized branch of physical theory—with accompanying mathematics—will successfully apply to.

strong reductions of the sort Kim contemplates—require that nearly all the notions used in the to-be-reduced science be amenable to strong reductions.[28]

It's worth noting again that strong reductions, if they existed in empirical science, would be as valuable to scientific practitioners as the actual existence of them in mathematics *is* to professionals in mathematics. Strong reductions, in the context of mathematics, were handed to philosophers by mathematicians (and logicians). Such wasn't the case with strong empirical "intertheoretic" reductions. This should have raised red flags. So consider: any set-theory book, selected nearly at random, is likely to contain "strong reductions," for example, definitions of counting number, rational number, and real number in (one or another) set-theoretic terms.[29] One searches in vain for the corresponding strong reductions of macro-physical notions or those of chemistry to particle physics via quantum mechanics.[30] (For additional discussion of this, see Azzouni 2000a, part I.)

Qualifications of the "red flag" remark in the last paragraph. In all fairness to those early philosophers of science who were focused on models of theoretical reduction (that were in the neighborhood of strong reductions): a large number of them did notice the indispensable role of approximation methods in these so-called intertheoretic reductions.[31] One thing, however, that clearly kept the notion of something like a deductive relation as being behind the "reduction" of scientific theories to other scientific theories philosophically alive for them was an unholy meshing of two ideas that should have been kept distinct: deduction and approximation. I'll briefly illustrate what I mean.

28. One fears that philosophers who think chemistry has been "substantially reduced" to particle physics via quantum mechanics are thinking neither of the rich indispensable vocabulary of actual chemistry nor of the actual quantum mechanical theories of particle physics, but of something like the periodic table.

29. For example, Azriel Levy, *Basic set theory* (Berlin: Springer-Verlag, 1979); Herbert B. Enderton, *Elements of set theory* (New York: Harcourt Brace Jovanovich, 1977).

30. For example, one doesn't find them in books on fluid dynamics or in continuum rational mechanics. More important, one doesn't find them in books dedicated to quantum physics (and related fields). Such are not to be found, for example, in W. Greiner and J. Reinhardt, *Quantum electrodynamics*, 2nd ed. (Heidelberg: Springer-Verlag, 1994); W. Greiner and A. Schäfer, *Quantum chromodynamics*, 2nd corrected ed. (Heidelberg: Springer-Verlag, 1995); W. Greiner and B. Müller, *Quantum mechanics: Symmetries*, 2nd ed. (Heidelberg: Springer-Verlag, 1994); or even in W. Greiner, *Quantum mechanics: An introduction*, 3rd ed. (Heidelberg: Springer-Verlag, 1994). Nor can such be found in L. D. Landau and E. M. Lifshitz, *Quantum mechanics (non-relativistic theory)*, 3rd ed. (Oxford: Pergamon Press, 1977)—not even in an appendix. Worse, not even hints of what these reductions could look like are provided. (Philosophers can search for either strong reductions or hints of such in other books and articles, of course, but they won't find them.) Ironically, even a book like Donald A. McQuarrie, *Quantum chemistry* (Sausalito, Calif.: University Science Books, 1983), is missing such strong reductions (or even hints of such). Instead, what one finds (everywhere) are highly specialized techniques of limited application accompanied by broadly sketched physical models that are useful but highly idealized. The reason (again) is the (mathematical) intractability of the underlying fundamental physical theories accompanied with massive ignorance about the details of the complex phenomena that such theories are applied to that force the development of macro-physical subjects in an autonomous fashion.

31. Glymour (1970, 340) notes that Kemeny and Oppenheim (1956) express awareness of it, and that Putnam and Hempel suggest treating the appropriate reductions as deductions of laws that only approximate the laws that are being "reduced." The notion of a law L_1 approximating another L_2, however, can only be parasitically defined on the basis of certain predictions of L_1 approximating (quantitatively) those of L_2. See my comments on "approximate truth," forthcoming below. Note as well the already observed mathematical and empirical intractability of underlying theories making impossible (in general) deductions even of laws approximating those of the to-be-reduced science.

Although it was recognized very early that there seem to be no good examples of strong reductions in the sciences, it continued to be thought that there were a lot of items that were pretty close, what I'll call "approximation reductions."[32] These, contrary to the views of those philosophers, can't be treated along models of "deduction." One does find everywhere in the sciences, the construction of theories from other theories via mathematical tools like letting limits go to infinity, turning various discrete sums into integrals, removing the (infinite) tail-end of infinite series, and so on. In this sense, Newtonian mechanics can be constructed from special relativity (by letting $c \rightarrow \infty$), and a theory of macro-thermodynamics can be constructed from theories of molecular kinematics. But these are not reductions (of the former to the latter) in any genuine sense. In particular, they are misdescribed as "approximative deductions" because these constructions aren't even remotely truth-preserving. To repeat, they are constructions of theories from other theories, often by the mere removal of certain terms that belong to the "reducing theory." That is, a deliberate falsification is introduced.[33] Similarly described is the introduction (via a limit process) of a theoretically exploitable falsification in what the theory represents (e.g., the replacement of granularity or discreteness, in some sense or other, by smoothness assumptions).

These deliberately introduced falsifications are usually motivated because they lead to a more mathematically tractable (and/or applicable) theory than the original. Furthermore (and crucial to this practice) is that how far the resulting (constructed) theories deviate in their predictions from the theories they're constructed from can (but only in certain cases) be mathematically constrained and calculated—for example, by bounding the dropped terms of a Taylor series.

No doubt some philosophers thought of these as "approximative deductions" along the lines of "approximate truth." But "approximate truth" and other such notions ("degrees of truthlikeness") are promissory notes that no one has ever managed to make good on (suggest an approach, that is, not obviously riddled by counterexamples). There is no workable idea of "approximate truth" available except by such a notion being parasitic on an antecedent idea of it being true (simplicter) that such and such is approximately so and so. In these cases, as just noted, a particular method of constructing a false theory from another theory that's taken to be true (e.g., by removing the infinite tail of a Taylor series) comes thus equipped with a mathematical method by which it can be calculated how far the false theory's quantitative answers deviate from the right answers. In this way, a class of theorems of the constructed theory, $\text{Th}(x_1, x_2, x_3, \ldots, x_m) = \mathbf{R}(x_1, x_2, x_3, \ldots, x_m)$ can be marked out as "approximately true." More accurately, theorems that are strictly true of the form $\text{Th}(x_1, x_2, x_3, \ldots, x_m) = \mathbf{R}(x_1, x_2, x_3, \ldots, x_m) \pm n$, where $\pm n$ bounds the range of error, can be deduced from the false simplified theory.

32. See, for example, Sklar (1967), 116. Glymour (1970, 342) treats the "taking of limits" as a syntactic device.

33. A deliberate "falsification," of course, from the point of view of the theory that the terms in question are being excised from.

Three last points about this issue. First, a device is needed to detach from a false theory the truths deducible from that theory, and the device in question is blind truth-ascription. (I discuss this further in section 4.8.) Second, an important complication that probably contributed to philosophers confusing genuine deductions with these sorts of theory constructions is that in any case, there isn't a simple one-to-one correlation between scientific theories and formal (logical) theories. Many scientific theories are couched in terms of differential equations, so that the target theory characterizing a phenomenon can be "several integrations away" from the presented set of differential equations. Such integrations, however, introduce constants, and terms, that are governed by families of parameter conditions (that can vary widely). By contrast, formal (axiomatized) theories are individuated by, among other things, the specific terms that appear and the specific axioms that govern those terms. Thus scientific theories—in practice—are at best open-ended families of formal (axiomatized) theories that vary greatly in their metalogical properties.

Third, the following historical point should be noted. Feyerabend (1962), notably, denied the existence of "strong reductions" in science precisely because of his recognition of the role of approximation in the shifting from a scientific theory to its successor theory. (In particular, he described successor theories as "replacing" earlier theories precisely because the earlier theories at best approximated their successors.) But his heavy (although unnecessary) use of meaning-holism perhaps obscured how fatal his counterexamples were to "strong reduction" (deduction) models of the relationship between scientific theories and their successor theories, and with respect to "micro-reductions."

4.3 Supervenience

So strong reductionist approaches to the unification of scientific laws and regularities won't work. But how the contours of the refutation of an approach to a task are characterized invariably affects the range of solutions to it that philosophers will think of. Multiple realizability, when mistakenly centralized as the problem for the reduction of scientific predicates to other scientific predicates, directly invites supervenience as a solution. That is, if—despite the indications in section 4.1 of the widespread use of domains of discourse (for theories) that are recognized by most scientists to contain things that don't exist—philosophers nevertheless construe the domains of the various theories of the various sciences as codifying the collective ontological commitments of those sciences, then despite the irrelevance of strong "theoretical reductions" to the practices of science, those philosophers will still be motivated to somehow "reduce" or eliminate specialized (inappropriately swollen) domains of discourse, so that only one domain of discourse (containing all and only the items that science is taken to be truly committed to) remains.

That is, even though nearly everyone has given up on projects of defining the predicates of one or another special science in terms of the predicates of an underlying more fundamental science, many still hope to show that any domain of discourse of a special science can be massaged so that it contains nothing other than what (is composed of what) occurs in the domain of that fundamental science—for most philosophers, (a branch of) physics. To this end, a weaker family of conditions of supervenience are introduced, in the hopes of motivating a "nonreductionist" or "token" physicalism.[34]

Such supervenience conditions involve claims to the effect that although the taxonomies (the predicates) of the various theories of the various special sciences aren't definable in terms of (or strongly reducible to) more fundamental underlying sciences, the domains of discourse nevertheless are. That is, even if a class K of mental events, characterized, say, as the perceivings of an orange, isn't strongly reducible to (definable in terms of) one or more classes of neurophysiological (or physiological, or physical) events, still (the proponent of supervenience will say), any such item within that class K of mental events is one or another event of one or another neurophysiological (or physiological, or physical) type. That is, supervenience (or "weak reducibility") allows that the various languages of the special sciences can retain their own autonomous sets of predicates as long as the quantifiers of all those languages range over and only over what's real (which, again, many philosophers concerned with this literature take to be "physically real" events).

One or another version of a supervenience thesis can be described in a vanilla fashion that physicalists of almost any stripe (including minimal physicalists) won't deny. Writing of mental properties and "physical/biological" properties, Kim (2005, 33) characterizes the supervenience of the former on the latter this way: "*Supervenience.* Mental properties strongly supervene on physical/biological properties. That is, if any system s instantiates a mental property M at t, there necessarily exists a physical property P such that s instantiates P at t, and necessarily anything instantiating P at any time instantiates M at that time."[35] He (34) elucidates mind/body supervenience further, by noting that he understands "supervenience as an ontological thesis involving the idea of dependence—a sense of dependence that justifies saying that a mental property is instantiated in a given organism at a time *because*, or *in virtue of* the fact that, one of its physical "base" properties is instantiated by the organism at that time" (emphasis in original). Many creatures of varying sorts—that is—have "mental" properties; they have desires, are aware of things, and so on; each of these (time-linked) properties is

---

34. See, for example, the papers in Jaegwon Kim, *Supervenience and mind: Selected philosophical essays* (Cambridge, Mass.: Cambridge University Press, 1993c), and the many papers and books of other philosophers cited therein; and Fodor (1974).

35. Kim describes this as "strong supervenience" because of the presence of the word "necessarily" in the formulation. He also notes that there are a number of "not quite equivalent" alternative formulations of mind-body supervenience, and refers the reader to Brian McLaughlin, "Varieties of supervenience." in *Supervenience: New Essays*, ed. Elias Savellos and Ümit Yalçin (Cambridge: Cambridge University Press, 1995), 16–59. The distinctions among these formulations—many of them differing only with respect to how modality manifests in the condition—will not matter to the issue I raise in this section.

taken at a time to supervene on one or another physical property (e.g., involving the state their brains are in) that are had by the organism at that same time.

Another common way of stating mind/body supervenience is that (Kim 2005, 14), "systems that are alike in intrinsic physical properties must be alike in respect of their mental or psychological character."

Quine (1978, 98) puts a similar—but broader—supervenience sentiment somewhat more eloquently: "Nothing happens in the world, not the flutter of an eyelid, not the flicker of a thought, without some redistribution of microphysical states."

Such physicalistic expressions of faith truly are "minimal"—even more minimal than the demands of minimal physicalism, as described in section 4.1—if only because it's unclear what bearing (if any) they have on questions of the working relationships between different sciences, and different scientific theories. There is a hint that somehow one's direct studies of biological/physical states of conscious things (or more generally, one's direct studies of microphysical states) bears on one's study of mentality (or, more generally, on one's study of everything). As so far stated, such is surely compatible with minimal physicalism. However, a more specific characterization of supervenience is to be found in the literature, one that's compatible with the above sentiments but truly goes beyond them and beyond minimal physicalism. It does so by placing specific conditions on the relationships between the predicates (or properties) of the "special sciences"—for example, psychology—and those of a designated fundamental science (i.e., "physics").

A predicate P is said to supervene on a set of predicates P_1, P_2, . . . , iff (for any b) whenever Pb holds, then there is an n ($n = 1, 2, 3, . . .$) such that P_nb holds as well.[36] Correspondingly, we can say that the regularity $(x)(Px \rightarrow Qx)$ supervenes on a set of regularities $(x)(P_1x \rightarrow Q_1x)$, $(x)(P_2x \rightarrow Q_2x)$, . . . , if P supervenes on P_1, . . . P_n, . . . and Q supervenes on Q_1, . . . , Q_n, . . .[37] We can describe the predicates P_1, . . . P_n, . . . , the supervenience base of the predicate P, and (similarly) we can call the regularities $(x)(P_1x \rightarrow Q_1x)$, $(x)(P_2x \rightarrow Q_2x)$, . . . , the supervenience base of the regularity $(x)(Px \rightarrow Qx)$. We can therefore say that a true regularity (x) $(Px \rightarrow Qx)$ is *supervenient reducible* to regularities of an underlying science—ultimately physics—if its predicates have supervenience bases of predicates from that underlying science, and the regularity itself has a corresponding supervenience base of true regularities from that underlying science couched in the supervenience bases of its predicates.

One thing that motivates cashing out the vague supervenience sentiments quoted above in terms of supervenience reducibility is that despite an absence of

36. This is a weak supervenience condition on predicates. As already noted, stronger refinements are possible, for example, invoking various necessity conditions. See, for example, Jaegwon Kim, "Concepts of supervenience," in *Supervenience and mind: Selected philosophical essays* (Cambridge, Mass.: Cambridge University Press, 1993b), 309–35. As I've already noted, the problems to be subsequently raised will affect all the versions of such supervenience conditions.

37. This picture of the relationships of the regularities of the "special sciences" to those of a more fundamental science, ultimately physics, is found in Fodor (1974).

strong reducibility, the satisfaction of supervenience reducibility with respect to predicates, $P, Q, P_1, \ldots P_n, \ldots, Q_1, \ldots Q_n, \ldots$, and regularities, $(x)(Px \rightarrow Qx)$, $(x)(P_1x \rightarrow Q_1x)$, $(x)(P_zx \rightarrow Q_zx)$, $\ldots$, can be taken to establish that the regularity $(x)(Px \rightarrow Qx)$ is true just because the set of regularities, governing the supervenience bases of its predicates, are true. Given an item b, it can be claimed that if Pb and Qb are true, they are true precisely because, for some n, P_nb and Q_nb are true.[38]

The rubric "token physicalism" is often used to describe the claim that non-physicalistic predicates, for example, ones corresponding to mental properties, have supervenience bases of physical predicates. This doctrine is taken to have independent philosophical interest—apart from the supervenience reducibility of "special science" regularities—because of a metaphysical concern with properties. But an important accompanying motivation for interest in token physicalism is that expressed by Fodor (1974): the supervenience reducibility of true special science regularities and laws to those of physics being a suitable characterization of "physicalism."

Required, however, for such supervenience reducibility (in any of its forms—that is—using any of the various definitions of the supervenience of predicates on their supervenience bases) to even get started, is an *already-in-place* assimilation of the domains of discourse of the supervening predicates and regularities to the domain of discourse of the supervenience base predicates and regularities. The supervenience approach isn't even an option if there are items in a domain of discourse of a regularity of a special science that can't be identified (in some way) with the items in the domain of discourse of the underlying science.

If, however, the results of the second chapter are right (and, more generally, if the descriptions of the domains of discourse of scientific theories sketched earlier in section 4.1 are right), then ineliminable from the various psychological sciences (and all sciences, for that matter) are regularities that require quantification over the nonexistent. But such regularities—if they remain in a form involving such quantification—cannot satisfy the conditions of supervenience reducibility. Consider, for example, the following candidate regularity cribbed and modified from chapter 2: "Every hallucinated object that presents itself as a hobbit to anyone either presents itself as resembling some movie character in a movie that person has seen, or it presents itself as resembling a hobbit in a calendar poster that person keeps by his bed."[39] Such a regularity quantifies over nonexistent hallucinated objects and uses predicates that hold of those nonexistent hallucinated objects. These objects are not the sorts of things that have biological/physical properties (because, actually, they haven't any properties at all).[40] Before regularities of this sort can be made amenable to supervenience reducibility, they

---

38. The position must be supported by additional metaphysical arguments about various dependence and/or identity relations among the properties such predicates correspond to, the properties corresponding to the predicates in their supervenience bases, and the items instantiating these predicates, that I here omit.

39. I'm pleased to say that this generalization is false. But that doesn't affect its force as an example.

40. Note the point. The attribution of truth-based properties to hallucinated objects that present as hobbits is required by the indispensability of reference to them and the indispensability of regularities about them. But such

must be put in a form where quantification over hallucinated objects that present as hobbits has been eliminated. The discussion in chapter 2, however, established the likelihood that such a thing is impossible. Similarly, if for certain sociological purposes, we find the following regularity to be both valuable and true: "For any fictional character depicted in a short story as living in London, there is a movie such that he or she is depicted as living in New York," then we are again forced—in the sociological sciences—to include a regularity, with predicates (e.g., "depicted in a short story"), that fails to be supervenience reducible to regularities in the underlying sciences (e.g., psychology, and ultimately, biology and physics).

Even token physicalism, therefore, must fail because nonexistent entities (hallucinated objects that present as hobbits) cannot be composed of elements from the domains of discourse of the physical sciences. This is not to deny that the domains of the physical sciences don't have their own nonexistent objects. As they were described in section 4.1, they obviously do. But for any theory, the nonexistent contents of a domain of discourse are clearly included because of the indispensable purposes of the theory in question that requires them. No physical theory (that I know of) requires hallucinated objects that present as hobbits to their experiencers. In any case, my polemical point is meant to apply narrowly against the proponent of supervenience as a tool for token physicalism. That proponent needs to have one or another story about the mathematical abstracta that are quantified over in physical theories. Perhaps she thinks they can be eliminated à la Field, or perhaps she thinks such abstracta really exist. The burden of chapter 2 is that no strategy to eliminate quantification over hallucinated objects is plausible, and any proponent of token physicalism is unlikely to think such hallucinated objects exist in addition to the abstracta indispensable to physics, and therefore that such should be included in the domain of discourse of a fundamental (physical) science. (If she does think that objects that present as hallucinated hobbits exist, it's unlikely she would also be a "physicalist" who is interested in employing supervenience as a metaphysical tool to support her version of physicalism.)

I hasten to stress again that the failure of "token physicalism" needn't be regarded as a failure of "physicalism." Still sustainable—at least in principle—are the two demands of minimal physicalism: first, to claim that everything (real) is composed of, and only of, certain designated (physically real) items, however those are to be identified; second, to claim that (certain) physical laws nevertheless apply to everything (real). Because the domains of discourse of scientific theories aren't to be taken as describing the ontology of those theories, these physicalistic allegiances can't be elucidated in terms of domains of discourse: that such contain all and only compositions of certain designated (physically real) items. That's false; and the falsity of such leads to the demise of programs of supervenience reducibility.

---

indispensability doesn't extend to the underlying science—for example, biology and/or physics. To project the quantification of such objects to the underlying sciences (to preserve supervenience reducibility) would be daft.

4.4 Gross Correlational Regularities

Two older approaches to the unification of scientific theories have been discussed in the last two sections.[41] I turn now to responding to the question, raised at the end of section 4.1, of how—despite the specialization of scientific languages with their accompanying (and varying) discourse-domains—scientific regularities nevertheless manifest so much widespread evidential and theoretical applicability. This question can be put another way: if connections between scientific theories aren't to be achieved by strong intertheoretic reductions nor by (one or another version of) supervenience reduction, then how are such managed?

One aspect of scientific practice that can help contribute an answer to this question has to do with the ontology presupposed by scientists as operative in different subject areas—what scientists take there to be (with respect to a certain phenomenon). More specifically, what's often relevant is what functionally relevant parts researchers take what they're studying to have, and consequently, how those parts are understood to causally impact on other parts, and on the wholes that they are the parts of. Such background ontological considerations have just been rather broadly described—but it's important to stress that it's often precisely just such a broad construal of what's under study that successful science operates on the basis of.

One of the two conditions of minimal physicalism, recall, is a composition-claim about aggregates. The other is that (some) physical laws apply to whatever there is. These conditions generalize to theories of other sciences—to relations between more fundamental sciences and less fundamental, more specialized, ones. Biological entities, for example, are aggregates of chemicals; chemical laws and regularities thus apply to the molecular parts of biological entities, and therefore correspondingly apply to items composed of such molecular parts, and thus to the biological entities themselves.[42] My claim is that what's often operating in the bringing to bear of different scientific theories on one another are (i) ontological assumptions of this sort (about composition) coupled with (ii) corresponding claims about how a science's regularities and laws apply to the elements making up aggregates of such and such sorts (and the aggregates themselves) coupled in turn to (iii) sophisticated instrumental interactions with the targeted objects, and their functionally relevant parts. What follows in the rest of this section is an extended illustration.

Start with the truism that animals have parts. "Part," of course, is vague insofar as any spread (contiguous or otherwise) of molecules that are definitely contained within an animal can be regarded as a "part" of it. Parts, so called, aren't studied by anyone. Rather, it's only those "parts" that have been empirically discovered to be

---

41. My thanks to Patrick Forber for some discussion of some of the material in this section.

42. Ernst Mayr, *The growth of biological thought* (Cambridge, Mass.: Harvard University Press, 1982), 60, describes "constitutive reductionism" as accepted by modern biologists, and as asserting "that the material composition of organisms is exactly the same as that found in the inorganic world. Furthermore, it posits that none of the events and processes encountered in the world of living organisms is in any conflict with the physico-chemical phenomena at the level of atoms and molecules."

functionally significant that are of interest, and that (one or another) scientific practice attempts to single out for research. Often, these functionally significant parts are recognized by their functional roles, and only later (sometimes) can they be parsed as physical parts of the animal and directly studied as such.

"Genes" were initially characterized, purely functionally, as information-carrying "bits" that are the mechanisms behind the inheritance of traits. Only slowly were such bits localized and characterized physically. Let's—with a little inaccuracy—describe genes as segments of DNA.[43] Chains of DNA are contained in certain cell parts, called chromosomes. Subsequent to Watson and Crick, we know enough about the molecular structure of DNA to understand why it can function both to carry information about genotypes (inheritable traits) that contribute to the traits expressed by an organism and why it can replicate (with errors), so that such genetic information can be (more or less) passed on to the descendants of an organism, or to the daughters of a cell. We also know—in principle—how the "information" contained in a chain of DNA leads to phenotypes, what the mechanisms of communication are between what a gene codes and what traits the (resulting) organism embodies; it occurs via the production of mRNA (messenger RNA), which in turn serve as templates for protein synthesis.

A rapidly growing body of knowledge composed of correlations between genes (here described as combinations of alleles present at loci in chromosomes) and phenotypes (manifest characteristics of organisms) is being established. One important fall-out effect of these correlations is the emerging availability of numerous genetic tests, which can be administered to adults, children, and the unborn, to reveal the presence of and propensities to various phenotypes—a tendency to obesity, say, diabetes, other specific diseases, certain psychological capacities or traits, facts about ancestry, and so on.

It would be a definite mistake to think that our knowledge about DNA and other molecular-biological, chemical (and even physical) laws and regularities suffices to deduce these correlations between genotypes and phenotypes. There are successful cases of reasoning from one to the other that are close to deductions, of course. A surprisingly early success story is the explanation of how the mutation

---

43. One contemporary descendant of the earlier functional notion of a gene is the "cistron"—a sequence of bases in the DNA that codes for a single polypeptide chain or stable RNA molecule. Notice that the definition of a cistron is deliberately open-ended as to how many bases are involved, is not sufficiently general (the genetic material of some viruses is RNA), and isn't a definition in terms of such and such chemicals (or a set of such) but rather in terms of what such and such a sequence of bases does, that is, participates in transcription. The notion, therefore, comes apart from a strict characterization of a "gene," say, as an inherited sequence of DNA. Because only a small amount of the DNA in any cell is ever transcribed, the inherited DNA in a cell includes enormous amounts of apparently role-less DNA, as well as DNA that serves nontranscriptional roles in the cell. Notice, however, that mutation can lead to cistrons (in descendants or in daughter cells) ceasing to be cistrons, or other DNA segments becoming cistrons. Arguably, one result of the discovery of the actual mechanisms of inheritance and cell replication is the splintering or even the demise of the classical functional notion of a "gene," and its replacement by a family of notions that are theoretically related. (Such, though, is usually the way with initial functional characterizations of entities in science.) On the difficulties facing various candidate definitions of the classical notion of "gene" in the language of molecular biology, see Kitcher (1984), 343–46. For an accessible history and characterizations of the evolving gene concepts, see Paul E. Griffiths and Karola Stoltz, "Gene," in *The Cambridge companion to the philosophy of biology*, ed. David L. Hull and Michael Ruse (Cambridge: Cambridge University Press, 2007), 85–102.

in a particular gene leads to sickle-cell anemia. Kitcher (1984, 360), drawing on Watson (1976) and Maugh (1981), writes:

> The hemoglobin molecule—whose structure is known in detail—is built up from four amino-acid chains (two "α-chains" and two "β-chains"). The mutant allele results from substitution of a single nucleotide with the result that one amino acid is different (the sixth amino acid in the β-chains). This slight modification causes a change in the interactions of hemoglobin molecules: deoxygenated mutant hemoglobin molecules combine to form long fibres. Cells containing the abnormal molecule become deformed after they have given up their oxygen, and because they become rigid, they can become stuck in narrow capillaries, if they give up their oxygen too soon. Individuals who are homozygous for the mutant gene are vulnerable to experience blockages of blood flow. However, in heterozygous individuals, there is enough normal hemoglobin in blood cells to delay the time of formation of the distorting fibres, so that the individual is physiologically normal.[44]

There are many other such detailed success stories—where one can (just about) deduce the phenotypic trait from a molecular description of the genotype.[45] However, as Kitcher (1984, 367) notes—and this is still true—the reason such near deductions of correlations between genotypes and phenotypes are possible (when they are) is because in such cases "[t]he details of the process of development can be ignored" (emphasis in original)

However,

> most structural genes code for molecules whose presence or absence makes subtle differences. Thus, typically, a mutation will affect the distribution of chemicals in the cells of a developing embryo. A likely result is a change in the timing of intracellular reactions, a change that may, in turn, alter the shape of the cell. Because of the change of shape, the geometry of the embryonic cells may be modified. Cells that usually come into contact may fail to touch. Because of this, some cells may not receive the molecules necessary to switch on certain batteries of genes. Hence the chemical composition of these cells will be altered.[46]

44. Also see Rosenberg (1985), 74–88.

45. Notice, however, that the deduction in question is not a pure deduction from molecular biology up to higher levels. Instead, one deduces the expressed phenotype from the genotype by crucially utilizing other regularities at various physiological levels of description, for example, "deoxygenated mutant hemoglobin molecules combine to form long fibres," "getting stuck in narrow capillaries," and the "experience [of] blockages of blood flow." It would be a mistake to think that the invocation of such macro-descriptions on Kitcher's part are due to him providing an accessible description of a process that can—by professionals—otherwise be described entirely in molecular-biological terms. Such is never the case.

46. Kitcher (1984), 367. There are, it must be added, many places where attempts at near-deduction from the structural/chemical facts about (various segments of) DNA to one or another inheritable trait will fail (require, that is, one or another only to be empirically established step). Some of these occur right at the beginning, when proteins are synthesized. To a very large extent, what (specific) proteins can do arises from their three-dimensional shapes—how they "fold." But the three-dimensional shape of a protein cannot (generally) be predicted from its amino acid sequence. How a protein folds, of course, is precisely due to its amino acid sequence (e.g., to the electrostatic attractions and repulsions resulting from the charge distribution on its amino acid R-groups); but there are no decision procedures for determining the resulting three-dimensional contours of a protein from this initially given information.

As a result, near deductions of genotype–phenotype correlations from genotype structure account for very few of the correlations that are being discovered. The scientific establishment of genotype–phenotype correlations is galloping along not via deductions or near deductions from theory but in a different way entirely.

Here's an illustration. We read in the abstract to Gerken et al. (2007, 1469), that "Variants in the *FTO* (fat mass and obesity associated) gene are associated with increased body mass index in humans." The first couple of lines of the article amplify the point by giving statistical detail and citations. There are numerous valuable results of just this sort being established daily. (Many of them appear in *Science*.) They are results—nearly enough—established by sheer empirically established correlations: such and such "genes" appearing in the population occur simultaneously with such and such expressed traits. Notice that the correlations in question are not absolute. (i) They are often species-specific (the same genes needn't do the same things when located in a different genetic environment)—the correlations are hedged ones—and (ii) the associations in question by no means presuppose that the isolated genes express the traits in question all on their own.[47]

What has made it possible to establish so many empirical correlations? I'll explain what's made it possible in this and in the next few paragraphs. Chromosomes, and the DNA they contain, are physically located in cells. Furthermore, we now have a physical picture of the actual shape of DNA—it can be depicted in visual models— and one can see how various important properties of DNA arise directly from its shape.[48] Furthermore, not only do we have a physical picture of its shape, we have a physical picture of how—spatially—it's composed of its functionally pertinent chemically active parts: the two backbones of a strand of DNA, which spiral around each other, are made up of sugars and phosphates from which molecules of adenine, cytosine, guanine, and thymine, project inward, "like the rungs of a ladder." DNA is held together in a double helix (by hydrogen bonding between the nitrogenous bases) where cytosine is always opposite guanine, and adenine is always opposite thymine. This is because these pairs are capable of forming hydrogen bonds between them. Hydrogen bonds are relatively weak (but strong when there are large numbers of them); cytosine forms three hydrogen bonds with guanine, and adenine two such bonds with thymine—this numerical difference in the number of hydrogen bonds is often significant. The DNA helix always has a width of approximately 2 nm. Drawings of this structure are ubiquitous.[49]

47. I stress again that there can be no real (general) theory of how these correlations arise. (There can be no general theory correlating genetic structure with expressed traits—that they "code" for—that enables such correlations to be deduced—or nearly so.) This doesn't mean, of course, that more local generalizations encompassing a number of these correlations won't be established (and, of course, this being empirical science, my claim that no general theory is forthcoming, for the reasons cited by Kitcher, and the various factors like the one I've noted in notes 45 and 46, is nevertheless what should be described as a "sure bet").

48. Arguably, the discovery of the double-helix shape of DNA is the most celebrated aspect of Watson and Crick's discovery precisely because it enabled an understanding of what DNA does. Of course, "shape" when applied to molecules is an idealization.

49. See, for example, M. Thain and M. Hickman, *The Penguin dictionary of biology*, 10th ed. (London: Penguin Books, 2001), 189. Diagrams that more dramatically accentuate the ladder-like structure are also available (and more common); see, for example, Philip Kitcher, *The lives to come* (New York: Simon & Shuster, 1996), 30; or J. Nicklin, K. Graeme-Cook, and R. Killington, *Instant notes in microbiology*, 2nd ed. (Oxford: BIOS Scientific Publishers, 2002).

The importance of the depiction of the units of inheritance as they are laid out in space—and as they shift in space and time—should not be underestimated. Just as the process of the mitosis of a cell is described as an event involving specific geometrical changes—it's literally understood as a series of physical movements of designated parts of the cell[50]—so, too, is the molecular process of transcription (the process by which mRNA and stable RNA molecules are synthesized from a DNA template) chemically and geometrically described. The DNA is (literally) unwound—in small sections at a time—and a complementary copy of RNA is polymerized. This is a chemical event, with specific (and changing) geometric contours, that takes place over space and time.

All of these visual depictions of DNA, its molecular parts, those of other significant molecules that DNA interacts with (e.g., proteins and RNA), and the chemical events that these molecules participate in, although not metaphors, are nevertheless idealized or schematized in various fashions.[51] Nevertheless, the chemical/geometrical properties of these complex molecules and of the events they participate in, have been described in enough detail to allow, in the subsequent decades (and especially in the last couple), the development of techniques for manipulating such physically and chemically, so that (i) they can be recognized as occurring in the cells of organisms (or in groups of such), and (ii) so that they can be modified in specific ways, and (iii) so that the effects of those modifications can be empirically determined in the resulting organisms (e.g., DNA molecules can be "subjected to deliberate sequence modifications and then introduced back into host cells so that the effects of the *directed mutations* can be assessed").[52] More generally, the genomes (of humans, and of other organisms) are being cloned, sequenced, and mapped. The word "mapped," as used here, is literal—the maps are physical ones that depict how the molecules are laid out in space.

50. Here are some descriptions from Eeva Therman and Millard Susman, *Human chromosomes: Structure, behavior, and effects*, 3rd ed. (Berlin: Springer-Verlag, 1993), 28 (emphasis in original): "In prophase, the chromosomes first become visible as long thin threads that gradually shorten and thicken as the diameter of the chromosomes coil increases. . . . At the same time that the threads are shortening, the nucleoli vanish. . . . Prophase is followed by a short prometaphase. During this period, the nuclear membrane dissolves and the chromosomes, which are nearing their maximum condensation, collect on a metaphase plate . . . Outside the nucleus, an organelle, called the *centriole* or *centrosome*, has divided and the mitotic spindle develops between the centrioles. The centromeres of the chromosomes collect halfway between the poles (centrioles) to form a metaphase plate. . . . Long chromosome arms may stick out of the plate. Even though plants do not possess defined centrioles, the spindle arises between two polar areas." And so on. Notice that the objects described here are not that far away from molecules—and indeed, the mechanism by which these items are taken to move are seen to be (directly) molecular ones, specifically: chemical/geometrical.

51. It's not just that the shapes and stability attributed to various molecules and their bonds don't "scale down," but that even at the level of description that occurs in molecular biology, they cannot be treated as accurate. This, as noted already, prevents strong reductions of the concepts involved here to those of (particle) physics. Nevertheless, the research tools these models supply suffice amply for molecular biology, and more generally, for chemistry. Part of the reason for this is that the relevant causal interactions between molecules due to the strength of their bonds, the kinds of attractions parts of them exemplify, and their (idealized) shapes, are—largely—insensitive to finer details about their actual shapes and stability.

52. Therman and Susman (1993), 52, emphasis in original. See Philip Kitcher, "Who's afraid of the human genome project?" (1995), in *The philosophy of biology* (1998), ed. David L. Hull and Michael Ruse (Oxford: Oxford University Press, 1998), 522–27, for a nice accessible description of some of these techniques (circa 1994). I've also found Gérard Lucotte and François Baneyx, *Introduction to molecular cloning techniques* (New York: VCH Publishers 1995), helpful. In the subsequent decade the number of techniques has greatly increased; the general description of how they operate—in terms of the actual chemical/geometrical properties of the items they are applied to—is unchanged.

The way that specific "techniques exploit the chemical and geometric properties of their targets is often pretty transparent. The early methods of Sturtevant and Morgan, for example, turn on exploiting the molecular distances (on chains of DNA) between alleles at loci. The further apart such are from one another, the more likely recombinations involving them will be. The technique of gel electrophoresis relies on the fact that smaller negatively charged molecules (smaller bits of DNA) move through an electric field faster than larger ones.[53] Chemistry and geometry in combination are systematically exploited in molecular biology to directly manipulate genotypes; the subtle interactions of chemistry and geometry needed cannot be deduced from "first principles." Rather, in accord with the dictates of minimal physicalism (and corresponding doctrines, such as "minimal chemicalism") the results of the underlying sciences are applied piecemeal whenever possible (e.g., the strength of hydrogen bonding plays a qualitative role in descriptions of how the DNA molecule is broken apart during transcription), but a great many of the properties of these molecules are—and can only be—empirically shown.

This gives us the answer to the question asked a few paragraphs back: what has made it possible to establish so many empirical correlations? It's by means of the physicochemical manipulation of genes that most of the correlations between genes and phenotypic traits are established[54]—and not by anything like a deduction of phenotypic traits from one or another genotype. That is, such correlations are established by circumstantial evidence: the presence of a sheer correlation between, say, certain mutations in certain loci, and the presence of certain traits in a population. Only after the correlation has been circumstantially established—most of the time—can other background chemical, physiological, molecular biological knowledge be brought to bear to enable researchers to establish some of the properties and aspects of the biochemical mechanisms that underlie that correlation.

These correlations between genotypes and phenotypes, therefore, are examples of what I call *gross correlational regularities*. Here are some crucial characteristics of such regularities.[55] (i) They cross domains of discourse. For example, genotypes are described in the terminology of molecular biology: as physical (three-dimensional) configurations of such and such molecules. Phenotypes, on the other hand, are described using terms from any number of disciplines—a phenotype can be characterized in terms of (say) the presence or absence of certain

53. Techniques that explicitly rely on the geometry of these molecules are ubiquitous. For example, in Lucotte and Baneyx (1993), 163, we read: "A useful method for the cloning of cDNA fragments consists of artificially elongating their extremities with complementary *homopolymeric sequences*" (emphasis in original). Of course, the importance of the geometric properties of molecules is significant everywhere in chemistry. (Again, I should note—parenthetically—that most of such geometric properties of molecules are not directly derivable from the underlying, quantum mechanical, physics; this is both because of the intractability of the physics, and also because such geometric properties are idealized.)

54. As noted earlier, these correlations are often not of genes per se with phenotypic traits, but of genes as they are located in a genetic environment—as they are located in chains of DNA relative to other segments of DNA. Although there is enormous overlap in genes among species, it's not the case that genes express the same traits wherever they appear. For example, genes that express aspects of our immune system are shared with the sponge. Whether the same genes as present in the sponge express (similar) aspects of their immune systems, express traits of some other sort entirely, or express nothing at all, is (I believe) currently unknown.

55. See my earlier (Azzouni 2000a) discussion of the broader class of gross regularities.

protein structures in certain cells, or (on the other hand) as having blue eyes. (ii) For the most part, such gross correlational regularities are not established by deductions from background scientific theories (hence the adjective "gross"). (Again, this is not to say that subsequent developments in theory might not lead to some of them being so deducible from one or another broad-scale theory.) Rather, (iii) the discovery of gross correlational regularities is enabled by the instrumental manipulation of both sets of items and/or events that are to be linked via a regularity (e.g., the instrumental cloning, sequencing, and mapping techniques of molecular biology on the one hand, visual or anatomical inspection of an organism, or population studies of a group of such on the other),[56] and (iv) they are established by the sheer (statistical) recognition of correlations between sets of characteristics. (v) Research programs to establish certain kinds—or classes—of gross correlational regularities are motivated by one or another broad background causal or ontological assumption, often of a compositional nature, such as that DNA is the primary molecular medium for inheritable traits.

A field in the midst of a robust program of the establishment of gross correlational regularities develops a distinctive look: (i) the publication of numerous specific results that researchers cross-index in their papers (which, consequently, exhibit long bibliographical tails), when they provide evidential arguments for and against more general theories, and that are also cited in the justification and descriptions of applications; and (ii) the description and development of numerous specific instrumental techniques for manipulating objects and events (based on empirically discovered properties of such) that are described in either the antecedents or the consequents of the resulting gross correlational regularities.

It's also worth noting that when philosophers (of science) take note of gross correlational regularities (which they rarely do), because such regularities cross terminological barriers, there is a tendency to attempt to assimilate them to "bridge laws." But gross correlational regularities are usually far too specific in content—and in the specific (empirical) ways that they are hedged—to be sensibly characterized this way.[57]

4.5 Neurological/Psychological Gross Correlational Regularities

Given the contents of chapter 2, a perhaps more pertinent example of a subject area—that involves research primarily directed toward the establishment of gross correlational regularities—are the neurosciences (neurophysiology, neuroanatomy, cognitive science, and so on) where one is often engaged in the discovery of gross

---

56. The items described in the antecedents and consequents of such gross correlational regularities are ones to which we forge what I have elsewhere called (instrumental) *thick epistemic access*. See Jody Azzouni, "Theory, observation and scientific realism," *British Journal for the Philosophy of Science* 55 (2004b), 371–92.

57. Even professional scientists sometimes describe gross correlational regularities with the nomenclature of "bridge laws," although usually only when indicating a programmatic hope of a more general theoretical underpinning for such gross correlational regularities. See, for example, Stanislas Dehaene and Lionel Naccache, "Towards a cognitive neuroscience of consciousness: Basic evidence and a workspace framework," in *The cognitive neuroscience of consciousness*, ed. Stanislas Dehaene (Cambridge, Mass.: MIT Press, 2001), 4.

correlational regularities between specific loci of activity in the brain, and manifest psychological traits had or psychological events experienced by individuals. As in the genotype/phenotype case, motivating such studies is a broad ontological correlation between the psychological states of a person, psychological experiences had by such a person, and activities of parts of that person's brain.[58] As in the case of the establishing of gross correlational regularities between segments of DNA (in specific genetic environments) and the phenotypic traits such DNA expresses, so, too, gross correlational regularities are established by instrumental interactions, of various sorts, with parts of the brain, to discover correlations between various kinds of brain activity, changes in the physiology of the brain, and so on, and induced psychological events of various sorts.

Here, too, not much background theory is available by which these gross correlational regularities can be established, and so the methods of choice is that of establishing sheer correlations by independent (and instrumental) access to differently described events (neurological events and states on the one hand; psychological events and states on the other).[59]

---

58. Dehaene and Naccache (2001), 3, write: "Within a materialistic framework, each instance of mental activity is also a physical brain state [i.e., any configuration of neural activity, whether stable (a fixed point) or dynamic (a trajectory in neural space)]."

As with phenotypes, there is slippage in background ontological assumptions. Just as other aspects of the molecular biology of the individual are relevant to the traits exhibited by that individual (the phenotypes exhibited are affected by factors other than genotypes), so are other aspects of an individual's physiology, apart from the brain, relevant to the psychological traits expressed by that individual.

59. Jaegwon Kim, *Physicalism, or something near enough* (Princeton, N.J.: Princeton University Press, 2005), 12–13, attributes to William James the recognition that "thoughts and sensations, that is, various modes of mentality and consciousness, arise out of neural processes in the brain." Kim adds, on behalf of William James, that:

But we can only make a list of, or "write down empirically" as he says, the observed de facto correlations that connect thoughts and sensations to types of neural processes. Making a running list of psychoneural correlations does not come anywhere near gaining an explanatory insight into why there are such correlations; according to James, "no glimmer of explanation" is "yet in sight" as to why these particular correlations hold, or why indeed the brain should give rise to thoughts and consciousness at all.

It's very important to separate two issues that Kim (and perhaps James) seem to be confounding. One is the "hard question" of consciousness: why should any neurophysiological event ever give rise to any sort of conscious psychological event—pain, the experience of blue, and so on? That, in the absence of a general theory from which gross correlational regularities (between psychologically described events and neurophysiologically described events) can be deduced, such regularities are largely empirically established independently of one another, has nothing whatsoever to do with this problem. Were the structure of the brain extremely simple, and were one or two simple generalizations discoverable that connected (all) psychologically described states and events to (a subset of) neurophysiologically described states and events, the epistemic need for the independent empirical establishing of gross correlational regularities between neurophysiologically described events and states and psychologically described events and states would be absent. However, we could still face the more general question of why any conscious experience should arise when a neurophysiologically described event occurs. (Why should these—simple—correlation generalizations be true?) The ontological identification of biological entities with structured chemicals of such and such sorts seems to leave—in principle—no dangling peculiarities, no puzzles about why the gross correlational regularities that are established should be. This isn't the case with respect to "mind" and "body." A person reflexively moves her arm. We have a rough (but satisfying) story of how descriptions of muscles, cells, and their activities scale up to the arm-moving event, as described globally. A person intentionally moves her arm to grab a cup. Many philosophers argue that we don't have a (satisfying) story of how what happens in the arm and the brain scales up to this event, as described globally, and as including her experience of the color, and so on, of the cup. I should add that these hard problems of consciousness are not among the topics of this book.

The pertinent functionally relevant parts of the brain aren't a priori given, but are discovered in the course of empirical exploration. Molecules, synapses, neurons, other cells, local circuits, large-scale networks, various organs, and larger areas of the brain (and other parts of the body) that are singled out and individuated by coined terminology, are recognized geometrically, functionally, and by the causal powers that they have been shown to have. To distinguish and manipulate these neurologically described aspects of the brain, techniques are developed (physical probes of various sorts directed toward causing more or less precise stimulations of more or less specific parts of the brain, visualization tools possessing various degrees of accuracy).[60] This (largely coined) terminology usually appears in the antecedents of the gross correlational regularities that are established.

The psychological terms used in these gross correlational regularities fall—roughly—into two classes.[61] First, there is the psychological-attitude talk—directed toward consciously accessible contents—that's adopted (pretty much unchanged) from ordinary (folk-psychological) ways of speaking. ("I noticed that blue object," "I hear a sound," "I recognize John," "I remembered an episode from my childhood," as well as third-person descriptions, "he noticed green lines," etc.) These provide various phenomenological descriptions (of the content) of conscious experience ("subjective reports," or "introspection"). Second, there are various unconscious states and events: various kinds of unconscious "mental representations." Such mental representations are also described by practitioners in the folk-psychological content-laden intentional language of "perception of," "responses to," "recognition of," "inferences about," content (numbers, objects, schematic types, etc.), and such mental representations are attributed to individuals (as occurring at such and such times) on the basis of various kinds of evidence—behavioral, neuropsychological, brain-imagining methods.[62]

As noted, both conscious and unconscious psychological states and events have substantial and rich content attributed to them; therefore, descriptions of such states and events indispensably take the form of their being "about" various events, objects, properties, as well as letters, numbers, words, concepts, and so on. And, as also noted, the working background assumption behind the search for gross correlational regularities between various mental representations, as so described, and various neurologically described events and states, is that the latter "give rise to" or are "associated with" the former, so that each "instance" of an occurrence of the latter is identified with an "instance" of the former.[63]

---

60. That is, the coined neurological terminology is—over time—partially and progressively "operationalized": it's associated (defeasibly) with various sorts of instrumental interactions (e.g., brain-imaging methods), behavioral symptoms, etc. (See Azzouni [2000a], part IV, for a discussion of the general case of the partial and progressive operationalization of "theoretical terms.")

61. By no means am I suggesting that the division of psychological events and states into these classes is either sharp, or (in all cases) straightforward.

62. Dehaene and Naccache (2001), 5. They write: "The current evidence indicates that many perceptual, motor, semantic, emotional and context-dependent processes can occur unconsciously."

63. To identity each and every mental event as one or another neurophysiological event is not—as we saw in section 4.3—to contemplate the supervenience of all the predicates required in the full vocabulary of psychology to that neurophysiology, if only because the instances of (content-laden) predicates of mental representations are not themselves identified with neurologically described events or entities in the brain. At the very best, therefore, this characterization amounts only to one of the two conditions of a doctrine of minimal neurophysiology/biology.

The gross correlational regularities in these areas of study, therefore, often have neurologically described antecedents, and intentional, content-laden, psychological-attitude consequents. Many of them are established by "subjective reports," a subject simply describing his experiences during the event of the instrumental interaction with his brain (e.g., probing or brain imaging).[64] In addition, there are numerous studies that describe gross correlational regularities between the presence of neurologically described lesions and other sorts of damage in specified parts of the brain, and resulting complexes of psychological symptoms. The resulting gross correlational regularities have, as antecedents, these neurologically described states—and various specific instrumentally recognized neurological events—and as consequents, various intentionally, content-laden folk-psychologically described conscious and unconscious states of the individual, evaluations of long and short-term changes in various capacities to manipulate and understand mental representations (of various sorts), and so on.[65]

It's precisely because the gross correlational regularities that are being established in these research areas are ones which correlate events described neurophysiologically with psychological changes—described folk-psychologically—that this literature has been so easy to popularize. One end of the correlation—the details of lesions, the range of sophistication of the visualization techniques, the relevant parts of the brain—tends to be vaguely described in popular writing. The other end of the regularity, however, is usually characterized in pretty much the same way it's characterized in the clinical literature. The utilized vocabulary—folk-psychological descriptions of the experience of an individual, or folk-psychological descriptions of the (unconscious) mental representations of an individual—is drawn from the only language that's available for psychological descriptions.

Just as with genotype/phenotype regularities, no strong or supervenience "reductions" of the folk-psychological terminology (that's needed to express these gross correlational regularities) are entertained by researchers. Thus, the gross correlational regularities of neuroscience necessarily cross vocabulary barriers as

---

64. Examples: Wilder Penfield and Phanor Perot, "The brain's record of auditory and visual experience," *Brain* 86 (1963), 595–696; G. D. Honey et al., "The functional neuroanatomy of schizophrenic subsyndromes," *Psychological Medicine* 33 (2003), 1007–18; Christian Plewnia, Felix Bischof, and Matthias Reimold, "Suppression of verbal hallucinations and changes in regional cerebral blood flow after intravenous lidocaine: A case report," *Progress in Neuro-Psychopharmacology and Biological Psychiatry* 31 (2007), 301–3; results described and summarized in Nancy Kanwisher, "Neural events and perceptual awareness," in *The cognitive neuroscience of consciousness*, ed. Stanislas Dehaene (Cambridge, Mass.: MIT Press, 2001), 89–113; Dahaene and Naccache (2001); Jean Decety and Thierry Chaminade, "The neurophysiology of imitation and intersubjectivity," in *Perspective on imitation: From neuroscience to social science*, vol. 1, ed. Susan Hurley and Nick Chater (Cambridge, Mass.: MIT Press, 2005), 119–40; chapter 3 of Friedemann Pulvermüller, *The neuroscience of language: On brain circuits of words and serial order* (Cambridge: Cambridge University Press, 2002).

65. For example, results described and summarized in John Driver and Patrik Vuileumier, "Perceptual awareness and its loss in unilateral neglect and extinction," in *The cognitive neuroscience of consciousness*, ed. Stanislas Dehaene (Cambridge, Mass.: MIT Press, 2001), 39–88; in chapter 3 of Pulvermüller (2002); as well as the numerous results popularized in Antonio Damasio, *Descartes' error* (New York: G.P. Putnam's Sons, 1994), and in the works of Oliver Sacks. I should note that such gross correlational regularities are invariably cited in almost any article in this area because they are the primary evidence available for broader theories of brain function.

dramatically as the gross correlational regularities established between genotypes and phenotypes do. In the abstract of Shinosaki et al. (2003, 88), for example, we read: "Desynchronization in the right auditory cortices, including the transverse gyrus of Heschl, planum temporale and supramarginal cortex, occurred during musical hallucinations in a 78-year old woman." Similarly,[66] we read: "During hallucinations, compared with the post-lidocaine state (with suppressed hallucinations), enhanced rCBF was found in the right angular and supramarginal gyrus, right inferior frontal gyrus, orbitofrontal cortex and in major parts of the cingulate cortex."

Penfield and Perot (1963) is full of correlations of this sort—ones determined, however, by the use of probes during brain surgery. In each of the sixty-nine cases that are given, we are told which part(s) of the brain are probed or otherwise affected; these neurological events are correlated with the simultaneous content of the hallucinatoric experiences had by the subject.

Consider the intricate combination of phenomenological and neurophysiological language in the following piece of reasoning. I quote it in full because several comparisons are made, several gross correlational regularities are alluded to, and it illustrates how these are used as evidence for and against broader functional claims about aspects of the brain (Almen and Larøi 2008, 160–61):

Lennox, Park, Jones, and Morris (1999) imaged a hallucinating schizophrenic patient with fMRI. This patient hallucinated with consequent intervals: For approximately 26 seconds he heard a "voice," followed by a comparable period in which hallucinations were absent. As was the case in the Silbersweig et al. (1995) study, the patient indicated with a key press when he heard the voice, which enabled a within-subject comparison between hallucinatory periods and hallucination-free periods. The results revealed strong activity in the right middle temporal gyrus In the same way, using the button-press method, Dierks et al. (1999) managed to scan 3 patients with fMRI. Besides recording brain activity during hallucination periods, they also measured brain activity in response to acoustic stimulation (speech in one condition and a tone in another condition). They observed hallucination-related activity in Broca's area, in the temporal gyri, and in the primary auditory cortex (Heschl's gyrus). A striking observation of this study was that the highest correlation of the fMRI signal time course with acoustic stimulation was observed in the transverse gyrus of Heschl, at the same location as the focus of activation during hallucinations. Because inner speech in normal people is not associated with activity in primary auditory cortex (Aleman et al., 2005; McGuire et al., 1996), it could be suggested that it is the abnormal occurrence of activity in primary cortex that lends such inner speech the quality of a real, external sound, and hence leads hallucinating patients to infer a nonself perceptual source (Dierks et al., 1999; Frith, 1999). On the other hand, selective attention towards perceiving an expected auditory stimulus can by itself increase activation of primary auditory cortex (Jäncke, Mirzazade, & Shah, 1999), which is consistent with the top-down perceptual expectation account described in chapter 4, this volume.

---

66. Plewnia e. al. (2007), 303.

It's worth noting that gross correlational regularities are also empirically established between such and such (non-neurological) physiological events, and various psychologically described events. For example, auditory hallucinations are often accompanied by electrical activation of the speech muscles ("subvocalization").[67] Another example (Bentall 1990, 84): "Toone, Cooke, and Lader (1981) found that hallucinating patients had higher levels and greater fluctuations of skin resistance than did controls. More recently, Cooklin, Sturgeon, and Leff (1983) were able to demonstrate a direct relation between changes in skin conductance and the onset of hallucinations."

I should note that there are attempts to ground specific gross correlational regularities in broader ones that can be used to predict those specific correlations (and others). Nevertheless, these broader (hypothesized) regularities exhibit the same character as the more specific regularities: the correlation of events and states characterized in neurological terms with those characterized in folk-psychological/phenomenological terms.[68]

4.6 The Logical Form of Gross Correlational Regularities

The last two sections were dedicated to describing two empirically established sets of gross correlational regularities. The point being illustrated was how such operate to bring different scientific theories (and languages) with very different domains of discourse to bear on one another evidentially and deductively. In doing so, I've also illustrated the point that gross correlational regularities (usually) involve, respectively in their antecedents and consequents, vocabulary from different areas (theories) of science, or even from ordinary life. I turn now to the question of what logical form these gross correlational regularities take. This question will bring in its train a question about the logic that must be employed along with such gross correlational regularities.

Recall that an essential element of the old positivistic view of scientific laws was that such were of the generalization-form: $(x)(Px \rightarrow Qx)$. We can correspondingly

67. André Almen and Frank Larøi, 2008, *Hallucinations: The science of idiosyncratic perception* (Washington, D.C.: American Psychological Association, 110).

68. Another example. Almen and Larøi (2008), 97, write:

[Nico J. Diederich, Christopher G. Goetz, and Glen T. Stebbins, "Repeated visual hallucinations in Parkinson's disease as disturbed external/internal perceptions: Focused review and a new integrative model," *Movement Disorders* 20:2 (2005), 130–40] suggested that visual hallucinations should be considered a dysregulation of the gating and filtering of external perception and internal image production. Contributive elements and anatomical links for their model include poor primary vision, reduced activation of primary visual cortex, aberrant activation of associative visual and frontal cortex, lack of suppression or spontaneous emergence of internally generated imagery through the ponto-geniculo-occipital system, intrusion of rapid eye movement dreaming imagery into wakefulness, erratic changes of the brainstem filtering capacities through fluctuating vigilance, and medication-related overactivation of mesolimbic systems. Not all of these have to be present, and different combinations will lead to differences in phenomenology.

ask: What (syntactic) form—in general—do the gross correlational regularities I've been describing take? A number of them, I think, can be described as taking the form: $(x)(t)(Pxt \rightarrow (\exists y)Qyt)$, where the variables x and y range over different discourse-domains, and the variable t ranges over times.[69] Notice that the "predicates" P and Q must be understood to be fairly complicated in structure—they are not only to characterize the kind of event involved (e.g., such and so neurons firing; seeing a blue elf), but they are also to characterize the events they range over as temporally, and perhaps spatially, cross-linked to one another, as I've partially indicated.[70]

Both the extended quotation from Aleman and Larøi (2008), in the last section, which described a number of gross correlational regularities between hallucinated content and activations of certain brain areas, and the extended quotation from Kitcher, in section 4.4, illustrate the striking and widespread practice of "mixed deductions"—that gross correlational regularities are used in patterns of inference in which the vocabulary barriers (that philosophers are apt to be sensitive to) are entirely ignored. This scientific practice raises two issues, one regarding the (implicit) background logic involved in such reasoning, and thus generally across our scientific web of propositions, and one regarding our use of the truth idiom. The second issue, regarding truth, I'll take up in sections 4.8 and 4.9; certain questions about the (implicit) logic will be addressed here and in section 4.7.

Let's assume (for the moment) that there is one background logic that's presupposed across the theories and vocabulary areas of the different sciences, and let's presume further that the logic in question is the ordinary traditional first-order logic. Given all this, we can ask: how is reasoning across vocabulary barriers to be managed when the scientific theories—as exhibited in previous sections—have different discourse-domains? In particular, how is the notion of validity—characterized as it is in terms of models—to be implemented? The answer to this question is very easy: quantification over different discourse-domains can be replaced by one discourse-domain coupled with the assimilation of the differing quantifiers to one quantifier using predicate relativization. That is, general and existential regularities and laws of the form $(x_d)(\ldots x_d \ldots)$ and $(\exists x_d)(\ldots x_d \ldots)$, where the subscripted variables range over different discourse-domains, can be replaced, respectively, by regularities of the form, $(x)(Dx \rightarrow \ldots x \ldots)$ and $(\exists x)(Dx \& \ldots x \ldots)$, where only one discourse-domain is involved.

Therefore, given,

---

69. For example, if such and such a set of neurons fire, then such and such an auditory hallucination—with so and so phenomenological content—occurs. This regimentation faces the same problem the original positivistic characterization faces: the generalization is empirically hedged in ways that can't be captured in the formulation. For simplicity, I've used the same variable, t, twice, but linked variables—for example—of the form: t, $t + n$, could be used as well.

I should add that although I've described—in the last section—the correlational regularities as containing neurological terminology in their antecedents, and psychological terminology in their consequents, the regularities can (and do) run the other way. Ones of biconditional form, for example, $(t)((\exists x)Pxt \leftrightarrow (\exists y)Qyt)$, are also possible. For simplicity of exposition, I stick to the simplified form I initially gave.

70. Howsoever this is to be done, by quantification over moments and locations, or in some other way involving a coordinate system. I've notationally suppressed the additional complications.

$$(x_d)(t)(Px_d t \to (\exists y_e)Qy_e t),$$

where the variables, x_d and y_e, are indicated by their subscripts to range over different domains, we can introduce one-place predicates D and E with extensions identical to those of the discourse-domains of x_d and y_e, and replace (1) with:

$$(x)(t)(Dx \to (Pxt \to (\exists y)(Ey \& Qyt))),$$

A couple of amplifications. It's worth noting (again) that these discourse-domains will contain large numbers of nonexistent entities. But there is now an additional wrinkle. This is that such domains will also contain a large number of (existing and nonexisting) items that appear, as it were, twice, although (often) with conflicting properties attributed to them. For example, suppose that for the purposes of one theory, Jupiter is treated as a point-mass; within the confines of another theory, the same planet is treated as a homogenous spheroid. If the domain-discourses of these two theories are predicate relativized into one domain, then Jupiter will appear twice. Thus, it can be the case that we have $(\exists x)(Dx \& Px)$ and $(\exists x)(Ex \& \neg Px)$, and that these can be instantiated to j_d and j_e, to yield $Dj_d \& Pj_d$, as well as $Ej_e \& \neg Pj_e$, and thus $Pj_d \& \neg Pj_e$, although j_d and j_e are both taken to co-refer (to Jupiter).

The solution to this conundrum is to take very seriously the claim that the discourse-domains (of scientific languages) are not to be understood as indicating the ontology of the sciences. It's to be recognized, outside of the context of these scientific languages, and therefore, outside of the context of this domain-discourse, that j_d and j_e both refer to Jupiter. But within the context of these languages, and their (joint) domain-discourse, no substitution of j_d for j_e (or vice versa) is admissible. From within these discourse(s), these terms are not treated as co-referential.

But this solution seems to raise in turn a second conundrum. This is that if both Pj_d and $\neg Pj_e$ are nevertheless true, then science is inconsistent. I agree: such a result is unappealing.[71] The solution is to realize that one (or both) of the two theories (about Jupiter) must be false. Following the details of this example, to treat Jupiter as a point-mass or to treat it as a homogenous spheroid is—strictly speaking—in both cases to attribute falsities to it. However, that's hardly the end of the matter. The point of such "idealizations" is always that from (appropriately selected) falsities, valuable truths may follow. By treating Jupiter in such and such contexts as a point-mass, one may be able to deduce predictions of approximations of how it moves.[72] These approximations, although deduced from (some)

71. Science may well be inconsistent—but it's not to be presumed inconsistent on these grounds. (See Azzouni forthcoming [c] on this.)

72. Is this to introduce a notion of "approximate truth"? No. Notice that if we claim that "It's approximately true that Jupiter is spheroid," we can just as well say "It's true that Jupiter is approximately spheroid." Similarly, and more significantly, for quantitative approximations, we can say, "It's approximately true that p is three inches," or we can say, "It's true that p is approximately (within such and such margins of error) three inches." I claim (but will not show here) that (i) all uses of "approximate truth" can—and should—be described instead as ordinary truths about what things are approximately like (in such and such respects); and, (ii) attempts to instead implement one or another notion of "approximate truth" creates problems with the truth predicate because the latter's role makes it indispensably qualitative.

falsities, are true simpliciter; therefore, they can be attributed to Jupiter independently of any theory. In particular, they can be emancipated from the false theories that spawned them.[73]

What's ultimately behind the refusal to allow unrestricted substitutions of j_d for j_e (and vice versa) is that one or both of these terms occur in the context of a (strictly) false theory. The truths that follow from these false theories, are typically applied to the objects of which they are true, independently of such theories. There is no resulting inconsistency in doing so, and indeed, for those purposes (outside the specific theories that yielded these truths, that is), j_d may be co-substituted with j_e, or—more likely—a single term ("Jupiter") will be used across the board.

There is the always possible trade-off between statements being taken to be (generally) false of something, or of those statements being taken to be true of something else. As noted in note 5 of section 4.1, it's possible to treat the two theories in question as about their own exclusive objects, so that j_d and j_e, respectively, are about[e] a point-mass and a different homogenous spheroid. The objects in question, however, are regarded as mathematical abstracta, and the theories are, respectively, applied to Jupiter (by treating it as if it's a point-mass or homogenous spheroid), and so the application yields truths that also hold of Jupiter when so applied. In this case, substitutions of j_d for j_e are barred simply because they are taken to refer[e] to different (nonexistent) objects. As in note 5, either approach comes to the same thing.

Notice that the approaches described here are not "intentional" ones. That is, no intentional operators are involved—just ordinary (first-order) logical tools plus the truth idiom (for purposes of the emancipation of truths). All and only what's distinctive about this approach to the discourse-domains of scientific languages is that the contents (the referents[e]) of those discourse-domains aren't being treated ontologically; thus, the facts about what's real and what isn't, and therefore, what's to be "identified" with what, aren't (directly) pertinent to the contents of these discourse-domains.[74]

The characterization of the discourse-domains—that I've given in this section—isn't problematic, as long as the actual scientific ontology (what the sciences currently take to exist, and what they currently take to be distinctive or to be identified) isn't (explicitly or implicitly) taken to be all and only what's contained in those domains. The kinds of scientific theories there are, and specifically, what they quantify over, is governed (of course) by scientific needs, and in particular, by the shared scientific need to understand and characterize the machinations of what exists. This need only indirectly bear on the contents of the discourse-domain of a scientific theory.

---

73. What enables the emancipation of truths deducible from false theories, so that they can be used without having to ascribe the accompanying false theories is the use of the blind-ascription role of the truth idiom. See section 4.8.

74. See chapter 5 for more details on this.

4.7 The Refutation of (Certain Versions of) Logical Pluralism

A picture, such as the one I've given of various scientific theories/languages with varying discourse-domains, contrary to my initial monistic assumption of a uniform logic, may seem to instead invite "Carnapian pluralism" with respect to logic—that is, just as discourse-domains shift from one theory/language to another, so does the (implicit or explicit) logic employed. Many such pluralist views of (applied) logic similarly presuppose a "cottage industry" view of scientific theories and languages—and, indeed, of natural languages per se. It seems reasonable to many philosophers that just as specific assumptions can be in play in some scientific theories, and not in others, so, too, specific logics can be in play in some discourses and not in others. Fictional discourse, for example, seems to invite the adoption of one or another paraconsistent logic. Pure mathematical discourse, moral discourse, and so on, seem to some to operate under the jurisdiction of "different" logics.[75] One may also think that certain empirical sciences require classical logic, but that other ones require one or another version of quantum logic. So, too, certain views about the nature of mathematical practice (e.g., that it operates not in terms of "objects" but in terms of "concepts" or "meanings") may motivate the suggestion that pure mathematics should be governed by intuitionism. This logical pluralist picture is one of varying applications of logical principles just in the same way that there are varying applications of mathematics, and varying empirical assumptions (e.g., ones about granularity as opposed to continuity) applied to some phenomena and not to others.

Fatal for this version of logical pluralism, however, is the external discourse demand—more specifically, the ubiquitous mixed deduction patterns that blend vocabulary from any discourse (both for deductive as well as for evidential purposes). We have no model for how evidential considerations and deductions are to cross discourse barriers other than as governed by a single deductive logic (accompanied with a notion of validity). Anyone, for example, who suggests that some of the pure mathematics that is based in a nonclassical logic can nevertheless be applied in the logically classical setting of empirical science has not offered a coherent "logical pluralism." For it's not just the conclusions of mathematical proofs that appear in empirical settings. Mathematicians routinely reconstruct physical reasoning as involving a complex combination of mathematical proof and empirical addition.

---

75. Pure mathematics—all by itself—does involve many different logics on sheer stipulative grounds: one can (and does) axiomatically base a mathematical subject-matter on one or another logic. But these studies really are logically isolated ones. See Jody Azzouni, *Metaphysical myths, mathematical practice: The ontology and epistemology of the exact science* (Cambridge: Cambridge University Press, 1994), for a general description of mathematical practice that takes specific account of the "logic-pluralism" of pure mathematics. Some have attempted to describe the isolated portions of (classical) mathematics as quite broad by noting how little of it actually is empirically applied. But the amount of (classical) mathematics applied at a time is (naturally) a moving target: it expands constantly. As the argument forthcoming in this section shows, however, any such applied mathematics—however rich in content—must nevertheless occur in the context of one logic, the same one that's operative throughout empirical science, on pain of violating the external discourse demand.

Furthermore, the implications of any nonclassically based mathematical result will shift as soon as it's moved to an empirical setting; as deductions from that mathematics coupled with an empirical subject matter are made explicit, the classical logic in the background will bring into play classical implications of that mathematics that are barred in its original nonclassical setting. The "cottage industry" picture of pure mathematics and empirical science—having one consequence relation, governed by one logic, in the pure setting, but having a different consequence relation in one or another empirical science—is, as I have just said, simply incoherent.

The same point, of course, applies to the idea that one empirical realm of study can be based on one logical practice (with one consequence relation) while another is based on a different logical practice (with a quite different consequence relation). Again, this cannot be so if these empirical fields are to be brought to bear on one another—deductively and evidentially.

The cottage industry isolated discourse picture may seem more suitably applied to the practices of fiction. But chapter 3 made clear that the external discourse demand is just as operative with respect to truth-apt fictional discourse as it is in the case of mathematics. Where genuine pretence is operating—for example, during the presentation of a play, or when tokens of sentences appear in novels—anything can go. But that's not a matter of a different logic being in place because in fact a different kind of speech act is in play altogether—not a truth-apt one. Where truths and falsehoods are required, as we've seen, mixed deductions involving—for example—comparisons of fictional and real objects are ubiquitous. The logic, therefore, must be uniform across truth-apt fictional discourse and the other empirical discourses. The logical monist has this advantage over the Carnapian pluralist; the former can explain how evidence and deduction crosses vocabulary barriers; the latter has no explanation for this whatsoever.[76]

Still remaining, however, is the task of discharging the assumption I started section 4.6 with: that the monistic logic in question should be taken to be the first-order predicate calculus. I understand this assumption to involve a certain amount of "free play." That is, I mean the logic in question to be one or another that imposes the consequence relation of the first-order predicate calculus on the propositions or sentences of the sciences. The assumption, therefore, lacks specificity insofar as, first, there is more than one way—semantically and proof theoretically— to impose a first-order consequence relation on an assertion-practice. Second, there is more than one way to treat (i.e., regiment) the propositions or sentences of the sciences—couched as they are in the vernacular—in first-order form. Nevertheless, despite the suggestion allowing wiggle room in these ways, it provides real constraints, and is open to (empirical) refutation.

In particular, the first-order thesis faces threats from at least two directions. First, there is the possibility of "consequence pluralism," the view that the

---

76. The point has been made before. See Jc Beall and Greg Restall, *Logical pluralism* (Oxford: Oxford University Press, 2006), 102. Also see Azzouni (1994), part II, where this point about logic is made utilizing the nomenclature *topic-neutrality*.

consequence relation(s) exhibited by deductive and evidential reasoning in the sciences is open to incompatible analyses—where the incompatibility emerges as differences in what are taken to be the consequences of particular sets of propositions or sentences that are nevertheless supposed to involve the "same form," to involve, that is, the same logical idioms. One version of this consequence pluralism—one that corresponds to Carnapian-style pluralism—may be set aside because it faces exactly the same problems that Carnapian-style pluralism with respect to logic faces. Sentences and sets of sentences are routinely exported from one discourse context to others; therefore, their consequences cannot shift.[77]

A second kind of consequence pluralism may still seem possible, one based on the apparent vagueness of the notion of "consequence" as it operates in ordinary language, in contrast to formal precisifications of it.[78] This is the suggestion that there is more than one suitable precification, and that these give different answers with respect to the consequences of one or another sentence or proposition form. This kind of pluralism is compatible with a generally monist take on logical laws (that such laws, whatever they are, apply to all sentences or propositions of the same form): the claim simply is that deduction practices in the vernacular (specifically, in the sciences) underdetermine a unique set of logical laws.[79]

At this stage in the argument, I must largely defer further discussion to other (already published) work.[80] Let me, however, sketch the line of argument that I believe refutes this form of logical pluralism. The first point to make is that

---

77. Notice the pragmatic importance of this constraint (one that I've been relying on throughout this book): a scientist cannot borrow results from other disciplines, or even from other theories in her own discipline, if she cannot rely on the known consequences of those results remaining the same.

78. Alfred Tarski ("On the concept of logical consequence," in *Logic, semantics, metamathematics*, ed. J. Corcoran [Indianapolis, Ind.: Hackett, 1983a], 409) writes:

> With respect to the clarity of its content the common concept of consequence is in no way superior to other concepts of everyday language. Its extension is not sharply bounded and its usage fluctuates. Any attempt to bring into harmony all possible vague, sometimes contradictory, tendencies which are connected with the use of this concept, is certainly doomed to failure. We must reconcile ourselves from the start to the fact that every precise definition of this concept will show arbitrary features to a greater or less degree.

See Beall and Restall (2006) for an attempt at logical pluralism based on consequence vagueness in this sense. They seem to base their argument for their version of logical pluralism on the (sheer) formal existence of at least two ways of construing the consequence relation: along the lines of Tarski or compatibly with one or another relevance constraint. I suspect they need to say more about how these various formal construals of the consequence relation fit the patterns of deduction in the vernacular before they can be said to have successfully made a case for their position.

79. It must be noted (again) that any view that tries to treat the "vagueness" of the consequence relation as leading to a Carnapian pluralist position: that in one context sentences of such and such a form have such and such (logical) consequences, but in another context have different ones fails in the face of the exportation of sentences and propositions from one context to another—as dictated by the external discourse demand.

80. Jody Azzouni, "Is there still a sense in which mathematics can have foundations?" in *Essays on the foundations of mathematics and logic*, ed. Giandomenico Sica (Milan, Italy: Polimetrica S.a.s., 2005), 9–47; Jody Azzouni, *Tracking reason: Proof, consequence, and truth* (Oxford: Oxford University Press, 2006), part II; and Jody Azzouni, "Why do informal proofs conform to formal norms?" *Foundations of Science* 14 (2009b), 9–26.

mathematics is applied in the sciences—and in ordinary life—ubiquitously. Consequently, the logic (implicitly) required in mathematical reasoning is normatively applied everywhere because of the indispensable mixed deduction patterns that mathematics intrudes into. The use of the phrase "normatively applied" is meant to indicate that such a logic is applied across the board to our reasoning in the vernacular even if the actual "logical" idioms of the vernacular are themselves clearly not ones that belong to classical "first-order logic."[81] But it can be shown that the consequence relations among mathematical propositions can be regimented compatibly with classical first-order logic, and only incompatibly with a number of other options, for example, intuitionism, relevance logics, and paraconsistency approaches. This forces an imposition of something in the neighborhood of classical first-order logic on our entire scientific (and ordinary language) discourse.[82]

4.8 The Blind-Ascription Role of Truth

Just as "logical pluralism" is an option that some philosophers have embraced, so is "truth pluralism."[83] However, the very same considerations that rule out logical pluralism also rule out truth pluralism: the external discourse demand and the ubiquitous presence of mixed deduction patterns that systematically ignore vocabulary barriers. This section and the next are dedicated to providing details.

Truth pluralism is gripped by the very same cottage industry perspective of our assertion practices with respect to different subject areas that moves logical pluralism.[84] One often starts motivating truth pluralism with the observation that there are a number of different perspectives on "truth"—correspondence, coherence, one or another version of minimalist or deflationist truth—and then noting that these different approaches to truth, although suitable to certain domains of discourse,

81. My understanding is that the linguistic study of the quantifiers of natural languages shows conclusively that such are generalized quantifiers, and that therefore they generally have far more content than first-order construals of them (first-order quantifiers plus predicates) can capture. (See Jon Barwise and Robin Cooper, "Generalized quantifiers in natural language," *Linguistics and Philosophy* 4 [1981], 159–219; Jon Barwise and S. Feferman, eds., *Model-theoretic logics* [Berlin: Springer-Verlag, 1985]; E. L. Keenan and D. Westerståhl, "Generalized quantifiers in linguistics and logic," in *Handbook of logic and language*, ed. Johan van Benthem and Alice ter Meulen [Cambridge, Mass.: MIT Press, 1997], specifically 863–66.) Among the differences are their very different metalogical properties—for example, various categoricity results not holding of them—and more important, a general failure of overlap between the deductive tools possible for recognizing the consequences of statements couched in these idioms and what those consequence relations are taken to be (failure of completeness results). The usual (implicit) strategy pursued in mathematical work is to drain that content out from the logical idioms of the vernacular, and instead explicitly axiomatize it in what amounts to a first-order setting. For details, see Azzouni (2005).

82. I should note that classical higher order logics are an interesting case: In practice—for example, with respect to mathematical axiom systems at particular times—they can offer no additional proof-theoretic content over and beyond that available in first-order logical systems. Consequently they are not the alternative option they appear at first glance to be. See Azzouni (2006), 197.

83. In general, it's not the case that the same philosophers need be (or are) both logical and truth pluralists.

84. See, for example, Crispen Wright, *Truth and objectivity* (Cambridge, Mass.: Harvard University Press, 1992). Also see Michael P. Lynch, "Truth and multiple realizability," *Australasian Journal of Philosophy* 82:3 (2004), 384–408, and Douglas Edwards, "How to solve the problem of mixed conjunctions," *Analysis* 68:2 (2008),

seem contradicted by others.[85] For example, a "traditional" causal/correspondence view that takes sentence (tokens) to be true or false by virtue of their causal relations (or the causal relations of the terms appearing in them) to mind-independent items in the world[86] does well for tables and chairs, but poorly with respect to mathematical abstracta (on most views of them). Similarly, "epistemic and response-dependence theories of truth" seem to nicely fit social or legal truths, but not truths about the stars that are outside of our light cone (that are causally inaccessible). Lynch (2004, 385) writes: "Once again, an explanation that works for some propositions fails for others."

A conclusion that can be drawn is that these different theories of truth aren't competing and incompatible characterizations of truth as it's employed globally but are instead suitably locally applied notions of truth, ones that are successful when restricted to specific kinds of discourse.[87] For example, one might think that one or another robust conception of correspondence truth applies adequately to (some of) the propositions of the empirical sciences, but that such a conception can't be applied to moral discourse or to mathematical discourse. Instead (perhaps) a response-dependence notion of truth is suitable for moral discourse, and a coherentist notion of truth is appropriate for mathematical discourse.

Crucial to truth-pluralist views (and contributing—in fact—to the claim that such views are all views about one thing: truth) is that the many purported truth idioms are all to be minimally governed by the Tarski biconditionals. These are statements of the form S is true iff p, for each statement of the language p, where S is a name of p, for example, *"Snow is white," is true iff snow is white*. One reason that the Tarski biconditionals are singled out as so significant is that many see truth—just as Tarski (1944) did, citing Aristotle—as engaged in "saying it like it is."[88] *"Snow is white," is true iff snow is white* indicates this role neatly by connecting the truth of a particular sentence to (an aspect of) "like it is."

But on pluralist views, to fully characterize each of the different truth idioms, the Tarski biconditionals must be supplemented with one or more additional (and differing) conditions—sometimes called "platitudes." So, for example, correspondence

---

143–44, for similar presentations of what I've called "the cottage industry" view of propositions. Edwards speaks of "different domains of discourse"; Lynch (2004, 399) speaks of different domains of propositions that are individuated by the use of different (moral, aesthetic, empirical, mathematical) concepts. In what follows, I will use the phrases, "proposition-domain" or "domain of propositions" to distinguish the discourses governed by different truth concepts (on the view of discourses generally taken in the pluralist truth literature) from the very different discourse-domains that were discussed in section 4.1.

85. Lynch (2004), 385. He calls it "the scope problem." I follow, to some extent, his (standardized) motivation of truth pluralism.

86. Lynch (2004), 385 cites Michael Devitt (*Realism and truth*, 2nd ed. [Princeton, N.J.: Princeton University Press, 1997]) and Hartry Field ("Tarski's theory of truth," *Journal of Philosophy* 69 [1972], 347–75) as examples.

87. Lynch (2004), 386, calls this position strong alethic pluralism (SAP), and notes that Wright (1992) and Crispen Wright ("Truth: A traditional debate reviewed," in *Truth*, ed. S. Blackburn and K. Simmons [Oxford: Oxford University Press, 1999], 203–38) often—but not always—writes as if he's committed to the position. SAP is to be contrasted with a different view that takes there to be only one truth-concept or truth-role but many truth-properties that instantiate that role. I discuss this second position in section 4.9.

88. Lynch (2004), 391, using the quoted phrase, describes this as part of the functional role of true propositions.

truth requires an additional notion of "fact," "object," or whatever; the additional condition to be added to the Tarski biconditionals must require in addition to those biconditionals that certain words (e.g., "snow" and/or "white") appearing in any sentence (that correspondence truth applies to) must refer to objects, or that (perhaps) that the proposition (as a whole) must correspond to a "fact." Alternatively (and incompatibly), an additional condition may require that the sentence in question have certain "coherence properties" with respect to a class of other sentences (e.g., observational ones). A yet different truth concept may require an additional condition that alludes to ideal epistemic conditions under which sentences would be confirmed. (I'm not suggesting, of course, that these various notions of truth are to be defined by the addition to the Tarski biconditionals of only single conditions.[89])

Further details about how all this should go don't really matter because the problems of (all versions of) strong alethic pluralism are so basic. Some of the linked claims I want to press against this family of views are these. (i) The truth idiom is indispensable for blind truth-ascription, (ii) blind truth-ascription (of sentences within one's own language) requires unrestricted Tarski biconditionals, and thus (iii) the truth idiom can have no additional topic-specific (discourse-specific) constraints placed on it. Therefore, given the previous arguments in this book about empty terms, and the truth-apt statements such terms appear in, (iv) the

89. It should be stressed—although I won't make a big deal of it in this book—that this is a misleading way of describing strong alethic pluralism. One cannot add conditions to the Tarski biconditionals to inflate the resulting truth predicates; one can only restrict those biconditionals. For example, to require of a truth predicate that the sentences it applies to correspond to facts (where, that is, such a correspondence is not had by all "true" sentences) is to replace the biconditional *S is true iff p* with the biconditional *S is true iff (p & C)* (and similarly for the other conditions one might consider). This point, apparently, isn't noted in the pluralist-truth literature—but it ought to be. In fact, weirdly, T. Horgan ("Contextual semantics and metaphysical realism: Truth as indirect correspondence," in *The nature of truth: Classic and contemporary perspectives*, ed. M. P. Lynch [Cambridge, Mass.: MIT Press, 2001], 73) writes: "Although contextual semantics asserts that the operative semantic standard governing truth (semantic correctness) can vary from one context to another, it also asserts that contextually operative metalinguistic semantic standards normally require truth ascriptions to obey Tarski's schema T." One wonders how certain conditions on truths are to vary from domain to domain, and yet Tarski's biconditional constraint—as applied to these different truth-concepts—is to remain unaffected. One unsavory—but consistent—way to pull the trick off is to grammatically isolate the various truth predicates from one another: T_1 is not to apply at all—falsely or truly—to the sentences in the domain of a different truth predicate T_2. Thus, we can neither say T_1 nor $\neg T_1$ of a sentence S outside of the domain of T_1. This amounts to treating the different domains of propositions as separate languages—at least as far as truth predicates are concerned; that fits somewhat badly with, for example, our being able to nevertheless assert conjunctions of sentences where each conjunct is from a different domain. Another family of ways to pull the trick off is to (i) change the logic by adopting three values: T_1 does apply to S but the result is neither true nor false; or (ii) deny that T_1S, although grammatical, expresses a proposition. All these ways of making pluralism compatible with Convention T saddle truth pluralists with additional constraints that they clearly don't want advertised loudly.

Joking aside, the difficult fit between truth pluralism and the Tarski biconditionals simply seems to have gone utterly unnoticed among truth pluralists; this is bizarre if only because Tarski—long ago—showed that truth predicates (obeying Criterion T), and operating on the same domain of sentences, have to agree with one another in their extensions (over those sentences).

If the Tarski biconditionals really are the minimal requirement for something to be a truth predicate, then one should be distressed at the prospect of having to hedge them. More important, I think, is that to so hedge them is to unfit the resulting truth predicate for blind truth-ascription. (See the discussion that follows.) The same point holds, by the way, of the other methods of making Convention T fit in with truth pluralism that are mentioned two paragraphs back in this note. (I should add that I press considerations similar to those of this footnote against truth pluralism in Azzouni [2000a]. Also see J. Azzouni and O. Bueno, "On what it takes for there to be no fact of the matter," *Noûs* 42:4 [2008], 753–69.)

truth idiom can have no correspondence constraints, or ontological constraints, placed on it.[90] This will suffice to rule out strong alethic pluralism. Some further considerations will be brought to bear against Lynch's (2004) descendent approach to truth that uses multiple property realizability. I take up (i) and (ii) in the rest of this section, and then continue the discussion in section 4.9.

To begin with (i), let's return to the cases, mentioned in section 4.6, where scientific theories—that are recognized to have one or more false assumptions—nevertheless have (some) truths as consequences. I noted that such truths can be emancipated from the false theories that may be (indispensably) required to deduce them. The truth idiom is (indispensably) required for this purpose. Consider a theory TH that characterizes Jupiter as a point-mass. Such a theory cannot be trusted to describe most of Jupiter's intrinsic properties correctly—for example, that it's largely made up of gases, that its shape becomes distorted in such and such ways due to its rotation—but if TH is judiciously constructed, it may successfully predict, within certain parameters of error, Jupiter's gravitational effects on the Sun. The truths in question can have those parameters of error explicitly included as part of their content—so that they are truths simpliciter. Let us label those true consequences of TH (consequences that usually involve the employment of other physical theories, and some mathematics) with the predicate P.[91] Then we can commit ourselves to the following statement:

All the consequences of TH that are P are true.[92]

Quine long ago distinguished between use and mention. To assert "John is running" is to "use" the sentence "John is running." To assert "John is running" is true, isn't to use the sentence, "John is running," at least not in the way that it's used in the first assertion; it's to mention it. Quine's distinction comports nicely with one of the insights Geach (1965) attributes to Frege. Assertoric force—the assertoric *use* of a sentence—represented explicitly by Frege's coined "assertion sign" does not already appear symbolized in natural languages because, in the language of Geach (1965, 458), any such symbol can appear in a sentence "now asserted, now unasserted."[93] Quine's use of the word "use" is slightly misleading; after all, the sentence "John is running" is used—at least in some sense of "used"—in the sentence "'John is running' is true," but as long as we keep clear that Quine

90. I'm attempting a careful but otherwise "reader's digest" version of the arguments for these claims. The full argument, coupled with the detailed complications, is available: Azzouni (1994), part II, §§3 & 4; Azzouni (2000a), part II, §7; Azzouni (2006), part I.

91. We can, that is, characterize with a predicate, P, those and only those consequences of TH that we regard as true. This is crucial to the forthcoming application of the (blind-ascription) role of truth.

92. This is a blind truth-ascription because a set of sentences (that aren't explicitly exhibited) are described as true, in contrast to "'John is running,' is true," where the sentence to which truth is attributed is explicitly exhibited in the truth ascription itself.

93. Geach notes that Frege, in his *Begriffsschrift*, mistakenly thought of his assertion sign as a "common predicate." P. T. Geach ("Assertion," *Philosophical Review* 74 [1965], 458) writes: "In later works Frege saw his mistake, and gave up any attempt to explain the assertion sign by classifying it as a predicate, or as any other sort of sign; it is necessarily *sui generis*. For any other logical sign, if not superfluous, somehow modifies the content of a proposition; whereas this does not modify the content, but shows the proposition is being asserted."

specifically means "assertoric use" by his generic (but technical) use of "use," there should be no problem.

It's important to realize that the discovery of scientific truths—of all sorts—is motivated not by the (mere) need to be aware that such things are true, nor by the (mere) need to contemplate the discovered truths, but by the need to *use* them in Quine's sense: to assertorically assert them. I can assert, one after another, the following three sentences (and speech-acts like this are fairly typical):

All persons are mortal.
I'm a person.
I'm mortal.

In such cases, sentence tokens of the three sentences whose tokens appear just before this (very) sentence token are used (asserted); it's clear in such cases that the conclusion can be asserted (is being asserted) because it follows from the two previous assertions. In the same way, generally, when a deduction is exhibited, one commits oneself to all the sentences that appear in it. To deduce a conclusion C from the premises, $Pr_1, \ldots, Pr_n$, one (needs to) assert $Pr_1, \ldots,$ assert Pr_n, and then rely on the truth-preserving property of deduction to (consequently) be able to assert C.

In the case of the false theory TH, however, one can escape this apparent need to assert the (false) premises of TH in order to conclude C (truly) by instead using (Quine 1953) "semantic ascent": one notes *that* C follows from TH (one notes that there is a deduction of C from TH), one notes further that C is P, and therefore, because all the consequences of TH that are P are true, one concludes that C is therefore true.

As noted, one usually can't rest with the mere contemplation of the fact that C is true. Science is an assertoric practice of *using* truths in deductions, in evidential arguments, and as representing aspects of the world; it isn't merely a practice of *mentioning* such truths (as one discovers them). One needs (therefore) to assert the sentence C like so: C. Thus, one needs to deduce C from "C is true."[94]

The reverse deduction, from *C* to *C is true*, is needed almost as often to enable the expression of blind truth ascriptions. I recommend a book to a friend. Such a thing is full of asserted statements or propositions that I approve of. I can long-windedly

---

Geach doesn't note (as he should have) that Frege's assertion sign, being a type, can no more indicate that a token of the proposition following a token of that sign is being asserted than any other symbol can; indeed, the use of such an assertion sign can do no better job than the mere appearance of an unadorned token of the sentence appearing on a page. In demonstrating what Frege's notation looked like, I may write a sentence—prefixed by the assertion symbol—to so demonstrate; doing so isn't to assert the sentence that follows the assertion symbol. One understands what Frege was worried about. In setting out results on the page, he wanted it understood that he wasn't merely depicting these results: he was asserting them. But inventing an "assertion sign" for such is incoherent. To assert a sentence is to do something with a sentence token; this can't be transformed into something one achieves by the sheer presentation of a symbol.

94. I've obviously been, in the foregoing, sloppy in my use of use and mention (although—I hope—not in what I've mentioned about use and mention).

recommend it by uttering each of them (ad nauseum)—by assertorically using each one. Although some unpopular people are rather like this, most prefer to employ blind truth ascription and say instead: "Everything in this book is true" (or perhaps to hedge: "Almost everything in this book is true," or perhaps still more guardedly, "Everything in this book about the Bush administration is true").

The foregoing has been a proof that if the truth idiom is to be used in blind-truth-ascription practices, then it must be governed by the Tarski biconditionals. Many philosophers—especially self-styled deflationists—have instead offered the Tarski biconditionals all on their own as an analytic condition on the notion of truth: as part (or all) of what the word means, or as some other kind of fundamental constraint on the concept. This approach to the Tarski biconditionals is unsatisfactory if only because one can then naturally contemplate changing the meaning of the word "true," as one does so often with other words. If a word's role isn't indispensable to some unavoidable task, the word with its fundamental constraint can be dropped altogether. But if blind-truth-ascription practices are indispensable (as they are), and the Tarski biconditionals are needed to facilitate blind-truth-ascription practices (as they also are), one can bypass considerations of the "meaning" of the truth idiom altogether and instead justify the truth idiom as needing to obey Tarski biconditionals by virtue of its blind-truth-ascription role. That is, some idiom or other is indispensable for blind truth ascription. And the truth idiom (of ordinary language, no less), because it's governed by unrestricted Tarski biconditionals, is equipped for just that purpose.

A different role for "true"—but one just as crucial (one might think)—has already emerged in the foregoing. This is that "valid" deductions are to be truth-preserving. Is this really a distinct (independent) role for "true?" No—it can be shown to follow rather directly from the Tarski biconditionals, which in turn have been shown to be required by blind truth ascription. Consider any deduction that's structured as a series of used (not mentioned) sentences, for example,

> All persons are mortal.
> I'm a person.
> I'm mortal.

Given that a person asserts "All persons are mortal," and "I'm a person," she must be allowed[95] to assert "I'm mortal." But given that a person asserts "All persons are mortal," and "I'm a person," because of the Tarski biconditionals, she is also allowed to assert "'All persons are mortal' is true," and "'I'm a person' is true." For the same reason (coupled with her license to assert "I'm mortal"), she can also assert "'I'm mortal' is true." Thus, it follows that legitimate deduction is truth-preserving.

Notice the point. Deductive rules are taken—by many philosophers—to be "justified" by their truth-preservation properties. My countersuggestion is that (to be nice about it) this is a particularly empty form of justification. After all, if a particular pattern of deduction (a particular pattern of asserted sentences of such

---

95. "Allowed," not "required." She might simply not notice that something follows from something else.

and such form) is always regarded as legitimate in a discourse-practice, then in the presence of a truth idiom that obeys the Tarski biconditionals, it simply follows that the pattern in question is "truth-preserving." Still unanswered, that is, is the hard question (that's faced by anyone who takes the possibility of alternative logics seriously) of which patterns of deduction those should be. Truth-preservation considerations cannot help adjudicate this question.[96]

4.9 Blind Truth Ascription, Truth Idioms, and the External Discourse Demand

Let us turn now to my claim (iii), of section 4.8, that the truth idiom can have no additional topic-specific (discourse-specific) constraints placed on it. Broadly speaking, much of the literature evinces some awareness of the problems facing the idea that there can be varying notions of truth that supplement the Tarski biconditionals with additional discourse-specific constraints. Two problems have been raised by Christine Tappolet (1997, 2000) that are described, respectively, as the mixed inference problem and the mixed conjunction problem. The first problem focuses on the role of truth as what's preserved in inference. The second focuses on the question of the assignment of truth values to sentences when they are conjunctions of sentences from different proposition domains.

Consider Tappolet's (1997, 209) example:

Wet cats are funny.
This cat is wet.
Ergo, this cat is funny.

By assumption, this deduction is truth preserving; but we can ask: what kind of truth is it exactly that's being preserved? The second sentence, presumably, is true in the ordinary correspondence sense. But the third sentence isn't; it's assumed to be true in some alternative "lightweight" sense.[97]

Beall (2000) responds to Tappolet's example by invoking many-(truth-)valued logic. Validity is truth preserving, but this can be generalized (in a context with more than one kind of truth) to its being designated-truth-value preserving.[98] Truth pluralism is thus revealed to be naturally accompanied by the employment

---

96. There is more to say, for example, about model-theoretic validity (see Azzouni [2006], part III), but it should be already clear from the line of thought just completed that attempts to justify deductive rules via truth-based notions are deeply misguided. Truth idioms are promiscuous: provide a(ny) deductive system, and introduce into that environment an idiom that fulfills the blind-truth-ascription role, and that idiom will flourish.

97. The predicates, in this case, are dictating the kind of truth the statement involves. Christine Tappolet ("Mixed inferences: A problem for pluralism about truth predicates," *Analysis* 57:3 [1997], 210) makes her point this way: "For the conclusion to hold, some unique truth predicate must apply to all three sentences. But what truth predicate is that? And if there is such a truth predicate, why isn't it the only one we need?"

98. In a number of approaches to many-valued logic, a number of values are truthlike, designated, and the rest are falselike. A deduction can be defined to be valid in such a context if, for any assignment of designated truth values to the premises, the conclusion has a designated truth value as well.

of multiple truth-values. In the context of one or another many-valued logic, the designated truth values don't all operate the same way truth functionally. (If they did, there would be no reason to treat them as distinct truth values.) But in a context where truth pluralism is to be unaccompanied by logic pluralism, all the truth values in question must operate indistinguishably with respect to deduction. This invites precisely the response to Beall that we find in Tappolet (2000): why treat these designated truth values as distinct truth values? After all, their distinctions are invisible to logical deduction, and it's only the disjunction of all of them that's preserved in mixed inferences; why not take the disjunction of all of them to be the truth value that's preserved in deduction?

This somewhat rhetorical question can be given a bit more force if it's coupled with the observations of section 4.8, that in fact the truth preservation of deductive forms falls out of blind truth-ascription (in turn, because the latter requires the Tarski biconditionals). Blind truth-ascription cannot be satisfied with locally restricted truth predicates if only because not only are there mixed inferences but there are mixed lists of statements that one may need to blindly truth-ascribe. Therefore: *only* the disjunction of all the truth predicates will be a useful device for blind truth-ascription.[99] If blind truth-ascription is the reason for a truth predicate, then only a global truth predicate will actually be a truth predicate.

Let's turn to the mixed conjunction problem (also found in Tappolet 2000). This can be put simply. Choose two sentences S_1 and S_2 from two different proposition-domains governed by two different truth predicates. Suppose S_1 is T_1 and S_2 is T_2. Consider S_1 & S_2. Tappolet's challenge is this: what kind of truth does the conjunction have? If one is approaching this via a question about truth-predicates, one is forced to introduce a nonsymmetric truth conjunction predicate: $T_1 \cap T_2$. But this truth conjunction predicate is just the first of a wearily long list of coined truth predicates that one needs. For there are all sorts of ways of combining sentences from different domains (using disjunction, negation, material implication, and so on)—not just conjunction is involved. The construction of numerous (compositional) truth predicates must similarly follow suit.[100]

One way that some of the pluralist truth literature has attempted to escape these problems—that strong alethic pluralism (SAP) faces—is to replace talk of different truth predicates (or different truth "concepts") with talk of different truth properties. After all (one can say) the issue ultimately isn't over the word "true": one can grant that the previous considerations (including the difficult item raised in note 89) necessitate a single truth predicate. But still possible is that the propositions of different proposition-domains have—or lack—different truth properties,

---

99. This is especially the case because blind truth-ascriptions can be not only grammatically blind but epistemically blind. Someone can blind truth-ascribe the remarks of someone else without knowing what kinds of truths (or what range of truths) that person has uttered. The same is true of the implications of a theory that one blind truth-ascribes. As we've seen amply illustrated in previous sections, gross correlational regularities cross vocabulary barriers.

100. Actually, the problem is much, much worse. No doubt the different truth predicates must correspond to different satisfaction predicates. So different open sentences that are joined by a conjunction might in turn be bound by the same quantifier. What kind of truth do the resulting sentences like that have? It's striking how the pluralist literature, in responding to Tappolet's examples, doesn't remark on how easily her examples can be generalized.

that a sentence (from one proposition-domain) can be true because it has one property, whereas a different sentence (from another proposition-domain) can be true because it has a quite different property.

Switching the pluralism from truth predicates (or concepts) to truth-properties strikes me as so much more appealing than SAP, in a number of ways. First, as just noted, we can have a single truth predicate, utilized for blind truth-ascription for all propositions, regardless of their "home proposition-domains." Second, that truth idiom can be governed solely by unrestricted Tarski biconditionals (which neatly avoids the problems raised in note 89). Third, the so-called platitudes that are supposed to differ from proposition-domain to proposition-domain (and that were originally supposed to fill out the minimal conception of truth into a richer conception) can now be treated not as conditions on the truth predicate but instead as varying conditions or facts about different classes of truths.[101] Thus, there can be—compatibly—a number of different "truth-properties" that truths have: some (say) correspond to the facts, others cohere with other truths (of such and such kinds), and so on.

Lynch, and other philosophers in this tradition, continue to associate specialized subject matters with specific kinds of truth properties. But it's desirable to snap that particular connection, to allow that some truths in the moral domain (say) have the fact-correspondence truth property, whereas others have the response-dependence truth property (or something like that). Truth properties, on this generalization of the view, would simply be common ways that some truths (but not all) are true, regardless of what subject areas such truths were drawn from. (Some statements are true because they correspond to external mind-independent objects, others because . . .).

Despite my airing some sympathies with this "multiple realization" picture of the concept of truth, it won't work. The problem is that—even as generalized in the last paragraph—such truth property views still rely far too much on the cottage industry picture of our (overall) discourse practices. Such views, that is, rely on the mistaken impression that each proposition that we use can—for the most part—be illuminatingly classified as drawing all its concepts from one specialized

---

In a sense, the truth-pluralist literature seems to be (strangely) operating at a superficial level of analysis that corresponds (roughly) to the sentential calculus. Of course, if it's "concepts" from different subject areas that appear in propositions that are pertinent to classifying the kind of truth that's applicable to those propositions, propositions that pose classification problems like the ones generated by Tappolet's mixed conjunctions can be easily generated by syntactic constructions that occur within the scope of quantifiers—not, that is, just by the utilization of truth-functional connectives between propositions. Indeed, once one starts to think at all carefully about the issues regarding the contents of the discourse-domains that were raised earlier in this chapter (e.g., the presence of mathematical abstracta in the discourse domains of scientific theories), one begins to suspect that truth pluralists have hardly noticed the numerous and complex kinds of counterexamples (i.e., sentences constructed using the predicates of various subject areas but that in addition quantify over objects drawn from those areas: fictional beings, moral values, abstracta, tables and chairs) that their family of views face. I say a little more about this later in this section.

101. A valuable distinction, if one is out to avoid confusions in this area, is that between a theory of "true" (a theory about the word "true" or about the concept of truth), and the very different theories of truth that are theories about the uniformities—if any—among truths. (See Azzouni [2006], 1.8.) The Tarski biconditionals, talk of blind truth-ascription, and so on, should be regarded as part of the theory of "true." Many of the "platitudes"—that some truths are correspondence truths, others are (say) "response-dependence" truths, and so on—are part of the theory of truth.

domains (e.g., the "moral," the "aesthetic," the "empirical," the "mathematical") so that it can be similarly classified. Exceptions are recognized, but as we've seen, they are invariably tame concoctions of mixtures of concepts from more than one domain of discourse.[102]

For example, we find Lynch (2004, 399) writing this:

> Propositions are in turn individuated by the concepts (moral, legal, mathematical) that compose the propositions. This means that ultimately, what makes one domain different from another derives from differences in the concepts we employ in thinking about different subject matters. This should be uncontroversial. In so far as it makes sense to distinguish our thought about morality as different from our thought about physics (and surely it does make sense), that distinction must ultimately derive from differences between the concepts that are distinctive of each domain. In this way, our reflections, e.g., on the concept of number, impacts how we understand the difference between mathematical propositions and propositions about the physical world.

Let us lay aside the vague term "concept" and notice what's really going on here. Propositions, that is, sentence-sized vehicles (and their correspondingly different truth properties), are not doing the hard work to distinguish themselves from one another. What's doing the hard work here are terms—vocabulary items such as predicates and names. Classes of propositions ("mathematical," "moral," etc.), in turn, enjoy derived individuation conditions based on the kinds of terms that appear within them. But names and predicates can appear within sentences in an utterly indiscriminate fashion. Consider any sentence of the form $S(n_1, \ldots, n_m, P_1, \ldots, P_o)$, containing m names and o predicates (of varying places). Any such sentence can contain—arbitrarily—m names drawn in any which way from any "conceptual domain" whatsoever, and o predicates similarly haphazardly drawn from any number of such "conceptual domains." What sense, therefore, is there in trying to determine the "truth properties" of the resulting sentences?

There *is* sense—or some sense, anyway—in so classifying the names and the predicates. The predicate "is a fictional character" can be classified differently from "is a neutron," differently again from "is immoral." So, too, "Sherlock Holmes," "John Buridan," and "the number nine." But to go this classificatory route is to drop the focus on truth properties altogether and replace it with a study in the neighborhood of ontology.

The truth property pluralist has one slender reed left. This is to argue that although propositions can in principle be ever so indiscriminant in the vocabulary

---

102. For example, Tappolet's examples of mixed conjunctions and mixed inferences, already described, are widely disseminated and responded to. But they provide an illusion, for example, that the problem is only one of conjunctions of propositions—from differing propositional domains—or (on the other hand) a problem with certain predicates, moral or humorous ones, as opposed to correspondence-suitable ones: for example, "funny," as opposed to "wet." This way of narrowing the apparent range of potential counterexamples to the pluralist cottage industry picture of our discourse practices—common both to proponents of truth pluralism and to opponents of such views— is already quite visible in Wright (1992), and in earlier work by other philosophers that influenced Wright—for example, Dummett.

they are made up of (indiscriminant enough to make useless any attempt to classify them as coming from various specific proposition-domains), in practice the propositions we are focused on (the ones we take to be true) are much better behaved.

Precisely here is where a too-meager diet of examples can be the source of so much mischief.[103] Consider the following illustrations:

- Sherlock Holmes is more famous than any real detective; in fact, he's even more famous than the number π (and, as you know, whole books have been written about π).
- Euler was confused about complex numbers, but this didn't stop him from using them in calculations that successfully predicted the stress points in several kinds of bridges.
- Because numbers aren't in space and time (like neutrinos are), some philosophers think they no more exist than moral values do.
- Good men often do stupid things. Because Peter was a good man, and because (in addition) he was a utilitarian, he eventually starved to death.
- If such and such specific parts of a person's brain are stimulated by a C-probe, then he will see hallucinated objects that will all appear to him to be colored in shades of green. Interestingly, the number of such hallucinated objects (on an occasion) correlates positively with the cross-section diameter of the probe used.

I've made these up. But the earlier discussion in this chapter of the various ways that gross correlational regularities cross vocabulary barriers indicates—I would think—that the cottage industry picture of propositions so inaccurately portrays the vocabulary mixture of most of the purported truths that we are concerned with[104] that it—and the truth-property views that accompany it—should be quietly retired.

4.10 Some Concluding Remarks

The external discourse demand has been a centerpiece of this chapter, and indeed, of the book as a whole. I should note that an ancestor of the external discourse demand is Quine's old "web of belief" claim—what he described as his "holism." The web of belief was—and remained in Quine's hands—a metaphor; one thing Quine surely intended was that logical deduction be the cement of that web. He was aided in this perception of the matter, in part, by a residual commitment to

103. The proposition-domain illusion, I think, is helped along by the fact that one learns subject matters in fairly compartmentalized ways in high school and college. Applying one's acquired knowledge (assertorically), however, is a different matter entirely.

104. This is especially the case with moral reasoning. It's striking how moral disagreements—about right and wrong—and arguments about such, seamlessly include both normative and non-normative vocabulary. There may be a gulf between the normative and the non-normative, but one isn't going to locate it by isolating propositions that fail to contain descriptive vocabulary. Only a few moral platitudes ("The good is the right") will look like that.

something like a covering law model for the application of scientific theories, but also in part because he saw deductive relations as crucial to the application of mathematics to the sciences.[105] Regardless, Quine never provided much in the way of further details.[106] In particular, there is pretty much no discussion in his corpus of how statements with varying vocabulary are supposed to deductively interlock. This is surely a nontrivial issue.[107] Nevertheless, Quine was quite sensitive to the fact that statements were brought to bear on one another outside of discourse demarcations. Another point should be made: Quine tended to speak of his holisms, both confirmation and meaning, as if they were "warm baths" that covered huge (but indeterminately shaped) swathes of propositions in the web of belief. This is—generally—not the case, and that it's not the case can be seen even if we restrict our attention to cases where confirmation relations are running roughly along deductive lines. Even in such cases, an event will confirm some aspects of a theory (some propositions of a theory), and not others. In part this is because confirmation is content-specific.[108]

I regard the development and deployment of the external discourse demand—throughout the course of this book—to be (now that I've cleared my conscience by airing some disagreements) broadly compatible with Quine's "holism." One of the burdens of this chapter is that if such a holism with respect to our discourse-practices is an insight, then it's one that's been widely disregarded. Pluralist views of truth and logic (in particular)—which are currently enjoying a bit of a vogue—cannot possibly be right if the interconnections between "proposition-domains" are as widespread and thorough as I have indicated them to be.

Congeniality toward my Quinean ancestry has never extended to his criterion for what a discourse is committed to nor to companion doctrines about singular idioms. I have tried to illustrate how the ubiquitous use of "idealizations" in the sciences amounts to a systematic and sensible violation of Quinean ontological dicta. Scientists formulate domains of discourse—and the vocabulary items that refer$^{(r/e)}$ to the contents of those domains of discourse—in ways that maximize successful applications of scientific doctrine to phenomena studied. That what is in those domains doesn't—strictly speaking—exist, is of no scientific concern. To say this is not to say that ontology is of no interest to science: we (philosophers) must just learn to be just a little less doctrinaire when we try to recognize how

---

105. Deduction, although important, is hardly the primary tool by which scientific (and mathematical) theories are applied. See Azzouni (2000a), part I, for details.

106. Most of what he had to say about the model is contained in W. V. Quine and J. S. Ullian, *The web of belief*, 2nd ed. (New York: Random House, 1978)—a book originally intended for freshman English courses.

107. Requiring, I claim, a fairly radical solution: gross correlational regularities.

108. There is no successfully worked out "theory" of confirmation. As noted, the difficulty is that confirmation relations—when they exist—are content-specific: they are sensitive to what the parts of a theory (its sentences) say. To recognize how the parts of a theory have been confirmed, one needs to look at the details of the theory and how it has been applied. An effect of the subtlety of this is that professionals often presume a whole theory has been confirmed by a series of empirical results, although close inspection usually shows otherwise. For a detailed illustration of these aspects of confirmation with respect to Newton's inverse square law, and the third law of motion, see George Smith, "Pending tests to the contrary: The question of mass in Newton's law of gravity," forthcoming. It's Goodman's (1983) toy examples of "grue," and so on, that first revealed the content specificity of confirmation.

scientists commit themselves ontologically. The same point, it should be said, holds when it's directed toward the ontological commitment practices of ordinary people. This should be no surprise, I think, since everyone in our culture commits themselves ontologically in pretty much in the same way.[109]

A stiff-necked attitude about the ontological commitments of scientific doctrine has been somewhat disastrous for philosophy. An intense focus on empirical strong reductions—which turned out not to exist—was motivated in the final analysis by ontological misgivings about the apparent terminological commitments of the special sciences (i.e., anything but "physics"). Philosophers should have detected the irrelevance of their concerns by the absence of any echo of a search for strong reductions on the part of scientists. The subsequent focus on supervenience—still a very active field in philosophy to this day—is equally irrelevant to and unreflective of actual scientific practice. If the gross correlational regularities that scientists find so valuable indispensably quantify over things that every scientist recognizes not to exist, how can supervenience constraints on special science terminology have a point?

Oddly enough, the (very simple) lesson seems to be this: philosophers haven't really taken talk of what doesn't exist (indeed, talk of what doesn't exist in any sense at all) seriously enough. And of course, you would have thought that they were the intellectual professionals who would have been the mostly likely to have done this.

---

109. See Jody Azzouni, "Ontological commitment in the vernacular," *Noûs* 41 (2007), 204–26, and Jody Azzouni, "Ontology and the word 'exist': Uneasy relations," *Philosophia Mathematica*, forthcoming (a).

5

Truth Conditions and Semantics

5.0 An Overview for Browsers, Grazers, and People Who Hate Surprises

The point of this chapter is to show that if idioms that don't refer[r] to anything occur in a language, then they must occur in the (meta)language used to depict the semantic properties of that language. In a way, this claim shouldn't be surprising. Tarski's original work—the source of contemporary semantics—required a replication (plus additional resources) of the referential resources of the targeted object language in the metalanguage. One result of this chapter is a corollary: if the resources of a targeted object language are referential[e], they, too, must be replicated in the metalanguage that provides the semantics for that object language.

I start by giving a simple traditional example of a truth-conditional theory for a first-order language L, and I show that if the quantifiers of that language are ontologically neutral, then such neutrality can be replicated by the quantifiers of the metalanguage, without affecting in any negative way the semantic theory (S) couched in that metalanguage. Along the way, I indicate why the truth conditions of sentences (of L) containing empty singular names can be easily given by metalanguage sentences containing appropriately empty singular names. In section 5.3, I unravel several tangles involving use and mention, disquotation, and ontology that many able practitioners in the philosophy of language have tripped over; in particular, certain arguments directed toward certain kinds of semantic theories (model-theoretic ones, structural ones) due to Lewis, Higginbotham, and others, are shown to miss their targets once these tangles are straightened out.

In section 5.4, I show that the ontological neutrality of objectual first-order quantifiers extends to set theory, and thence to the semantic analysis of generalized quantifiers. (It also applies to semantic theories that can't be housed in standard set theory.) I then provide a baby case of a truth-conditional semantic theory that operates by assigning values to the nodes of the syntactic trees of sentences (of a language), and I illustrate how such an assignment of values is also ontologically neutral: nothing in what such semantic theories are supposed to do—by way of explanation of the understanding of languages—requires those values to exist. In section 5.5, finally, I sketch how singular phenomena—for example, demonstrative expressions—change nothing ontological in the foregoing picture. That is to say, on any of a variety of approaches to complex demonstratives (e.g., using demonstratives in the statement of the truth conditions; using only descriptions in conditionalizations of such truth conditions), no ontological requirements arise by virtue of the semantic theories themselves.

Notice the claim to be established in this chapter: the various approaches to semantics respect whatever ontological commitments already appear or don't appear in the object language. They needn't add additional ones.

5.1 Introduction

This chapter is essentially a technical addendum to the book. I've claimed that empty singular locutions are indispensable to daily life and to the sciences. This is part of a broader thesis of the book: that locutions that quantify over or refer^e to the nonexistent are indispensable. This thesis, I've argued, is distinct from any of those in the family of Meinongian views that take there to be objects that "don't exist." Such Meinongian views often look highly nonconservative in appearance when the semantics of expressions referring to Meinongian objects is given. Two styles of quantifiers, for example, may be described as required: one that quantifies over what's real, and one that doesn't. Other approaches, however, may take the quantifiers to be "ontologically neutral" and shift the work of making needed ontological distinctions to certain designated predicates (e.g., "exist").

The often made remark (among certain Meinongians) that their quantifiers are "ontologically neutral" sounds rather like remarks I've long made about (ordinary first-order objectual) quantifiers. The difference, however, is that when the Meinongian makes this claim, he intends to say that the quantifier in question is neutral with respect to two kinds of objects, existing ones and nonexisting ones, both of which the quantifier ranges over, both of which have properties, and the properties of which—in turn—are crucial to the truth conditions of statements: those about real objects, those about unreal objects (and those about both).

I mentioned that Meinongian approaches to semantics often look nonconservative. But to read this as indicating their genuine unorthodoxy is to overlook their fundamental compatibility with semantics as it's almost universally understood and practiced today. Semantic theories are—almost universally—taken as requiring genuine sentence/world relations, and more specifically, as requiring genuine term/ object relations of various kinds. This is because semantics—as it's almost universally understood and practiced today—takes the notion of truth to be its fundamental tool. In turn "truth" so understood employs (descendants of) the formal devices invented by Tarski (and introduced into the study of semantics by Davidson).[1] Almost as universally, the "truth tools" so employed are taken to involve genuine language/world relations. A sentence (proposition, etc.) is true in such and such circumstances ("circumstances" being understood in a way specific to the semantic theory in question) because its compositional structure (the language/world relations of some of its functionally significant parts: names, quantifiers, etc.) induces (recursively) such and such relations between the containing sentences and those circumstances. In these respects Meinongian views are entirely traditional: the terms referring to Meinongian objects, and the properties those objects have, similarly induce truth relations between sentences and the world (understood broadly as containing what doesn't exist in addition to what does).

In contrast: I've stressed repeatedly that on my view, we must distinguish between terms that refer[r] and terms that refer[e]. Reference[r] is a term/world relation between terms, names, demonstrative expressions, pronouns, and so on, and items in the world. Truth conditions of statements containing terms that refer[r] take account of—at least in principle—the items those terms refer[r] to. In the paradigmatic case, "John is running," is true just when what "John" refers[r] to (John) has the property (Running) that the statement "John is running" attributes to him.[2]

Reference[e], on the other hand (and as I've stressed), isn't a relation at all. A term that refers[e] bears no referential[r] relation to anything, and consequently it isn't about[r] anything either. (Aboutness[e] is no more a real relation things have to other things than reference[e] is.) Therefore (presupposing, for example, a nominalist view about numbers), "Nine is a number" cannot have truth conditions that takes account of an object (nine) that "Nine" refers[r] to. What on Earth can its truth conditions look like, therefore? Some philosophers will be quick to suggest that the only alternative is to drop truth conditions (and truth) entirely, and supply instead something like "verification" or "assent" conditions."[3] This tempting proposal characterizes—in a broad way—sets of circumstances in which the "assertability conditions" of the sentence "Nine is a number" (and other sentences in which the word "Nine" appears) are to be evaluated and indicates in which of those circumstances it's appropriate to assent to those sentences and in which of those circumstances it's not appropriate to assent to those sentences.

1. See Alfred Tarski, "The concept of truth in formalized languages," in *Logic, semantics, metamathematics,* ed. J. Corcoran (Indianapolis, Ind.: Hackett, 1983b), 152–278, and the papers in Donald Davidson, *Essays on actions and events* (Oxford: Oxford University Press, 1980) and Donald Davidson, *Inquiries into truth and interpretation* (Oxford: Oxford University Press, 1984).

2. Putting it this way may make it sound like taking account of the truth conditions of sentences like "John is running," requires commitment to properties (or things coextensive to such, e.g., sets). I don't think it does—but this tangle of issues cannot be discussed in this book. Nothing I say turns crucially on how these issues are resolved.

3. The idea is to drop truth conditions along with truth, with respect to statements about numbers. Such sentences are, therefore, appropriately assertable, appropriately assentable, or something like that.

Exploring this tempting suggestion further, we can take ourselves to be (collectively) engaged in a communitywide mathematical practice involving mathematical proof. One then suggests that the "assent conditions" for mathematical statements (including "Nine is a number") are something like this:

(1) S is appropriately assertable iff there is a proof of S.

The proposal, as it stands, invites a great deal of philosophical scrutiny and development; indeed, there are many (different and incompatible) ways to do so. For example, there are issues about how to understand "there is a proof": is this the ordinary classical quantifier, and are the proofs as so described therefore timeless Platonist objects? Or must it be a time-linked quantifier because proof practices involve human constructions that take place over time? Different answers to this question push the suggestion in different directions, and in ways that seem to impact on the logic of mathematics. Second, formal proofs are relative to axiom systems that provide decision procedures for their proprietary notions of "proof" and that are, in general, incomplete. How is "proof" as it occurs in (1) to be taken? If it's relative to an axiom system, or even to an open-ended family of such (recursive) axiom systems, then the "appropriate assent" conditions aren't bivalent.

Considerations roughly of this sort have convinced many philosophers that the logic of pure mathematics isn't bivalent, and that therefore the logic of mathematics can't be the standard classical one. I've argued, however, that the external discourse demand requires that something in the neighborhood of classical first-order logic must be the logic of pure—but applicable—mathematics. In general, it has to be noted (and as the previous comments briefly indicated) that the replacement of truth conditions for a discourse practice with "assertability conditions" almost invariably requires a change in the logic. It also—as Benacerraf (1973) noted—forces the semantics attributed to mathematical statements to deviate from the (truth-conditional) semantics otherwise (widely) taken as the appropriate semantics for our sentences.

I started the discussion of this illustration by observing that many philosophers see the denial of referents[r] to mathematical terms, the denial of referents[r] to any terms for that matter, as forcing the desertion of traditional truth-conditional semantics for mathematical languages and, more generally, for all languages with nonreferring[r] terms. What it is, precisely, that seems at work in forcing this desertion of truth-conditional semantics—recall—is the rigorous imposition of the claim that some terms (e.g., mathematical terms) don't refer[r]; in saying so, it's meant that there are no objects (of any sort) with any properties that can be treated as pertinent to the truth conditions of those statements. The Meinongian, as noticed, seems to be in a position to help himself to (some version of) traditional semantics even though his objects "don't exist." This is because these nonexisting objects have properties, and those properties are pertinent to the truth conditions of the sentences that terms referring[r] to those objects appear in.

My aim in the rest of this chapter is to show that discourses that contain both terms that refer[r] and terms that refer[e] can be given a uniform truth-conditional semantics with clauses that are indistinguishable from those found in the standard truth-conditional theories. Semantic theory has no genuine referential[r] requirements of any sort: that is, the truth-conditional theories—in the forms they already take—are ontologically neutral: not in the Meinongian sense that they can provide truth conditions for sentences that refer[r] to Meinongian objects, but in the sense that they can provide truth conditions for sentences in a way that's insensitive to whether the terms in those sentences refer[r] or refer[e].[4] The key to understanding this surprising thesis is to take note of how truth-conditional semantic theories provide truth conditions for sentences: that they do so by the theories in question providing sentential formulations of those truth conditions. But these sentential formulations of truth conditions—it will be revealed—are themselves ontologically neutral. I undertake the task of showing this in the sections to follow.

5.2 An Example of a Truth-Conditional Theory

I start by providing a (fairly standard) set of truth conditions for a simplified formal language. Let L be the targeted language (the "object language") for which a truth-conditional semantics is to be given. L is a standard interpreted first-order language (with the quantifier, $(\exists\#)$, the conjunction, $\#\&\#$, and the negation $\neg\#$). The domain of L (what its quantifiers range over) is, let's say, a subselection of items from the world. Its nonlogical vocabulary is a single one-place predicate, P, and a single name, b. P has a subset of the domain of L as its extension, and b designates some object in that domain. L^M is the "metalanguage" in which the truth-conditional semantic theory of L is to be given. It's also a standard interpreted first-order language. It contains enough nonlogical resources to describe the semantics and syntax of L; in particular, the concept of a well-formed formula (wff) of L is definable in L^M. I'll informally (and sloppily) depict the description of the syntax and semantics of L (in L^M) using quotation, and without explicit definitions. Any professional will know how to replace my informal locutions with the real things, and (I think) those unfamiliar with the formal technicalities will see the points being made—ones that don't require much in the way of technical detail to see.[5]

---

4. In this sense, therefore, we can say that truth-conditional theories characterize the truth-conditions of the sentences they are applied to in terms of reference[(r/e)] (recall section 1.7) where "reference[(r/e)]" is neutral with respect to either a reference[r] relation (to objects) or for the reference[e] property. In what follows, I usually, but not always, suppress the superscript "(r/e)," and just use "refer," as it's done in ordinary English, and as I've done pretty much throughout this book.

5. There are numerous books (and articles) that provide truth-conditional theories of meaning along the lines I'm sketching, and that—in particular—spell out the notion of satisfaction satisfactorily. A tiny (fairly arbitrary) list: John Etchemendy, *The concept of logical consequence* (Cambridge, Mass.: Harvard University Press, 1990); Wolfgang Künne, *Conceptions of truth* (Oxford: Oxford University Press, 2003), 175–202; W. V. O. Quine, *Philosophy of logic*, 2nd ed. (Cambridge, Mass.: Harvard University Press, 1986), chapter 3; and Scott Soames, *Understanding truth* (Oxford: Oxford University Press, 1999), chapter 3. An excellent book, presenting a truth-conditional semantics that's informed by contemporary (1995) linguistics, is Richard Larson and Gabriel Segal, *Knowledge of meaning* (Cambridge, Mass.: MIT Press, 1995).

The domain of L^M includes all the items in the domain of L, but contains in addition various sets and functions that are needed to refer to the specific vocabulary items of L and (more generally) that are needed to characterize the syntax and semantics of L. That domain also contains the name b^M and the predicate P^M. The former is stipulated to co-refer with the term b of L and the latter is stipulated to have the same extension as the predicate P of L. Crucial to the recursive characterization of the truths of L is the previously noted notion of a wff of L. Among these are the sentences of L, but in addition the wffs include those items with free variables that are generated from the sentences in L by substituting occurrences of any of one or more of the variables x_1, x_2, . . ., x_n, . . ., in place of (some but not necessarily all) occurrences of the constant b in those sentences. We say that a wff has no free variables if every variable that appears in it appears within the scope of some quantifier containing that same variable. If and only if a wff has no free variables is that wff a sentence.

Preliminaries. Consider the set of variables x_1, x_2, . . ., x_n, . . . of L. Call a mapping I of these variables to the domain of L an *interpretation* of the variables. (An interpretation treats each variable of L as if it's a name of the item the interpretation maps the variable to.)

The resulting semantic theory is a *recursion* on the wffs of L:

(S) Given an interpretation I, a variable x_i of L, and wffs F_1 and F_2 of L:

(S_1) "Px_i" is satisfied by I iff $P^M I(x_i)$,

(S_2) "Pb" is satisfied by I iff $P^M b^M$,

(S_3) "F_1 & F_2" is satisfied by I iff "F_1" is satisfied by I and "F_2" is satisfied by I,

(S_4) "¬F_1" is satisfied by I iff "F_1" is not satisfied by I,

(S_5) "($\exists x_i$)F_1" is satisfied I iff there is an interpretation I*, where $I^*(x_j) = I(x_j)$
        for $j \neq i$, and "F_1" is satisfied by I*.

Definition. A *sentence* (a wff without free variables) is true iff it is satisfied by every (any) interpretation I.

Discussion. It's already been noted—in section 4.1—that the domains of scientific theories can contain a great deal more than what there is. Semantic theory is surely to be no exception among the sciences. Semantic theory can help itself to (its sentences can quantify over), for example, interpretations. These are mathematical functions that map terms to the world; they are items that—from the nominalist's point of view—don't exist.[6] Something more specific, however, should be said about the clauses of (S). Their surface appearance indicates correctly that (S) is a theory that can provide truth conditions on a one-by-one basis for each sentence

---

6. For that matter, the nominalist can take a similar attitude toward the wffs themselves—the items of the language. She can regard these, for example, as mathematical substituents for the actual physical embodiments of speech events.

of L. Just as we have (S_2): "Pb" is satisfied by I iff P^Mb^M, which is an axiom of (S), we have (as a theorem of (S)):

(2) "$(\exists x_i)Px_i$" is true iff there is something that is P^M.[7]

Results of the form (2), for every sentence of L, are theorems of (S).[8] These (collectively) are the desired truth conditions (stated in L^M) for the sentences of L.

A general point immediately follows from this: the truth conditions of sentences are related to actual objects and their machinations only to the extent that such relations are expressed by the metalanguage statements of the form (2) that provide those truth conditions, and (more generally) only to the extent that such relations are expressed by (S) and the other statements (in background theories) that are needed to prove statements of the form (2). That is, if—for example—the quantifiers that appear in the metalanguage are ones that don't quantify over anything real, then (at least as far as the quantifiers dictate these matters) those truth conditions don't involve objects.

As I've said, to note this is to note nothing beyond what was shown in section 4.1. But more should be said about (S) than this. (S) is—famously—a recursive providing of the truth conditions for the sentences of L. That is, and using satisfaction, it provides satisfaction conditions (and derivatively, truth conditions) for the wffs of L step by step in terms of the satisfaction (or not) of subwffs of those wffs. For example, the wff $(Px_1 \& Qx_2)$ is satisfied by I iff Px_1 is satisfied by I and Qx_2 is satisfied by I. The satisfaction conditions are "buck-passed" from the wffs of L to other subwffs of L. However, and crucial to the approach, is that because all wffs of L are finite in length, although the satisfaction conditions of complex wffs of L are buck-passed to subwffs of those wffs, these satisfaction conditions must eventually be passed off to a characterization of the satisfaction conditions of the basic wffs of L. These, in turn, cannot buck-pass the satisfaction conditions of those wffs to yet other wffs of L, but must give them outright in terms of (certain) sentences of L^M.

It can be proven (by induction) that the satisfaction conditions for *any* wff of L are buck-passed (eventually) to those wffs governed by (S_1) and (S_2). (S_1) and (S_2) provide satisfaction conditions for wffs of L of the form Px_i and Pb in terms of $P^MI(x_i)$ and P^Mb^M. That is, if $I(x_i)$ is in the extension of P^M, then (and only then) is Px_i satisfied by I. Similarly, if b^M is in the extension of P^M, then (and only then) is Pb satisfied by I. And this is *all* that the semantic theory (S) (plus other background

7. Informal proof: "$(\exists x_i)Px_i$" is true iff there is an interpretation I that satisfies "$(\exists x_i)Px_i$" iff there is an interpretation that satisfies "Px_i" iff $P^MI(x_i)$ iff there something that is P^M.

8. These truth conditions, Tarski biconditionals, that link each sentence of L to a sentence of L^M that gives its truth condition, follow from (S) by ordinary logic. However, if (S)—or corresponding semantic theories—are to be taken as characterizing the semantic knowledge had by speakers of a (natural) language, it may not be desirable to allow such theories to be closed under the consequence relation of logic. This is for, pretty much, the same reasons that if one is out to characterize what someone (consciously) knows, the set of representations of such will be inaccurate if those representations (of his knowledge) are taken to be closed under logical implication. (See chapter 2 of Larson and Segal [1995] for a nice discussion of this.) Given this restriction, additional principles (of one or another sort, and that I don't specify here) must be added to (S) to allow the derivation of sentences of the form (2) for each sentence of L.

theoretical results, such as those from set theory) has to say about the satisfaction (respectively, the truth) of Px_i and Pb.

The result I've just described is clear (and widely known). The truth (satisfaction) of the sentences (wffs) of L are necessarily and sufficiently described in terms of a specific body of truths of L^M. More specifically, the truths about what the predicate P holds of (and doesn't hold of) are buck-passed to truths about what its sibling metalanguaged predicate P^M holds of (and doesn't hold of). Correspondingly (and more generally), truths about the domain of L are buck-passed to truths about the domain of L^M.

The initial description of the domain of L, which I just gave, was that it was a subselection of the real world. In turn, the interpretation function I was taken to map the variables of L to that domain. P was taken to be a subset of that domain, and P^M was stipulated to co-refer with P. Consequently, (S_1) guarantees that Px_i is satisfied by I if indeed the item that I maps the variable x_i to falls in the extension of P. We need to ask: "What, in (S), is sensitive to the domain of L being a subselection of the real world, I mapping the variables of L to real things, and P holding of a subset containing real things?"

Nothing.[9] Given that statements of L^M (like the statements of any language) can be true, despite their referring to nothing at all, it can certainly be that the domain of L (and the entire domain of L^M, for that matter) is actually empty, and that P, correspondingly, has no extension. The metalanguage L^M is designed to provide the semantics of L. To that end, it's required to be a language taking a certain form, and the resulting theory must have truths of a certain form. In particular, it must be true that P^M has the same extension as P, and that b^M refers to the same thing that b does. It must be true that the various interpretation functions I_j map the variables of L to the domain of L. To satisfy these requirements, it's not needed for P^M or P to have extensions; it's not needed that b and b^M refer^r to anything at all; it's not even needed that there be a domain. What is needed is that (S) involve certain true statements, for example, that $b = b^M$, and that $(x)(Px \leftrightarrow P^Mx)$.[10]

We have seen this kind of thing before: theories and languages that must be true and that have terms that co-refer^e (are about^e) the same things, even though the terms in question don't refer^r. The only difference in this case is subject matter: that the theories in question are about (to put it accurately: about$^{(r/e)}$) other theories, and what those theories refer$^{(r/e)}$ to. But if ordinary theories/languages (of science) can contain truths and yet refer^r to nothing at all, then the same is true at the metalanguage level. Here, too, theories can be true and yet the terms in them not refer^r. More pointedly,

---

9. What follows replicates, in slightly different language, a point I've made in Jody Azzouni, *Deflating existential consequence: A case for nominalism* (Oxford: Oxford University Press, 2004a), and indeed, first made in Jody Azzouni, "Applied mathematics, existential commitment and the Quine-Putnam indispensability thesis," *Philosophia Mathematica* 3:5 (1997), 193–209 and Jody Azzouni, "On 'on what there is,'" *Pacific Philosophical Quarterly* 79:1 (1998), 1–18.

10. Strictly speaking, these statements are in the metametalanguage, one that contains (and can use) both the terms of L and those of L^M. What's required, of course, is that b and b^M co-refer$^{(r/e)}$, and similarly, that P and P^M co-refer$^{(r/e)}$. L^M can say something in the neighborhood of these things: that P holds of something x iff P^Mx is true, (e.g., (S_1) and (S_2)).

such theories can contain terms that although they refer^r to nothing at all, nevertheless co-refer^e with other terms (that also refer^r to nothing at all).[11]

It's true that in initially setting out L and L^M, I described and contrasted their discourse-domains (and I did so deliberately). What the preceding paragraph indicates is something that we can otherwise independently see: all this talk of domains is, in any case, superfluous. Worse, it's misleading because it invites the reader to indulge in Meinongian imagery (various containers filled with brightly colored existing and nonexisting objects). One can, however, easily expunge all references to domains: talk about the variables of L^M and L, and officially design those of L^M on the basis of those of L.[12] The point comes down to a description of the terms of L and the terms of L^M, and how these are to be stipulated to co-refer$^{(r/e)}$.[13]

But wait. *Surely* (some philosopher is likely to protest) this much of the referential apparatus of L^M must be taken seriously: there are terms in L^M that refer^r to the syntactic elements of L; they don't refer^e to them. No—a final position on that question is to be resolved pending one's view of the ontological status of the syntactic elements of L. If one thinks that the language of L is real (although, say, what its terms refer$^{(r/e)}$ to isn't real) then one will so characterize reference of the terms in L^M to the sentences of L: they refer^r to the wffs of L, although they only refer^e to the items that the terms of L also refer^e to. Otherwise (if one is nominalistic about L as well), it's reference^e in L^M across the board.

One point about exposition, here and in what follows. It's somewhat desirable—in philosophical settings—to avoid explicit talk of discourse-domains ("universes") if only because in philosophical settings the tendency to read such talk as ontologically committing (as reference^r) is almost automatic. But avoiding the "material mode" of speech, and speaking of the existential truths of such and such sorts of quantifiers, is extremely awkward. So I'm not going to do it systematically. In what follows I instead speak of "universes" or "domains" containing things "that don't exist." The reader who has reached this point in the book should be quite aware that nothing even faintly Meinongian is in the offing: such remarks aren't to be read as a (metalanguage) quantification over things that don't exist; they're to be understood as ontologically neutral uses of quantifiers—uses that, in general, have been shown to be indispensable. A common family of locutions I consistently avail myself of—and have in the foregoing already availed myself of—are these: *items of such and such that don't exist. This is a discourse-domain containing items that don't exist*, and so on. These are of the form: there are so and sos, and some (or all) such don't exist (or do exist); these forms of speech (on my reading) couple ontologically neutral quantifiers with a contrastive existence predicate. "There are so and sos that don't

11. Terms in mathematics, that the nominalist denies refer^r to anything, nevertheless co-refer^e as we've seen, for example, "2" and "1 +1".

12. For example, one can write: $(x_L)((Px_L \vee \neg Px_L) \leftrightarrow (x_M)(Dx_M \rightarrow (Px_M \vee \neg Px_M))$ in the metametalanguage. As noted, the quantifiers of L^M must be involved in more truths than the quantifiers of L.

13. It's worth stressing again: the truth-conditional semantics is indifferent as to whether what's going on is reference^r or reference^e; thus, the appropriateness of the nomenclature "reference$^{(r/e)}$."

exist," is not to be read as contradictory, as views that analytically identify the particular quantifier and ontological commitments, must so read it. Nor is it to be read Meinongistically: as the claim that there are objects, but they don't have the property of nonexistence.[14]

5.3 Getting Clear about Use and Mention in Disquotational Theories of Truth

A number of professionals seem to think that the very form of (S) enables it to deliver "language-world" connections. Ludlow (1999, 36), for example, writes: "Crucially, the theorems of a truth-conditional semantics are also disquotational. That is, they express relations between expressions of the object language and the world." What Ludlow is pointing to is something operative not in every clause of (S), but specifically in those clauses ((S$_1$) and (S$_2$)) of (S), here repeated:

(S$_1$) "Px_i" is satisfied by I iff P^{M}I(x_i),

(S$_2$) "Pb" is satisfied by I iff P^{M}b^M,

In contrast, (S$_3$), here repeated,

(S$_3$) "F$_1$ & F$_2$" is satisfied by I iff F$_1$ is satisfied by I and "F$_2$" is satisfied by I,

connects the satisfaction of one wff of L to the satisfaction of other wffs in L. All three clauses, (S$_1$), (S$_2$), and (S$_3$), of course, are statements in the metalanguage; but only (S$_1$) and (S$_2$) are "disquotational": although their antecedents talk about the sentences of the object language, their consequents don't. Those consequents simply lay down conditions. Notice that all the desired truth-conditional theorems of the form (2), here repeated,

(2) "(∃x_i)Px_i" is true iff there is something that is P^M,

are similar to (S$_1$) and (S$_2$). Each such theorem mentions an object-language sentence, and biconditionally connects it to a statement in the metalanguage that's used.

This property of truth-conditional semantic theories has been invoked in polemics against other (nondisquotational) semantic theories to argue that the latter cannot provide models of "understanding a language" that truth-conditional semantic theories can provide. This point is usually tightly coupled with the idea that such nondisquotational theories cannot do this precisely because their semantic analyses of the sentences (of the object language) don't say what those sentences are about: only a disquotational theory reveals what the object language sentences are about.

14. Recall note 104 of section 2.11.

For example, consider the "structural semantic theories" of Katz (1972), Katz and Fodor (1963), and Jackendoff (1972). Such theories are designed to provide mappings of each natural-language expression to those of a representational language, either a language of thought, (as in Fodor 1975) or an abstract language (as in Katz 1981). Lewis (1970) influentially argued that such mappings provide no interpretation of a natural language because such mappings are from one system of notation to another; but that tells us nothing about what either system is about.[15] We lack what Ludlow (1999, 29) regards as a "language-world" connection. Lepore (1983) and Higginbotham (1990) direct similar objections toward model-theoretic semantics. Such a semantics supplies theorems such as: "The content of the Italian word 'fragola' is the extension of 'fragola' in every possible world." But this doesn't tell us—with respect to *any* of the worlds in question—what that extension is.

This family of objections, coupled as it is with implicit constraints on successful theories of understanding and "language-world" connections, involves subtleties of use and mention, as well as ontology, that must be separated out. Chierchia and McConnell-Ginet (1990, 82) write: "What a Tarski-style definition of truth does is to associate sentences with a description of the conditions under which they are true *in a certain metalanguage*. It thereby seems to shift the issue of meaning from the object language to the metalanguage without really telling us what meaning is" (emphasis in original). Ludlow (1999, 37) responds that the "truth conditions are *stated* in the metalanguage" (emphasis in original), and that "'Snow is white' is true iff snow is white," is more informative than "'Snow is white' is associated with the metalanguage expression 'snow is white.'" Ludlow takes the former statement to provide "language-world" connections whereas the second only provides language-metalanguage connections.

What's going on here? Well, certainly Chierchia and McConnell-Ginet (1990) have put the matter a little sloppily. Truth-conditions of the form (2) don't say what the meaning of the object-language sentences are,[16] but that person who already knows the metalanguage is able to grasp those meanings regardless. The reason they can do so, however, is noticed by Chierchia and McConnell-Ginet (1990): the extension of P and the referent of b are respectively buck-passed to the extension of P^M and the referent of b^M by the latter items being used (not mentioned) in the clauses (S_1) and (S_2). However (and this is the point of their remark "without really telling us what meaning is"), no analysis of how P^M and b^M have, respectively, the extension and referent they have is given by those clauses: (S_1) and (S_2) describe no mechanism by which P^M has the extension it has. (S_1) and (S_2) describe no mechanism by which b^M refers to what it refers to. Nor does anything else in such semantic theories so describe.

15. Someone can know the mappings in question without knowing what the sentences in either language mean. A neat exemplification of the point is the possibility, described in Larson and Segal (1995), 561–62, note 22, of a useless version of the Rosetta Stone, because (say) it has three passages translated into three different languages that no living person knows.

16. Perhaps, though, they "show" such. See, for example, John McDowell, "On the sense and reference of a proper name," in *Reference, truth and reality*, ed. Mark Platts (London: Routledge and Kegan Paul, 1980) or Gareth Evans, *The varieties of reference* (Oxford: Oxford University Press, 1982).

Once it's seen clearly how use and mention are playing out in disquotational truth-conditional theories, one can see how these objections raised against structural and model-theoretic semantics score only a small technical point but otherwise essentially miss their mark. Consider the internal (I-language[17]) IN of a speaker S of a natural language L. And consider a theorist T who is studying S, IN, and L, and who speaks her own language, TH.[18] By assumption, IN is not spoken by the theorist, T. T may formulate theories about the mechanism by which S understands L. And T may hypothesize that the psychologically real mechanism by which S understands the sentences of L is by a mapping MM of the sentences of L to the language IN. Indeed, T may formulate MM in her own language TH. Such a description of the mapping MM (in TH) may take a recursive form and have theorems like this: "F" is true in L iff "F*" is true in IN. Furthermore, it should be part of T's theory of S's understanding of L (via MM) that the speaker S understands IN. For the theorist T to know this is not for T herself to understand IN, but it is for T to understand that it is S's understanding of IN that enables his understanding of L (via MM).

Of course, if T then learns (or realizes that she already understands) IN, she can then go on to disquote the consequents of the theorems of MM; doing so is not to modify T's theory of S's understanding of L (a theory that includes MM as a central part), nor is it appropriate to claim that T only now has a theory of S's understanding of L, one that she lacked before. The difference is solely that now she can use IN—and what's stated in IN—whereas before she couldn't. My claim is this: it cannot be that a theory of understanding is only a theory of understanding when all of it can be used. That's a bit crazy as a demand on theorizing. Let C be a theory of chemistry. This is true: if I don't know the language a crucial part of C is couched in, I can't use it. But being unable to use C (because I can't use this crucial part) doesn't make it—just by virtue of that—not a theory of chemistry. In that case it's a theory of chemistry all right, but it's one I can't use in certain ways.

It's important to realize that just because a theory is couched (in part) in language that someone doesn't know doesn't make that theory entirely useless.

17. See Noam Chomsky, *Knowledge of language* (New York: Praeger, 1986). Understand the I-language to be a speaker's internal neurologically based language of thought.

18. I'm taking care to precisely distinguish the subject S, the theorist T, and the respective languages involved so that explicit account can be taken of when the discussion is second-person ("our language") and when it's third-person ("their language"), when a language is being used (and by whom), and when it's being mentioned. See Peter Ludlow, *Semantics, tense, and time: An essay in the metaphysics of natural language* (Cambridge, Mass.: MIT Press, 1999), for illustrations where—especially in chapters 1 and 2—the discussion shifts without warning or acknowledgment from one focused on "the internal languages (I-languages) of speakers" (where such internal languages are different from one another and so must be described—necessarily—from a third-person point of view, where the languages in question must be mentioned) to second-person discussions of the disquotational nature of truth-conditional theories providing theory/world connections by virtue of their intrinsic property of disquotation (where talk of disquotation indicates the perspective of someone using the theory). Not being careful about these shifts leads almost irresistibly to confusions. This is despite the fact that the identification of the author and the reader with two of the subjects whose I-languages are being studied is otherwise legitimate. As I've indicated, I intend the confusions in question to be ones that can be attributed not just to Ludlow but to Lepore, Higginbotham, Lewis, and many others.

There are characterizations of objects in science that can't be written down (explicitly) in a theory. Nevertheless, the existence of such theories, and that they take certain forms, can be exploited for useful information. This, in fact, is extremely common.[19]

One might try to argue that truth-conditional semantic theories are different. After all the form of:

"F" is true in L iff "F*" is true in L*

is different from the form of:

"F" is true in L iff F*.

This observation is correct, and so a subtlety must be introduced in how the theorist T should describe her theory of S's understanding of L. In particular, if pressed on her theory of how MM is employed by S in his understanding of L, she should say that she can exhibit how that's done. Her theory of S's understanding of L is that he employs a disquotational theory (M) in IN. T, in turn, can exhibit that very theory (M), but she can't use it (because (M) is in a language IN that T doesn't understand). T's exhibition of (M) (in TH) goes something like this.

Here is the theory in IN that S uses to understand L:

(M)   Given an interpretation I, a variable x_i of L, and wffs F_1 and F_2 of L:

(M_1)   "Px_i" is satisfied by I iff $P^{IN}I(x_i)$,

(M_2)   "Pb" is satisfied by I iff $P^{IN}b^{IN}$,

(M_3)   "F_1 & F_2" is satisfied by I iff "F_1" is satisfied by I and "F_2" is satisfied by I,

(M_4)   "$\neg F_1$" is satisfied by I iff "F_1" is not satisfied by I,

(M_5)   "$(\exists x_j)F_1$" is satisfied I iff there is an interpretation I*, where $I^*(x_j) = I(x_j)$ f or $j \neq i$, and "F_1" is satisfied by I*.

(M_6)   A *sentence* (a wff without free variables) is true iff it is satisfied by every (any) interpretation I.

Notice: T is exhibiting (M); she is not using (M). (Think of (M) as flanked, as it were, by quote marks.) As it turns out, T can be taken to understand most of (M). That's because most of (M) is couched in terms that can be easily translated to her language TH. I'm speaking specifically of all the terms of IN that refer to the syntax of L. She can also be taken to have no problem understanding the connectives

---

19. I'm alluding, in particular, to theories that are indicated by sets of differential equations. Such equations, when meeting such and such conditions, indicate that a solution (a theory) of so and so form exists—although no one may be able to write that theory down. But as I've indicated, that doesn't stop anyone from successfully milking for useful empirical results the fact that such a theory can be shown (without explicitly exhibiting it) to have thus and that properties.

and quantifiers of IN. As a consequence she can understand pretty much everything that's being done in (M) via the mapping MM. Indeed, she fully understands clauses (M_3)–(M_6), because appropriate translations of them from IN into her language TH are available to her. (Such translations are available to her precisely because (M_3)–(M_6) aren't disquotational.) But she doesn't take herself to (fully) understand the crucial (M_1)–(M_2) because they employ the mapping MM explicitly, and disquote it: use words of IN in the language IN to give truth conditions for wffs of L. IN is not the language of T. So T's theory of S's understanding of L comes to this. There is a mapping MM, which can be stated in TH, and MM is used by S in his internal language IN to give a truth-conditional theory of L of the form (M). It's not obvious, to put it mildly, why T's theory of S's understanding of L (using MM) fails as a theory of understanding. That it doesn't provide the language/world connections cannot be claimed. It does provide such—at least it does so as well and as much as any truth-conditional theory does—and T can even point to exactly where the purported language/world connections are made: in clauses (M_1)–(M_2). What she can't do, of course, is indicate exactly what those language/world connections are.

Actually, not even that description of what T can't indicate is correct. T can say—by description—what the language/world connections are. She can say, for example, that b (in L) refers to what b^{IN} refers to.[20] To complain that such a description doesn't "appropriately" supply the language/world connections needed in a theory of understanding of a language L is to stipulate that the language/world connections must be given by disquotation (that is, by the use of terms—a second-person characterization of the theory) and to rule out—by fiat—third-person descriptions of what those terms refer to. But ruling out third-person descriptions of what terms refer to needs independent justification; such justification is not provided by unsupported claims that nondisquotational theories will not allow "us to reason between language and the world in the way required of semantic knowledge."[21]

So much, therefore, for what is right and wrong about the criticisms of Lewis, Higginbotham, Lepore, and others, of structural or model-theoretic semantic theories. What about the positive bit used in the foregoing polemics, that disquotational semantic theories do provide the needed language/world connections? Well, the mere fact that a theory uses certain sentences to state truth conditions does nothing toward indicating a robust language/world connection. There is no necessary connection between using a sentence and thereby indicating a language/world connection. That depends entirely on the sentence being used!

Consider the classic example:

(3)   *"Snow is white," is true iff snow is white.*

Many proponents of truth-conditional semantics say that the truth conditions of the sentence "Snow is white," are given by (3) in terms of some way that the

---

20. Compare: "neutrino," as I use it, refers to what particle physicists refer to by means of it.
21. Larson and Segal (1995), 51.

world is described to be, in particular, that snow is white. That is, the topics of the consequent of (3) (snow, whiteness) are what's pertinent to determining the truth conditions of "snow is white."[22] But truth conditions can be given of sentences that provide no such descriptions of "the world": "Sherlock Holmes is depicted in fiction as a great detective," is true iff Sherlock Holmes is depicted in fiction as a great detective, "11 is a prime number," is true iff 11 is a prime number, and so on. If sentences that refer[r] to nothing at all can be used (and sustain truth values), as argued in this book, then truth-conditional semantics can use such sentences to give truth conditions; yet no language/world connection (at least of a direct sort based on what the terms of the sentences in question refer to) will be vouchsafed as a result. It's just a peculiar presumption of the truth-conditional semantic literature that disquotation (the shift from mention to use) has an automatic onto-logical reach into the world.

The word "peculiar" is suitable precisely because nothing in the resulting semantic theories requires that such a presumption be assumed by theorists. Dis-quotation is thus burdened with a role it cannot sustain but that isn't needed. The slender shift from talking about a sentence to using it cannot support doctrines to the effect that language/world connections are therefore operative, or to sustain the requirement that theories of understanding must disquote—as opposed to the far weaker assumption that theories of understanding require that disquotation be used (internally, say) by a subject whose understanding of a language is being characterized by a truth-conditional semantic theory.

5.4 Ontological Presuppositions and Truth-Conditional Semantics

I've been arguing—in the last two sections—that despite characterizing the semantics of L (in L[M]) in a way that's ontologically neutral, nothing, nevertheless, out of the ordinary occurs. The theory (the true theory) describing the truth-con-ditions of L is entirely standard. Imagine, therefore, that L is a (small) piece of ordinary language: that P is the predicate, "flies," and b is the name "Pegasus."[23] We can also take the domain of the quantifiers of L to be genuinely empty (or not—it doesn't matter to the example). Crucial to the resulting theory (S) is a bit of set theory (encapsulated, in particular, in the existence and properties of the mapping functions I_j from the variables of L to the domain of L). But, some may

---

22. Larson and Segal (1995), 50, write of the sentence, "La neige est blanche is true if and only if snow is white," that this "T sentence, like all T sentences, goes from the mention of linguistic expressions to their use; it relates language to the nonlinguistic." Some lines earlier, they write that if "we know the meaning of a sentence and we are told that it is true, then we learn something about how things stand in the world." Also see Ernest Lepore, "What model theoretic semantics cannot do," *Synthese* 54 (1983), 167–87; Ernest Lepore and Barry Loewer, "Trans-lational semantics," *Synthese* 48 (1981) 121–33; and Ernest Lepore and Barry Loewer, "Three trivial truth theories," *Canadian Journal of Philosophy* 13 (1983) 433–47. Ludlow (1999, 37), as mentioned, stresses that disquotational theories provide "language-world" connections.

23. The point of the example is that "Pegasus" is to be a nonreferring[r] expression. Pagans, therefore, should choose a different example.

worry, {Pegasus} = {},[24] and therefore, the needed truths about these mappings I_j from the variables to the domain of L aren't forthcoming.

The concern presupposes placing an illicit constraint on the quantifiers involved in this piece of set theory with urelements.[25] This illicit constraint is that the quantifiers aren't ontologically neutral, so that $(x)(x \neq$ Pegasus). On the contrary: this particular application of set theory (with urelements) has quantifiers that "range over" items like Pegasus, and so, in this particular application of set theory, we have {Pegasus} $\neq$ {}.

"But wait," someone may protest, "isn't it really the case that {Pegasus} = {}?" After all, Pegasus *doesn't* exist. I agree. What is true is that Pegasus doesn't exist. But we don't capture that claim by the formulation: $\neg(\exists x)(x =$ Pegasus); instead we invoke an existence predicate E, and capture it this way: $\neg(\exists x)(Ex \ \& \ x =$ Pegasus). If, therefore, while using ontologically neutral quantifiers in one's set theory, one nevertheless wants to distinguish those cases where the items in question really exist from the cases where they don't, one employs an existence predicate. The situation, again, is identical to cases in the sciences (discussed in section 4.1) where specialized quantifiers range over more (and less) than what exists. In such cases, the mathematics employed similarly operates in tandem with the quantifiers: functions are defined over everything that has such and such properties (and regardless of whether or not what the functions operate on exists). It's precisely the quantifiers' studied ontological neutrality that makes this cogent. The same occurs with respect to set theory with urelements that's applied in the context of semantics—specifically truth-conditional semantics. The quantifiers of the applied set theory are (again) neutral, and that means that they "range over" both the nonexistent and the existent, and all such "objects" are the urelements that sets are defined in terms of.

This point about the ontological neutrality of the quantifiers of set theory—both pure and applied—has wide scope and impact on ontological evaluations of the study of the semantics of natural languages. Consider generalized quantifiers in natural languages.[26] The background logical setting for these is a given universe E of objects. Noun phrases, NPs (e.g., *John, Neither Frodo nor Samwise, All hobbits, No healthy doctor, More philosophers than accountants, Few dragons*), combine with predicate phrases, P_1s (e.g., *worked hard, laughed, is depicted in fiction as a detective, is a hallucinated object*), to form sentences, Ss (*John is a hallucinated object, More philosophers than accountants are depicted in fiction as detectives, Neither Frodo nor Samwise worked hard*). The semantics treats P_1s as denoting subsets of E, Ss denoting the truth values, 1 (true) or 0 (false), and NPs as denoting type $\langle 1 \rangle$ quantifiers over E: functions from $P(E)$ (the power set of E), to the set of truth values $\{0, 1\}$. Notice that so described, the semantic study of generalized quantifiers is a straightforward application of the mathematics of sets defined on an arbitrary universe E. No

---

24. {} is the null set. Jan Cover has raised this particular worry to me (personal communication).

25. Urelements are the nonsets—for example, ordinary physical objects—that are contained in sets.

26. For concreteness, I'm restricting expository attention to Type $\langle 1 \rangle$ quantification. But my observations will clearly apply beyond that case. I follow the exposition of type $\langle 1 \rangle$ quantifiers found in E. L. Keenan and D. Westerståhl, "Generalized quantifiers in linguistics and logic," in *Handbook of logic and language*, ed. Johan van Benthem and Alice ter Meulen (Cambridge, Mass.: MIT Press, 1997), 837–93.

requirement need be in place that E, in general, must contain only items that exist. Indeed, as my deliberately chosen examples indicate, ordinary speakers often rely on a universe E that contain many things that don't exist or that's entirely empty.[27]

Consider, as another illustration, a version of truth-conditional semantics that operates via the assignment of values to the sentences (and their functionally significant) parts.[28] Let L* be a language with proper names (*Albert Einstein, Sherlock Holmes*, etc.) and with verb phrases (*is intelligent, is depicted as a detective in fiction*, etc.). Let the production rules for L* be these:[29]

S → NP VP
NP → {*Albert Einstein, Sherlock Holmes*, . . . }
VP → {*is intelligent, is depicted as a detective in fiction*, . . .}

Let the semantic theory for L* be this:

(S*)
Val (*x, Albert Einstein*) iff x = Albert Einstein,
Val (*x, Sherlock Holmes*) iff x = Sherlock Holmes,

.
.
.

Val (*x, is intelligent*) iff x is intelligent,
Val (*x, is depicted as a detective in fiction*) iff x is depicted as a detective in fiction,

.
.
.

Val (*x*, NP) iff Val (*x, n*) and n is a daughter node of NP,
Val (*x*, VP) iff Val (*x, n*) and n is a daughter node of VP.
Val (t, S) iff NP and VP are daughter nodes of S, and for some x,
    Val (*x*, NP) = Val (*x*, VP).

The simple language L* contains only proper-name/predicate-phrase sentences of the form: "Sherlock Holmes is intelligent," "Albert Einstein is depicted as a detective in fiction," and so on. The syntactic form of each sentence is a

---

27. I should add that what's obviously doing the work here is the ontological neutrality of the quantifiers, not the background set theory as a whole. Therefore, similar considerations apply to semantic theories that may elude characterization in standard set theory, for example, approaches via structured propositions (as they appear in the work of Braun, King, Richard, Salmon, Soames, and others), those of possible-world semantics (Lewis, Stalnaker, and others), or versions of situational semantics (Barwise, Perry, and others). All such theories are best viewed—pace, for example, David Lewis, *On the plurality of worlds* (Oxford: Basil Blackwell, 1986)—as theoretical characterizations of various kinds of abstracta, and therefore as branches of mathematics that are applied to natural languages (and specifically to prima facie semantic phenomena). One should not recognize the ontological commitments of the resulting theories (propositions, relations, possible worlds, mappings, objects referred to, etc.), therefore—no more than one should in any other science—by merely listing what falls under the quantifiers of such theories.

28. See Larson and Segal (1995); Ludlow (1999).

29. What follows is one way to go; there are others (see Larson and Segal [1995], chapter 4). The points I need to make can be made in the terms of any of the approaches that they describe.

simple tree with S at the root node, with two branches to NP and VP as daughter nodes of the S node, followed by branches to terminal nodes with the vocabulary items, "Albert Einstein," "Sherlock Holmes," and so on, as the possible daughter nodes of the NP node, and the vocabulary items, "is intelligent," "is depicted as a detective in fiction," and so on, as possible daughter nodes of the VP node.

In turn, the semantic theory is understood as supplying values to each node so that parental nodes are given semantic values, based on the values of the daughter nodes. In particular, the NP node of a tree inherits Albert Einstein as a value iff "Albert Einstein" occurs below it; the VP node inherits everyone who is intelligent as values iff "is intelligent" occurs below it. In turn, the node S gets the value true if there is a shared value among its daughter nodes; otherwise, it gets the value false.[30]

The same concern can now be raised about both the semantic theory just presented for L*, and the earlier one given for L. The concern is with what happens (with respect to L) when the term b^M fails to refer; in the case of L* the concern—similarly—is with what happens when names such as "Sherlock Holmes" arise. It seems that in both cases the compositional mechanisms of the respective semantic theories go idle (grind to a halt). Let's consider (S*) first. In this case, values are supposed to be passed from node to node; but if the clause "x = Sherlock Holmes" is unsatisfied because there is no Sherlock Holmes, then there is—correspondingly—no Val $(x, Sherlock Holmes)$. Consequently, no values are handed up to the higher nodes in the tree, and so the other semantic clauses cannot finish their jobs by assigning the node S a truth value (of any sort) when S is, for example, "Sherlock Holmes is depicted as a detective in fiction." This problem looks very acute if (S*) is taken as representing the semantic module of the I-language of a speaker. For then—on some views—(S*) is supposed to represent a psychologically real mechanism operating (subpersonally) in the speaker that enables that speaker to understand L*. But how is the speaker to attribute values to those sentences of L* when the semantic system (S*) assigns no values (as in the case of "Sherlock Holmes is depicted as a detective in fiction")? It seems we get just the result many philosophers think we have to get when empty names show up: sentences without truth values.

The corresponding worry can be raised for the language L in cases where (as I've allowed) the domain of L is empty. Consider (2), of section 5.3, repeated here:

(2)   "$(\exists x_i)Px_i$" is true iff there is something that is P^M.

The corresponding concern is that such a theorem is deduced via a series of other theorems and assumptions of L^M with respect to interpretation functions, and the satisfaction of wffs.[31] It's not that a sentence of L is simply paired (by the semantic theory (S)) with another sentence of L^M, where the latter is to be taken to be true (and so the former can be taken to be true as well). It's that such is done via

---

30. Ludlow (1999, 66) reads "Val $(x, \underline{snow})$ iff x = snow)" as short for: "For all x, Val $(x, \underline{snow})$ iff x = snow." He then introduces ontology into semantics by reading the quantifier as ontologically committing.

31. Recall the informal proof of note 7 of section 5.2.

the satisfaction mechanism of L^M. But this semantic machinery seems to be spinning in an entirely idle way because there are no such interpretations (and no domain). One can say, rather dramatically, "The whole satisfaction mechanism is just a series of connected gears that emptily turn nothing at all."

The key to seeing through this extremely seductive analogy with idle gears in a machine is to first note that actual gears in a piece of machinery do something to the world that in turn can (physically) affect those gears. If, for example, the gears are transferring force due to steam to lift a lever (to move a rock), things can go very wrong. This is because the transfer of force to the lever can be insufficient to move the rock. Then, for example, the gears will grind uselessly against one another (and perhaps get stripped). Or something else physically unpleasant can result.

The interaction of (S*) with its values is nothing like this. (S*) ascribes values to the functionally significant parts of the sentences of L* (the names and the predicate phrases) as well as to the other nodes in the tree via ascriptions that are characterized in IN. The ascription of values will occur regardless of whether the ascriptions in IN pick out anything at all. In particular, the terms "t" and "f" that are used to ascribe values to the sentences of L needn't be real. The background language IN, for example, may quantify over truth values, objects, and whatever else, without those quantifiers actually picking out anything at all. The psychologically real mechanism doing this, the semantic module, need only be "assigning values" by virtue of the psychological content of representations of IN. In turn, the results that the semantic mechanism yields by manipulating those representations can be "handed over" to other modules, for example, the perception module,[32] or to modules that operate to support processes of conscious ratiocination, or whatever. The operations of these modules can occur—and be psychologically real—without the Val function picking anything out, without (correspondingly) the ascriptions of particular values to the Val function on the part of representations of IN referring to anything. Reference[e] suffices. It's precisely because the physical machinery that gears are in (as cogs) makes physical contact with objects (and that those objects in turn physically respond—usually by Newton's third law—to that physical machinery) that it's possible for a machine to have gears that are idly turning. We can trace the genuine lines of transmission of force through the functionally relevant parts of a machine, and thus discover that some gears are "outside the loop": they're not doing anything. It's precisely this palpable contact with reality that the semantic module is missing.

"But that's just wrong," some philosophers are sure to protest. We often learn that we're asserting falsehoods about the objects we are actually referring to, and we then correct ourselves. We see that the rock is blue (not red), and we adjust our recognition of the truth values of the corresponding sentences (of L*) to suit such corrections. In this way, in exactly this way, the gears and cogs of semantic theory touch base with real objects. We recognize that we have attributed the wrong

---

32. There is no "perception module"; rather, there are a number of such (more or less well-defined) modules. For simplicity of exposition, and because it doesn't mislead in this context, I continue to speak of the "perception module."

values to a node S because, for some x, and for its daughter nodes NP and VP, we wrongly took it that Val $(x, NP) = $ Val (x, VP).

To argue this way is to continue to be seduced by the gear picture. Imagine that S is looking at a rock and that he recognizes that the rock is red. A result that was (subpersonally) handed over to his perception module requires the co-reference[e] of certain terms appearing in representations that are the results of computations in the semantics module with terms that appear in other representations that are to serve as inputs to the perception module. Of course, the reverse happens: representations resulting from computations in the perception module have terms that are taken to co-refer[e] to terms that serve as input for the semantics module.

That co-reference[e] can suffice, that none of this transference of representations between subpersonal modules requires actual reference[r] to actual objects, can be recognized by the success of the interaction of such a set of modules in dramatic cases of hallucination—for example, brains in a vat.[33] The interaction of the semantic module—indeed, of all of the language modules—with the perception module (indeed, with any module that manipulates representations), can occur without there being any actual referents[r] of the terms of either the language L* or the language IN.[34] External input, of course, is required—but such input (various stimulations of nerve endings, say) isn't the appropriate sort of thing to serve as the values Val (x, p) that the language IN attributes to L*.

Part of what makes the view that genuine reference[r] assumptions are essential to truth-conditional semantic theories so seductive is a kind of bottom-up picture of how such models work. Returning to the example of L (and the corresponding semantic theory (S) in L^M), there is a strong tendency among those familiar with such models to read the "flow of mechanism" from the domain up to the sentences assigned truth values by that domain. This makes it seem like the whole machinery of semantics must run idle if there is no domain at the bottom (turning the semantic levers, as it were). And this perception of how truth-conditional theories like (S) work, in turn, drives (some) philosophers to Meinongianism. If some objects, that we say truth-apt things about, don't exist, nevertheless, the cogency of what we say must—on pain of the vice of idleness—require a discourse-domain in which those (nonexistent) objects appear.

In point of fact, as should already be quite clear, the "domain" plays no role whatsoever in the semantics. What does play a role is the ascription of objects to the domain (and the corresponding ascription of properties to those objects) by sentences in L^M. One can fail to see this if one thinks too much along the lines of foundational epistemic models based on perception. In such cases, one is prone to think of the objects (in the domain) as items we see the properties of. In this way, our independent access to the domain—and what's in it—enables us to recognize what the truths of L^M are.

---

33. Consider a case where the brains know the situation they're in. They can refer[e] to their collective hallucinations—more accurately, to what the hallucinations are of—with no difficulty.

34. Some philosophers are likely to try to deny this. But in this context, such a denial would be begging the question. The point is that the machinations of the relevant modules, for example, the semantic module, are starkly disanalogous to machinery of any sort that actually makes physical contact with the world.

However, apart from the fact that this picture only transfers (surreptitiously) ontological assumptions from the semantic theory to the perceptual module,[35] something that's already been noted to be illicit, there is in addition a mistake about our epistemic practices. The model of us seeing a rock, recognizing that it's round, and deriving the corresponding truth is only one way that things can go. Another is that the truths can come first (by testimony, by deduction, etc.) and the contents of the domain designed on the basis of those truths. "There are a lot of people in China," is something I've heard. Thus my semantics module ascribes as in the discourse-domain (of the language that sentence is in) lots of people with the property of living in China. I hear that Sherlock Holmes is depicted in Conan Doyle's short stories as a detective. My semantics module ascribes as in the discourse-domain (of the language that sentence is in) a character Sherlock Holmes with the property of being depicted in Conan Doyle's short stories as a detective. With respect to both truths, the discourse-domain is correctly characterized by the semantics module; but only in the case of the truth about China are real entities required to appear in that domain.

We can think of the semantics module as assuming there are objects, properties, more general semantic values, and so on; we can think that those values are passed on to other modules. But this is a use/mention conflation: the values themselves aren't passed on, regardless of whether or not there are such. Only a mechanism of co-identifying[(r/e)] the terms in the representations of different modules can actually occur. (It's a use/mention error to think that values—actual objects, say—are themselves moved from one module to another.) But in a context where we are trying to evaluate exactly what ontological presuppositions are needed to get the whole thing to work, speaking of the semantic module so assuming things is just inviting philosophical confusion. It's better to focus directly on the representations of IN, and recognize the semantic module value-ascription system as operating via the manipulation of those representations, concomitantly with the stipulation of equivalencies and identifications between representations (in the semantics module), terms in those representations, and representations (and terms) in other modules. For any of this, reference[e] is every bit as good as reference[r].

I've just discussed what may be described as a "coming to a halt" concern: that where there are no values for terms (e.g., "Sherlock Holmes") values cannot be assigned to representations further up in the tree. The response, briefly, is that the system can work entirely well even if there are no values; the ascription of values on the part of the IN is insensitive to ontology. Another worry—which can also be called a "coming to a halt" concern—is with respect to the biconditional theorems of (S). Such a truth-conditional semantic theory can yield theorems of the form (2), repeated here:

(2)   "$(\exists x_i)Px_i$" is true iff there is something that is P^M,

---

35. This is one reason it's often so hard to get philosophers to see that they are presuming (without argument) the necessity of real objects (and reference[r] to them) in their characterizations of the workings of semantics, perception, and so on. The question-begging ontological assumptions are presupposed, by virtue of their being borrowed from another module (that isn't the current focus of attention).

but so what? If there are no objects corresponding to the terms in these sentences, how is one to go on? (Whatever is one to do with these results of (S)?)

The appropriate response has already been made in the foregoing chapters; but it's perhaps illuminating to reprise it again in the specialized jargon of "modules" that's come up here. In some cases, the results of the semantic module are "input" into the perception module. One therefore adjusts one's claims about what is true by coordinating the representations of the semantic module (more broadly, the language module) with those of the perception module. Perhaps certain terms in certain representations in the language module are stipulated to co-refer$^{(r/e)}$ to facilitate this; in that way, epistemic considerations stemming from perception become relevant to the statements that are to be taken to be true. These results then percolate via (S*) to the other statements of L, as well as to assertions about the properties to be ascribed to the items that terms refer$^{(r/e)}$ to. In other cases (e.g., in fiction or mathematics), the results of the semantic module are interchanged with other broader psychological modules to take account of various deference or deduction practices. I attribute "being depicted in the short stories of Conan Doyle as a superhero" to Sherlock Holmes. But I can learn that I'm wrong, that in fact various comic books I read as a child misled me, and that he is not so depicted. Similarly, the appropriate evaluation of mathematical truths takes place by a combination of ratiocination on my part (by my own proof practices) coupled with a great deal of deference to other results held in common in the mathematical profession. We thus take every such sentence to be either true or false and regard ourselves as ignorant of the truth values of those statements that neither we (nor anyone else we know of) can successfully sort.[36]

Worries about the semantics module grinding to a halt or otherwise failing to provide truth conditions for its object language are misguided because they fail to recognize how limited the job of the semantics module actually is. Its job is to supply truth conditions, and to do so in a way that connects the truth conditions of sentences to other sentences, and more broadly to other functionally significant parts of those sentences. If in the process of doing so, the semantics module is required to supply semantic values to items such as noun phrases and verb phrases, it does so by virtue of metalanguage ascriptions of those values to the appropriate items. Such ascriptions however, can be manipulated (psychologically) regardless of whether there really are values that correspond to them. The reality that grounds our semantic practices (and our semantic modules) comes into the picture only via other modules and only indirectly in many of those cases as well. The ontological situation—therefore—is identical to the one we've found operative in all the other sciences, and indeed, in daily life as well.

I should observe again, as I did in the general introduction, that "truth condition semantics," in my view, is unfortunate terminology, especially when it's presumed (as it almost universally is) that such "truth conditions" are supposed to supply necessary and sufficient conditions for the truth (and falsity) of the

---

36. Recall the discussion of this in section 2.10.

statements of a language for which they are the truth conditions. There is a subtlety here that must be teased out. So understanding truth conditional semantics builds in the unfortunate ontological commitments that I have argued are not appropriate. Purging these ontological commitments from semantic theory (in general) results in a "truth-conditional semantics," as we've seen here, that's indistinguishable from such semantics when construed as involving (say) quantifiers in the metalanguage that are ontologically committing. However, semantics construed ontologically neutrally, although it does still provide necessary and sufficient truth conditions, doesn't do so in a way that necessarily assigns truth values to the statements these truth conditions are given for.

How is this possible? Very easily, actually. The truth conditions in question are necessary and sufficient conditions for an object language in terms of a metalanguage. But it's a separate and distinguishable question whether the statements in the metalanguage (that provide these truth conditions) actually determine the truth values of the statements they provide these truth conditions for. In cases where only reference^r is at work in the metalanguage, and where certain other conditions apply,[37] they do indeed determine such truth values. However, where reference^e is instead at work, what must provide the actual truth values are the truth-value inducers of the object language statements (and, correlatively, the same truth-value inducers provide the truth values for the metalanguage statements corresponding to these object language statements as well).

So "truth conditions," given the ontologically neutral reading of the quantifiers and the other idioms of the metalanguage, do provide necessary and sufficient conditions for truth values for the sentences of the object language in terms of metalanguage idioms. But this doesn't necessarily determine truth values for those sentences. It does determine such values when only reference^r is involved in the language (and when the quantifiers of that language range over only what's real). Otherwise those conditions are compatible with the truth values that are otherwise determined by the truth-value inducers of those sentences.

I round out this section with the discussion of one last issue. Some philosophers may understand truth-conditional semantics (or semantic theories, more generally) as meant to be applied to "public languages." They may not be, therefore, sympathetic to the idea of (S*) as characterizing the operations of an internal semantic module in the mind. In this case, those same philosophers may argue, the story—that I've told about how Val (x, p) can operate psychologically even if there are no values that it assigns to anything—isn't going to quite work because the psychological element that Val (x, p) is supposed to correspond to is missing. Instead, the view is that some public language L* has the semantics (S*)—but on the view being pushed here, aspects of that semantics correspond to nothing at all. Claim: the idle gear issue is still with us in the context of the semantics of public languages.

---

37. Such other conditions include, for example, that the logic of the object language and the logic of the metalanguage (supplying the truth conditions for the object language statements) is the same one. See Jody Azzouni, "Alternative logics and the role of truth in the interpretation of languages," in *New essays on Tarski and philosophy*, ed. Douglas Patterson (Oxford: Oxford University Press, 2008), 390–429, for details.

In response, I claim that the study of public languages occurs via the application of a branch of mathematics to language phenomena. Functions of various sorts are introduced, a domain containing the needed values for theory is stipulated; but (as described in section 4.1) it doesn't follow, and anyway never happens, that everything that appears in that domain need exist. Semantics as a science is driven by the need to characterize in a lawlike fashion a body of human behavior. In doing so, it's indispensable to describe items—types (such as sentences or propositions) as having syntactically significant parts, and those parts as having certain semantic values. The theory as a whole is successfully applied to the relevant kind of human behavior (language behavior); this doesn't require that the items quantified over by the theory have to exist or have to play a genuine causal role. That quantifiers in semantic theories "range over" items that themselves cannot be playing a genuine causal role in how people understand language is no more shocking than the phenomena of physical theories indispensably quantifying over items (e.g., space-time points) that cannot be playing a genuine physical role in how objects move.[38]

5.5 Demonstratives

It may seem, even if the foregoing is correct, that the semantics of certain singular locutions pose fresh obstacles to the semantic characterization of statements or thoughts that contain empty singular terms because such—like names—are not quantificational expressions.[39] In particular, a truth-conditional semantic theory must provide truth conditions for demonstrative expressions. Although names clearly pose no problems because a metalanguage name that's taken to co-refer[(r/e)] with an object language name can correspondingly be taken to have exactly the same semantic properties as that object-language name it's coined to match,[40] this perhaps isn't possible in the case of demonstratives.

Let's look into this a little. One nontraditional approach to the semantics of demonstratives is relatively direct.[41] Motivated by the claim that a truth-conditional semantics is (often) to be supplied by an internal I-language of the speaker for

38. Indeed, the analogy between the "propositions" quantified over by a semantic theory and a coordinate system of (space-time) points is one that's extremely natural in many respects. This, however, isn't the time or place to give details.

39. Well, there is a bit of a debate about this. See Ernest Lepore and Kirk Ludwig, "The semantics and pragmatics of complex demonstratives," *Mind* 109:434 (2000), 199–240, for discussion of the literature up to the date of their article. Also see Jeffrey C. King, *Complex demonstratives* (Cambridge, Mass.: MIT Press, 2001). For illustrative purposes (and because my claims about the ontological neutrality of demonstratives and names doesn't require it), I assume that the foregoing results about the ontological neutrality of quantifiers, specifically generalized quantifiers, doesn't directly show the same is true of either names or demonstratives.

40. In the foregoing illustrative semantic theories (S) and (S*), names are provided with truth conditions via corresponding metalanguage names that co-refer[(r/e)] with them. If the object-language name is rigid, so may its metalanguage companion be taken to be rigid. If the object-language name is instead semantically construed in the metalanguage via a description, then its rigidity may be handled via the rigidification of the metalanguage description its semantics is given in terms of—for example, by an actuality operator. I'm leaving aside any further discussion of this because it doesn't affect the points—about the ontological commitments of truth-conditional semantic-theories—that I'm making in this chapter.

41. See Ludlow (1999), chapter 3.

herself, indexical expressions that appear on both sides of the biconditional can be treated as co-referring[r/e]. That is,

(4)   "That vase is ugly," is true iff that vase is ugly,

(5)   "She is an hallucinated object," is true iff she is an hallucinated object,

(6)   "The hobbit over here isn't real," is true iff the hobbit over here isn't real,

(7)   "I am hungry," is true iff I am hungry,

are various truth-conditions the theory is supposed to yield. A variant, taking account of the context of the interpreter being different from that of the utterer of the utterances in question, is to appropriately shift the indexicals like so:

(6*)   "The hobbit over here isn't real," is true iff the hobbit over there isn't real.

(7*)   "I am hungry," is true iff he is hungry.

To provide a truth-conditional interpretation of someone else's utterances (at the moment that person is making them) may acceptably include indexical uses on the right side of the biconditionals that are appropriated saturated by items in the interpreter's context. Truth-conditional clauses of either sort, however, allow empty singular terms to appear on both sides of the appropriate truth conditions. If (as has been argued in chapter 2) one can be in a context where it makes sense to gesture toward one's (or someone else's) hallucinated object and utter a truth-apt demonstrative sentence about[e] that hallucinated object, then a truth-condition clause can be supplied that avails itself of exactly the same resources. Contexts—the background from which interpretations for indexicals are supplied—needn't be restricted to what's real.

The foregoing sketch of an approach to truth-condition clauses using indexicals is, however, not the standard approach. The standard approach is one that—as Ludlow (1999, 57) puts it—the "character" or "role" of the indexical is excluded from the right side of the truth condition. More to the point, indexicals do not occur at all on the right side of the truth condition. Instead, their content is expressed in a "conditionalization": a description of their referents. Instead of (4), (5), (6), and (7), we have:

(4**)   An utterance u, at time t, by speaker s, of "That vase is ugly" is true iff there is an object (a vase) o, designated by s by her use of "that vase" at time t, and o is ugly.

(5**)   An utterance u, at time t, by speaker s, of "She is an hallucinated object," is true iff there is an object o designated by s by her use of "she," at time t, and o is an hallucinated object.[42]

(6**)   An utterance u, at time t, by speaker s, of "The hobbit over here isn't real," is true iff the object o indicated by s by her use of "over here," at time t, (presents as a hobbit) and isn't real.

---

42. It may be that the content of "she"—being female—must be demoted to "presents as female."

(7**) An utterance u, at time t, by speaker s, of "I am hungry," is true iff if s, at time t, is hungry.[43]

(5**)–(7**) use quantifiers. Doing so, however, doesn't require that such quantifiers be ontologically committing (no more so than their appearance in the object language implies such). Nothing, therefore, prevents such a quantifier "ranging over" hallucinated object, or hallucinated objects that present themselves as hobbits.

5.6 Concluding Remarks

The general lesson should be clear: the almost universal assimilation of singular expressions to "object-dependent" expressions—where the objects that the expressions are so dependent on are required to be real—sloganistically encapsulating the requirement that the truth conditions for statements (and more generally, thoughts) containing such expressions must take account of actual objects is utterly unjustified. Views to the contrary often presuppose a false dichotomy: that either (i) a term have semantics—specifically truth-conditional semantics—that characterize its appearance in statements and thoughts via concepts (descriptions) that are taken as associated with it (e.g., "Vulcan" being associated with "the planet between Mercury and the Sun"); or instead, (ii) that term have semantics to be characterized in terms of an actual object to which the term refers[r]. This false dichotomy is usually accompanied with the (surreptitious) assumption that any singular term used in the metalanguage (or any quantifier so used, for that matter) must be ontologically committing: a singular term must refer[r] to an object to function successfully; such quantifiers must range over, and only over, what's real. But if this is false of the object language, if the object language can have meaningful truth-apt terms that refer[r] to nothing all, the same is possible of the metalanguage.

The burden of this chapter has been to indicate why one cannot respond to the suggestion that an object language has truth-apt statements containing empty singular terms, and has quantifiers that range over things that exist (in no sense at all), by claiming that such cannot be the case with respect to the language that is to supply the truth conditions for such statements. The arguments for there being—indispensably—truth-apt statements with terms (singular ones, among others) that

---

43. (4**)–(7**) are meant to be simple illustrations of a broadly characterized family of approaches. In particular, and among other things, in formulating it, I'm not attending to issues about exactly how conditionalizations are supposed to be characterized and in what detail; I'm skirting over issues about exactly how content that appears in the utterance (e.g., "vase," "he") is supposed to contribute to the truth conditions of the utterance; I'm skirting over mismatch issues between demonstrative expressions being vacuous—not because a hallucinated object is demonstrated, but because (say) the object someone intended to demonstrate was moved elsewhere—and the definite description on the right-hand side being false as a result. The data is complicated, and the options are numerous and debatable. See Lepore and Ludwig (2000), 230–38 for discussion and criticism of various approaches to the conditionalizations of complex demonstratives. "Designated" is my stand-in (or cover-up) for a fuller explication in terms of gestures, intentions, speech acts, and so on. It should be clear, however, that my points about the ontological neutrality of the resulting truth-condition clauses will be unaffected by the replacement of my (4**)–(7**) with appropriately complicated alternatives.

refer to nothing at all can just be repeated against this claim in the rarefied setting of a discussion of the language presupposed in the study of semantics.

Some see as what's essential to the successful functioning of singular expressions to be that the objects referred to take precedence over the user's conceptualization of those objects. Correlated with this view is that names, demonstratives, and other singular expressions operate (to various degrees) independently of the descriptive content associated with them. Laboring under such an impression allows one to comfortably call singular terms "object-dependent." But in this way referentialism, direct reference, and other such views wed together as the same phenomenon, several different semantic processes that we now see how to separate. A name can operate independently of the descriptive content a user associates with it, either because—semantically speaking—the object it refers^r to takes precedence over the description associated with it (as with demonstratives directed towards a perceived object), or because the descriptive content that's public or held by experts takes precedence over the description a user associates with that term (as with certain artificial-kind terms, or certain names), or because the name functions in a practice where no fixed description is relevant to that function (named hallucinated objects, names of fictional objects not otherwise described).

Call nondescriptivism the view that certain terms operate (semantically) independently of descriptive content that can be associated with them (either by individual users or by publicly deferred experts). Nondescriptivism is the view that such content isn't contributed by those terms to the statements they appear in. Call direct reference ("Millianism") the view that certain terms operate (semantically) by contributing only the object they refer^r to. Nondescriptivism is a more general property terms can have, one that includes direct reference as a special case. If we are to have a general semantic theory governing all terms, both those that refer^r and those that don't, it must be based not on Millianism but on nondescriptivism. This chapter has indicated how such an approach must work.

The remarkable fact about nondescriptivism is that adopting it has no downside: semantic theories—specifically truth-conditional semantic-theories (and regardless of which of the many ways that truth-conditional semantical theories are formulated), but not just those—are couched in metalanguages that have access to exactly the same referential$^{(r/e)}$ resources possessed by the targeted object languages. Thus contemporary formulations of semantic theories are already ontologically neutral. Only what may be described as "ontological marginalia" are affected by the adoption of nondescriptivism. The substantial content of any truth-conditional semantic theory (for example) is insensitive to ontological issues precisely because any ontological imposition on such theories requires insisting that quantifiers (of various sorts) are ontologically committing, or that singular expressions (of various sorts) are object dependent, when such appear in the semantic theories in question. There is nothing in what the quantifiers or singular expressions do in semantic theories that's any different from what they do anywhere else. This enables the successful deflection of the attribution of ontological commitments to a semantic theory when such is attempted on the basis (alone) of the quantifiers or singular expressions of that theory.

Let me conclude this section by discussing a concern some philosophers may have about whether my empty singular views can be made to fit with the role that structured propositions have in certain linguistic theories—more specifically, that they have in certain theories of speakers' understanding of sentences, ones that characterize such an understanding in terms of speakers grasping the structured propositions that sentences mean, or that are the meanings of such sentences. The way I think structured propositions should be approached is clearly implied by the foregoing discussion in this book, especially in earlier sections of this chapter. Nevertheless, it's worth going over this particular matter explicitly.

It may be thought that to grasp a sentence such as "Bertrand Russell is tall," is to grasp a structured entity represented like so: <Bertrand Russell, *Tallness*> which contains both Bertrand Russell and the property *Tallness*. Such a view, it may be thought, cannot be carried over to sentences like "Sherlock Holmes is tall," because the corresponding structured proposition will have a blank where Bertrand Russell appears in the first structured proposition I exhibited, that is, it will appear like so: <, *Tallness*>, and therefore it will be indistinguishable from the structured proposition corresponding to the sentence "Pegasus is tall."

It may seem that my approach must reject structured propositions as what speakers grasp when they grasp the meaning of sentences. I think, however, that my empty singular view is neutral about this. What it does require is the rejection of the view that every structured proposition is a real entity that a human being who understands a sentence enjoys a relationship with. It is not possible to enjoy a relationship—a real relationship, anyway—with something that doesn't exist. In the case of one's grasp of the sentence "Sherlock Holmes is tall," what such a theory will describe the speaker as grasping is the structured proposition <Sherlock Holmes, *Tallness*>. That is, the characterization of structured propositions used to represent the understanding of singular sentences is one that itself treats nonexistents as appearing in those structured propositions.

Now to do so means that the theory of linguistic understanding here described will help itself to quantification over nonexistent entities in the same way as how I've described other scientific theories to so help themselves. Doing so is not to engage in Meinongianism; it's not to treat the nonexistent entities as truth makers for statements of the theory. It's simply to allow certain truths of the theory not to have truth makers at all but only truth-value inducers. A theory of linguistic understanding that helps itself to structured entities that are characterized by that theory as the theoretical relata of a speaker's understanding of sentences, but yet are entities that don't exist, is no different than a physical theory that quantifies over spacetime points. (I'm assuming, of course, that if Sherlock Holmes doesn't exist, neither does any structured proposition that contains him.) Such a theory can be as valuable as any physical theory in providing explanations and predictions, and in enabling an understanding of the phenomena it's applied to, despite its quantifying over (at least in part) nothing at all.

My own longstanding nominalist views, of course, preclude my taking it that structured propositions, properties, and so on, exist in any case. But I am not presupposing those views here. The only point I am making now is that a theoretical construal of the semantics of sentences, in terms of structured entities, doesn't require that all of these entities, or their constituents, that are relevant to the theory, exist.

A remaining worry may be what might be described as a "ground floor concern": that characterizing a speaker's understanding of a sentence in terms of the grasping of a structured proposition that doesn't exist (because it contains nonexistent entities) cannot be what is "really" going on with respect to that speaker's understanding. This is true, however, only if "grasping" is required to be a theoretical relationship between speakers and real entities. But to demand that of a theoretical relationship that is the focus of scientific study—that it only be a relationship between real things—is to demand something that in general cannot be satisfied. Any scientific theory may indispensably require its descriptions of a phenomena to involve the characterization of relationships between entities some of which don't exist. A special science, such as semantics, is no different in this respect.

A second remaining concern may be that if structured propositions are allowed to contain nonexistent entities they cannot have the truth properties that such entities are required to have by that theory. This, however, is simply false; and this is a matter that this chapter has been dedicated to showing is false in some detail. What is true is that the truth values of such structured propositions will not be determined by their truth conditions. Such truth values, or some of them, anyway, will instead be determined by truth-value inducers. (My thanks to Gary Ostertag who posed a question to me, on December 29, 2009, that led to my writing these explicit concluding remarks on structured propositions.)

General Conclusion

It's so easy to miss the target in ontology: to presume there is more (or less) than there actually is. More to the point (of this book), it's easy to presume that we must (or that we do) commit ourselves to more (or less) than we actually have to (or do). I mean this not merely in the straightforward sense of getting it wrong, thinking that there is something (over there) when there isn't. I mean this also in the more dramatic sense that's been central to the topic of this book: to think it's required of us to think a certain class of items exist when we already know that they don't. The ways we talk about the world invite missing the target in this latter dramatic fashion. If we let grammar—or more refined versions of grammar (logical form, regimented language)—dictate our commitments, we find ourselves by virtue of similarity of language forms officially committed to fictional characters, hallucinated objects, numbers, and myths by the very same forms of words we use to deliberately commit ourselves to tables, chairs, and neutrinos. If we focus on the ways we seem forced by matters outside of our control to assert certain things and not other things, we again seem forced to take so and so and not such and such to be true of numbers, fictions, and myths just as we seem forced to assert this and that, and not that and this, to be true of tables, chairs, and neutrinos.

Ontology is a real mess. It would be an avoidable mess if it simply didn't matter. But it does matter, and it matters for the very simplest and most obvious of reasons: we want to know what's out there, and we want to distinguish what's out there from what we've made up—even if what we've made up we had to make up to successfully talk about what's out there. Not to want to distinguish what's real from what we've made up is to deliberately choose to lose touch with reality. On good days. we all know what a mistake that would be.

The topic of ontology would dissolve as a suitable topic of study if there was—in principle—no distinguishing between our creative contributions (what we've made up) and the world's contributions (what there is) as they are joined together in our true theories and representations of the world, and indeed, as they are joined together in our more fundamental (and automatic) perceptual interactions with the world that our theories are largely based on. This would be a result in philosophy: we can't distinguish what's out there from our own contributions.[1] Something that we (ordinarily) want, we can't have. Scepticism is a similar position: we'd like to distinguish the cases where we know things from cases where we don't. The sceptic—or at least certain straightforward versions of the sceptic—tries to show that we can't have what we want in this case either.

That we couldn't distinguish what's part of the world from what's only our creative contribution to our worldview was the position of the dominant American philosophers of the latter half of the past century: Quine and Putnam. Versions of the position run squarely back to Kant, and indeed, many of the arguments used by the latter-day American philosophers to attempt to establish their positions are eerily similar to his.

This book has not been dedicated to facing those arguments directly. I've already done that elsewhere. Instead I've undertaken the job of illustrating in fair detail—in three (fairly) clear cases—how requirements on taking certain statements or thoughts to be truth-apt come apart from the requirement that the terms in those statements refer[r] to objects in the world. Consequently, although we must take such statements to be true or false (and although we must do so because of demands of our theorizing about and our representations of ourselves and our world), those statements are not true or false by virtue of states of affairs enjoyed by the referents[r] of the terms in those statements. There are (to speak plainly) sometimes no such items to be referred[r] to, and so there is nothing to be said about[r] them, either correctly or incorrectly.

That such truth-apt statements are indispensable to our theorizing is nevertheless reflected not only in what we take to be true or false, but must also be reflected in our understanding of how we theorize about the world, and what it is about the world that forces the truth values we take our theorizing sentences to have. I have tried to show how this works in these cases.

One point I want to keep stressing is that the theories of (and representations utilizing) terms referring[e] to numbers, hallucinations and fictions are contrast cases. Not all true statements (or thoughts) are like these in having no referential[r] connections to the world. Carefully formulated representations about ordinary objects ("Many chairs are made of wood," "Great apes are going extinct") are truth-apt precisely because they describe (accurately) a state of affairs: the ways that certain objects are. I've not established—in this book—that the cases of statements about

---

1. Hilary Putnam, *The many faces of realism* (LaSalle, Ill.: Open Court, 1987), 16, has as a subtitle: "The Trail of the Human Serpent Is Over All."

numbers, hallucinations, and fictions contrast with these sorts of statements. In part, to establish that is to establish that the kind of linguistic idealism of philosophers like Quine and Putnam is wrong. That's work for another book. A previous book. Two previous books.[2]

A couple of (last) words about the aboutness intuitions that bedevil our talk about what doesn't exist. It's notorious that intuitions are often selectively chosen by philosophers to support otherwise broad-ranging philosophical positions. How are we to get past the methodological blunders that such an approach to intuitions can lead to? One thing to do is to get a principled idea of the sources of the intuitions. In the case of aboutness intuitions, for example, that "Pegasus doesn't exist," and "Vulcan doesn't exist," are—respectively—about two different things, I take it that the intuitions arise from central special cases, where a number of factors that can come apart haven't come part. The factors I mean to point to are (i) the truth-aptness of the statement, (ii) the grammatical subject of the statement referring[r] to something. These are the central cases our intuitions (unsurprisingly) are honed on, and that our involuntary object-directed psychological proclivities—discussed in section 1.4—incline us to focus on. Given the parochial nature of these intuitions, they are (evidentially) no better than similar intuitions (based on similarly innate psychological proclivities) that moving objects naturally come to a stop after an initial impetus sets them going. The question remains: how do we proceed to generalize beyond these intuitions?

I have nothing fresh, methodologically speaking, to offer. One must—I think—focus on broad aspects of our linguistic practice to determine what aspects of that practice are explained, and how, by the various competing theories. Consider—therefore—a brief comparison of my approach with opposing approaches. (i) I leave intact the truth-aptness of indispensable sentences. (I don't want to treat them as empty propositions that are pragmatically provided with meanings, nor do I want to treat them as part of a global pretence practice.) (ii) I leave intact the commonsense ontological picture of certain items not existing. (Fictions, myths, and hallucinated objects.) (iii) As a cost, my approach violates the "intuition" that statements and thoughts are always true by virtue of what they are about[r]. This intuition is not sacrificed altogether; rather, it is demoted to a special case: where the demands on ontology don't come apart from the demands on truth. It doesn't violate the aboutness intuitions, however, in the following ways. There are sentences within which "Santa Claus" and "Pegasus" appear that are true, and they aren't the same sentences, for example, "Santa Claus is depicted in American mythology as wearing a beard," and "Pegasus was believed by the ancient Greeks to be a flying horse." If someone points at an hallucinated elf, and says "That doesn't exist," his statement parallels the content of what it is he's focused on. (Even though nothing is there.) The way that the aboutness intuition is violated—if it is—is that there isn't anything that the statements in question are

---

2. Jody Azzouni, *Knowledge and reference in empirical science* (London: Routledge, 2000a; paperback edition with important corrections published in 2004), and Jody Azzouni, *Deflating existential consequence: A case for nominalism* (Oxford: Oxford University Press, 2004a).

"about," and our story about how those statements get the truth values they get doesn't turn on the properties of the items that (intuitively) the statements in question seem to be about^r. Perhaps that violates aboutness intuitions—but only if those intuitions have a genuine metaphysical component.

Do they have a genuine metaphysical component? The discussion of our capacity, in chapters 1 and 2, to, despite the involuntary psychological responses to hallucinations, be able to recognize that there is nothing there at all suggests that they don't have such a metaphysical component. The same person who says that "Pegasus is a flying horse" is about Pegasus is also firm that there is no Pegasus. This, I claim, is naturally captured by distinguishing between aboutness^r and aboutness^e.

Notice also that such aboutness intuitions, when their "metaphysical component" is indulged in by the ordinary speaker, leads straight to the use/mention errors discussed in the general introduction. My approach is compatible with this; but it seems that realist and Meinongian approaches are not. After all, the ordinary person wouldn't flounder for a subject for vacuous singular terms to be about if those views were the right ones (at least as descriptions of the ordinary speaker's practices).

If my approach does violate intuitions, how costly is this violation? In terms of our truth-assertion (representation) practices and our deduction practices, not costly at all.[3] Indeed, the only downside to my approach is its opposition to the long-entrenched philosophical tradition in metaphysics that regards the guide to the real to be the true (and therefore regards the guide to what we must take to exist to be what we must say about it). Even this long-entrenched methodological proposal isn't entirely jettisoned on my view, but only qualified: it's treated as a special case.[4]

---

3. That, I think, is another way in which it shows its superiority to alternative approaches, for example, Meinongian and realist ones. My approach doesn't make "Sherlock Holmes is an abstract object," true, and "Sherlock Holmes doesn't exist" ("exist" understood ontologically), false (against the realist); it also doesn't require the double-talk of the Meinongian. On my view, Sherlock Holmes doesn't exist (ontologically speaking). Period. The End. (He *really* doesn't exist.) It shows its superiority to pretence views by allowing us to say straight: "Sherlock Holmes is depicted in fictions as a detective." (See? It's all about being able to say stuff that's true with a clear metaphysical conscience.)

4. "Long-entrenched" is no exaggeration. A translation of a fragment of Parmenides reads: "It must be that what is there for speaking of and thinking of is; for it is there to be" (Parmenides, *Parmenides of Elea* [Toronto, Canada: University of Toronto Press, 1984]). One also reads in Plato's Sophist ("The sophist," in *Plato: The collected dialogues*, ed. Edith Hamilton and Huntington Cairns [Princeton, N.J.: Princeton University Press, 1963], 957–1017) 237D–E an apparent commitment to the claim that if a use of "something" fails to refer then it fails to be meaningful:

> *STRANGER:* Surely we can see that this expression "something" is always used of a thing that exists. We cannot use it just by itself in naked isolation from everything that exists, can we?
>
> *THEAETETUS:* No.
>
> *STRANGER:* Is your assent due to the reflection that to speak of "something" is to speak of "some *one* thing"?
>
> *THEAETETUS:* Yes.
>
> *STRANGER:* Because you will admit that "something" stands for one thing, as "some things" stands for two or more.
>
> *THEAETETUS:* Certainly.
>
> *STRANGER:* So it seems to follow necessarily that to speak of what is not "something" is to speak of no thing at all.
>
> *THEAETETUS:* Necessarily.
>
> *STRANGER:* Must we not even refuse to allow that in such a case a person is *saying* something, though he may be speaking of nothing? Must we not assert that he is not even saying anything when he sets about uttering the sounds "a thing that is not"? (emphasis in translation)

I want to make some brief (concluding) remarks about how ordinary people talk to each other about ontology and truth: how, in particular, they presuppose the nonexistence of things that they talk about, and how they indicate that they so presuppose the nonexistence of these things. Our ordinary ways of speaking are treacherous. In particular, these ways of speaking are often used by philosophers to argue that ordinary speakers actually have ontological commitments to things they don't actually have any commitment to—fictional objects, say. These ways of speaking also motivate certain approaches to ontology that are—or so I've argued—misguided.

Let's start with how ordinary people indicate that they aren't committed to fictional objects. Braun (2005, 612) considers the statements: "There is no Sherlock Holmes. Sherlock Holmes does not exist. Sherlock Holmes is just a fictional character."

Braun considers this series of remarks inconsistent; indeed, he claims that "Most ordinary speakers' beliefs about fiction really are (deep down) confused and inconsistent" (Braun 2005, 613). Really? Before drawing this conclusion, shouldn't we consider how contextual shiftings play into what people say? (Shouldn't we further charitably notice how such contextual shiftings occur in automatic ways that ordinary people aren't capable of taking account of should they be in the position of trying to defend themselves against inconsistency charges brought against them by, say, philosophers?) Sometimes we—when speaking ordinarily—try to quantify over only what exists. We then say: *There are no Bs. Bs do not exist.* Other times, when our subject matter is in regard to one or another fictional subject, we may use "there is" or "exists" in an ontologically neutral way: *No Disney characters that are talking yaks exist, although there certainly are plenty of talking sheep.* Sometimes, we switch in what amounts to the very same sentence (as above: *There is no Sherlock Holmes; Sherlock Holmes is just a fictional character*). This is no more inconsistent than if a terrorist were to say (to a good friend who could successfully contextualize what she had said): "After I blew up the bank, I went fishing by the bank." In many contexts, that remark would be misleading (in addition to being disturbing); but it wouldn't be inconsistent.

If someone says, in the course of betraying that he thinks Sherlock Holmes was real, "Sherlock Holmes lived in London in the nineteenth century," we may dislodge his presupposition by saying: "No, Sherlock Holmes is a fictional character." If that person clearly knows that Sherlock Holmes is fictional but says, falsely, "Sherlock Holmes lived in New York in the eighteenth century," he'll be corrected with: "No, he lived in the nineteenth

---

See Peter Ludlow, *Semantics, tense, and time: An essay in the metaphysics of natural language* (Cambridge, Mass.: MIT Press, 1999_, 219–20, note 1, where these antecedent philosophical views are quoted with approval. See Jody Azzouni, "Proof and ontology in Euclidean mathematics," in *New trends in the history and philosophy of mathematics*, ed. Tinne Hoff Kjeldsen, Stig Andur Pedersen, and Lise Mariane Sonne-Hansen (Denmark: University of Southern Denmark, 2004c), 117–33, for a discussion of how such ontological assumptions influenced both the interpretation of and the direction of Euclidean geometry: that is, how this truth-maker assumption directly led to the ontological positing of abstracta.

century."[5] Neither way of speaking requires an interpretation that implies that the sentence, "Sherlock Holmes lived in London in the nineteenth century," presupposes—ontologically speaking—a fictional object. Rather, what is the case is that in different contexts different things are presupposed by speakers making mistakes, and the corrections of those speakers by others track these presuppositions, whether or not they are explicitly represented in the semantic structure of the statements uttered. To say that Sherlock Holmes is a fictional character is not to commit oneself to fictional characters. To say that Sherlock Holmes didn't live in New York isn't to imply that he lived somewhere else, in contrast to statements otherwise identical in form, such as "Churchill didn't live in New York during World War II" where there *is* an implication (or an "implicature") that Churchill indeed did live somewhere else during that time.

Similar, suppose we learn that Vulcan doesn't exist. So it's true that: "Vulcan isn't between Mercury and the Sun." Saying this isn't meant to give listeners the impression that Vulcan is to be found somewhere else (between Mars and Saturn, say) any more than my dramatic remark to someone that the number 2 isn't hiding under my bed is meant to give that person the impression that it might be found hiding somewhere else (in my closet, for example).

These forms of speech are read by Meinongians (and those who want fictional objects, mathematical objects, etc., to be abstracta) in ways that motivate their views. Only a broader examination of the evidence of usage can successfully overturn the apparent usage evidence that's apparently in favor of the Meinongian position. To dismiss ordinary intuitions as inconsistent (without undertaking to explain their sources) is to deliberately immunize one's views against the evidence that such intuitions contain; it also prevents finding evidence for one's views.[6]

A different collection of ordinary ways of speaking explains, I think, the popularity among philosophers of handling otherwise truth-apt sentences about the nonexistent via modifications of truth idioms (e.g., lightweight truth, pretence, etc.), instead of approaching such directly via nonreferring[r] terms. When the ordinary person tries to indicate that he's exaggerating something, or more generally, that an idealization of some sort is involved, he invariably falls back on the notion of truth to do so: he describes what he's saying as "not quite right," or as only "approximately true." This intuitive utilization of the notion of truth is similarly behind the philosophical tendency to make the word "true" do work when it's recognized that a simple correspondence relationship between certain sentential vehicles and the

---

5. Part of the complication here is the tendency to speak directly of Sherlock Holmes living in the nineteenth century, rather than as depicted in such and such fictions as living in the nineteenth century. The tricky philosopher can annoy the ordinary person by pointing out that she has said: "Sherlock Holmes lived in London in the nineteenth century." The tricky philosopher can arch his eyebrow, and say, in a particular tone of voice, "Where, *exactly*, in London did he live?" The exasperated ordinary person can respond: "Of course Sherlock Holmes didn't live in London. There was no Sherlock Holmes." The tricky philosopher can then arch his eyebrow again and say: "Oh? Then what are we talking about, exactly?" (And so on.) Perhaps more people would like philosophers if they didn't find this kind of thing so entertaining.

6. Noam Chomsky (*Knowledge of language* [New York: Praeger, 1986], 36) describes the judgments of native speakers as "the result of an experiment, one that is poorly designed but rich in the evidence it provides."

world isn't to be had. When philosophers take up this loose and innocent way of speaking, and attempt to make it do philosophical work, they oblige themselves to characterize the sentences in question in some other way: such sentences are pretended-true, or they're fiction, or they're approximately true, or they're true relative to a practice (e.g., mathematics); similarly, philosophers may suggest that there are many kinds of truth, with rather different properties.

So much trouble stems from the fact that we tend to ordinarily and automatically think of our sentences as either successful (true), and thus sticking onto the world correctly (as wholes), or as failures, and thus as not fully sticking onto the world. We don't ordinarily have the vocabulary (beyond phrases like "that's not exactly true") to investigate the functionally significant pieces of such sentences, and see what those are doing in the cases where we have become uncomfortable just saying that "It's true that . . ." "True" is, for all its indispensability, a relatively primitive and simple device. Truth idioms exist in our language solely because we need blind truth endorsements. Otherwise we would get on in life with just the sentences themselves (that we want to utter).[7] As was illustrated in chapter 4, it's because of this that the truth idiom is governed by (unrestricted) Tarski biconditionals. Those unrestricted Tarski biconditionals pretty much all by themselves put a stop to philosophical attempts to add bells and whistles to the truth idiom to manufacture more sophisticated descendent notions.

Nevertheless, the many ways that assertorically used truths don't "fit" the world—as neat correspondence views would have it do—are crying out for taxonomy. It's philosophy's job[8] to supply this taxonomy if only because the job in question is so close to the traditional topic of "ontology." We don't have natural ways of describing what we do in the vernacular, but a major part of a successful methodology is to construct true sentences that involve clever ways of talking about nothing at all, ones that nevertheless successfully target aspects of the world that we want to study (and manipulate), and that we have no other way of reaching. When we try to informally talk about our methods for doing this, we end up saying things like: "It's not really true that Jupiter is a sphere; it's only approximately true," or "it's not really true that molecules have shapes, but it's approximately true." In many of these cases, "approximately true" hardly gets at what's going on (in what sense is an electron approximately a singularity?). Instead something rather subtle is called for, descriptions of how we use carefully chosen falsehoods to deduce truths about things, and descriptions of how we pad our models of what there is with nonexistent items to facilitate our understanding of the former.

I've been suggesting that ordinary (and sloppy) ways of speaking are sometimes helpful when they're cleaned up by the philosopher; but sometimes they're not. "Approximate truth," I want to claim, isn't helpful no matter how much philosophers polish it; distinguishing between what exists and what there is,

---

7. It should be noted that even normative-sounding pronouncements like "We should only believe true sentences," are blind truth-ascriptions, amounting just to (in a formulation taking liberties with use/mention and quantifiers): for all p, we should believe p iff p. See Azzouni forthcoming(b) for further discussion on this.

8. At the moment, anyway. The "job" of philosophy—at least when one takes a long enough view—changes rather dramatically over time.

when suitably regimented, *is* helpful. With care, we can—using it—avoid turning whole bodies of indispensably truth-apt thought and speech into pretence. But we can also be seduced into attributing to the ordinary person (or adopting ourselves) the belief that there (really) are all sorts of things that lack the existence property.

The ordinary person doesn't usually think to fall back on this way of putting the matter: there are ways of talking that are indispensable, that look and function semantically just like other ways of talking (ones that are about objects) but nevertheless contain terms that don't refer to anything. Sometimes an ordinary person is moved to say: *But this is all just a way of talking*, but usually he will fumble much the way that Braun (2005, 613) says he will, utter "all sorts of (usually incoherent) claims about what he or she really meant and thought." These "material modes of speech" similarly invite philosophers to engage in all sorts of misguided studies of ontology: extended taxonomies of all sorts of (let's be frank) bizarre "objects," ones that go well beyond what we should take there to be. One theme of this book is that all such ontologizing is quite unnecessary and unmotivated. Instead (or so I've argued) we should try to make good on the ordinary person's initial outburst: this is all just a way of talking. In doing so, however, I've tried to avoid the other horn of the dilemma, ending up with a philosophical position that leaves no place at all for metaphysics. Sometimes it's all just a way of talking, sometimes we're really referring' to things, sometimes it's both, and very often, it's all just a way of talking that gets us to things (although not directly by way of what we say about them). The hard task is seeing when what is doing which.

Bibliography

Aleman, André, E. Formisano, H. Koppenhagen, P. Hagoort, E. H. F. de Haan, and R. S. Kahn. 2005. The functional neuroanatomy of metrical stress evaluation of perceived and imagined spoken words. *Cerebral Cortex* 15: 221–28.

Aleman, André, and Frank Larøi. 2008. *Hallucinations: The science of idiosyncratic perception.* Washington, D.C.: American Psychological Association.

Allaire, E. B. 1963. Bare particulars. *Philosophical Studies* 14: 1–18.

———. 1965. Another look at bare particulars. *Philosophical Studies* 16: 16–21.

Austin, J. L. 1962. *Sense and sensibilia.* Oxford: Oxford University Press.

Azzouni, Jody. 1994. *Metaphysical myths, mathematical practice: The ontology and epistemology of the exact science.* Cambridge: Cambridge University Press.

———. 1997. Applied mathematics, existential commitment and the Quine-Putnam indispensability thesis. *Philosophia Mathematica* 3(5): 193–209.

———. 1998. On "on what there is." *Pacific Philosophical Quarterly* 79(1): 1–18.

———. 2000a. *Knowledge and reference in empirical science.* London: Routledge. (Paperback edition with important corrections published in 2004.)

———. 2000b. Stipulation, logic, and ontological independence. *Philosophia Mathematica* 3(8): 225–43.

———. 2003. Individuation, causal relations and Quine. In *Meaning*, ed. Mark Richard, 197–219. Oxford: Blackwell Publishing.

———. 2004a. *Deflating existential consequence: A case for nominalism.* Oxford: Oxford University Press.

———. 2004b. Theory, observation and scientific realism. *British Journal for the Philosophy of Science* 55: 371–92.

———. 2004c. Proof and ontology in Euclidean mathematics. In *New trends in the history and philosophy of mathematics*, ed. Tinne Hoff Kjeldsen, Stig Andur Pedersen, Lise Mariane Sonne-Hansen, 117–33. Denmark: University of Southern Denmark.

———. 2005. Is there still a sense in which mathematics can have foundations? In *Essays on the foundations of mathematics and logic*, ed. Giandomenico Sica, 9–47. Milan, Italy: Polimetrica S.a.s.

———. 2006. *Tracking reason: Proof, consequence, and truth.* Oxford: Oxford University Press.

———. 2007. Ontological commitment in the vernacular. *Noûs* 41: 204–26.

———. 2008. Alternative logics and the role of truth in the interpretation of languages. In *New essays on Tarski and philosophy*, ed. Douglas Patterson, 390–429. Oxford: Oxford University Press.

———. 2009a. Empty *de re* attitudes about numbers. *Philosophia Mathematica* III(17): 163–88.

———. 2009b. Why do informal proofs conform to formal norms? *Foundations of Science* 14: 9–26.

———. 2009c. Evading truth commitments: The problem reanalyzed. *Logique et Analyse* 206: 139–76.

———. forthcoming (a). Ontology and the word "exist": Uneasy relations. *Philosophia Mathematica*.

———. forthcoming (b). Deflationist truth. In *Handbook on truth*, ed. Michael Glanzberg. Oxford: Blackwell Publishing.

———. forthcoming (c). A new characterization of scientific theories. *Synthese*.

Azzouni, J., and O. Bueno. 2008. On what it takes for there to be no fact of the matter. *Noûs* 42(4): 753–69.

Baker, Alan. 2008. Mathematical skepticism. In *Scientific papers of Latvia*, vol. 739, ed. Jurģis Šķilters, 7–21. Riga, Latvia: Latvijas Universitāte.

Barnes, J., L. Boubert, J. Harris, A. Lee, and A. S. David. 2003. Reality monitoring and visual hallucinations in Parkinson's disease. *Neuropsychologia* 41: 565–74.

Barwise, Jon, and Robin Cooper. 1981. Generalized quantifiers in natural language. *Linguistics and Philosophy* 4: 159–219.

Barwise, Jon, and S. Feferman, eds. 1985. *Model-theoretic logics*. Berlin: Springer-Verlag.

Batchelor, G. K. 1967. *An introduction to fluid dynamics*. Cambridge: Cambridge University Press.

Beall, Jc. 2000. On mixed inferences and pluralism about truth predicates. *Philosophical Quarterly* 50: 380–82.

Beall, Jc, and Greg Restall. 2006. *Logical pluralism*. Oxford: Oxford University Press.

Benacerraf, Paul. 1973. Mathematical truth. *Journal of Philosophy* 70: 661–80.

Bentall, R. P. 1990. The illusion of reality: A review and integration of psychological research on hallucinations. *Psychological Bulletin* 107(1): 82–95.

———. 2000. Hallucinatory experiences. In *Varieties of anomalous experience: Examining the scientific evidence*, ed. E. Cardeña, S. J. Lynn, and S. Krippner, 85–120. Washington, D.C.: American Psychological Association.

———. 2003. *Madness explained: Psychosis and human nature*. London: Penguin Books.

Black, Max. 1952. The identity of indiscernables. Reprinted in *Problems of analysis* (1954), 204–16. Ithaca, N.Y.: Cornell University Press.

Blanke, Olaf, Stéphanie Ortigue, Theodor Landis, and Margitta Seeck. 2002. Stimulating illusory own-body perceptions. *Nature* 419: 269–70.

Block, Ned. 1990. Can the mind change the world? In *Meaning and method: Essays in honor of Hilary Putnam*, ed. George Boolos, 137–70. Cambridge: Cambridge University Press.

Braudel, Fernand. 1981. *Civilization and capitalism: 15th–18th century. Volume 1: The structures of everyday life: The limits of the possible*. New York: Harper & Row.

———. 1982. *Civilization and capitalism: 15th–18th century. Volume 2: The wheels of commerce*. New York: Harper & Row.

———. 1984. *Civilization and capitalism: 15th–18th century. Volume 3: The perspective of the world*. New York: Harper & Row.

Braun, David. 1993. Empty names. *Noûs* 27: 443–69.

———. 2005. Empty names, fictional names, mythical names. *Noûs* 39: 596–631.

Brody, Baruch A., ed. 1970. *Readings in the philosophy of science*. Englewood Cliffs, N.J.: Prentice Hall.

Bueno, Otávio, and Edward N. Zalta. 2005. A nominalist's dilemma and its solution. *Philosophia Mathematica* 3(13): 294–307.

Burge, Tyler. 1974. Truth and singular terms. *Noûs* 8: 309–25.

———. 1977. Belief de re. In *Foundations of mind* (2007), 44–64. Oxford: Oxford University Press.

———. 1979. Sinning against Frege. In *Truth, thought, reason* (2005), 213–39. Oxford: Oxford University Press.

———. 1992. Frege on knowing the third realm. In *Truth, thought, reason* (2005), 299–316. Oxford: Oxford University Press.

———. 2005. Postscript to "Frege and the hierarchy." In *Truth, thought, reason* (2005), 167–210. Oxford: Oxford University Press.

———. 2007a. Introduction. In *Foundations of mind* (2007), 1–31. Oxford: Oxford University Press.

———. 2007b. Postscript to "belief de re." In *Foundations of mind* (2007), 65–81. Oxford: Oxford University Press.

Butterfield, Brian. 1999. *The mathematical brain*. London: Macmillan.

Byrne, Alex, and Heather Logue. 2008. Either/or. In *Disjunctivism: Perception, action, knowledge*, ed. Adrian Haddock and Fiona Macpherson, 1–24. Oxford: Oxford University Press.

Carey, Susan. 2009. Where our number concepts come from. *Journal of Philosophy* 106(4): 220–54.

Cartwright, Nancy. 1983. *How the laws of physics lie*. Oxford: Oxford University Press.

———. 1999. *The dappled world: A study of the boundaries of science*. Cambridge: Cambridge University Press.

Cartwright, Richard. 1960. Negative existentials. In *Philosophical essays* (1987), 21–31. Cambridge, Mass.: MIT Press.

Castaneda, Carlos. 1968. *The teachings of Don Juan: A Yaqui way of knowledge*. New York: Washington Square Press.

Causey, Robert. 1972. Attribute identities in microreductions. *Journal of Philosophy* 69: 407–22.

Chappell, V. C. 1964. Particulars re-clothed. *Philosophical Studies* 15: 60–64.

Chierchia, Gennaro, and Sally McConnell-Ginet. 1990. *Meaning and grammar: An introduction to semantics*. Cambridge, Mass.: MIT Press.

Chisholm, Roderick M. 1972. Beyond being and nonbeing. In *Metaphysics: The big questions* (2008), ed. Peter van Inwagen and Dean W. Zimmerman, 40–50. Oxford: Blackwell Publishing.

Chomsky, Noam. 1986. *Knowledge of language*. New York: Praeger.

Cohen, L., S. Dehaene, F. Chochon, S. Lehéricy, and L. Naccache. 2000. Language and calculation within the parietal lobe: A combined cognitive, anatomical and fMRI study. *Neuropsychologia* 38: 1426–40.

Collerton, Daniel, Elaine Perry, and Ian McKeith. 2005. Why people see things that are not there: A novel perception and attention deficit model for recurrent complex visual hallucinations. *Behavioral and Brain Sciences* 28: 737–94.

Cooklin, R., D. Sturgeon, and J. Leff. 1983. The relationship between auditory hallucinations and spontaneous fluctuations of skin resistance in schizophrenia. *British Journal of Psychiatry* 142: 47–52.

Crittenden, Charles. 1991. *Unreality: The metaphysics of fictional objects*. Ithaca, N.Y.: Cornell University Press.

Damasio, Antonio. 1994. *Descartes' error*. New York: G.P. Putnam's Sons.

Darton, Robert. 1984. Peasants tell tales: The meaning of Mother Goose. In *The great cat massacre and other episodes in French cultural history*, 8–72. New York: Random House.

Davidson, Donald. 1980. *Essays on actions and events*. Oxford: Oxford University Press.
———. 1984. *Inquiries into truth and interpretation*. Oxford: Oxford University Press.

Davies, Robertson. 1982. Revelation from a smoky fire. In *A gathering of ghost stories* (1995), 10–18. New York: Penguin Books.

Decety, Jean, and Thierry Chaminade. 2005. The neurophysiology of imitation and intersubjectivity. In *Perspective on imitation: From neuroscience to social science*, vol. 1, ed. Susan Hurley and Nick Chater, 119–40. Cambridge, Mass.: MIT Press.

Dehaene, Stanislas. 1997. *The number sense: How the mind creates mathematics*. Oxford: Oxford University Press.
———. 2002. Single-neuron arithmetic. *Science* 297: 1652–53.

Dehaene, Stanislas, and Laurent Cohen. 1997. Cerebral pathways for calculation: Double dissociation between rote verbal and quantitative knowledge of arithmetic. *Cortex* 33: 219–50.

Dehaene, Stanislas, Nicolas Molko, Laurent Cohen, and Anna J. Wilson. 2004. Arithmetic and the brain. *Current Opinion in Neurobiology* 14: 218–24.

Dehaene, Stanislas, and Lionel Naccache. 2001. Towards a cognitive neuroscience of consciousness: Basic evidence and a workspace framework. In *The cognitive neuroscience of consciousness*, ed. Stanislas Dehaene, 1–37. Cambridge, Mass.: MIT Press.

Dehaene, Stanislas, Manuela Piazza, Philippe Pinel, and Laurent Cohen. 2003. Three parietal circuits for number processing. *Cognitive Neuropsychology* 20(3–6): 487–506.

Dennett, Daniel. 1991. *Consciousness explained*. Boston: Little, Brown.

De Ridder, Dirk, Koen Van Laere, Patrick Dupont, Tomas Menovsky, and Paul Van de Heyning. 2007. Visualizing out-of-body experience in the brain. *New England Journal of Medicine* 357: 1829–33.

Deutsch, Harry. 2000. Making up stories. In *Empty names, fiction and the puzzles of non-existence*, ed. Anthony Everett and Thomas Hofweber, 149–81. Stanford, Calif.: CSLI Publications.

Devitt, Michael. 1997. *Realism and truth*, 2nd ed. Princeton, N.J.: Princeton University Press.

Diederich, Nico J., Christopher G. Goetz, and Glenn T. Stebbins. 2005. Repeated visual hallucinations in Parkinson's disease as disturbed external/internal perceptions: Focused review and a new integrative model. *Movement Disorders* 20(2): 130–40.

Dierks, T., D. E. Linden, M. Jandl, E. Formisano, R. Goebel, H. Lanfermann, and W. Singer. 1999. Activation of Heschl's gyrus during auditory hallucinations. *Neuron* 22: 615–21.

Donnellan, Keith. 1966. Reference and definite descriptions. *Philosophical Review* 75: 281–304.

———. 1974. Speaking of nothing. *Philosophical Review* 83: 3–32. Reprinted in *Naming, necessity, and natural kinds* (1977), ed. Stephen P. Schwartz, 216–44. Ithaca, N.Y.: Cornell University Press.

Driver, Jon, and Patrik Vuilleumier. 2001. Perceptual awareness and its loss in unilateral neglect and extinction. In *The cognitive neuroscience of consciousness*, ed. Stanislas Dehaene, 39–88. Cambridge, Mass.: MIT Press.

Dummett, Michael. 1983. Existence. In *The seas of language* (1993), 277–307. Oxford: Oxford University Press.

Edwards, Douglas. 2008. How to solve the problem of mixed conjunctions. *Analysis* 68(2): 143–49.

Enderton, Herbert B. 1977. *Elements of set theory*. New York: Harcourt Brace Jovanovich.

Etchemendy, John. 1990. *The concept of logical consequence*. Cambridge, Mass.: Harvard University Press.

Evans, Gareth. 1973. The causal theory of names. Reprinted in *Collected papers* (1985), 1–24. Oxford: Oxford University Press.

———. 1982. *The varieties of reference*. Oxford: Oxford University Press.

Everett, Anthony. 2000. Referentialism and empty names. In *Empty names, fiction and the puzzles of non-existence*, ed. Anthony Everett and Thomas Hofweber, 37–60. Stanford, Calif.: CSLI Publications.

Feigenson, Lisa, Stanislas Dehaene, and Elizabeth Spelke. 2004. Core systems of number. *Trends in Cognitive Sciences* 8(7): 307–14.

Feigl, H., and M. Brodbeck, eds. 1953. *Readings in the philosophy of science*. New York: Appleton-Century-Crofts.

Feyerabend, P. K. 1962. Explanation, reduction, and empiricism. In *Minnesota Studies in the philosophy of science*, vol. III, ed. Herbert Feigl and Grover Maxwell, 28–97. Minneapolis: University of Minnesota Press.

Field, Hartry. 1972. Tarski's theory of truth. *Journal of Philosophy* 69: 347–75.

———. 1980. *Science without numbers*. Princeton, N.J.: Princeton University Press.

Fleming, Ian. 1959. *Goldfinger*. London: Pan Books, 1961.

Fodor, Jerry A. 1974. Special sciences, or the disunity of sciences as a working hypothesis. In *Representations* (1981), 127–45. Cambridge, Mass.: MIT Press.

———. 1975. *The language of thought*. Cambridge, Mass.: Harvard University Press.

Frith, C. 1999. How hallucinations make themselves heard. *Neuron* 22: 414–15.

Gaddis, William. 1955. *The recognitions*. New York: Penguin Books.

Geach, P. T. 1965. Assertion. *Philosophical Review* 74(4): 449–65.

Gerken, Thomas, Christophe A. Girard, Yi-Chun Loraine Tung, Celia J. Webby, Vladimir Saudek, Kirsty S. Hewitson, Giles S. H. Yeo, Michael A. McDonough, Sharon Cunliffe, Luke A. McNeill, Juris Galvanovskis, Patrik Rorsman, Peter Robins, Xavier Prieur, Anthony P. Coll, Marcella Ma, Zorica Javanovic, I. Sadaf Farooqui, Frances M. Ashcroft, Stephen O'Rahilly, and Christopher J. Schofield. 2007. The obesity-associated

FTO gene encodes a 2-Oxoglutarate-dependent nucleic acid demethylase. *Science* 318: 1469–72.

Glymour, Clark. 1970. On some patterns of reduction. *Philosophy of Science* 37: 340–53.

Goodman, Nelson. 1978. *Ways of worldmaking*. Indianapolis, Ind.: Hackett.

———. 1983. *Fact, fiction, and forecast*, 4th ed. Cambridge, Mass.: Harvard University Press.

Greiner, W. 1994. *Quantum mechanics: An introduction*, 3rd ed. Heidelberg: Springer-Verlag.

Greiner, W., and B. Müller. 1994. *Quantum mechanics: Symmetries*, 2nd ed. Heidelberg: Springer-Verlag.

Greiner, W., and J. Reinhardt. 1994. *Quantum electrodynamics*, 2nd ed. Heidelberg: Springer-Verlag.

Greiner, W., and A. Schäfer. 1995. *Quantum chromodynamics*, 2nd corrected ed. Heidelberg: Springer-Verlag.

Griffiths, Paul E., and Karola Stotz. 2007. Gene. In *The Cambridge companion to the philosophy of biology*, ed. David L. Hull and Michael Ruse, 85–102. Cambridge: Cambridge University Press.

Grossberg, Stephen. 2000. How hallucinations may arise from brain mechanisms of learning, attention, and volition. *Journal of the International Neuropsychological Society* 6: 583–92.

Haddock, Adrian, and Fiona Macpherson. 2008. Introduction: Varieties of disjunctivism. In *Disjunctivism: Perception, action, knowledge*, ed. Adrian Haddock and Fiona Macpherson, 1–24. Oxford: Oxford University Press.

Halmos, P. 1957. Nicolas Bourbaki. *Scientific American* 196: 88–99.

Harman, Gilbert. 1990. The intrinsic quality of experience. In *Reasoning, meaning, and mind* (1999), 244–61. Oxford: Oxford University Press.

Hellman, Geoffrey, and Frank Thompson. 1975. Physicalism: Ontology, determination, and reduction. *Journal of Philosophy* 72: 551–64.

Hempel, Carl G. 1965. Studies in the logic of confirmation. In *Aspects of scientific explanation and other essays in the philosophy of science*, 3–46. New York: Macmillan.

Higginbotham, J. 1990. Contexts, model, and meanings: A note on the data of semantics. In *Mental representations: The interface between language and reality*, ed. R. Kempson, 29–48. Cambridge: Cambridge University Press.

Hinton, J. M. 1967. Visual experiences. *Mind* 76: 212–27.

Hirsch, Eli. 1993. *Dividing reality*. Oxford: Oxford University Press.

Honey, G. D., T. Sharma, J. Suckling, V. Giampietro, W. Soni, S. C. R Williams, and E. T. Bullmore. 2003. The functional neuroanatomy of schizophrenic subsyndromes. *Psychological Medicine* 33: 1007–18.

Horgan, T. 2001. Contextual semantics and metaphysical realism: Truth as indirect correspondence. In *The nature of truth: Classic and contemporary perspectives*, ed. M. P. Lynch, 67–95. Cambridge, Mass.: MIT Press.

Husserl, Edmund. 1900. *Logical Investigations* (1970) (trans. J. N. Findlay). London: Routledge & Kegan Paul.

Irving, Washington. 1820. *Rip van Winkel and The legend of sleepy hollow*. New York: Penguin Books, 1995.

Jackendoff, R. 1972. *Semantic interpretation in generative grammar*. Cambridge, Mass.: MIT Press.

Jäncke, L., S. Mirzazde, N. J. Shah. 1999. Attention modulates activity in the primary and the secondary auditory cortex: A functional magnetic resonance imaging study in human subjects. *Neuroscience Letters* 266: 125–28.

Johnson, M. K., S. Hashtroudi, and D. S. Lindsay 1993. Source monitoring. *Psychological Bulletin* 114: 3–28.

Kalderon, Mark Eli. 2005. Introduction. In *Fictionalism in metaphysics*, ed. Mark Eli Kalderon, 1–10. Oxford: Oxford University Press.

Kant, Immanuel. 1781. *Critique of pure reason* (1998), ed. Paul Guyer, trans. Allen W. Wood. Cambridge: Cambridge University Press.

Kanwisher, Nancy. 2001. Neural events and perceptual awareness. In *The cognitive neuroscience of consciousness*, ed. Stanislas Dehaene, 89–113. Cambridge, Mass.: MIT Press.

Katz, Jerrold J. 1972. *Semantic theory*. New York: Harper & Row.

———. 1981. *Language and other abstract objects*. Totowa, N.J.: Rowman and Littlefield.

Katz, Jerrold J., and Jerry A. Fodor. 1963. The structure of a semantic theory. *Language* 39: 170–210.

Keenan, E. L., and D. Westerståhl. 1997. Generalized quantifiers in linguistics and logic. In *Handbook of logic and language*, ed. Johan van Benthem and Alice ter Meulen, 837–93. Cambridge, Mass.: MIT Press.

Kemeny, J. G., and P. Oppenheim. 1956. On reduction. *Philosophical Studies* 7: 6–19.

Kim, Jaegwon. 1993a. Multiple realization and the metaphysics of reduction. In *Supervenience and mind: Selected philosophical essays*, ed. Jaegwon Kim, 309–35. Cambridge, Mass.: Cambridge University Press.

———. 1993b. Concepts of supervenience. In *Supervenience and mind: Selected philosophical essays*, ed. Jaegwon Kim, 309–35. Cambridge, Mass.: Cambridge University Press.

———. 1993c. *Supervenience and mind: Selected philosophical essays*. Cambridge, Mass.: Cambridge University Press.

———. 2005. *Physicalism, or something near enough*. Princeton, N.J.: Princeton University Press.

King, Jeffrey C. 2001. Complex demonstratives. Cambridge, Mass.: MIT Press.

Kitcher, Philip. 1984. 1953 and all that: A tale of two sciences. *Philosophical Review* 93: 335–73.

———. 1995. Who's afraid of the human genome project? In *The philosophy of biology* (1998), ed. David L. Hull and Michael Ruse, 522–35. Oxford: Oxford University Press.

———. 1996. *The lives to come*. New York: Simon & Shuster.

Kripke, Saul. 1972. *Naming and necessity*. Cambridge, Mass.: Harvard University Press.

Kroon, Fred. 2000. Negative existentials. In *Empty names, fiction and the puzzles of nonexistence*, ed. Anthony Everett and Thomas Hofweber, 95–116. Stanford, Calif.: CSLI Publications.

Künne, Wolfgang. 2003. *Conceptions of truth*. Oxford: Oxford University Press.

Landau, L. D., and E. M. Lifshitz. 1977. *Quantum mechanics (non-relativistic theory)*, 3rd ed. Oxford: Pergamon Press.

Larson, Richard, and Gabriel Segal. 1995. *Knowledge of meaning*. Cambridge, Mass.: MIT Press.

Laurence, Stephen, and Eric Margolis. 2005. Number and natural language. In *The innate mind: Structure and contents*, ed. Peter Carruthers, Stephen Laurence, and Stephen Stich, 216–35. Oxford: Oxford University Press.

Lemer, Cathy, Stanislas Dehaene, Elizabeth Spelke, and Laurent Cohen. 2003. Approximate quantities and exact number words: Dissociable systems. *Neuropsychologia* 41: 1942–58.

Lennox, B. R., S. B. Park, P. B. Jones, and P. G Morris. 1999. Spatial and temporal mapping of neural activity associated with auditory hallucinations. *Lancet* 353: 644.

Lepore, Ernest. 1983. What model theoretic semantics cannot do. *Synthese* 54: 167–87.

Lepore, Ernest, and Barry Loewer. 1981. Translational semantics. *Synthese* 48: 121–33.

———. 1983. Three trivial truth theories. *Canadian Journal of Philosophy* 13: 433–47.

———. 1989. More on making mind matter. *Philosophical Topics* 17: 175–92.

Lepore, Ernest, and Kirk Ludwig. 2000. The semantics and pragmatics of complex demonstratives. *Mind* 109(434): 199–240.

Levy, Azriel. 1979. *Basic set theory*. Berlin: Springer-Verlag.

Lewis, David. 1970. General semantics. In *Philosophical papers*, vol. 1 (1983), 189–229. Oxford: Oxford University Press.

———. 1978. Truth in fiction. In *Philosophical papers*, vol. 1 (1983), 261–75. Oxford: Oxford University Press.

———. 1983. Postscripts to "Truth in fiction." In *Philosophical papers*, vol. 1 (1983), 276–80. Oxford: Oxford University Press

———. 1986. *On the plurality of worlds*. Oxford: Basil Blackwell.

Lucotte, Gérard, and François Baneyx. *Introduction to molecular cloning techniques*. New York: VCH Publishers.

Ludlow, Peter. 1999. *Semantics, tense, and time: An essay in the metaphysics of natural language*. Cambridge, Mass.: MIT Press.

Lynch, Michael P. 2004. Truth and multiple realizability. *Australasian Journal of Philosophy* 82(3): 384–408.

Malvern, Lawrence E. 1969. *Introduction to the mechanics of a continuous solid*. Upper Saddle River, N.J.: Prentice Hall.

Mandler, George, and Billie Jo Shebo. 1982. Subitizing: An analysis of its component processes. *Journal of Experimental Psychology: General* 111(1): 1–20.

Manning, Sylvia Bank. 1971. *Dickens as satirist*. New Haven, Conn.: Yale University Press.

Martin, M. G. F. 2006. On being alienated. In *Perceptual experience*, ed. Tamar Szabó Gendler and John Hawthorne, 354–410. Oxford: Oxford University Press.

Maugh, T. H. II. 1981. A new understanding of sickle cell emerges. *Science* 211: 265–67.

Mayr, Ernst. 1982. *The growth of biological thought*. Cambridge, Mass.: Harvard University Press.

McDowell, John. 1980. On the sense and reference of a proper name. In *Reference, truth and reality*, ed Mark Platts. London: Routledge and Kegan Paul.

———. 1986. Singular thought and inner space. In *Subject, thought, and context*, ed. Philip Pettit and John McDowell, 137–68. Oxford: Oxford University Press.

McEvoy, Mark. 2004. Is reliabilism compatible with mathematical knowledge? *Philosophical Forum* 35(4): 423–37.

McGuire, P. K., D. A. Silbersweig, I. Wright, R. M. Murray, A. S. David, R. S. Frackowiak, and C. D. Frith. 1996. The neural correlates of inner speech and auditory verbal imagery in schizophrenia: Relationship to auditory verbal hallucinations. *British Journal of Psychiatry* 169: 148–59.

McLaughlin, Brian. 1995. Varieties of supervenience. In *Supervenience: New essays*, ed. Elias Savellos and Ümit Yalçin, 16–59. Cambridge: Cambridge University Press.

McQuarrie, Donald A. 1983. *Quantum chemistry*. Sausalito, Calif.: University Science Books.

Moore, G. E. 1962. *Commonplace book 1919–53*, ed. Casimir Lewy. London: George Allen and Unwin.

Moreland, J.P. 1998. Theories of individuation: A reconsideration of bare particulars. *Pacific Philosophical Quarterly* 79: 51–63.

Nagel, Ernest. 1961. *The structure of science*. New York: Harcourt, Brace and World.

Nagel, Thomas. 1986. *The view from nowhere*. Oxford: Oxford University Press.

Nicklin, J., K. Graeme-Cook, and R. Killington. 2002. *Instant notes in microbiology*, 2nd ed. Oxford: BIOS Scientific Publishers.

Ohayon, Maurice M. 2000. Prevalence of hallucinations and their pathological associations in the general population. *Psychiatry Research* 97: 153–64.

Oppenheim, Paul, and Hilary Putnam. 1958. Unity of science as a working hypothesis. In *Minnesota studies in the philosophy of science*, vol. II, ed. Herbert Feigl, Michael Scriven, and Grover Maxwell, 3–36. Minneapolis: University of Minnesota Press.

Parfitt, Derek. 1971. Personal identity. *Philosophical Review* 80(1): 3–27.

Parmenides. 1984. *Parmenides of Elea*. Toronto, Canada: University of Toronto Press.

Parsons, Charles. 1971a. A plea for substitutional quantification. In *Mathematics in philosophy: Selected essays* (1983), 63–70. Ithaca, N.Y.: Cornell University Press.

———. 1971b. Ontology and mathematics. In *Mathematics in philosophy: Selected essays* (1983), 37–62. Ithaca, N.Y.: Cornell University Press.

———. 1979–80. Mathematical intuition *Proceedings of the Aristotelian Society* NS 80: 145–68.

Parsons, Terence. 1980. *Nonexistent objects*. New Haven, Conn.: Yale University Press.

Penfield, Wilder, and Phanor Perot. 1963. The brain's record of auditory and visual experience. *Brain* 86: 595–696.

Plantinga, Alvin. 1974. *The nature of necessity*. Oxford: Oxford University Press.

Plato. 1963. The sophist. In *Plato: The collected dialogues*, ed. Edith Hamilton and Huntington Cairns, 957–1017. Princeton, N.J.: Princeton University Press.

Plewnia, Christian, Felix Bischof, and Matthias Reimold. 2007. Suppression of verbal hallucinations and changes in regional cerebral blood flow after intravenous lidocaine: A case report. *Progress in Neuro-Psychopharmacology and Biological Psychiatry* 31: 301–3.

Pulvermüller, Friedemann. 2002. *The neuroscience of language: On brain circuits of words and serial order*. Cambridge: Cambridge University Press.

Putnam, Hilary. 1967. The nature of mental states. In *Mind, language and reality: Philosophical papers*, vol. 2 (1975), 429–40. Cambridge: Cambridge University Press.

———. 1981. *Reason, truth and history*. Cambridge: Cambridge University Press.

———. 1987. *The many faces of realism*. LaSalle, Ill.: Open Court.

Quine, W. V. O. 1953. On what there is. In *From a logical point of view* (1980), 1–19. Cambridge, Mass.: Harvard University Press.

———. 1958. Speaking of objects. In *Ontological relativity and other essays* (1969), 1–25. New York: Columbia University Press.

———. 1960. *Word and object*. Cambridge, Mass.: MIT Press.

———. 1978. Goodman's ways of worldmaking. In *Theories and things*, 97–99. Cambridge, Mass.: Harvard University Press.

———. 1981. What price bivalence? In *Theories and things*, 31–37. Cambridge, Mass.: Harvard University Press.

———. 1986. *Philosophy of logic*, 2nd ed. Cambridge, Mass.: Harvard University Press.

Quine, W. V., and J. S. Ullian. 1978. *The web of belief*, 2nd ed. New York: Random House.

Raley, Yvonne. 2008. Jobless objects: Mathematical posits in crisis. In *Philosophy of mathematics: Set theory, measuring theories, and nominalism*, ed. Gerhard Preyer and Georg Peters, 112–31. Frankfurt: Ontos-Verlag.

Reimer, Marga. 2001. A "Meinongian" solution to a Millian problem. *American Philosophical Quarterly* 38: 233–48.

Resnik, Michael D. 1997. *Mathematics as a science of patterns*. Oxford: Oxford University Press.

Rosen, Gideon. 2006. Review of "Deflating existential consequence: A case for nominalism." *Journal of Philosophy* 103: 312–18.

Rosenberg, Alexander. 1985. *The structure of biological science*. Cambridge: Cambridge University Press.

Routley, Richard. 1980. *Exploring Meinong's jungle and beyond: An investigation of non-eism and the theory of items*, interim ed. Philosophy department monograph 3. Canberra: Research School of Social Sciences, Australian National University.

Routley, Richard, and Valerie Routley. 1973. Rehabilitating Meinong's theory of objects. *Revue Internationale de Philosophie* 27: 224–54.

Russell, Bertrand. 1905. On denoting. *Mind* 14: 479–93.

———. 1919. *Introduction to mathematical philosophy*. London: Routledge.

Ryder, John D. 1991. Electron tubes. In *Encylopedia of physics*, ed. Rita G. Lerner and George L. Trigg, 317–20. New York: VCH Publishers.

Sainsbury, R. M. 2005. *Reference without referents*. Oxford: Oxford University Press.

Salmon, Nathan. 1987. Existence. In *Metaphysics, mathematics, and meaning* (2005), 9–49. Oxford: Oxford University Press.

———. 1998. Nonexistence. In *Metaphysics, mathematics, and meaning* (2005), 50–90. Oxford: Oxford University Press.

———. 2002. Mythical objects. In *Metaphysics, mathematics, and meaning* (2005), 91–107. Oxford: Oxford University Press.

Shapere, Dudley. 1971. Notes towards a post-positivistic interpretation of science. In *The legacy of logical positivism*, ed. P. Achinstein and S. Barker, 115–60. Baltimore, Md.: Johns Hopkins University Press.

Shinosaki, Kazuhiro, Masakiyo Yamamoto, Satoshi Ukai, Shunsuke Kawaguchi, Asao Ogawa, Ryouhei Ishii, Yuko Mizuno-Matsumoto, Tsuyoshi Inouye, Norio Hirabuki, Toshiki Yoshimine, Tetsuji Kaku, Stephen E. Robinson, and Masatoshi Takeda. 2003. Desynchronization in the right auditory cortex during musical hallucinations: A MEG study. *Psychogeriatrics* 3: 88–92.

Silbersweig, D. A., E. Stern, C. Frith, C. Cahill, A. Holmes, S. Grootoonk, et al. (1995, Nov. 9). A functional neuroanatomy of hallucinations in schizophrenia. *Nature* 378: 176–79.

Sklar, Larry. 1967. Types of inter-theoretic reduction. *British Journal for the Philosophy of Science* 18: 109–24.

Smith, A. D. 2002. *The problem of perception*. Cambridge, Mass.: Harvard University Press.

Smith, George. Forthcoming. Pending tests to the contrary: The question of mass in Newton's law of gravity.

Snowdon, Paul. 1980–81. Perception, vision, and causation. *Proceedings of the Aristotelian Society* 81: 175–92. Reprinted in *Vision and mind: Selected readings in the philosophy of perception*, ed. Alva Noë and Evan Thompson, 151–66. Cambridge, Mass.: MIT Press, 2002.

Soames, Scott. 1999. *Understanding truth*. Oxford: Oxford University Press.

Stebbins, G. T., C. G. Goetz, M. C. Carrillo, K. J. Bangen, D. A. Turner, G. H. Gover, and J. D. E. Gabrieli. 2004. Altered cortical visual processing in PD with hallucinations: An fMRI study. *Neurology* 63: 1409–16.

Strawson, P. F. 1956. On referring. In *The philosophy of language*, 2nd ed. (1990), ed A. P. Martinich, 219–34. Oxford: Oxford University Press.

Tappolet, Christine. 1997. Mixed inferences: A problem for pluralism about truth predicates. *Analysis* 57(3): 209–10.

———. 2000. Truth pluralism and many-valued logics: A reply to Beall. *Philosophical Quarterly* 50: 382–83.

Tarski, Alfred. 1944. The semantic conception of truth. *Philosophy and Phenomenological Research* 4: 341–75.

———. 1983a. On the concept of logical consequence. In *Logic, semantics, metamathematics*, ed. J. Corcoran, 409–20. Indianapolis, Ind.: Hackett.

———. 1983b. The concept of truth in formalized languages. In *Logic, semantics, metamathematics*, ed. J. Corcoran, 152–278. Indianapolis, Ind.: Hackett.

Taylor, Kenneth A. 2000. Emptiness without compromise: A referentialist semantics for empty names. In *Empty names, fiction and the puzzles of non-existence*, ed. Anthony Everett and Thomas Hofweber, 17–36. Stanford, Calif.: CSLI Publications.

Thain, M. and M. Hickman. 2001. *The Penguin dictionary of biology*, 10th ed. London: Penguin Books.

Therman, Eeva, and Millard Susman. 1993. *Human chromosomes: Structure, behavior, and effects*, 3rd ed. Berlin: Springer-Verlag.

Thomasson, Amie L. 1999. *Fiction and metaphysics*. Cambridge: Cambridge University Press.

Toone, B. K., E. Cooke, and M. H. Lader. 1981. Electrodermal activity in the affective disorders and schizophrenia. *Psychological Medicine* 11: 497–508.

Truesdell, C. 1991. *A first course in rational continuum mechanics*, 2nd ed. San Diego, Calif.: Academic Press.

Truesdell, C., and K. R. Rajagopal. 2000. *An introduction to the mechanics of fluids*. Berlin: Birkhäuser.

Urmson, J. O. 1976. Fiction. *American Philosophical Quarterly* 13: 153–57.

Van Fraassen, Bas. C. 1980. *The scientific image*. Oxford: Oxford University Press.

Van Inwagen, Peter. 1977. Creatures of fiction. In *Ontology, identity, and modality* (2001), 37–56. Cambridge: Cambridge University Press.

———. 1983. Fiction and metaphysics. *Philosophy and literature* 7: 67–77.

———. 2000. Quantification and fictional discourse. In *Empty names, fiction and the puzzles of nonexistence*, ed. Anthony Everett and Thomas Hofweber, 235–47. Stanford, Calif.: CSLI Publications.

Walton, Kendall L. 1973. Pictures and make-believe. *Philosophical Review* 82: 283–319.

———. 1978. Fearing fictions. *Journal of Philosophy* 75: 5–27.

———. 1990. *Mimesis as make-believe*. Cambridge, Mass.: Harvard University Press.

———. 2000. Existence as metaphor? In *Empty names, fiction and the puzzles of nonexistence*, ed. Anthony Everett and Thomas Hofweber, 69–94. Stanford, Calif.: CSLI Publications.

Waters, C. Kenneth. 1990. Why the antireductionist consensus won't survive the case of classical Mendelian genetics. *PSA 1990*, Philosophy of Science Association, 1: 125–39.

Watson, James D. 1976. *Molecular biology of the gene*. Menlo Park, Calif.: W. A. Benjamin.

Williamson, Timothy. 1994. *Vagueness*. London: Routledge.

Wilson, Mark. 2006. *Wandering significance: An essay on conceptual behavior*. Oxford: Oxford University Press.

Wright, Crispen. 1992. *Truth and objectivity*. Cambridge, Mass.: Harvard University Press.

———. 1999. Truth: A traditional debate reviewed. In *Truth*, ed. S. Blackburn and K. Simmons, 203–38. Oxford: Oxford University Press.

Zalta, Edward, N. 1983. *Abstract objects: An introduction to axiomatic metaphysics*. Dordrecht: Reidel.

———. 1988. *Intensional logic and the metaphysics of intentionality*. Cambridge, Mass.: MIT Press.

Index

CPSIA information can be obtained
at www.ICGtesting.com
Printed in the USA
BVHW01s0618060218
507131BV00011B/28/P